TRANSITIONS

Transitions

The Development of Children of Immigrants

Edited by

Carola Suárez-Orozco, Mona M. Abo-Zena, *&* Amy K. Marks

NEW YORK UNIVERSITY PRESS

New York and London

NEW YORK UNIVERSITY PRESS
New York and London
www.nyupress.org
© 2015 by New York University
All rights reserved

References to Internet websites (URLs) were accurate at the time of writing. Neither the author nor New York University Press is responsible for URLs that may have expired or changed since the manuscript was prepared.

ISBN: 978-0-8147-8944-5 (hardback)
ISBN: 978-0-8147-7017-7 (paperback)

For Library of Congress Cataloging-in-Publication data, please contact the Library of Congress.

New York University Press books are printed on acid-free paper, and their binding materials are chosen for strength and durability. We strive to use environmentally responsible suppliers and materials to the greatest extent possible in publishing our books.

Manufactured in the United States of America

10 9 8 7 6 5 4 3 2 1

Also available as an ebook

To all the children of immigration and their families—in hopes that your journeys will be better understood

CONTENTS

FOREWORD

CYNTHIA GARCÍA COLL

In the life of an academic, sometimes—not often—we come across a book that we immediately sense will make a seminal and long-noted contribution. This is the case with this volume. Let me briefly explain why.

As we know, migration has been a major source of population growth and cultural change throughout the history of the United States. What is unique about this particular historical period is the rate and projection of growth of immigrant-origin children and youth in the United States in comparison to the White middle class.

First- and second-generation children of immigrants are (or will soon become) the majority of children in many districts, cities, and towns and, in the next fifty years or so, in the whole country. Moreover, these children are not only growing up in contexts very different from the contexts of those who migrated in earlier times, but they are also changing the landscapes of our schools and our neighborhoods. They are placing demands on our institutions that have catered in the past to "mainstream" populations or used assimilative theoretical models that heralded quick, unilateral assimilation as the way to integrate these newcomers into our country.

Families no longer migrate as a whole, as Ellis Island records portrayed for earlier, "similar" massive waves of immigration. Some migrants are refugees; some come through family reunification processes, some for education or employment purposes. Parents might not have legal status in the U.S., while their children are U.S. citizens. Siblings might differ in language capabilities, and schooling. There is not a typical immigrant-origin child, family, or successful adaptation. The phenomenon is full of complexities and often contradictions.

What this book does is bring clarity to a seemingly chaotic topic. It comprehensively disentangles the myriad of influences, experiences, and outcomes observed in this population. It uses our most recent understanding and data from a variety of academic fields to ascertain what these children need in order to become productive, healthy members of our communities. In particular, it looks at the environments in which these children live and examines what works and what does not. In some cases, children and youth are just that, regardless of where they were born, and where they are growing up. They need consistent, loving, and stimulating caretaking and schools and neighborhoods that are safe and enriching in particular ways that allow them to be competent in those settings and beyond. All children, after all, need opportunities to grow, develop, and flourish.

But the unique circumstances of these children put further demands on those who care for them. Parents who speak a language other than English and who have not been educated in the U.S. are expected to help their children with homework. Teachers have to instruct children who barely understand the content of a lesson. Older children become brokers for their parents into "strange" cultural practices. Families have loved ones deported, leaving behind children to take care of each other. Community organizations see their numbers dwindle unless they cater to newly arrived populations.

This book elucidates both the commonalities and differences in developmental processes, outcomes, and settings between children of immigrant backgrounds and all other children. It contributes to our knowledge of universal and community-specific developmental outcomes and processes, thus informing mainstream theories and investigations. And moreover, it gives us an understanding that can be used to promote healthy outcomes, to prevent misguided interventions, and to support families, teachers, and community leaders in the important work of bringing up this next generation.

My hope is that this insightful book will be read not only by those of us who are interested in children's development from a scholarly perspective but also by those who play pivotal roles in the lives of these families, children, and youth through their practices and policies. Knowledge is to be used. Knowledge can serve as a catalyst of change, as a base for instituting practices and policies that help and not harm. We certainly hope this is the case.

This wish is not a new one. In 1936, the scholar Pauline V. Young expressed this sentiment clearly and precisely: "The situation has been complicated by the fact that schools and social agencies have attempted to solve the problems of the immigrant without an adequate knowledge of the life within the immigrant community and without . . . research which would provide them with the knowledge of 'what works' and 'does not work' in the adjustment of the immigrant" (429).

Once again, the future of this country depends on fulfilling precisely this goal.

REFERENCES

Young, P. V. (1936). Social problems in the education of the immigrant child. *American Sociological Review, 1*(3), 419–442.

ACKNOWLEDGMENTS

We want to first and foremost thank all of the immigrant children, adolescents, and young adults who have shared with us their stories over the years. In this book, we have done our best to tell your story in a way that captures a complex, multidimensional reality in an accurate and empathic way.

We want to thank all of the authors who contributed to this volume. We asked you to write to a very specific task in a somewhat prescribed way so we could present the most coherent volume possible. Thank you for sharing your wisdom and bearing with us.

We are extraordinarily grateful to Cynthia García Coll for taking time to write her gracious and inspiring foreword. The words coming from her are particularly appreciated given her groundbreaking and inspiring work with immigrant-origin children.

We thank Jennifer Hammer at NYU Press for having confidence in this complicated project and for so painlessly ushering us through the process.

We thank Vici Casas for the painstaking line editing she did to the first draft of the manuscript. We were committed to having a coherent, "readable" social science book, and with Vici's keen eye, by Jove, I think we have got it!

I, Carola, thank my many students over the years—most of whom are the children of immigrants. You have inspired me and kept me engaged and passionate about what I do. It excites me to see you take the work to the next level. Mona, thank you for coming to me with the idea of doing this book, and Amy, thank you for your always cheerful can-do attitude—not only are you thoughtful developmentalists, but you are lovely colleagues. Thank you, Marcelo, for being my first student of ESL, my best teacher of immigration theory, as well as the love of my life. And Marisa and Lucas, my adored children, thank you for always keeping me grounded.

I, Amy, wish to thank foremost my students, research participants, community members, and friends whose immigration stories continue to inspire me. I also wish to thank you who are reading this book. It means you share some interest, curiosity, commitment, or passion for the subject matter bound in this cover. I am hopeful we can work together to improve the lives of immigrant families in the U.S. For my mentors and colleagues who support me and our work, I am forever grateful. In particular, I have been gifted to know and work alongside Carola and Cynthia García Coll, whose leadership in this field is truly inspiring. You are both masters at your work; you are beacons on behalf of immigrant youth. Your depth of character, wisdom, and care are truly outstanding. Mona, what a gift it has been to work with you on this project, which you conceived. Your passion and commitment made this work a reality. Lastly, my deepest felt thanks to my family. My husband, Kevin, and my daughters, Isabel and Evelyn—you are my light, my everything. Your love is my eternal guidepost; because of you I continue my own most fulfilling development.

I, Mona, wish to thank the many students, family members, research participants, friends, mentors, and colleagues who have shared their personal and professional perspectives on immigrant-origin youth. Your reflections and candid statements about how it is to be an immigrant-origin youth or to work with children and families in a variety of capacities have provided me insights into the strengths of the youth and those who support them, as well as the challenges they face. I hope that we have represented you and your stories well and that you will help us continue to refine these images. I have been fortunate to have Carola as a mentor and colleague in my own development as I seek to infuse scholarship with lived experiences of diverse youth; thank you for believing in me and the idea for this book and for always being able to ground scholarship in the details of family life. Like heritage language should be for immigrant-origin youth, your feedback and encouragement are music to my ears. Amy, thank you for your collegiality, your astute feedback, and the boundless energy you give our work. I thank each of our contributors for their willingness to dedicate their expertise to this collective project, and NYU Press, particularly Jennifer Hammer, for support of this volume from inception to completion. My interest in studying immigrant families originated with my own parents, and I thank them, Mahmoud Abo-Zena and Fifi Elshaarawey, for their guidance in every step of my own development. I am humbled by their efforts as my husband, Mohamed Hassan, and I strive to support our own children, Abdelrahman, Mariam, Noor, and Abdallah. Your reactions keep me puzzling and inspire me, and I thank you for your patience and engaging practically in this work. I wish all our families, wherever the locations and constellations, the best of multiple worlds.

Introduction

Unique and Shared Experiences of Immigrant-Origin Children and Youth

CAROLA SUÁREZ-OROZCO, AMY K. MARKS, AND MONA M. ABO-ZENA

The moment I open my mouth, they know I am not one of them.
—16-year-old first-generation Russian-origin adolescent girl
who arrived at age 13

Before I came, I missed my parents; now I miss my grandparents.
—9-year-old first-generation Guatemalan-origin girl

I worry every day when my father drops me off at school that he
won't be there to pick me up. What if ICE has taken him away?
—11-year-old first-generation Mexican-origin boy

I am African American. My parents are African, and I was born
in America, so I am not fully American, and I am not fully African. Sometimes I get confused about what to call myself. But I
am African American.
—15-year-old second-generation African American boy

The words in the epigraphs provide glimpses into the worlds, preoccupations, and complexities of the "children of immigration"[1] from a variety of origins. In 2001, Carola Suárez-Orozco and Marcelo Suárez-Orozco coined that phrase and took stock of a nascent field. Using an interdisciplinary lens, they explored what was known about the experience of immigrant-origin children[2] from a childcentric point of view. The overarching goal of their 2001 book was to assess the state of the field at the time. As the population of immigrant-origin[3] children has

1

increased, so has the study of immigrant children across a variety of disciplines. The social science research base has grown immensely over the past decade and a half, and it is again time to take stock, now showcasing the wisdom provided by many experts across multiple research domains. When compiling this new volume, we turned to domain-specific scholars to succinctly review the latest research critical to understanding the development of immigrant-origin children and youth who share one thing in common—a parent of immigrant origin.

The Demographic Imperative

Immigration to the United States has reached historic numbers—currently 40.4 million (or approximately 12.5 percent) of people residing in this country are foreign born.[4] As the foreign-born population has increased over the past few decades, so too has the number of their children. Currently 25 percent of children under the age of 18, a total of 18.7 million children, have an immigrant parent.[5] This growth has been extremely rapid—in 1970, the population of immigrant-origin children stood at 6 percent of the total population of children. It reached 20 percent by 2000 and is projected to be 33 percent by 2050.[6] These children have become an integral part of the national tapestry. The majority of them are *citizen-children*, that is, children born in the United States, who are automatically citizens. The bulk of the expansion of this population during the past decade has been in the second generation—that is, children who are born in the United States to immigrant parents.[7] Notably, this increase has occurred at a faster rate than the birth rate of children who are not of immigrant origin. Thus, the well-being of immigrant-origin youth has implications for a large swath of our child population and is deeply intertwined with the future of our nation.

Immigrants are an extraordinarily heterogeneous group. The previous wave of migration to the United States, which lasted from the 1880s to the 1920s, brought immigrants who were primarily of European origin (97 percent from Europe or North America and 3 percent from Latin America, Asia, Africa, Oceania, or the Caribbean). Today only 11 percent of migrants originate from Europe or North America, while 89 percent arrive from Latin America, Asia, Africa, Oceania, or the Caribbean.[8] This migratory flow is a significant factor in the United States' becoming a "majority-minority" country. Because this new migratory stream is primarily non-European in origin, the majority of immigrant-origin children and youth in the United States will remain visible minorities and be at risk of being treated as perpetual foreigners.[9]

Parents are motivated to migrate for a variety of reasons. Though on a case-by-case basis migration may seem to be born of individual decisions, when it occurs en masse, there typically are economic, historical, and political influences and pressures behind the parents' decisions.[10] The decision to migrate is never the child's, but it is the child who must navigate their[11] development within a disoriented family in a new land. The primary incentives for migration are typically the search to reunify with family members who have previously migrated, the search for work, and the search for relief from political or social strife.

Since 1965, citizens or permanent lawful residents of countries of origin who have close relatives in the United States have been given priority to immigrate. Currently some two-thirds of all migrants in the United States have entered via family reunification laws. A second pathway to entry is available to individuals with skills or resources deemed essential to the workforce, such as specialized workers (including those coming into the country under temporary worker programs); highly educated and skilled professionals; and entrepreneurs who invest considerable resources in the U.S. economy. The third lawful mechanism for entry includes humanitarian relief provided to those seeking refuge from their homelands due to "a well-founded fear of persecution."[12] These are the "legal" mechanisms, which allow entry into the country. Even so, adults and children are also likely to seek entry in order to be reunited with family members who have previously migrated, especially when there are significant pressures in their home countries in the form of violence and rampant unemployment, even when there are no legal pathways available to them (as in the case of the crisis of unaccompanied Central American children in 2014).[13]

Immigrant parents arrive in the new land with great diversity in levels of education. At one end of the spectrum are highly educated immigrant adults; at the other are many immigrant parents with educational levels far below those of their U.S.-born contemporaries.[14] Some immigrant parents are among the most educated people in our nation: immigrants comprise a quarter of all physicians, 47 percent of scientists with doctorates, and 24 percent of science and engineering workers with bachelor's degrees.[15] Others work for sectors of the U.S. labor market that greatly rely on "low-skilled" immigrant adults, such as agriculture, service industries, and construction.[16]

Immigrants come from every part of the world, and they bring with them their religious beliefs and practices. Newly arrived immigrant adults and children, feeling disoriented in their new land, are particularly likely to turn to their religious communities in times of transition.[17] Consequently, the current new wave of immigration is contributing to the revitalization and diversification of our religious institutions.[18] Although U.S.-born residents' participation in the Catholic Church has decreased in recent decades, the participation of Latin American and Caribbean immigrants has increased.[19] Central Americans and Caribbeans who converted to evangelical churches before migrating tend to continue their participation in them after migration, and networks of relatives perpetuate additional conversions as immigrants are drawn to religious institutions in search of support networks in the new land.[20] Membership in non–Jewish or Christian religions (such as Islam, Hinduism, Sikhism, and Buddhism) in the United States has particularly grown in recent decades as a result of migration.[21]

Immigrant parents living in the United States represent the Tower of Babel—460 languages are currently spoken in homes across the country.[22] The percentage of children who speak a second language at home increased from 9 percent in 1979 to 21 percent in 2008.[23] Of those individuals speaking a language other than English at home, 62 percent speak Spanish, 19 percent speak another Indo-European language, 15 percent speak an Asian or Pacific Island language, and the remaining 4 percent speak a different language.[24] Many of the nonnative English speakers have varying degrees of fluency and language skills, with higher levels of education and longer residency in the United States generally correlating with greater fluency.[25] The classification of immigrant parents as fluent in English (40 percent) or as English-language learners (44 percent) is often a subjective distinction between those who speak English "very well" and those who speak "well." Additionally, 14 percent of families have parents with mixed English-language skills. Of all immigrant-origin children ages 0 through 17, 81 percent have parents who speak English and another language at home, and 5 percent live in a home where no parent or caregiver speaks English.[26] Whether they are newcomers themselves or the children of immigrants, many immigrant-origin children face the psychological and academic issues associated with speaking limited or "accented" English.

Common Denominators of Experience

What can children growing up in such an array of diverse households possibly have in common? Clyde Kluckholm and Henry Murray long ago reflected that all humans are at once like all others, like some others, and like no others.[27] How are immigrant-origin children like all other children, like some other children, and like no other children? What challenges as well as what opportunities do their circumstances present for their development? How are immigrant children like all other children, and how are they unique? What characteristics are they likely to share because they have immigrant parents, and what characteristics are unique to specific groups of origin? How are children of first-generation immigrants different from those of second-generation immigrants? These are the questions we will grapple with throughout this text. In doing so, we not only reflect on the uniqueness of immigrant children's experiences but also observe fundamental experiences that promote a deeper understanding of child development more broadly.

Immigration as Both Growth Enhancing and Stressful

Immigrant parents would not embark on the venture of leaving their countries of origin without being highly motivated to do so. Immigration results in tremendous opportunities to provide for loved ones left behind by making remittances or to secure educational pathways for one's children. It can be an escape from turmoil caused by war or political upheaval or a means to avoid religious or ethnic persecution.[28] It is almost always a journey laced with great hope and optimism,[29] factors that can serve to inoculate migrants against the adversity that is part of the process. The very voyage of migration can be "growth enhancing"[30] for many members of the family. At the same time, immigration is by every measure a highly stressful endeavor.[31] Immigrants leave behind many of their most important relationships with extended family members, neighbors, and friends. They are stripped of familiar roles and can no longer take for granted the most basic of social rules. Others' perception of their competency is undermined since their basic thoughts can no longer be readily communicated.

How the children of immigrants cope with their families' migratory transition is in a large part determined by a constellation of factors associated with both the *premigration* circumstances leading up to the journey and the *postmigration* experiences.[32] A family's particular premigration resources—financial, educational, social, and psychological—will provide very different starting points for children of different families as they enter the host country. These factors provide an array of tools with which children can navigate the new land. Further, the contexts into which children and youth arrive—the economic, legal, neighborhood, and school settings—will be in varying degrees welcoming and conducive to success. In some cases the reception is arid and daunting, while in others it is verdant and welcoming. Clearly, success will be more likely with a positive constellation of premigratory resources (along with a welcoming context) than with negative ones.

Thus, a six-year-old child whose parents both have college educations and speak English, arrive with secured green cards and a healthy bank account, have obtained jobs, and have family and friend networks residing in the area of settlement will have a very different experience than will a 15-year-old whose depressed mother is widowed, has a sixth-grade education, does not speak English, is undocumented, works in the fields by moving from place to place, migrated six years earlier to support her child, leaving him in her sister's care, and sent for him only when her sister was no longer able to care for him.

Multiple adversities that occur concurrently or at multiple junctures during a child's development lead to far less likely avenues of success than those available to children without such burdens.[33] Additionally, every child is in turn variably resilient and resourceful.[34] The immigrant-origin child's response to the stress they experience will be determined by an interaction between their individual characteristics (such as temperament and developmental stage, among others) and the manifold demands of their environment.[35] When the demands are optimally aligned, the child will fare well. Conversely, when the demands are misaligned and create a condition in which the child cannot flourish, they may languish.

The Immigrant Paradox: Taking a Generational Perspective

Many of the most socially and economically advantaged immigrant-origin youth perform extraordinarily well in their new land—regularly winning spelling bees and Intel prizes and becoming valedictorians.[36] Other immigrant youth with fewer advantages succeed valiantly against the odds.[37] A number of recent studies suggest that many immigrant-origin youth are successfully integrating into and adapting to their new land, faring as well as or better than their native same-ethnicity peers.[38] Other studies, however, point to problems in the educational adaptation of immigrant youth.[39] Many immigrant students struggle academically, leaving school without having acquired the tools they will need to function effectively in the highly competitive, knowledge-intensive U.S. economy,[40] in which limited education severely impedes social mobility over time.[41] In particular, students who immigrate as adolescents often have more trouble adapting to the new land since they must cope with transitions to adolescence and young adulthood as well as the challenges brought about by the transition of migration.[42] A constellation of factors that includes generational status, language proficiency, length of residence, gender, country of origin, access to support systems, and the attitudes and reception that immigrant students encounter in their new contexts results in various pathways of adaptation.

For many decades, researchers have noted that immigrant generation—whether children are born abroad (first generation), in the United States to foreign-born parents (second generation), or in this country to U.S.-born parents (third generation)—can be a powerful marker of developmental pathways and outcomes.[43] These population and group-level findings reveal striking developmental trends. Newcomer youth, who on average live in the poorest neighborhoods and families and attend the poorest schools, consistently compare favorably on health and behavioral attitude outcomes when compared to native-born peers. This phenomenon, termed the *immigrant paradox*, holds important implications in the study of immigrant youth development.

On one hand, newcomer youth on average appear to be faring better despite troubling receiving contexts and poor economic resources in the new land. On the other hand, U.S.-born children of immigrant parents and grandparents—who typically have more English-language skills, social capital, and economic resources—tend to struggle more with their education, health, and well-being. As we depict later in the book, these paradoxical patterns are extremely nuanced by culture of origin, gender, and developmental age groupings and carry implications for a variety of outcomes.

Thus, when considering immigrant-origin youth's patterns of adaptation, it is important to consider generational status. First-generation youth are born abroad, where they spend their childhoods and acquire the foundations of their education. Members of the 1.5 generation are born abroad but arrive in their new homeland prior to age 12, so they are exposed to the new country's schools and culture during their formative years. Second-generation youth are born in the new country to foreign-born parents. In terms of these groups' comparative advantages and disadvantages, first-generation students benefit from having immigrant optimism[44] and a dual frame of reference[45]—that is, immigrants tend to compare their current circumstances with those left behind and therefore tend to be more optimistic and hopeful even though their situations may not be ideal. Compared with native-born students, however, newcomer students tend to struggle more with English, particularly academic English. Research has shown that English proficiency that enables quality engagement with academic subjects takes up to seven years to acquire, even when students' English appears functional under other circumstances. Thus, language proficiency in the new language will have particular effects on academic outcomes.[46] The second and later generations, having been born in the new land, no longer have comparative points of reference, but they have the advantages of full citizenship and more consistent exposure to English, which facilitate both English fluency and better access to curricula.[47] For third- and later-generation students, recent research shows that length of residence often correlates with declining academic engagement and performance. This is a counterintuitive trend since one might assume that the longer immigrants have lived in the new country, the better they and their offspring will adapt. New research in this area, however, suggests that this outcome is often not the case and that factors such as racism, poverty, anti-immigrant sentiment, and acculturation to antiacademic peer norms may each play a role in diminishing the adaptability of young people of the third or later generations.

Navigating the New Land: Parents with Misaligned Compasses

Immigrant-origin children—the first and second generation, who both have immigrant parents—unlike their nonimmigrant peers, often do not have well-informed guides to help them acquire the cultural knowledge of the new society. Rather, the children themselves may serve as the "experts" who guide their parents with their newly acquired cultural and language skills. As immigrant-origin children navigate (or struggle to navigate) new schools, peers, and societal norms, they may concurrently feel pressured to acquire (or maintain) the skills and knowledge that are valued within their heritage culture. Immigrant-origin youth navigate two different worlds, sometimes benefiting from the enriching perspective that this position provides and sometimes facing the isolation of being marginalized.

All societies define parenting along shared scripts of safety, security, and emotional care for children.[48] Providing for the physical security of a child is but the most fundamental of parental responsibilities. The work of protecting children involves a range of domains: providing basic financial resources needed for food and clothing, providing educational opportunities, and caring for health. Parents also expect to provide their children with guidance on how to live as members of the larger community.

Immigrant parents, who are renowned for their work ethic and for valiantly striving to provide for their families, are often challenged in their roles as guides for their children in their new lands. Immigration is particularly stressful for parents when they are unable to draw on their usual resources and coping skills, especially when much is at stake for the balance and well-being of the family.[49] Immigration removes parents from many of the supports that are linked to community ties, jobs, and the main institutions of the new society. Stripped of many of their significant supports (e.g., extended family members, best friends, and familiar neighbors), immigrant parents may never fully develop the social maps needed to find their way in a foreign land. Lacking a sense of basic competence, control, and belonging, many immigrant parents feel marginalized. Thus, a new paradox becomes evident. Even as immigrant parents become more empowered economically by the opportunities in their new homeland, they experience a keen sense of inadequacy in their ability to effectively exercise their parenting authority. At a time when immigrant children and youth need extra guidance to navigate the difficult currents of the new country, many immigrant parents find themselves unable to guide their children.

Parenting involves a variety of roles and responsibilities. Beyond the fundamental economic and physical security that parents normatively provide, there are parental authoritative, socializing, and emotional roles essential for promoting optimal child development and well-being.[50] For various reasons, many (especially low-income) immigrant parents have strained available psychological and social resources to enable them to fulfill these roles.[51] Many work multiple jobs for long hours. Others find the stresses of learning a new language while performing on the job overwhelming. Most are mourning the losses of loved ones left behind. The cumulative stresses and losses of migration, while tempered by economic gains, leave many parents emotionally exhausted, anxious, depressed, and distracted. Therefore, although physically present in their children's lives, many parents may be psychologically elsewhere, unavailable to meet their children's emotional day-to-day needs.[52] Others are forced by circumstances to be physically separated from their children for extended periods of time as a result of the migratory process.[53] Thus, despite their best intentions, many immigrant parents find themselves unable to provide the physical presence, time, and energy required to optimally parent their children.

Numerous immigrants take jobs far beneath their qualifications and skills. The field of immigration is littered with examples of wasted talent: the doctor from China now working as a nurse, the nurse from El Salvador working as a cleaning lady, the engineer from Ghana working as a taxi driver. Even with a better salary, many immigrants find social demotions a hard pill to swallow. And while other immigrants may not suffer a reduction in job status, they nonetheless find themselves toiling at the most stigmatized, dangerous, and demeaning work. Narratives of immigrant workers often reveal a deeply felt sense that they, and only they, can and will endure the harshest, most unforgiving working conditions that the new land has to offer.[54]

Demoralization, uncertainty, and fear felt in the workplace are but part of the stress that worms its way into the heart of immigrant family life. Immigration also reverses the natural order of parental authority.[55] Nonimmigrant parents normally know the basic rules of socialization and ways to guide their children through the moral, social, and cultural etiquette required for membership and belonging.[56] They can wisely impart to their children the basic rules for respectful interaction with others, ways to complete school, and ways to get a job. However, in a new society, the rules of engagement have changed for immigrant parents, and they are no longer masters (or sometimes even players) of the game. For immigrants, "relinquishing the parental function" is a painful and reluctant process. Some do so out of a sense of helplessness and prematurely entrust their children with responsibilities beyond those appropriate for their years. Many parents find themselves turning to their children for help and guidance in the practical, cultural, and linguistic nuances of the new society. However, asking children to take on this mature role comes at a cost. Although some youth cherish this role and feel like they are responsible and active contributors to the family,[57] others feel burdened by these responsibilities and by their parents' inability to guide them confidently through their childhood and adolescence.[58]

The reversal of parental authority is most undermined by many immigrant parents' inability to master the language of the new land. The complexity of understanding and making oneself understood in a new language will define the lives of new immigrants at work; in dealing with institutions of the new society, including schools, health-care services, the police, and the judicial system; and with the very essence of social membership. Immigrant parents are overwhelmingly preoccupied with language, which they regard as essential to their advancement in the new society. Some are blessed with linguistic skills, previous education, and social contexts that can facilitate their rapid acquisition of the new language, but many others find themselves linguistically challenged and never fully master the intricacies of it.

Immigrant children, by contrast, more readily come into more intimate contact with the language and culture of the new society. Schools will immerse them in the new values and worldviews and, above all, will introduce them to the systematic study of the new language. Their teachers are often members of the majority culture who often do not speak the immigrants' native language. Other children who may not be immigrants will become the daily interlocutors with whom immigrant children will develop a new linguistic repertoire. The children watch television, see movies, listen to music, and are steeped in other media in their new land's language. Their parents, on the other hand, are removed from these new cultural routines, particularly if they work long hours and spend their time in enclaves with other immigrants who tend to be of the same linguistic, ethnic, and national background. The children's deep immersion in the new culture will facilitate their acquisition of the new language and will give them a course to chart in making their way in the new society.

As the children increasingly develop mastery of both the new language and the new culture, many experience feelings ranging from vague to intense embarrassment as they recognize their parents' inability to help them manage what appear to be simple tasks. Some immigrant parents rage against their loss of authority; overreaction is common. Hypervigilance, regimented routines, and policing children's peer influences as well as those of the media become preoccupations in many immigrant households. Parents feel threatened by the encroachment of new cultural values and behaviors in their children, so they often respond by tightening the reins. However, putting in place disciplinary sanctions from the "old country" opens a new cultural can of worms. While withholding a meal, pulling an ear, or requiring that a child kneel on rice are common practices in many countries of origin, they may not mesh with mainstream notions of proper discipline in the new land. A "good spanking" in the old country can be a reportable offense in the new. If immigrant parents do not learn alternative sanctioning mechanisms, they may lose control of their offspring. This outcome may severely impact the well-being of the children as it is essential for parents to maintain basic authoritative functions within the family. Parents' authority is not only symbolic but is also critical for imposing curfews, conveying values that promote respectful behavior toward others, establishing expectations for doing homework, and much more. When the voice of parental authority is undermined—and if the children lose respect for their parents—the very foundation of safety and family coherence is compromised.

Many parents, thus, come to face the paradox of parenting in a promised land. The country that offers them the dream of a better tomorrow and provides them with the opportunity to give their children greater economic security can become a battlefield over the children's identity and the coherence and cohesion of the family. The profound familial dislocations and the delegitimizing of parental authority can have a destabilizing effect on the development of immigrant children, undermining their educational and professional advancement in the new society.

Contexts of Reception

Even under optimal circumstances, immigration constitutes an abrupt and dramatic change in the ecological contexts of immigrant families and their children. Their subsequent exposure to a new cultural milieu may challenge their values and require shifts in cultural practices due to new and sometimes conflicting demands posed by new contexts. Although the parents may have chosen to migrate, newcomer children and youth generally have less agency; they are thrust into a foreign context that they need to make feel like home. Sometimes from birth and sometimes midway in their development, immigrant-origin children raised in a new society must learn to navigate the norms of their own heritage culture in addition to those in the "mainstream."

The contexts in which the immigrant family settles shape the experiences and pathways of their children. Arguably, three types of contexts matter most for the immigrant family: (a) the economic contexts and labor-market opportunities available in the new land; (b) the legal framework of the new community, including immigration policies granting and restricting the rights of new arrivals; and (c) the social context, including the general level of xenophobia and the level of acceptance and media representations of immigrants.

Economic Realities. Immigrant families generally leave their homelands to improve their lives and prospects. For many, immigration results in more economic opportunities and personal growth than they would have experienced in their country of origin. Securing work is an important motivation for immigrating, and the work setting is of paramount importance in understanding the immigrant experience. It is through the parents' work that immigrant families realize substantial benefits. Research demonstrates that the economic benefits of migration accrue first and foremost to the immigrants themselves: by crossing boundaries between nations with large wage differentials, immigrants are the biggest winners in the complex lottery of immigration.[59]

The broader economic context will shape the experience of immigration in a variety of ways—in the types of jobs that are available, in the stability of jobs, and in the opportunities to move up a status mobility ladder.[60] Skilled immigrants have been rapidly moving up into the upper echelons of the work hierarchy.[61] On the other hand, other immigrants, especially those with lower levels of education and skills, have struggled and stagnated, especially after the most recent economic recession.[62] The realities of the economy for parents, therefore, will shape outcomes for their children.

For many immigrant families, living in poverty is a significant concern.[63] Since 2007, the proportion of immigrant children living below the poverty level has increased considerably (from 22 percent to 31 percent).[64] First-generation immigrant children are significantly more likely than their nonimmigrant peers to be growing up in poverty (31 percent versus 20 percent).[65] Furthermore, another 26.7 percent of the first generation live at near-poverty levels.[66] The second generation fares only marginally better—27.9 percent live below the poverty level, and 27.9 percent live in near-poverty.[67] More than half of children with immigrant parents, then, are living in circumstances of poverty.

Living below the official poverty line is an important but not sufficient index of the economic realities of immigrant-origin children. Such figures reflect a developmental context whereby an insufficient income translates into a series of behavioral mechanisms and pathways, including having inadequate nutrition, contending with instability of residence, living in violent neighborhoods, and attending poor schools that provide limited learning experiences.[68] In addition, the timing of poverty in children's development and the consequences of enduring extreme poverty over many years appear to have distinct effects.[69]

The recency of migration considerably affects children growing up in immigrant homes. Children whose families are recent arrivals—those who have been in the new land less than 10 years—are the most likely to be living under the poverty threshold. However, they are also the most likely to have parents who are married and working (characteristics that serve as protective factors for other groups).[70] Families that have recently arrived also use food stamps less often and have lower levels of medical insurance than do nonimmigrant families.[71]

For immigrant-origin children, official calculations of family poverty fail to consider the economic complications of their families' transnational lives. Many immigrant families, particularly those who have recently arrived, maintain dual economic frames of reference, making remittances to spouses, other children, parents, siblings, and other family members in the country of origin for medical, educational, and other basic expenses.[72] These regular distributions to kin abroad result in fewer available resources for the family's children residing in the host country. Consequently, already thin resources are stretched even thinner.

Immigration Policies. It is also essential to consider the policies of the receiving nation. In the United States, immigration policy has largely focused on border control, with no consideration of a national integration policy for new immigrants.[73] Since 1988, when the amnesty provisions of the Immigration Reform and Control Act ended, U.S. immigration policy has restricted pathways to citizenship for the undocumented.[74] What in the public imagination are clearly demarcated lines of *legal* and *illegal* are in fact states of *liminal legality*.[75] Many families, children, and youth exist in a state of ambiguous documentation, fall out of legal status, or live in families of mixed status—in which some members are documented while others are not.[76]

Furthermore, during the past several years, the United States has become a "deportation nation," deporting 400,000 individuals a year. Concurrently, as attitudes toward undocumented immigrants have grown increasingly harsher, a spate of state and local laws were enacted targeting undocumented immigrants.[77] Long backlogs, a byzantine bureaucracy, and high rates of denials and deportations have cemented growing numbers of transnationally separated as well as mixed-status families. These contexts of development have unique consequences for the development of immigrant-origin children.

As noted earlier, there are widely differing ways in which immigrant families gain entry into the United States. Although approximately one-quarter of immigrants in this country are undocumented, most arrived through a variety of mechanisms, including the green-card lottery, work or study visas, family reunification visas, refugee status, and asylum status.[78] The migration experience is colored by the nature of immigrants' process of entry into the United States and has psychological effects on immigrant adults and their children. For example, some refugees may have had dire or traumatic experiences during their often prolonged migration from their nation of origin to this country but were subsequently able to find assistance in the United States and to make social and emotional connections with others from their heritage country. In contrast, those who leave their heritage country seeking asylum in the United States may be afraid to openly associate with others from that country for reasons similar to the ones that motivated them to seek asylum (for example, transgender individuals from nonsupportive cultural contexts may fear the same sort of previously experienced discrimination from fellow emigrants from that culture). The highly skilled, sponsored technology worker who can utilize the services of an accomplished immigration lawyer hired by his employer will have an entirely different experience than will the family with limited English proficiency that hires an attorney through the phone book in hopes of getting assistance with the complex, high-stakes forms and later discovers that the attorney has absconded with their fees and paperwork. These very different circumstances and associated stressors and their effects on family functioning are often not reflected in considerations of the immigrant family experience.

The Social Mirror. In addition to economic and policy contexts of reception, the social welcome mat can affect the development of immigrant-origin children. Immigrant identities will in no small part be shaped by their ethos of reception. The *social mirror*—the general social and emotional atmosphere and the collective representations of immigrants that new arrivals encounter upon their settlement in the new country—is an important context of immigration.[79] During times of socioeconomic and political anxiety, immigrants embody citizens' fear of the unknown. The recent rapid increase in immigration, the terrorist attacks on September 11, 2001, the persistence of unauthorized immigration, and the deep economic recession have aligned to stimulate U.S. citizens' unease concerning immigrants of color. *Xenophobia*, defined by psychologists as the fear or hatred of foreigners and their cultures, has been on the rise, especially as directed toward newer immigrants, particularly Muslims[80] and Latinos.[81] There is emerging evidence of negative media coverage of immigration[82] and an increase in hate crimes against immigrants,[83] as well as exclusionary legislation enacted on the municipal, state, and federal levels.[84] Furthermore, since the new immigrants are predominantly of non-European origin, their children will remain visible minorities for generations, subject to the ongoing racial climate of the nation. What are the developmental implications of such a context of development?[85]

Immigrant parents and their children face different tasks when crafting an identity and sense of belonging in the new society.[86] For immigrant parents and latecomer adolescents, a dual frame of reference that brings together "the here and now" and "the there and then" filters the ways in which they view themselves and their new lives. Family roles must be renegotiated. The challenges of providing for the family in a new country, contending with status demotions and promotions, navigating new gendered ideologies and practices, and learning to raise children according to new cultural expectations and standards all become central themes in the creation of these new identities.

For the children of these immigrants, the work of developing identities will, at different stages of development, involve "fitting in" with peers, struggling with issues of embarrassment about their parents' foreign ways (e.g., accents, dress, manners, and ethnic foods), and eventually synthesizing cultural currents from the parental tradition and the norms, values, and worldviews of the new society. *Hybridity*—the fusion of multiple cultural trends—characterizes second- generation immigrant-origin children's process of creating their new identities.[87]

Book Goals

Although immigrant-origin youth are the fastest growing sector of the child population in the United States, there are few resources that employ whole-child, developmental, and contextual approaches to understand their experience. In this book, we take a person-centered point of view that incorporates developmental, psychological, sociological, and anthropological perspectives. We have employed these interdisciplinary perspectives to better understand cross-cultural developmental psychology and to elucidate the multiple ways in which personal, social, and structural factors interact.[88] Preeminent and emerging scholars of the development of immigrant children and youth have highlighted the key aspects of a developmental perspective here by considering themes of continuity and discontinuity across the life span, by adopting a holistic and integrated perspective while also emphasizing specific domains of development, and by considering the many contextual variables and ways in which they interact with the person over time. It is beyond the scope of this book to provide an exhaustive and comprehensive review of every immigrant group or developmental domain. Rather, the goal is to identify ways in which the composite of developmental pathways vary within and across immigrant groups and to provide a framework for understanding child development and its outcomes.

Contextually Grounded

We employ an ecological perspective to frame this book. As theorized by Urie Bronfenbrenner[89] and others, we posit that children's outcomes are a result of reciprocal interactions between their experiences and their environment. Outcomes will vary over the course of time as a function of the child, their culture, and their environment. This book's chapters consider the roles of contextual risks and protective factors in hindering and enhancing adaption.[90] Thus, this text situates discussions of immigrant children in the many levels of context in which they live. Contextual considerations include an individual's interactions with their family, neighborhood, community, city, region, nation of origin, and host country. Central to the discussion of context is the goodness of fit between the individual and their contexts.

Integrated across Developmental Domains and Processes

The current literature on immigrant-origin youth is vastly informative and examines many developmental domains and processes such as cognitive development and academic achievement, identity development, and language acquisition. A holistic developmental perspective, however, would consider how growth and change within a particular domain are integrated across development. This text balances a focus on specific domains with an exploration of how development may occur across domains (e.g., how emerging bilingualism affects school achievement and ethnic identity development and how children's developmental trajectories may differ because of contextual variables such as socioeconomic status and school quality). This integrated focus on developmental processes pays particular attention to processes associated with acculturation, identity development, language development and bilingualism, and language brokering.

Developmental Outcomes across Childhood and Adolescence

This book examines the ways in which developmental contexts at multiple levels interact with particular developmental processes to produce a range of outcomes for immigrant-origin children and youth. Developmental perspectives are characterized by their examination of behaviors and attitudes considered normal for a particular developmental phase. Ironically, focusing on a specific developmental period can sometimes cause a theorist to lose a broader developmental perspective that considers how developmental phases are related to a person's life span. In addition to specifically focusing on what are perceived as qualitatively distinct developmental phases, this book integrates the developmental purview with discussions about early childhood to adolescence and beyond in order to consider developmental continuities and discontinuities with respect to the range of outcomes. While development may progress toward a range of culturally mediated outcomes, this text particularly focuses on the outcomes of physical health, mental health, behavior, academic achievement, and civic engagement.

Interdisciplinary Approaches and Future Considerations

The research and methods discussed by the authors draw from education, child development, psychology, sociology, public health, medicine, and family studies. Our focus on immigrant-origin children, families, and communities itself reflects both cultural and contextual diversity given the range of nations of origin, cultural variation within groups, and acculturative processes examined. Since this book concentrates on the United States as the host country, authors tend to discuss specific policies and conditions in this country. Whenever possible, however, contributors address practices that could support immigrant youth in other sociopolitical contexts.

Given the complexities of the puzzle of the development of immigrant-origin youth, we cannot fully address all the dimensions that influence their pathways. This book, however, strives to provide a developmental framework and food for thought for those who seek to support both culturally sensitive and conceptually thoughtful research, practice, and policy work with the children of immigrants.

NOTES

1. Suárez-Orozco, C., & Suárez-Orozco, M. (2001). *Children of immigration.* Cambridge: Harvard University Press.

2. Note that in this text when we say *immigrant child,* we are referring to the first generation; *immigrant-origin children* have at least one immigrant parent and thus may either be of the first or second generation. First-generation children are born abroad; second-generation children are born in the host country but have a parent who was born abroad. Third-generation children have grandparents who were born abroad and are not considered of immigrant origin for the definition used in this book since they do not have an immigrant parent.

3. By "immigrant origin," we specifically mean the children of immigrant parents— either the first or second generation.

4. Pew Hispanic Center. (2013). *A nation of immigrants: A portrait of the 40 million, including 11 million unauthorized.* Washington, DC: Pew Research Center. Notably, proportionally we have fewer children growing up in immigrant families today than we did at our previous peak a century ago (25 percent in 2011 versus 28 percent in 1910).

5. Child Trends. (2013). Immigrant children: Indicators on children and youth. Washington, DC: Author. Retrieved from http://www.childtrends. org/?indicators=immigrant-children.

6. Hernandez, D. (2014, February, 28). Lecture. UCLA Program on International Migration. Los Angeles. Based on 2005–2007 U.S. Census Bureau American Community Survey IPUMS; Hernandez, D., & Napierala, J. S. (2012). Children in immigrant families: Essential to America's future. *Child and Youth Well-Being Index policy brief.* New York: Foundation for Child Development. Retrieved from http://fcd-us.org/resources/children-im-migrant-families-essential-americas-future; Passel, J. S. (2011). Demography of immigrant youth: Past, present, and future. *Future of Children: Immigrant Children, 21*(1), 19–41.

7. Child Trends. (2013). The second generation increased from 14 to 21 percent from 1994 to 2012. The first generation, on the other hand, remained between 4 to 5 percent

throughout this period of time, peaking at 4.7 percent in 2005 and declining since then.

8. Ibid. In 2012, for the first generation, the four most common birthplaces were Mexico (28 percent), China, India, and the Philippines (each at 5 percent); for the second generation, the four most common birthplaces were Mexico (38 percent), El Salvador, India, and the Philippines (each at 5 percent). Note that the rate of Mexican migration has steadily dropped over the past decade for both the first and second generation.

9. Huynh, Q. L., Devos, T., & Smalarz, L. (2011). Perpetual foreigner in one's own land: Potential implications for identity and psychological adjustment. *Journal of Social Clinical Psychology, 30*(2), 133–162.

10. United Nations Development Program. (2009). *Human development report— Overcoming barriers: Human mobility and development.* New York: United Nations Development Program. While migration may be undertaken by individuals, when migration happens in large scale from one country to another, it is often shaped by deep historical and economic relationships between sending and receiving countries; Suárez-Orozco, M. M., & Suárez-Orozco, C. (2013). Taking perspective: Context, culture, and history. In M. G. Hernández, J. Nguyen, C. L. Saetermoe, & C. Suárez-Orozco (Eds.), *Frameworks and Ethics for Research with Immigrants: New Directions for Child and Adolescent Development, 141* (pp. 9–23). San Francisco: Jossey-Bass. These migration corridors—the dense networks of relationships based on trade, colonial ties, and war—come over time to channel migrations from discrete sending contexts into specific receiving nations. When citizens can lead productive lives, according to their prescribed cultural schemas and social practices, and have the resources to fulfill their roles and obligations to their families, migration is an option attractive only to adventurers. When conditions in a country become destabilized—and migration corridors and networks of relationships are in place—migration follows.

11. The editors of this book have chosen to use the gender-inclusive terms "their" or "they" throughout this book in place of using "his or her." We do this recognizing that, although grammatically incorrect, "their" is an inclusive term that does not reinforce a gender binary.

12. United Nations High Commissioner for Refugees (2003). Guidelines on international protection: Cessation of refugee status under article 1C(5) and (6) of the 1951. Convention relating to the status of refugees (the "Ceased Circumstances" Clauses). HCR/GIP/03/03.

13. Martínez, O. Why the children fleeing Central American will not stop coming. *Nation* (July 30). Retrieved from http://www.thenation.com/article/180837/ why-children-fleeing-central-america-will-not-stop-coming.

14. Portes, A., & Rumbaut, R. A. (2001). *Legacies: The story of the new second generation.* Berkeley: University of California Press.

15. Kerr, W. R., & Lincoln, W. F. (2010). *The supply side of innovation: H-1B visa reforms and U.S. ethnic invention.* Cambridge, MA: National Bureau of Economic Research.

16. Passel, J. S. (2011). *Unauthorized immigrant population: National and state trends 2010*. Washington, DC: Pew Hispanic Center. Retrieved from http://pewhispanic.org/files/reports/133.pdf; Schumacher-Matos, E. (2011). Consensus debate and wishful thinking: The economic impact of immigration. In M. Suárez-Orozco, V. Louie, & R. Suro (Eds.), *Writing immigration: Academics and journalists in dialogue*. Berkeley: University of California Press.

17. Levitt, P. (2007). *God needs no passport: Immigrants and the changing American religious landscape*. New York: New Press; Stepick, A. (2005). God is apparently not dead: The obvious, the emergent, and the still unknown in immigration and religion. In K. Leonard, A. Stepick, M. A. Vasquez, & J. Holdaway (Eds.), *Immigrant faiths: Transforming religious life in America* (pp. 11–38). Lanham, MD: AltaMira.

18. Eck, D. L. (2001). *A new religious America*. San Francisco: Harper; Levitt. (2007).

19. Eck. (2001).

20. Levitt. (2007).

21. Eck. (2001); Pew Forum on Religious Life. (2008). *U.S. religious landscape survey: Religious affiliation: diverse and dynamic*. Washington, DC: Author. Retrieved from http://religions.pewforum.org/pdf/report-religious-landscape-study-full.pdf.

22. Kindler, A. L. (2002). *Survey of the states' limited English proficient students and available educational programs and services, 2000–2001 summary report*. Washington, DC: National Clearinghouse for English Language Acquisition and Language Instruction Educational Programs.

23. U.S. Department of Education, National Center for Education Statistics. (2010).

24. Shin, H. B., & Komiski, R. B. (2010). *Language use in the United States*. Washington, DC: American Community Survey Reports. Retrieved from http://www.census.gov/population/www/socdemo/language/ACS-12.pdf; Bayley, R., & Regan, V. (2004). Introduction: The acquisition of sociolinguistic competence. *Journal of Sociolinguistics, 8*, 323–338. Though Spanish is the predominant foreign language spoken in the United States, there are two million speakers of Chinese (including its various dialects) and more than one million speakers of Tagalog, French, German, Korean, and Vietnamese. There are a total of 26 languages with more than 100,000 speakers over the age of five in the United States today.

25. Shin & Komiski. (2010).

26. Hernandez. (2014).

27. Kluckhohn, C. K. M., & Murray, H. A. (1948). *Personality in nature, society, and culture*. New York: Knopf.

28. American Psychological Association. (2012). *Crossroads: The psychology of immigration in the new century; APA Presidential Task Force on Immigration*. Washington, DC: Author. Retrieved from http://www.apa.org/topics/immigration/report.aspx.

29. Kao, G., & Tienda, M. (1995). Optimism and achievement: The educational performance of immigrant youth. *Social Science Quarterly, 76*(1), 1–19.

30. García Coll, C., & Magnuson, K. (1997). The psychological experience of immigration: A developmental perspective. In A. Booth, A. C. Crouter, & N. Landale

(Eds.), *Immigration and the family: Research and policy on U.S. immigrants* (pp. 91–132). New York: Routledge.

31. Suárez-Orozco & Suárez-Orozco. (2001).

32. Suárez-Orozco & Suárez-Orozco. (2013).

33. Evans, G. W., Li, D., & Whipple, S. S. (2013). Cumulative risk and child development. *Psychological Bulletin, 139*(6), 1342–1396.

34. Masten, A. S. (2001). Ordinary magic: Resilience processes in development. *American Psychologist, 56*(3), 227–238.

35. García Coll & Magnuson. (1997).

36. See, for example, the film *Spellbound* (2002; directed by Jeffrey Blitz).

37. Suárez-Orozco, C., Suárez-Orozco, M., & Todorova, I. (2008). *Learning a new land: Immigrant adolescents in America.* Cambridge: Harvard University Press.

38. García Coll, C., & Marks, A. (Eds.). (2011). *The immigrant paradox in children and adolescents: Is becoming American a developmental risk?* Washington, DC: American Psychological Association Press; Suárez-Orozco, C., & Suárez-Orozco, M. (1995). *Transformations: Immigration, family life, and achievement motivation among Latino adolescents.* Stanford: Stanford University Press.

39. Portes & Rumbaut. (2001).

40. Murnane, R. (1996). *Teaching the new basic skills: Principles for educating children to thrive in a changing economy.* New York: Free Press.

41. Portes & Zhou. (1993). The new second generation: Segmented assimilation and its variants. *Annals of the American Academy of Political and Social Science, 530*(1), 74–96.

42. Suárez-Orozco et al. (2008).

43. Marks, A. K., Ejesi, K., & García Coll, C. (2014). The U.S. immigrant paradox in childhood and adolescence. *Child Development Perspectives, 8*(2), 59–64.

44. Kao, G., & Tienda, M. T. (1995). Optimism and achievement: The educational performance of immigrant youth. *Social Science Quarterly, 76*(1), 1–19.

45. Ogbu, J. (1991). Immigrant and involuntary minorities in comparative perspective. In M. Gibson and J. Ogbu (Eds.), *Minority status and schooling: A comparative study of immigrant and involuntary minorities* (pp. 3–36). New York: Garland.

46. Walqui, A. (2000). *Access and engagement: Program design and instructional approaches for immigrant students in secondary school.* McHenry, IL: Delta Systems.

47. Suárez-Orozco & Suárez-Orozco. (2001).

48. Levine, R. A. (1993). *Worlds of childhood.* New York: HarperCollins.

49. Suárez-Orozco & Suárez-Orozco. (2001).

50. Maccoby, M. M. (1992). The role of parents in the socialization of children: An historical overview. *Developmental Psychology, 26*(8), 1006–1017.

51. Suarez-Orozco & Suarez-Orozco. (2001).

52. Boss, P. (1999). *Ambiguous loss: Learning to live with unresolved grief.* Cambridge: Harvard University Press.

53. Abego, L. J. (2013). *Sacrificing families, navigating laws, labor and love across borders.* Stanford: Stanford University Press; Coe, C. (2013). *The scattered family:*

Parenting, African migrants, and global inequality. Chicago: University of Chicago Press.

54. Orner, P., & Hernández, S. (2009). *En las sombras de los Estados Unidos: Naraciones de los immigrantes indocumentados.* San Francisco: McSweeney's Books.

55. Suárez-Orozco & Suárez-Orozco. (2001).

56. Maccoby. (1992).

57. Orellana, M. (2009). *Translating childhoods: Immigrant youth, language, and culture.* New Brunswick: Rutgers University Press.

58. Suárez-Orozco & Suárez-Orozco. (2001).

59. Hanson, G. H. (2010). *The economics and policy of illegal immigration in the United States.* Washington, DC: Migration Policy Institute.

60. Suárez-Orozco & Suárez-Orozco. (2013). During the past 40 years, the U.S. economy has had plenty of jobs for new immigrants. By 2010, more than 35 million immigrants were in the U.S. labor market, representing approximately 15.7 percent of the U.S. workforce, an increase from 9.7 percent in 1995. In some sectors of the economy, such as agriculture, the reliance on migrant workers has been continuous: generation after generation of growers have summoned migrant workers to tend American fields. In other areas, the reliance is more cyclical. Construction is an example—the real-estate boom of the 1990s created a voracious appetite for immigrant workers that has disappeared since the 2008 recession.

61. Hanson. (2010).

62. Suárez-Orozco & Suárez-Orozco. (2013).

63. Hernandez & Napierala. (2012).

64. Ibid.

65. Child Trends. (2013). The *poverty rate* is defined as the U.S. Bureau Census thresholds for poverty (e.g., $23,492 per year for a family of four).

66. Ibid. *Near-poverty* is defined as between 100 and 199 percent of official poverty rates.

67. Child Trends. (2013).

68. Brooks-Gunn, J., & Duncan, G. J. (1997). The effects of poverty on children. *Future of Children, 7*(2), 55–71; Milner, H. R. (2013). Analyzing poverty, learning, and teaching through a critical race theory lens. *Education in Research, 37*(1), 1–53.

69. Brooks-Gunn & Duncan. (1997).

70. Hernandez, D. J., Denton, N. A., & Macartney, S. (2009, April). Children in immigrant families—the U.S. and 50 states: Economic need beyond the official poverty measure. Child Trends & the Center for Social and Demographic Analysis, University of Albany, SUNY. The complex factors surrounding the measurement and effects of socioeconomic status generally are particularly relevant to the situation of immigrant and newcomer families. A research brief that draws on 2000 U.S. Census data to explore differences between poverty rates in children of immigrant families and children of native-born families highlights shortcomings in the official poverty measures.

71. Ibid.; Yoshikawa, H. (2011). *Immigrants raising citizens: Undocumented parents and their young children.* New York: Russell Sage Foundation.

72. Levitt, P., & Schniller, N. G. (2004). Conceptualizing simultaneity: A transnational social field perspective on society. *International Migration Review, 38*(145), 595–629; de Haas, H. (2005). International migration, remittances and development: Myths and facts. *Third World Quarterly, 26*(8), 1269–1284.

73. Suárez-Orozco & Suárez-Orozco. (2013). This stands in sharp contrast to Canada, for example.

74. Motomura. (2008). Immigration outside the law. *Columbia Law Review, 108*(8), 1–9.

75. Suárez-Orozco, C.,Yoshikawa, H., Teranishi, R., & Suárez-Orozco, M. (2011). Living in the shadows: The developmental implications of unauthorized status. *Harvard Education Review, 81*(3), 438–472.

76. Ibid.; Kanstrom, D. (2010). *Deportation nation: Outsiders in American history.* Cambridge: Harvard University Press; Menjívar, C. (2006). Liminal legality: Salvadoran and Guatemalan immigrants' lives in the United States. *American Journal of Sociology, 111*, 999–1037.

77. Preston, J. (2011, June 4). Immigrants are focus of harsh bill in Alabama. *New York Times*, p. A10.

78. American Psychological Association. (2012).

79. Suárez-Orozco, C. (2000). Identities under siege: Immigration stress and social mirroring Among the Children of Immigrants. In A. Robben & M. Suárez-Orozco (Eds.), *Cultures under siege: Social violence and trauma* (pp. 194–226). Cambridge: Cambridge University Press.

80. Sirin, S. R., & Fine, M. (2008). *Muslim American youth: Understanding hyphenated identities through multiple methods.* New York: NYU Press.

81. Chavez, L. (2008). *The Latino threat: Constructing immigrants, citizens, and the nation.* Stanford: Stanford University Press.

82. Massey, D. S. (2010). *New faces in new places: The changing geography of American immigration.* New York: Russell Sage Foundation; Suro, R. (2011). Preface. In M. Suárez-Orozco & V. Louie (Eds.), *Writing immigration: Academics and journalists in dialogue* (pp. ix–xxiii). Berkeley: University of California Press.

83. Leadership Conference on Civil Rights Education Fund. (2009). *Confronting the new faces of hate: Hate crimes in America—2009.* Washington, DC: Author. Retrieved from http://www.civilrights.org/publications/hatecrimes/lccref_hate_crimes_report. pdf.

84. Carter, A., Lawrence, M., & Morse, A. (2011). *2011 Immigration-related laws, bills, and resolutions in the states: Jan. 1–March 31, 2011.* Washington, DC: National Conference of State Legislatures. Retrieved from http://www.ncsl.org/default. aspx?tabid=13114.

85. García Coll & Magnuson. (1997); Suárez-Orozco & Suárez-Orozco. (2001).

86. Ibid.

87. Ibid.

88. Super, C. M., & Harkness, S. (1986). The developmental niche: A conceptualization at the interface of child and culture. *International Journal of Behavioral*

Development, 9(4), 545–569; Levitt, P., Barnett, M., & Khalil, N. A. (2011). Learning to pray: Religious socialization across generations and borders. In K. F. Olwig & M. Rytter (Eds.), *Mobile bodies, mobile souls* (pp. 139–159). Aarhus, Denmark: Aarhus University Press.

89. Bronfenbrenner, U., & Morris, P. A. (2006). The bioecological model of human development. In W. Damon & R. M. Lerner (Eds.), *Handbook of child psychology: Vol. 1, Theoretical models of human development* (6th ed., pp. 993–1023). Hoboken, NJ: Wiley; Serdarevic, M., & Chronister, K. M. (2005). Research with immigrant populations: The application of an ecological framework to mental health research with immigrant populations. *International Journal of Mental Health Promotion, 7*(2), 24–34.

90. Lerner, R. M., & Overton, W. F. (2008). Exemplifying the integrations of the relational developmental system: Synthesizing theory, research, and application to promote positive development and social justice. *Journal of Adolescent Research, 23*(3), 245–255.

PART I

Contexts of Development

An Ecological Framework

CAROLA SUÁREZ-OROZCO, MONA M. ABO-ZENA, AND
AMY K. MARKS

In this first set of contributions to the book, we consider several broad social contexts to set the stage for understanding the development of immigrant-origin children and youth. These contexts, derived from an ecological model of human development introduced by Urie Bronfenbrenner[1] are those that matter in unique ways to inform the overall functioning of immigrant families and the development of their children.

Like all children, immigrant children's experiences are a result of reciprocal interactions between their experience and their environment. Outcomes will vary as a function of the child, their culture, and their environment over the course of time. Each child has their own set of characteristics that when interacting with the environment will place them in varying positions of vulnerability or strength. Put simply, all children grow within cultural contexts that shape their future selves. By studying immigrant child development in new—and oftentimes competing—cultural environments, we learn more deeply about the ways all children make adaptations when faced with novel cultural contexts. For immigrant children, some critical individual characteristics shaping development are the child's age at migration, race and ethnicity, language skills, exposure to trauma, sexual orientation, and temperament. *Microsystems* are the settings and arrangements with which the child comes into direct contact, such as family, peers, community, and religious organizations. *Mesosystems* are the interconnections among the various microsystems (such as the relationship the parents have with school personnel); these have an indirect but nonetheless important effect on the child. *Exosystems*, another sphere of indirect effects, are the interconnections among settings and larger social structures that influence the child (such as the safety of a mother's work environment, which can in turn influence her mental health and her consequent psychological availability to her child). The *macrosystems* are the larger political, economic, or social forces that nonetheless have a distinct influence on the child's life (such as a political coups or the Great Recession). The *chronosystem* represents developmental changes over time. (See figure I.1, a depiction of the ecological model of immigration with a focus on adaptation to the new land.)

The chapters of this section consider some of the critical contexts of development that immigrant-origin children and youth navigate in ways that are distinct to their experiences. It is beyond the scope of this book to address all dimensions of the model that influence the immigrant child and youth experience. In this section, we feature dimensions that are particularly important and unique to their development. *Transnational familyhood* constitutes an ecological context specific to immigrant-origin children and youth that is both physical and emotional in nature, with varied effects on family functioning.[2] In two chapters of this section, we consider both family reunifications following separations during the initial migration of the parents and the process of maintaining communication with loved ones across transnational borders. Schools are the setting in which the immigrant child must first systematically cross the boundaries between the home culture and the host culture on a daily basis. Globally, religion plays an important role in the majority of people's lives; it does so in many immigrant families' lives, particularly since religious institutions provide a vital context as immigrants navigate the unfamiliar landscapes of a new homeland.[3] Lastly, national immigration policies provide a context of development that is unique to contemporary immigrant-origin children and youth.

In the study of transnational familyhood in chapter 1, Carola Suárez-Orozco describes how global migrations transform the shape and definition of a family. What does it mean to be a parent, a child, or even a "family unit" in the transnational circumstances of global migration? This chapter explores varieties of family relations, such as the biological parent who sends funds from the United States to support their children and the grandparent, aunt, or uncle in the home country who provides

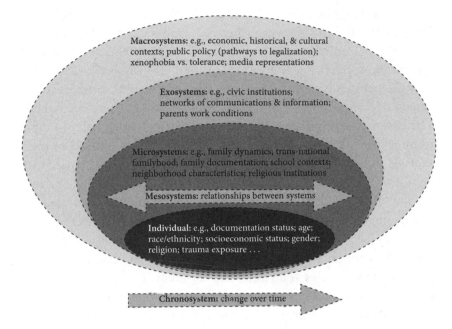

Figure I.1. An ecological perspective on adapting to a new land

for the children's daily needs. Is the children's attachment to the "functional everyday parent" different from that to the long-distance parent? This chapter draws from both qualitative and quantitative studies to illustrate both the joyful and the stressful reverberations of the reunification process for children and their families.

Connecting home and school settings, in chapter 2, Amy K. Marks and Kerrie Pieloch focus on the school contexts of immigrant youth in the United States. Regardless of cultural background, family economics, or documentation status, most immigrant-origin children and adolescents attend schools in the new land. This chapter explores the unique aspects of immigrant-origin children's preschool, primary school, and secondary school contexts, including school resources and language programs, student-teacher body characteristics, and issues related to differences between the family and school cultures. In addition, the chapter explores characteristics and challenges of school-level immigrant peer networks, such as segregation and discrimination, that immigrant children and youth encounter in the school climate.

While forging new connections at school, immigrant-origin youth also develop and maintain their heritage-country connections. Examining another unique manner in which family contexts are shaped by migration, in chapter 3, Gonzalo Bacigalupe and Kimberly Parker discuss the many ways in which immigrant-origin youth connect to the culture of their heritage country and with family members living there. The authors pay particular attention to the increasing use of digital technologies that both shape and maintain the quality of these connections. Historically, the parent generation tended to manage contact with families in the heritage country. However, within the time span of a generation, the handwritten letter that once took months to arrive and the costly long-distance telephone call have become obsolete. With changes in the availability and affordability of technology that now enable rapid and instant communication, Generation M members can now develop and maintain their own qualitatively different relationships with the heritage country and its residents. By analyzing the contexts created by satellite dishes, the Internet, and smartphones, this chapter shows how Generation M has been able to stay connected with others, resulting in altogether different social, cultural, economic, and political exchanges from those available to previous immigrant generations. This chapter also describes how such connections may affect family functioning and contribute to socioemotional development.

While religion and religious contexts play a prominent role in human development generally, in chapter 4, Mona M. Abo-Zena and Meenal Rana describe the multiple ways in which religion may be particularly salient for immigrant-origin families. Religious communities and faiths generally provide them with spiritual guidance and fellowship as well as material support. For immigrants, religious contexts are often coethnic and offer a space for religious, cultural, and ethnic socialization of children. Although a source of support, religion and religious contexts may also challenge the development of immigrant children and youth in various ways such as precipitating a crisis in faith, highlighting differences in degrees of religious commitment between an individual and their family or community, and contending with religious-based discrimination or alienation. The authors also provide examples of how religious content and immigrant context may interact, producing variations in practices that have implications for practitioners and researchers.

At the furthest levels of the ecological model, laws and macro-level contextual processes within a society can have a profound influence on the daily lives and functioning of immigrant-origin children and youth. In chapter 5, Carola Suárez-Orozco and Hirokazu Yoshikawa describe a context that is emotional rather than physical—the very palpable experiences that derive from living in a family with members who have various undocumented legal statuses. An estimated 5.5 million children and adolescents are growing up with unauthorized parents and are experiencing multiple and often unrecognized developmental consequences resulting from their family's existence in the shadow of the law. Although these youth are American in spirit and voice (and three-quarters are citizens themselves), they are nevertheless members of families that are considered "illegal" in the eyes of the law. The authors elucidate the various dimensions of documentation status—going beyond the binary of the "authorized" and "unauthorized." They show how undocumented status cuts across every sector of the ecological framework, influencing multiple developmental outcomes with implications for immigrant children's well-being as well as for the nation's future.

NOTES

1. Bronfenbrenner, U., & Morris, P. A. (2006). The bioecological model of human development. In R. M. Lerner & W. Damon (Eds.), *Handbook of child psychology: Vol. 1, Theoretical models of human development* (6th ed., pp. 793–828). Hoboken, NJ: Wiley.

2. Suárez-Orozco, C., & Suárez-Orozco, M. (2013). Transnationalism of the heart: Familyhood across borders. In D. Cere & L. McClain (Eds.), *What is parenthood?* (pp. 279–298). New York: NYU Press.

3. Levitt, P. (2007). *God needs no passport: Immigrants and the changing American religious landscape.* New York: New Press.

1

Family Separations and Reunifications

CAROLA SUÁREZ-OROZCO

Leticia[1] made the arduous journey from El Salvador, through Mexico, and into Los Angeles after her union-organizer husband had been killed in a demonstration. She left behind eight-month-old Joaquin and five-year-old Silvia in the loving care of their grandmother, planning to send for them as soon as she settled. After the crossing, she took any job she could find, dutifully sending half of her meager earnings to her children and their grand-parents. Though she immediately applied for asylum, her request worked its way slowly through the approval process, taking 11 years to be formally granted. Now remarried with two new children, Leticia had accumulated sufficient savings to send for the children. However, the adolescents rejoined their mother with mixed feelings. Twelve-year-old Joaquin had no recollection of her, as she had not been able to travel back and forth while awaiting asylum status; he was angry about being summoned to join a family to which he did not feel attached. Sixteen-year-old Silvia fondly remembered an idealized mother and eagerly looked forward to new opportunities, yet she deeply resented her stepfather and new siblings, whom she felt had unfairly stolen their mother's attention during the years of separation. Though the family awkwardly but lovingly reunited at the airport, the honeymoon of reunification was short. Both siblings missed their beloved grandmother, aunts, uncles, and cousins as well as their daily routines and found adjusting to their new home difficult. Joaquin was sullen and frequently had angry outbursts. Silvia quietly withdrew into herself, often crying herself to sleep. Their mother alternated between overindulgently trying to woo her children in an attempt to make up for lost time and angrily scolding them for being ungrateful and uncooperative.

Increasingly, global migrations have led to long-distance "familyhood" practiced across national borders. Transnational migration results in a cycle of "separation and reunification of different members of the family unit over time,"[2] beginning with a member's initial sacrifice to benefit other family members. Shortly after a Filipina nurse loses her husband to cancer, for example, she makes the migratory journey to Abu Dhabi, working long shifts to support her four young children, who have stayed behind in the care of her mother. A Haitian accountant from Port-au-Prince reluctantly leaves his family to find work as a taxi driver in Boston to save for his youngest daughter's costly medical treatment. The father of two toddlers, finding no work on his rancho in Mexico, makes his way north to Los Angles to labor as a landscaper, hoping to send for his wife and children before the children reach school age. Countless similar sacrifices constitute the ethical logic of family migration the world over. In most cases, the intention is to work hard, gather funds, and reunite with family soon either "here or there." The bittersweet paradox of immigration is that while undertaken for the well-being of the family, in reality transnationalism wrenches the family apart.

The international incidence of transnational families has garnered increasing recognition and interest, as noted by the United Nations Development Program on Human Mobility.[3] While it is difficult to establish the frequency of immigrant family separations, informed estimates can be made. There were 214 million immigrants and refugees in 2010. If, on average, each leaves behind two immediate family members,[4] at least 642 million individuals may be involved in transbordered, transnational family configurations.

Typically, migrations take place in a "stepwise" fashion, with one family member going ahead, followed later by others.[5] Historically, the male left first, establishing a beachhead in a new land while making remittances home. Over time, when financially feasible, the process of bringing relatives—wife, children, and others—began. But in recent decades, immigration has achieved a nearly perfect gender balance.[6] The first world's demand for service workers draws women[7]—many of them mothers—from a range of developing countries to care for "other people's children."[8] In countries with a rapidly increasing number of aging people, these immigrants also care for "other people's aging parents." When migrating mothers leave their children behind, often members of the extended family such as grandparents or aunts become the primary caretakers with the help of the father (if he remains local and is still part of the family). In other cases, both parents go ahead, leaving the children with the extended family.[9]

As migrant households gain a firmer footing in the country of immigration, new children are born. These complex blended families incorporate a variety of settled migrants, new arrivals, and *citizen-children* who are born in the new land.[10] In recent years, families with undocumented parents have been involuntarily wrenched apart by workplace as well as in-home raids conducted by immigration authorities. These result in citizen-children being left behind, sometimes in relatives' care or in foster homes, or being forced to relocate to a country they have never known (see Suárez-Orozco and Yoshikawa, "The Shadow of Undocumented Status," chapter 5 in this volume).[11]

The United Nations Human Development Report of 2009 suggests that family separations are widespread and have lasting repercussions. In a nationally representative survey of documented immigrants within North America, nearly a third of the six- to 18-year-olds had been separated from at least one parent for two or more years. Notably, the rates of separation were highest for children of Latin American origin, who account for more than half of all migrants to the United States.[12] Since separation rates are higher among the unauthorized or those in the process of regulating their documentation status, this is probably a low estimate. Many migrations result in protracted family separations that deeply threaten the identity and cohesion of the family, transforming well-established roles, creating new loyalties and bonds, and destabilizing cultural scripts of authority, reciprocity, and responsibility.[13] Even under the best of circumstances, the family is never the same after migration. While one family starts the migration process, an entirely different family completes it.

The Longitudinal Immigrant Student Adaptation Study

We conducted a U.S. bicoastal study with 400 recently arrived immigrant public school youth from China, the Dominican Republic, various countries in Central America, Haiti, and Mexico and found that the majority of the children had been separated from one or both parents for protracted periods of time—from six months to 10 years.[14] Nearly three-quarters of the youth had been separated from one or both parents during the migration process. Significant differences among ethnic groups regarding family separations emerged: Chinese families were the least likely to be separated over the course of migration (52 percent) while the vast majority of Central American (88 percent) and Haitian children (85 percent) had been separated from either one or both parents during the course of migration.[15] Approximately 26 percent of children in the study had been separated from both parents for some period of time, a pattern most often occurring in Central American families (54 percent). Separations from only the mother occurred most frequently among Dominican families (40 percent), whereas separations from only the father were found most frequently among Mexican families (33 percent).[16]

Some children reported being separated from one or both parents for nearly their entire childhood. The length of separation between parents and their children varied widely across regions of origin. Of the youth who had been separated only from their mothers, 54 percent of Central American children (approximately a third of both the Dominican and Haitian families) endured separations lasting four or more years. Chinese and Mexican children underwent fewer and shorter separations from their mothers. However, when separations from their fathers occurred during migration, these were often very lengthy or permanent (a total of 28 percent of the sample had separations from fathers that lasted more than four years—44 percent of these were Haitian; 42 percent, Central American; and 28 percent, Dominican).[17]

An interplay of cultural practices, political and economic pressures, and policy limitations contributed to these patterns.[18] The Chinese were most likely to be documented and had small families so were thus more likely to have the luxury of migrating as a family unit. Central Americans were often fleeing traumatic political conditions, ended up waiting in long bureaucratic lines to be granted refugee status, felt an obligation to send remittances to family members left behind, and simply did not have the funds to bring their children over. In the case of Haitians, the fathers often went ahead and formed new families; as political and economic chaos escalated in their native land, they sent for their biological children but not their former spouses. Mexicans, living across the U.S.

border and following a historical legacy of the bracero program,[19] have a long-standing cultural practice of fathers crossing the border to work and sending funds back.

What are the psychological effects of these separations? When comparing youth who had not been separated from family with those who had, youth who had arrived as part of a family unit were less likely to report symptoms of depression or anxiety in the initial years following reunification. Those who had undergone the longest separations from their mothers reported the highest levels of these symptoms five years later. Generally, the highest levels of distress were reported by youth who had experienced medium- and long-term separations.[20] Not surprisingly, youth who had been separated from their mothers for four or more years reported the greatest distress. Many of these children had stayed with their fathers rather than with both grandparents or with aunts and uncles and reported less stability of care. The lowest rates of psychological distress were observed among youth who had not undergone separations. Of those who had been separated, youth who had borne separations of less than two years from only their fathers fared best. The children who had remained with their mother while the father was away seemed to fare better; perhaps they had both continuity of care and the financial stability afforded by a father working to send funds back.[21]

The Separation Phase

The act of separation was often described by respondents in our study as one of the hardest aspects of coming to the United States. Jamisa,[22] a 14-year-old Dominican girl, said, "The day I left my mother I felt like my heart was staying behind. Because she was the only person I trusted— she was my life. I felt as if a light had extinguished. I still have not been able to get used to living without her."

In many cases, parents left their children when they were infants and toddlers. Carmen, the mother of 13-year-old Central American twins, shared, "It was very hard above all to leave the children when they were so small. I would go into the bathroom of the gas station and milk my breasts that overflowed, crying for my babies. Every time I think of it, it makes me sad."

Parents told us that although they had hoped to reunite quickly with their children, the separations turned out to be more protracted than anticipated. A host of other challenges associated with migration often compounded parents' separation from their children. These included barriers due to language and cultural differences, long hours working for low wages, displacement from familiar settings, cultural disorientation, and a limited social support system. Lack of documentation and concerns about security added exponentially to the distress of having the family torn apart.

Rosario, a Salvadoran mother of three, told us,

> I never thought it would be so long. But I had no choice. My husband had been killed, and my children had no one else. I had to make the journey to El Norte. I left them with my mother, hoping I could send for them in a few months, but life here is so expensive. I sent money back every month to take care of them and saved every dollar I could, and I spent nothing on myself. My life was better in El Salvador. Here I had no friends. I was always lonely. I miss my children desperately and my family. I worked all the time. But a safe crossing was so expensive for three children.

Parents, especially mothers, maintain contact with their children through a series of strategies that include sending regular remittances, making weekly phone calls, exchanging letters and e-mails, sending photos and gifts, using Skype (see Bacigalupe and Parker, "Transnational Connections through Emerging Technologies," chapter 3 in this volume), and occasionally making return visits as finances and documentation status allow. Over time, these contacts play an ever more important role in nurturing the memory of the absent parent in the child's mind.

Being able to send funds to support children and other family members is the core motivation for the majority of the parental absences.[23] A 15-year-old Guatemalan girl, Amparo, explained, "I remember that my grandparents would tell me that my parents had to go to work so they could send money for us to live on." Children recalled gifts that had been sent, sometimes on special occasions in the form of money so they could buy what they liked but also in the form of lovingly selected items sent with visitors. Lupita, a 12-year-old Mexican girl, recounted, "My parents would send dolls, necklaces, clothes, and perfume—things they thought I would like." For some, the gifts served to salve the absence of the parent. Leandro, a 12-year-old Mexican boy, explained, "[My grandparents] would say to me, 'Son, do you miss your mother?' I would say, 'Yes' and then go and play. With the video games she sent, I would forget everything."

Staying in touch by sending gifts is a tangible means of maintaining contact. Nevertheless, a few children reported that no number of material goods could provide what they wanted: a parent's presence and active involvement in their daily life. For example, 14-year-old Bao Yu said, "Even though he kept sending me new beautiful clothes—so what? I felt that he is my father, he should *stay* with me and see how I grow up." While some children had memories of their parents, for others, memories had begun to fade. Araceli, a 13-year-old Guatemalan girl whose mother had left when she was two (and whom Araceli did not see again until nine years later, when her asylum papers were finally granted), told us, "I would look at the pictures of my mother, and I would think that I would like to meet her because I could not remember her. . . . I would say, 'What a pretty mom—I would like to meet her.'" For a number of immigrant youth, the parents in the picture were parents in name only, long-distance benevolent figures ambiguously present but with whom the children had had few firsthand experiences.

Over the course of time, many families, especially those enduring long-term separations, find it difficult to maintain steady long-distance communication. Communication is hardest for parents who left children behind when they were very young. As the children grow up, the parent becomes an abstraction. As the mother of a 12-year-old Salvadorian boy, Manuel, explained, "They lived with my mother in El Salvador. I left when they were babies. I spoke to the eldest once a month by phone. As the little one grew, I spoke to him, too. But since he didn't know me, our communication was quite short. I really had to pull the words out of him."

As we listened to parents, it was evident that the absent child remained a daily sustaining presence in their lives. For children, however, the story was different. Especially with long-term parental absences, for many youth it was a case of out of sight, out of mind. Often the day-to-day caretakers took on the parenting function along with the psychological role of being the symbolic "mother" or "father."

The Reunification Phase

One might expect that after so many sacrifices, family reunification would be joyful. Indeed, many children, especially those whose separations had been short-term or from only one parent, described the moment of reunification with the word *happy*. A 13-year-old Guatemalan girl recalled the day she reunited with her mother: "[I was] so happy. It was my dream to be with her." Likewise, Yara, a 14-year-old Dominican girl, described her family's reunification: "We were so happy. We cried, talked a lot, and embraced."

Yet for many children who had endured protracted separations, the reunification was quite complicated. In almost all cases, the children remembered their parents receiving them in a highly emotional and tearful welcoming manner. The children's experience, meanwhile, was different—the parent had become a stranger. As Beatriz, a 14-year-old Guatemalan new arrival, recalled, "My mother was crying. She hugged me, . . . and I felt bad. Like neither my sister nor I *knew* her."

For parents, the reunification signified the joyful conclusion of a painful period of sacrifice and struggle to bring the family together. For the children, however, the reunification was the beginning of a new and emotionally laden phase. For them, it meant entering a new life in a new land to be raised by a new set of adults. They reported intense feelings of disorientation. Thirteen-year-old Celeste from Haiti confided, "I didn't know who I was going to live with or how my life was going to be. I knew of my father, but I did not know him." Even under optimal circumstances, migrating to a different country and adopting a new way of life are disorientating. Yet for many youth in our study, the process was complicated by uncertainty about whether they would feel comfortable in their own homes, get along with the people with whom they would be living, and know what their everyday routines would be. These children were experiencing two migrations—one to a new country and another to a new family.

Araceli, a cautious 13-year-old from Guatemala whose father had left before her birth and mother had left when she was a year old, not reuniting with her for nine years, recalled, "I felt very strange since I didn't know my mother. I saw a lot of women [at the airport] but didn't know who my mom was. And when she came to hug me, I said to her, 'Are you my mom?' I didn't hug her very hard because I didn't know her or anything. I didn't have that much trust or didn't feel that comfortable with her."

Upon reunification, these youth displayed emotions ranging from a short-term sense of disorientation to sadness to anger. For some, the extended absence led to a sustained rejection of the parent whom they perceived as having abandoned them. In such cases, the damage of the long absence led to rifts that were challenging to traverse. Some children were unforgiving; by the time parents reentered their lives, it was too late. These youth had grown accustomed to living without the missing parent; they were ready to assert greater independence and were unwilling to submit to the parents' authority after an extended separation. A 14-year-old Chinese girl, An, confided that after a nine-year absence, "Suddenly I had another creature in my life called 'father.' . . . I was too old by then, and I could no longer accept him into my life."

Some parents perceived the rupture in trust and patiently worked to rebuild a bridge across the emotional chasm. The mother of a 14-year-old Honduran, Felipe, told us, "It was really hard at the beginning because we had been separated for five years. . . . He barely trusted me, but now, little by little we are building something." But other parents were less patient and were hurt and indeed enraged that their children did not appreciate the sacrifices made on their behalf. A Haitian father who had worked years to bring his daughter over said between clenched teeth, "She barely looks at me. All she does is complain that she wants to be back with her aunt, and she just treats me like an ATM."

Parents and adolescents shared with us that reunifications were especially complicated when youth had to adapt to entirely new family members, particularly new stepparents (or partners) or new siblings (or stepsiblings). For example, 12-year-old Inez from Mexico explained why she had not wanted to migrate: "I did not know anybody, and I was going to live with a man [a new stepfather] I did not like." Many admitted outright jealousy. The mother of 13-year-old Nicaraguan Enrique disclosed, "We are getting used to each other. We are both beginning a different life together. . . . The kids are jealous of each other, and my husband is jealous of them. . . . Jealousy exists between those who were born here and those who were not."

It was not unusual for the youth to envy the attention lavished on new siblings (or stepsiblings). As 14-year-old Bao Yu articulated, "Now whenever I see how my father spends time playing with my younger sister, I always get mad that he never gave me fatherly love. Now I think he is trying to make up to my younger sister." This pattern of envy often led to tension and conflict among family members.

The moment of reunification was thus interlaced with contradictory emotions as children had to leave the caretakers who had become their de facto parents during the absence of the immigrant parent. A 16-year-old Guatemalan, Marisol, explained, "I loved living with them [the grandparents] because they were really sweet people. They were wonderful parents. For me they are not like grandparents[;] they are like my parents because they understand me [and] they love me. . . . I did not want to leave them."

Understandably, many adolescents described their bittersweet feelings upon reunification because of this loss of caretakers with whom they had had daily contact. Marisol told us, "I was sad because I had left my grandparents behind but happy to be together with my mother." Similarly, 11-year-old Honduran Juan recalled, "I was crying because I was leaving my grandfather. I had conflicting feelings. On the one hand, I wanted to see my mother, but on the other, I did not want to leave my grandfather." Such double separations and losses are major disruptions in the lives of these youngsters. In these situations, the grandparents also endure two sets of major separations. The elderly had said good-byes to their own children when the family migration began and then had to bid farewell to their grandchildren whom they had raised as their own children.

Many parents expressed guilt for having been away from their children while recognizing that their sacrifice was necessary for the good of the family. It often dawned on them that their children did not always understand this situation. The longer the parents and child were apart, the harder it was for the child to make sense of things and the more parental authority and credibility were undermined. Graciela, the insightful mother of a 13-year-old Central American girl, reflected on life since the reunification:

Our relationship has not been that good. We were apart for 11 years and communicated by letters. Now, we have to deal with that separation. It's been difficult for her and for me. It's different for my son because I've been with him since he was born. If I scold him, he understands where I'm coming from. He does not get angry or hurt when I discipline him, but if I discipline [my daughter], she takes a completely different attitude. I think this is a normal way to feel given the circumstances.

Further Issues to Explore

Both quantitative and qualitative data reflecting youth's and parents' points of view underscore their disorientation and distress during separations and reunification. Both parents and youth in our study described their acute discomfort in the initial months and years following reunification. Over time, however, most newcomer immigrant youth appeared to adjust to the loss and negative circumstances of separation resulting from migration, demonstrating remarkable strength, determination, resourcefulness, and resilience in dealing with the imposed challenges. This result is consistent with resilience research that suggests many youth and families have a noteworthy capacity to overcome negative circumstances in their lives.[24] We should caution, however, that while the specific psychological symptoms we measured—anxiety and depression—subsided over time, it remains an open question what the long-term developmental, psychological, and relational implications might be.[25]

Future research should attempt to establish prevalence rates for other high-intensity sending (e.g., the Philippines, India) and receiving (e.g., Canada, Australia) of other migrant populations across the globe. This line of inquiry would best be done by involving researchers on "both sides of the border." More research will be required to further unpack the short- and long-term effects of separations. Multiple outcomes beyond depression and anxiety should be considered, including academic performance, trust, family relations and conflict, and interpersonal relations, as these outcomes may be affected by disruptions in family relations. Studies should be developed to examine what the particular vulnerable stages of development for separations and subsequent reunifications are.[26]

Cross-cultural perspectives are critical to understanding these migration-related separations. Theories about parent-child relationships, such as attachment theory, predict that family separations lead to negative psychological outcomes. However, such frames of reference are limited since they were developed by Western-trained psychologists with the constricted lens of understanding that comes with that perspective. We are left with the question of whether such theories and principles might "apply to *many, most, or all* . . . irrespective of their national or cultural contexts and irrespective of income [and] education."[27] Although the exploration of country-of-origin differences in our study yielded limited distinctions in responses to parental separations, there was one key exception—while for other groups the psychological symptoms abated over time, the Mexican children reported short-term depression and anxiety as well as residual anxiety that was sustained over time the longer they were separated from their mothers. This finding suggests the possibility of cultural differences in patterns of normative acceptance of mothers leaving, a phenomenon to be explored in further studies.[28]

One way to avoid imposing ethnocentric outcomes would be to do initial qualitative work with professionals in the country of origin; considering outcomes of concern noted within that context would strengthen the constructs and instruments used. Culturally sensitive work should consider cultural norms of child care and the meaning of collective values of family in different cultures that are closely related to family separation issues.[29] Child fostering is a normative child-care practice in the Caribbean and African cultures.[30] For Chinese immigrants, it is now common practice to send infants back to China to be raised by grandparents until school age; they then are returned to the birth parents to begin their education in Canada or the United States.[31] For some other families, separation could be an intentional strategy to seek greater opportunities for children's futures as well as to secure and improve the family's collective position in this globalized 21st-century economy, as we can see in cases of "parachute children"[32] or independent child migrants (sometimes referred to as *unaccompanied minors*).[33]

Future research should consider developmental patterns since there are likely to be certain stages of development in which children may be more or less vulnerable during separation or reunification. Further qualitative research needs to be conducted to unpack the gendered processes behind the variations and nuanced sensitivities to separations from the mother or father. Further research should build on previous work that points to an association between complicated family reunifications and subsequent academic difficulties.[34] Evidence-based intervention studies should be developed to explore ways to reduce the negative effects of separation and to create strategies to help families manage the reunification process.[35]

On a cautionary note, those who conduct this kind of research must maneuver significant ethical land mines since participants are often both emotionally vulnerable as they speak of their significant losses and legally vulnerable as many have not achieved full documented status. Thus, researchers must proceed with extreme care as they begin researching this important domain affecting many families in our increasingly globalized world.[36]

For those who immigrate from many points of origin to a variety of destinations, transnational familism, separations, and (often complicated) reunifications create at least a temporary challenge for family relations and development. Children and youth talked about missing loved ones—their parents (during the separation phase) and their caretakers (during the reunification phase). Quite notably, however, transnational youth display remarkable resilience in the face of the adversities of family separation. Moving forward, those who serve immigrant communities should keep in mind the magnitude of the phenomenon of immigrant family separations. While recognizing the short-term challenges these present to families and youth, service providers and researchers must check their cultural biases, assumptions, and expectations regarding what a "typical" family looks like.[37] Providers also need to stand ready to supply supports that children, youth, and families require as they adapt to these challenges to the family system.

NOTES

1. All case studies are based on real examples from our research or experience but have been disguised and use pseudonyms.

2. Tyyskä, V. (2007). Immigrant families in sociology. In J. E. Lansford, K. D. Deater-Deckard, & M. H. Bornstein (Eds.), *Immigrant families in contemporary society* (pp. 83–99). New York: Guilford. (Quotation from p. 91.)

3. United Nations Development Program (UNDP). (2009). *Human development report 2009—Overcoming barriers: Human mobility and development.* New York: United Nations Development Program.

4. This is likely a conservative estimate. Most migrants tend to originate from settings with large families. Further, estimates of global remittances suggest that in some

South–North migration corridors, each migrant in the North who sends funds back to the South is supporting an estimated four family members remaining behind. World Bank, *World Bank Migration and Remittances Fact Book* (Washington, DC: World Bank, 2008).

5. Hondagneu-Sotelo, P. (Ed.). (2003). *Gender and U.S. immigration: Contemporary trends*. Berkeley: University of California; Orellana, M. F., Thorne, B., Chee, A. E., & Lam, W. S. E. (2001). Transnational childhoods: The participation of children in processes of family migration. *Social Problems, 48*(4), 572–591.

6. UNDP. (2009).

7. Abrego, L. (2009). Economic well-being in Salvadoran transnational families: How gender affects remittance practices. *Journal of Marriage and Family, 71*, 1070–1085.

8. Hondagneu-Sotelo, P., & Avila, E. (1997). "I'm here, but I'm there": The meanings of Latina transnational motherhood. *Gender & Society, 11*(5), 548–571. (Quotation from p. 548.)

9. Bernhard, J. K., Landolt, P., & Goldring, L. (2006). Transnational, multi-local motherhood: Experiences of separation and reunification among Latin American families in Canada. *CERIS, Policy Matters, 24*. Retrieved on July 15, 2009, from http://ceris.metropolis.net/PolicyMatter/2006/PolicyMatters24.pdf; Foner, N. (2009). Introduction: Intergenerational relations in immigrant families. In N. Foner (Ed.), *Across generations: Immigrant families in America* (pp. 1–20). New York: NYU Press.

10. Menjívar, C. (2006). Family reorganization in the context of legal uncertainty: Guatemalan and Salvadoran immigrants in the United States. *International Journal of Sociology of the Family, 32*(2), 223–245; Suárez-Orozco, C., Yoshikawa, H., Teranishi, R., & Suárez-Orozco, M. (2011). Living in the shadows: The developmental implications of unauthorized status. *Harvard Education Review, 81*(3), 438–472.

11. Capps, R. M., Castañeda, R. M., Chaudry, A., & Santos, R. (2007). *The impact of immigration raids on America's children*. Washington DC: Urban Institute; Chaudry, A., Pedroza, J., Castañeda, R. M., Santos, R., Scott, M. M. (2010). *Facing our future: Children in the aftermath of immigration enforcement*. Washington, DC: Urban Institute.

12. Gindling, T. H. & Poggio, S. (2009). Family separation and the educational success of immigrant children. Policy Brief. Baltimore: University of Maryland.

13. Suárez-Orozco, C., & Suárez-Orozco, M. (2013). Transnationalism of the heart: Familyhood across borders. In L. McClain & D. Cere (Eds.), *What is parenthood?* (pp. 279–298). New York: NYU Press.

14. Suárez-Orozco, C., Suárez-Orozco, M. M., & Todorova, I. (2008). *Learning a new land: Immigrant students in American society*. Cambridge: Harvard University Press.

15. Suárez-Orozco, C., Todorova, I., & Louie, J. (2002). "Making up for lost time": The experience of separation and reunification among immigrant families. *Family Process, 41*(4), 625–643.

16. Ibid.

17. Suárez-Orozco, C., Bang, H. J., & Kim, H. Y. (2011). "I felt like my heart was staying behind": Psychological implications of immigrant family separations & reunifications. *Journal of Adolescent Research, 25*(5), 222–257.

18. Coe, K. (2013). *The scattered family: Parenting, African migrants, and global inequality*. Chicago: University of Chicago Press.

19. The bracero (literally, one who works using his arms) program was a temporary contract-worker exchange program between the United States and Mexico that took place between 1942 and 1964.

20. Coe. (2013).

21. Ibid.

22. Pseudonyms are used for all names throughout this chapter.

23. Abrego, L. (2014). *Sacrificing families: Navigating laws, labor, and love across borders*. Stanford: Stanford University Press.

24. Masten, A. S. (2001). Ordinary magic: Resilience processes in development. *American Psychologist, 56*(3), 227–238.

25. Suárez-Orozco, Bang, & Kim (2011).

26. Ibid.

27. Arnett, J. J. (2008). The neglected 95%: Why American psychology needs to become less American. *American Psychologist, 63*(7), 602–614. (Quotation from p. 609.)

28. Suárez-Orozco, Bang, & Kim (2011).

29. Ibid.

30. Coe. (2013).

31. Bohr, Y., Whitfield, N. T., & Chan, J. L. (2009). Transnational parenting: A new context for attachment and the need for better models: Socio-ecological and contextual paradigms. Paper presented at the meeting of the Society for Research in Child Development, Denver, CO; Gaytán, F. X., Xue, Q., & Yoshikawa, H. (2006). Transnational babies: Patterns and predictors of early childhood travel to immigrant mothers' native countries. Paper presented at the annual National Head Start Research Conference, Washington, DC.

32. Parachute kids are a highly select group of foreign students who are sent abroad without their parents to seek a better education in schools in other countries; Zhou, M. (1998). Parachute kids in Southern California: The educational experience of Chinese children in Southern California. *Educational Policy, 12*(6), 682–704.

33. Orellana et al. (2001); Hernández, M. (2013). Migrating alone or rejoining the family? Implications of migration strategies and family separations for Latino adolescents. *Research in Human Development, 10*(4), 332–352.

34. Gindling & Poggio (2009); Suárez-Orozco et al. (2008).

35. Suárez-Orozco, Bang, & Kim (2011).

36. Ibid.; Suárez-Orozco, C., & Yoshikawa, H. (2013). Undocumented status: Implications for child development, policy, and ethical research. In M. G. Hernández, J. Nguyen, C. L. Saetermoe, C. Suárez-Orozco (Eds.), *Frameworks and Ethics for Research with Immigrants: New Directions for Child and Adolescent Development, 141* (pp. 61–78). San Francisco: Jossey-Bass.

37. Suárez-Orozco, Bang, & Kim (2011).

2

School Contexts

AMY K. MARKS AND KERRIE PIELOCH

Marissa is a 16-year-old attendee of a selective, urban, independent high school. The school's gleaming campus looks a lot like the liberal arts college nearby. She attends school on a hard-earned scholarship won for her high grades and exam scores during her attendance at a public middle school. Her family supports her greatly by providing the books and space she needs to study, though she wishes she had a computer at home. Having one would make her study evenings shorter—long nights at the library are taking their toll, complicated by a long city-bus commute each morning. When asked about her school's social climate, she says she tries to spend as little time at her current school as possible when the school day is officially over. She does this, she explains, because students "like me" (those on scholarship, who also tend to be students of color) get into big trouble for small transgressions. And, she adds, "My daddy can't pay my way out of it." She therefore does not take part in school fairs and activities but instead pours her energy into her studies and supporting her family. Besides, she notes, most of her friends attend the nearby public high school, where "no one cares what color you are, what language you are speaking, or how you dress." Their school is not as "nice," she continues, but why would she not rather hang out there? The students make her feel at home. It is her favorite place to go on Friday afternoons when she can give herself a little study break before the weekend.

Immigrant children and adolescents in the United States attend both public and private schools with widely varying economic resources, linguistic services, and student/teacher characteristics. In 2011, children from immigrant households constituted 20.6 percent of the total school-age population. Though they made up 21.5 percent of the total public school enrollment, they were only 6.6 percent of the students attending private schools for ages five through 19.[1] In 2006, immigrant children accounted for 22 percent of children in preschool and kindergarten, 22 percent of children in elementary school (grades one through five), 21 percent of children in middle school (grades six through eight), and 20 percent of children in high school (grades nine through 12). These data and others demonstrate a pattern of solid enrollment of immigrant children in educational institutions, with very little attrition over time from elementary school to high school graduation. Further, according to data from the Integrated Public Use Microdata Series (IPUMS), there was a decline in immigrant student dropouts from 1990 to 2000.[2]

Comparisons across immigrant generations show that first-generation children rather than second-generation or native-born children are the least likely to drop out. (See Marks, Seaboyer, and García Coll, "Academic Achievement," chapter 13 in this volume, for a more detailed examination of the experiences of both high-achieving and academically at-risk immigrant students.) Recent immigrants' optimism (positive attitudes and parents' determination that their children succeed) and cultural capital may at least partially account for this generational disparity.[3] More specifically, several studies have shown that after taking into account family socioeconomic status, children of Mexican, Hispanic, and Asian immigrants are less likely than either same-race U.S.-born or White native peers to drop out of high school.[4] With a strong presence in the public school system and little attrition through high school graduation, first-generation immigrant children and adolescents are in strong attendance at U.S. schools.

Importantly, until reaching the age of 18, immigrant children are entitled to a public education while residing in the United States, an opportunity protected by law regardless of the child's immigration legal status. Many immigrant youth make extraordinary use of both public and private schooling in the United States, with some newcomer youth outperforming native-born youth academically.[5] (See Marks, Seaboyer, and García Coll, "Academic Achievement," chapter 13 in this volume.) At the same time, many immigrant children attend schools that lack adequate resources and that are located in communities struggling with crime conditions that pose serious risks to students' well-being and achievement potential. This chapter examines the social and structural characteristics of preschool, primary school, and secondary school contexts that may promote or inhibit immigrant child development in the United States. We focus our review on the public school system, within which the majority of U.S. immigrant youth are educated, and on several themes that have emerged in recent decades of scholarship, including school characteristics related to discrimination and multiculturalism.

Early Education and Preschools

Most child-care researchers and professionals agree that the first five years of a child's life (before the official start of formal public schooling) are paramount to the child's future development and academic achievement.[6] While census data from early in the first decade of the 21st century revealed that immigrant families used more home-based care (42.5 percent) than out-of-home child care, more recent data from 2007 demonstrated that increasing numbers of immigrant families (68.3 percent) rely on child care and early education (i.e., preschools) outside of the home during this critical period of development.[7] More recent studies also have shown that immigrant families are now more likely to use center-based child care for children ages zero through four rather than care provided at home by a relative or other person.[8] Furthermore, the rate of use of center-based child care increases with a child's age, with about 13.2 percent of immigrant children ages zero through two, 44.9 percent of those age three, and 65.9 percent of those age four receiving center-based care.[9]

Given the growing frequency with which early education centers, center-based child care, and preschools are being utilized by immigrant families, it is important to understand the quality and availability of such out-of-home care. One possible reason for the increase in immigrant participation in preschool care is the expansion of state-funded programs.[10] Accessible, high-quality early childhood education programs, which have been linked to gains in immigrant children's reading, math, and English-language skills, may be an important policy tool to reduce school-readiness gaps faced by immigrant children.[11] Research on such gaps indicates that immigrant children who do not attend preschool are less likely to pass tests of English oral-language proficiency than are peers who experience early childhood educational settings.[12] Preschools, therefore, can be powerful contexts for promoting educational opportunity among immigrant children, particularly those in low-income families.

However, the decision to send children to out-of-home child care is not necessarily an easy one for parents—including immigrant parents—to make. A study of West African immigrant families showed that although the majority of the parents had wanted to have family members care for their children in their own homes, most parents had enrolled their children in child-care centers.[13] One of their reasons for doing so was to allow their children to socialize or interact with other children. The parents also found the center helpful for teaching their children English and preparing them for kindergarten.[14] Other studies have noted immigrant parents' desires to promote their children's biculturalism and bilingualism by enrolling them in English-language-based child care at an early age while also maintaining home traditions and languages from their countries of origin.[15] Furthermore, for immigrant families living in low-income communities where the need for both parents to work many hours per week is great, in-home care by relatives and center-based care such as Head Start may be used together out of necessity.[16]

Though immigrant families' use of out-of-home care is increasing, their preschool usage varies greatly across different ethnic groups. The California Health Interview Survey 2005 found that Asian immigrant families (59.2 percent) were more likely to use licensed child care than Latino (28 percent) or European (12.8 percent) immigrant families were and that their most popular form of child care was a preschool or nursery school (61.2 percent).[17] Latino immigrant families (55 percent) were more likely to use Head Start programs or state preschool than Asian (41.4 percent) or European (3.6 percent) immigrant families were, but their most common form of child care was that provided by a nonfamily member in the person's home (57.1 percent).[18] A study using data from the Early Childhood Longitudinal Study–Birth Cohort (ECLS-B) found that Mexican immigrant families placed their preschool-age children in center-based and home-based care settings at much lower rates than did immigrant families originating from other regions of the world. When using child care, Mexican families tended to use home care and Head Start programs more than center-based care.[19] Immigrant families from Africa, the Middle East, and Europe typically were more likely to use center care for their young children, whereas those from Latin America, the Caribbean, or U.S. territories were more likely to use Head Start programs.[20] Due to the fact that the most advantaged immigrant families more frequently choose center-based care and the least advantaged rely on parent care and Head Start, it is critical for further research to disentangle the influence of family factors, socioeconomic status, and child-care choices across ethnic groups when examining links between early education engagement and school readiness.

Primary Schools

As the contributors assert throughout this book, immigrant children in the United States must develop unique social and psychological competencies for optimal growth and academic achievement. These include developing bilingual and bicultural skills, forming positive ethnic and racial identities, and learning to navigate and overcome both interpersonal and systematic discrimination.[21] In each of these processes, schools play an integral part in facilitating child development. In the primary school years—roughly kindergarten (age five) through the eighth grade (age 13)—schools are a primary source of peer socialization and friendship as well as the central system for academic achievement. Children at this age also learn to interact with nonfamily adults (teachers and school staff) with increasing frequency. Since achievement in primary school is highly correlated with future success in high school and college and with career success and acquisition of personal economic capital, the qualities of primary school contexts are vitally important to the well-being of U.S. immigrant children.[22]

Once immigrant children enter the formal U.S. school system, what kind of environment are they experiencing? A study of the elementary school environments of first- and second-generation Mexican immigrant children found that when compared with a matched sample (indexed by family background characteristics) of U.S.-born White, African, Asian, and Latino children, Mexican immigrant children were more likely to attend an elementary school with a "problematic" school context. In this study a *problematic school context* was defined as one with a larger student body, less experienced teachers, a larger minority representation, a larger proportion of the student body living in poverty, and a greater number of problems such as crime in the neighborhood surrounding the school.[23] Inadequate school resources that create a stratified system around racial and economic disparities remain a pervasive problem in the U.S. educational system. A disproportionate number of racial-minority youth attend schools that do not have the necessary resources to realize the students' learning potential and do not have adequate staffing to ensure that students are provided with equal opportunities to prepare for a college education.[24] Such structural barriers pose strong threats to the welfare of immigrant children, who are more likely to be racial minorities and to live in low-income communities (see Suárez-Orozco, Marks, and Abo-Zena, introduction to this volume).

Although some studies, such as the one noted earlier, indicate that it may be problematic for a school to have a high percentage of ethnic- or racial-minority students, the effects of the ethnic and racial composition of elementary schools on immigrant children who are students there have been linked to different academic experiences and outcomes. Researchers studying Latino immigrant first graders found that having a high concentration of Latino students in the children's school improved their math and reading test scores. However, this result did not occur with U.S.-born White children or U.S.-born Latino children under similar conditions.[25] Another study of third and fourth graders found that Mexican immigrant children at schools with more Latino students perceived more teacher, peer, and community discrimination than children at schools with fewer Latino students did.[26] This outcome was also affected by the value that a school placed on multiculturalism, with children perceiving more discrimination if they felt that the schools devalued multiculturalism.[27]

The same study of Mexican immigrant third and fourth graders also found that children whose teachers valued diversity highly regarded their ethnic identities more positively and considered them more important than did children whose teachers devalued diversity. Additionally, the fourth graders regarded their ethnic identities more positively than the third graders did, but this finding may be related to the fact that these same fourth graders perceived less teacher discrimination than the third graders did.[28] Taken together, these studies indicate the importance of the intersection of school values and immigrant children's emerging ethnic and racial identities—particularly for first- and second-generation youth. As immigrant children become increasingly more aware of their identities, their perceptions of discrimination may negatively impact their self-esteem, physical health, and ability to achieve.[29] Therefore, one critical area of the primary school context that can support the success and development of immigrant youth is the practice and celebration of multiculturalism.

Secondary Schools

With conditions similar to those noted in primary schools, the secondary schools attended by many immigrant adolescents tend to be large, urban, relatively poor, and underresourced. For example, more than half of all teachers in urban schools have at least one English-language learner (ELL) student in their classes, but fewer than 20 percent of these teachers are certified to teach ELL students.[30] Despite such limitations, many first-generation immigrant adolescents, like Marissa in the chapter's opening narrative, excel in high school and beyond. As her story also illustrates, in addition to school resources, the social characteristics of high schools around multiculturalism contribute to a student's optimal achievement and development. During adolescence, a period when students explore their ethnic and racial identities with increasing frequency and intensity,[31] the detrimental effects of discrimination on their well-being and achievement intensify as well.[32] A recent study of 95 first- and second-generation immigrant adolescents found that more than 75 percent reported at least one incident of racial or ethnic discrimination by a peer at school, and more than 50 percent reported at least one incident of racial or ethnic discrimination by a teacher or other adult at school.[33] For second-generation immigrant adolescents (but not for first-generation), perceived discrimination by peers and adults at school was correlated with symptoms of depression. This correlation may indicate that different immigrant generations employ different means of self-protection, so schools, caregivers, and teachers may want to pay particular attention to addressing the discrimination-related mental health needs of second-generation immigrant youth.[34]

While many educators and researchers recognize the need for intervention to prevent discrimination at the school level, there have not been many studies of specific programs that support immigrant youth in this area. One promising approach is the participatory action researchers (PAR) model, which seeks to create ecologically valid and culturally responsive interventions that address immigrant students' immediate concerns while also fostering systematic social change. This model was established in an urban high school through an internship program for Asian immigrant adolescents. It provided the student researchers with a means to articulate the challenges they had been facing as immigrants in a new school. The PAR model also helped the students develop their language and communication skills, facilitated positive peer relationships and group closeness (something notably lacking in Marissa's story), and gave them a sense of pride about their involvement in a program that would help new immigrant students acclimate to life in the United States.[35]

Another noteworthy effort was a literacy-based after-school program that promoted collaboration among culturally and linguistically diverse students, particularly urban, low-income, immigrant youth. The students created a video targeting gossip in their school, specifically focusing on incidents in which students used different languages to spread rumors about each other. By putting the impetus for change in the hands of students, the program taught them to value not only their own language and literacy practices but also those of their diverse peers. Moreover, the students were empowered by this program because it enabled them to create their own solution for resolving a local conflict at their school.[36]

As many immigrant students struggle to adjust to life in U.S. schools, school programs that support their identities and achievements should also be considered by administrators and policy makers. To address the many difficulties being experienced by a large influx of Latino immigrant students, one high school started an after-school mentoring program that paired Latino immigrant students with local college students. After participating in this program, the immigrant students were more successful academically. (Previously they had regarded homework as a "hopeless task.") They had been provided with a safe haven where they felt empowered and comfortable discussing issues with their mentors and consequently felt more respected and valued.[37]

Another high school employed a multilingual drama intervention with two classrooms of immigrant students. This was a 12-week program for students and teachers that included theatrical exercises, language-awareness activities, and stories contributed by the students. Findings demonstrated that students who participated in this program experienced more solidarity with their peers, were enabled to disclose stories of loss and abuse through the supportive theater setting, were empowered, and felt pride in demonstrating their mastery of their own and other languages.[38]

High schools also have the important task of helping to support immigrant students when they move from high school to college or the workforce. Schools and teachers are key resources for graduating students, helping to provide references, write resumes, foster student-work contacts, and provide emotional support during this major life transition. One study compared the different school contexts of Korean immigrant youth at two high schools during this critical transitional period. The researchers found that the youth attending an elite public high school in New York City were steeped in a college-preparatory curriculum, had been assigned college advisers and counselors, and had teachers who helped them prepare college applications and wrote letters of recommendation for them. In contrast, the youth attending a neighboring poor, urban high school had very different experiences. When interviewed, these students consistently mentioned feeling isolated at their school and immersed in an ineffective learning environment with few opportunities for developing relationships with their counselors or teachers. Consequently, many of the immigrant students at the second school will likely quit school; some may even be advised to drop out and take the GED (general equivalency diploma) test instead.[39] Clearly, the quantity and quality of secondary school resources—and, perhaps most importantly, the social support received from teachers and peers—can profoundly influence the likelihood of immigrant adolescents' achieving their potential.

Beyond High School

If one of the primary goals of the U.S. public education system is to create the nation's next generations of workers, scholars, leaders, and parents, it is vital to understand how this educational system supports—or does not support—immigrant adolescents' transition to adulthood. An increasing amount of literature on emerging adulthood (roughly age 18 through the early to mid 20s) posits that the success or failure of immigrant young adults in the job market largely depends on their high school experiences.[40] Immigrant youth who attend elite public high schools or private schools already have networks in place to support their higher-education goals. Many immigrant young adults in these circumstances strive to find professional opportunities in the mainstream economy in order to move beyond the low-wage jobs and health or lifestyle prospects of their parents. These immigrant youth have internalized the value placed on hard work that is reflected in their parents' efforts laboring long hours at difficult jobs; the youth apply this work ethic in order to achieve economic and social mobility beyond that attained by their first-generation parents.[41]

On the other hand, immigrant young adults who drop out of high school usually do not have the opportunity to attend college, unless they earn a GED. Without a high school diploma, young adults who drop out are often relegated to low-wage jobs in ethnic enclaves (e.g., Korean youth working for Korean entrepreneurs), thus retaining their ties to the ethnic economy of their first-generation parents. These jobs are often easy for young immigrants to secure through their contacts in the ethnic and immigrant community, and employers value their bilingual skills.[42] Although there are advantages to working within an ethnic enclave, one downside that has been noted is that many immigrant young adults who leave high school before graduating falsely believe that they can earn an adequate living without a college degree. When they find that they cannot, those who have experienced occupational barriers try to go back to school, pass the GED test, and apply to vocational schools, community colleges, and city and state universities. This solution may not be the easiest or most direct route to upward mobility, but a low-paying job in an ethnic enclave may be the only steppingstone some immigrant young adults have.[43]

Another issue for immigrant young adults is the impact that their undocumented status has on their lives, educational opportunities, and economic prospects. For more than 2.1 million immigrant young adults, leaving high school means leaving their legally protected status and transitioning to undocumented or "illegal" immigrant status.[44] No longer possessing a legal right to attend public school, undocumented young adults also cannot legally work, vote, or receive financial aid, and they now must live with the constant threat of deportation. Sixty-eight percent of young adults who drop out of high school or do not continue on to college after graduating learn of their lack of legal status when they apply for their first job. About 60 percent of immigrant young adults who had planned on going to college discover that they are undocumented during the college application process.[45] Despite their success in high school or their aspirations, all undocumented young adults hit a brick wall of exclusion when they turn 18. This shocking discovery has serious negative effects on the identity formation and future plans of many immigrant young adults. The combination of scarce family resources and exclusion from financial aid at the state and federal levels makes the path to higher education very steep for undocumented high school students. Some states allow undocumented students to pay in-state college tuition, but many students are not aware of this option. Even if they are, many still cannot afford to pay the reduced fee.[46]

What choices do these undocumented immigrant young adults have? For youth who drop out of high school, typically the only option is to work illegally in order to provide for themselves and their families. Similar to other youth who drop out of high school, undocumented immigrant youth become part of the same low-wage job pool that contains their parents, who have much less education than their children do. For undocumented youth who can afford to finance higher education, college attendance is critical for avoiding legal trouble. Unfortunately, the combination of their need to work, the scarce availability of scholarships or financial aid, and the difficult nature of college academics leads many young immigrant adults to leave college prior to graduation.[47]

In the movement of immigrant youth from preschool through the U.S. public education system to young adulthood, they are strongly affected by school policies and contexts. Schools are therefore powerful and vital settings that profoundly influence the potential for success among immigrant youth.

NOTES

1. Camarota, S. (2012). *Immigrants in the United States: A profile of America's foreign-born population*. Washington, DC: Center for Immigration Studies.

2. Fischer, M. J. (2010). Immigrant educational outcomes in new destinations: An exploration of high school attrition. *Social Science Research, 39*(4), 627–641.

3. Perreira, K. M., Harris, K., & Lee, D. (2006). Making it in America: High school completion by immigrant and native youth. *Demography, 43*(3), 511–536.

4. Greenman, E. (2013). Educational attitudes, school peer context, and the "immigrant paradox" in education. *Social Science Research, 42*(3), 698–714.

5. García Coll, C., Patton, F., Marks, A. K., Dimitrova, R., Yang, H., Suarez-Aviles, G., & Batchelor, A. (2012). Understanding the immigrant paradox in youth: Developmental and contextual considerations. In A. Masten (Ed.), *Realizing the potential of immigrant youth* (pp. 159–180). Cambridge: Cambridge University Press; García Coll, C., & Marks, A. K. (2012). *The immigrant paradox in children and adolescents: Is becoming American a developmental risk?* Washington, DC: American Psychological Association; García Coll, C., & Marks, A. K. (2009). *Immigrant stories: Ethnicity and academics in middle childhood.* New York: Oxford University Press.

6. World Health Organization's Commission on the Social Determinants of Health. (2007). *Early child development: A powerful equalizer.* Washington, DC: World Health Organization.

7. Karoly, L. A., & Gonzalez, G. C. (2011). Early care and education for children in immigrant families. *Future of Children, 21*(1), 71–101.

8. Ibid.

9. Ibid.

10. Ibid.

11. Magnuson, K., Lahaie, C., & Waldfogel, J. (2006). Preschool and school readiness of children of immigrants. *Social Science Quarterly, 87*(5), 1241–1262.

12. Palacios, N., Guttmanova, K., & Chase-Lansdale, P. (2008). Early reading achievement of children in immigrant families: Is there an immigrant paradox? *Developmental Psychology, 44*(5), 1381–1395.

13. Obeng, C. (2007). Immigrants families and childcare preferences: Do immigrants' cultures influence their childcare decisions? *Early Childhood Education Journal, 34*(4), 259–264.

14. Ibid.

15. Uttal, L., & Han, C. Y. (2011). Taiwanese immigrant mothers' childcare preferences: Socialization for bicultural competency. *Cultural Diversity and Ethnic Minority Psychology, 17*(4), 437–443.

16. Conn, B. M., Marks, A. K., & Coyne, L. (2013). A three-generation study of Chinese immigrant extended family child care-giving experiences in the preschool years. *Research in Human Development, 10*(4), 308–331.

17. Santhiveeran, J. (2010). Child care preferences of foreign-born immigrant groups in California. *Journal of Family Social Work, 13*(1), 45–55.

18. Ibid.

19. Miller, P., Votruba-Drzal, E., & Coley, R. (2013). Predictors of early care and education type among preschool-aged children in immigrant families: The role of region of origin and characteristics of the immigrant experience. *Children and Youth Services Review, 35*(9), 1342–1355.

20. Ibid.

21. Marks, A. K., Godoy, C. M., & García Coll, C. (2013). An ecological approach to understanding immigrant child and adolescent developmental competencies. In L. Gershoff, R. Mistry, & D. Crosby (Eds.), *The contexts of child development* (pp. 75–89). New York: Oxford University Press; Marks, A. K., Ejesi, K., McCullough, M., & García Coll, C. (2015). The development and implications of racism and discrimination. In M. Lamb, C. García Coll, & R. Lerner (Eds.), *Handbook of child psychology: Vol. 3, Socioemotional processes* (7th ed.). Hoboken, NJ: Wiley.

22. Welsh, M., Parke, R. D., Widaman, K., & O'Neil, R. (2001). Linkages between children's social and academic competence: A longitudinal analysis. *Journal of School Psychology, 39*(6), 463–482.

23. Crosnoe, R. (2005). Double disadvantage or signs of resilience? The elementary school contexts of children from Mexican immigrant families. *American Educational Research Journal, 42*(2), 269–303.

24. Carter, P. L. (2009). Equity and empathy: Toward racial and educational achievement in the Obama era. *Harvard Educational Review, 79*(2), 287–297.

25. Lee, J. C., & Klugman, J. (2013). Latino school concentration and academic performance among Latino children. *Social Science Quarterly, 94*(4), 977–1015.

26. Brown, C., & Chu, H. (2012). Discrimination, ethnic identity, and academic outcomes of Mexican immigrant children: The importance of school context. *Child Development, 83*(5), 1477–1485.

27. Ibid.

28. Ibid.

29. Marks et al. (2015).

30. Urdan, T. (2012). Factors affecting the motivation and achievement of immigrant students. In K. R. Harris, S. Graham, T. Urdan, S. Graham, J. M. Royer, M. Zeidner (Eds.), *APA educational psychology handbook: Vol. 2, Individual differences and cultural and contextual factors* (pp. 293–313). Washington, DC: American Psychological Association.

31. French, S. E., Seidman, E., LaRue, A., & Aber, J. L. (2006). The development of ethnic identity during adolescence. *Developmental Psychology, 42*(1), 1–10.

32. Marks et al. (2015).

33. Tummala-Narra, P., & Claudius, M. (2013). Perceived discrimination and depressive symptoms among immigrant-origin adolescents. *Cultural Diversity and Ethnic Minority Psychology, 19*(3), 257–269.

34. Ibid.

35. Ching, A. M., Yeh, C. J., Siu, W., Wu, K. A., & Okubo, Y. (2009). Evaluation of a school-based internship program for Chinese immigrant adolescents in the United States. *Adolescence, 44*(175), 601–620.

36. Kelly, C. (2012). The cafeteria as contact zone: Developing a multicultural perspective through multilingual and multimodal literacies. *Journal of Adolescent & Adult Literacy, 56*(4), 301–310.

37. Diversi, M., & Mecham, C. (2005). Latino(a) students and Caucasian mentors in a rural after-school program: Towards empowering adult–youth relationships. *Journal of Community Psychology, 33*(1), 31–40.

38. Rousseau, C., Armand, F., Laurin-Lamothe, A., Gauthier, M., & Saboundjian, R. (2012). A pilot project of school-based intervention integrating drama and language awareness. *Child and Adolescent Mental Health, 17*(3), 187–190.

39. Lew, J. (2010). Asian American youth in poverty: Benefits and limitations of ethnic networks in postsecondary and labor force options. *Journal of Education for Students Placed at Risk, 15*(1–2), 127–143.

40. Perreira et al. (2006).

41. Perreira, K. M., Harris, K., & Lee, D. (2007). Immigrant youth in the labor market. *Work and Occupations, 34*(1), 5–34; Rumbaut, R., & Komaie, G. (2010). Immigration and adult transitions. *Future of Children, 20*(1), 43–66.

42. Lew. (2010).

43. Rousseau et al. (2012).

44. Gonzales, R. G. (2011). Learning to be illegal: Undocumented youth and the shifting legal contexts in the transition to adulthood. *American Sociological Review, 76*(4), 602–619.

45. Ibid.

46. Ibid.

47. Ibid.

3

Transnational Connections through Emerging Technologies

GONZALO BACIGALUPE AND KIMBERLY PARKER

In California's Bay Area, two teenagers huddle over a mobile phone. As they speak to their four-year-old sister and parents in Guatemala, their joy is palpable—the poor connection does not temper their excitement. As the boy clutches a prepaid calling card, his speech accelerates as an automated voice declares that only a minute remains on the call. It ends before he has a chance to say good-bye. Sometime later, at the teenage girl's 14th birthday party, the parents appear on a webcam watching from afar as their daughter blows out candles. They remain on the video call throughout the celebration, happily observing but not fully participating in the festivities. Their virtual presence is meaningful but perhaps not enough, we might surmise, as we look more closely at the birthday girl's face.

These scenes are taken from Theo Rigby's short documentary film *Sin País*, or *Without Country*,[1] which chronicles a mixed-status Guatemalan family's encounter with the U.S. immigration system. Their struggle culminates with the parents, Sam and Elida Mejia, and their four-year-old daughter leaving the two teenage children behind in the States. Emerging technologies, known as Internet communication technologies (ICTs), constitute an integral aspect of the family members' quotidian lives, easing the pain of transition while also complicating it in some ways. With the rapid evolution of emerging technologies, the experiences of immigrant youth in the United States have been transformed in significant ways. Participating in new media ecologies,[2] these "millennial" youth born at the turn of the century experience qualitatively different relationships with their heritage countries than did the generations of immigrants who preceded them before the advent and mainstreaming of these technologies.

Emerging technologies serve as the basis for financial, educational, and political attainment,[3] yet they can also act as "global drivers of migration" in their ability to foster the transnational transmission of information about economic opportunity and civic freedom.[4] Immigrants use mobile phones, text messages, e-mails, online instant messaging, and videoconferencing programs such as Skype, among other forms of electronic correspondence, to communicate with family and friends back home about a variety of topics ranging from ostensibly mundane information such as day-to-day weather to more serious reports about major life events such as births, deaths, and border crossings.[5] Some emerging technologies enable family members separated by time and space to be virtually present for extended periods of time, thereby allowing faraway relatives to "participate" in a household's occurrences. Emerging technologies create opportunities for togetherness between remote friends and relatives that never before existed: a separated mother and daughter can shop online together, a distant father can monitor his son's homework progress, and relatives in sending countries can watch immigrants select ways to decorate a house or can virtually attend family gatherings. The list of possible uses for emerging technologies is interminable, although different types of technologies are better suited for communication about certain activities. Moreover, various technologies combine in the form of polymedia to create different communicative environments especially suited to certain contexts.[6] For many transnational users of emerging technologies, the content of the communication is not nearly as important as its social, and often emotional, function.[7] The felt presence of another person that the technology enables is, in and of itself, significant for families' and children's development.

No single canon of literature exists that examines the phenomenon of emerging technologies and transnationalism, which, unlike the less inclusive notions of acculturation and assimilation, underscores the strengths that migrants demonstrate during geographical transition.[8] The current research on immigration and technology bridges disciplines. Transcending clearly defined borders that serve to demarcate academic fields, the literature in this way mirrors the experience of transnational migrants.

For both immigrants and their families left behind, emerging technologies change the meaning of migration, albeit in different ways. For some, these technologies help family members justify the decision to live apart;[9] for others, they help immigrants resituate themselves in their adopted lands, providing them with a familiar emotional connection as they strive to create new social networks in the United States.[10] For most immigrant families, emerging technologies allow a means to hear and see aspects of their heritage country that may otherwise have been forgotten, thereby partly mitigating some painful experiences of loss and loneliness. Whereas the use of emerging technology was once predominantly predicated on socioeconomic standing, these technologies are now more accessible than ever, even to immigrants with limited resources.[11] However, factors other than ICT access and cost may profoundly affect immigrants' ability to utilize or adopt the technology, including education level and literacy skills, generational status, gender, nativity, perceived social acceptability, physical security, English proficiency, and the economic, industrial, or sociopolitical climate of the heritage country.[12] Access may also vary tremendously across regions. Whereas immigrant youth from industrialized societies in Europe, North America, and Asia are likely to have relatives in their sending countries with easy access to emerging technologies, those who migrate from other countries, especially those in sub-Saharan Africa, may have relatives with little or no access to ICTs, even though their children living in industrialized countries do. It is important to consider whether children's native countries possess the infrastructure to support emerging technologies.[13] Latin American and African countries are, however, rapidly making inroads into ICT access and adoption. In some cases, wireless Internet and phone technologies have been made available in regions where phones were never available in the past. Finally, access is not the same as participation in terms of ICT use.[14] Access is only the first step—some catalyst (e.g., a child's desire to communicate with his distant grandparents or a teenager's motivation to use an online search engine to complete a school project) must be present for engagement with the technology to occur.

Children's Experience of Transnationalism: Why Should We Care?

Developmentally, children occupy a unique position that affords them a very different understanding of space and time than that possessed by adults. In fact, unlike their parents, children of immigrants occupy many different developmental positions within a short time span.[15] While adults "narrate their changing relationships with place and space in terms of what has already happened, children have their lives ahead of them."[16] Consequently, their understanding of time, space, and movement across them is largely present and future oriented rather than based predominantly in the past. For immigrant youth, especially the millennial generation, orientation to time and space inexorably impacts their experience and use of emerging technologies. Children have an "inherently physical nature" and likely experience a more "immediate relationship with their physical bodies and environment" than adults do;[17] this attribute and capacity influence the levels at which children are able to connect with their heritage lands and distant relatives by means of technology. As technologies continue to advance, the argument that they can reproduce sounds and sights but cannot fully stand in for various sensorial dimensions (taste, smell, and physical sensations) is increasingly contestable. Still, for children who have never set foot in their parents' homelands, the technologies' limitations may be more salient since the children have few or no physical experiences of those countries on which technology might help them expand. Moreover, the intensity of a child's desire to connect with their heritage country may change over time as they develop.[18]

Children's Agency

Children actively partake in the construction of their families' immigration narratives, and Internet communication technologies may contribute to children's ability to manage their relationships with the people and culture "back home." Emerging technologies provide children and youth the ability to reauthor migration stories in which they previously had little voice. In relation to transnationalism, children have traditionally been portrayed as being without agency. They have been depicted as stuck between the cultures of their native and host countries[19] or as too young to develop an awareness of the type of relationship they want to have with their heritage lands.[20] However, emerging technologies may empower children and adolescents to construct a grounded and relational cultural narrative. Despite traditional discourses' presentation of children as passive observers of an adult immigrant saga, children are full protagonists in their families' stories, and ICT may capitalize on their agency.

Whereas children have always been able to demonstrate agency in their relationships to their heritage countries, children's use of emerging technologies underscores how they dictate the terms according to the ways in which they want to relate to their—or their parents'—homelands. Children now assume greater agency in "negotiations of identity and belonging"[21] and find that with ICT they are able to "preserve those parts of their homeland that they miss most while being in full control of the frequency and intensity of their relationships with its virtual forms."[22] Haikkola contends that "second-generation children who are not migrants themselves act within a field of relations that their family's migration has produced."[23] While immigrant youth do not choose be "transnational," these millennials *may* choose how to negotiate their transnational identities, so technology makes acting on their choices much easier. For example, emerging technologies enable youth to be politically active in heritage countries in which they may never have set foot; the Internet itself may serve as an outlet for some second-generation youth to express their often conflicting feelings about events taking place in their heritage countries.[24] The Internet, then, serves as an alternate arena in which youth might explore and negotiate the world around them, especially the family's culture of origin, which becomes less distant and more tangible.

Finally, emerging technologies create opportunities for children to "participate in different forms of compliance, resistance or subversion" in relation to their own acculturation.[25] Immigrant millennials are "engaged in a selective acculturation process,"[26] so ICTs can introduce youth to and actively engage them in "a counter-discourse to the dominant one of separation and alienation from the family."[27] Emerging technologies provide a vehicle for resistance by allowing youth to act against the displacement they have experienced and the societal "structures" that may have necessitated their dislocation. Whereas parents once controlled family contact with the heritage land through traditional means such as periodic remittances and letters, children now can exercise agency by deciding when, how, and under what circumstances they wish to communicate with people back home. In allowing youth to autonomously negotiate unique acculturation or assimilation trajectories and in giving them ownership of the transition process itself, emerging technologies act as a form of social capital for children.[28] Ultimately, children's use of ICTs underscores their inherent agency and highlights their capacity to act, think, and feel autonomously.

Family Relations and Emerging Technology

Role Reconstruction

Immigrant youth are often early adopters of emerging media,[29] often orchestrating Internet use both at home and in their sending countries, enabling both sides to communicate with one another. Millennials are typically more knowledgeable than their parents in navigating these technologies,[30] a discrepancy in knowledge that can create structural changes within the family. Gender equality, for example, may become more pronounced, and children may assume more power.[31] Text messaging serves to test, if not altogether disrupt, family hierarchy in terms of social class, gender, and age.[32] For example, maintaining and managing social ties—a relational activity once considered women's work—may migrate into the domain of men's work as men become increasingly more proficient in communication technologies.[33] Importantly, families serve as information hubs, and children's involvement with emerging technologies may serve to encourage "educational aspiration" and to promote "civic inclinations" among older family members.[34] When children bring home technical skills learned in school, their parents' access to information about local, national, and global politics may increase.

Many immigrant children, often the firstborn, act as technology brokers within their families in the same way that they may serve as linguistic or cultural brokers in helping their parents navigate U.S. society. Once a child has acquired the role of technology broker, it quickly becomes fixed, often remaining even after the child leaves home. For example, an older sibling who has moved out of the household may, over consecutive visits home, continually introduce her parents and younger siblings to new technologies.[35] That immigrant families are dependent on their millennial children for their technology use may warrant concern, however.

Family Processes

Internet communication technologies impact the interactional patterns within immigrant youths' families. The family is an arena for information exchange. Information "must flow through the family for it to be meaningfully shared, evaluated, comprehended, and acted upon,"[36] and emerging technologies serve as points of entry into the family system for new information. The adoption of technology may, therefore, compromise some of the existing boundaries supporting the family identity and the outside world, thereby transforming families into more permeable systems. Moreover, emerging technologies and their associated media create dialectical processes in which communication technologies and social environment inevitably act on one another, highlighting the ways in which "communication technologies and relationships are mutually constitutive" since relationship itself is "intrinsically mediated."[37] In examining family process among Filipino mothers parenting from afar, Uy-Tioco found that technology use impacts family dynamics and that family dynamics in turn influence technology use.[38] Moreover, "power relations and structures" are "reproduced, rejected, or reinforced" by a family's use of ICT.[39]

Some authors have found that immigrant youths' information ecology is qualitatively different from that of their parents, a conclusion suggesting that children can form connections with their heritage countries independently of their parents.[40] Therefore, millennials' transnational relationships are likely to be distinct from those of their parents since emerging technologies grant youth the autonomy to control the connections they make back home. In contrast, in a study of transnational computer use by immigrant adolescent Latinas, Sánchez and Salazar found that online computer use is likely to reflect the entire family's involvement, not just the individual's.[41] Family-to-family communication has been a common practice as opposed to the more typical person-to-person communication for which computers are often used. For families in which members use the Internet together, connecting with shared family friends, not just individual friends, is possible. According to these researchers, a parallel exists between the ways that people choose to use technologies and the values they hold (e.g., communalism).[42] For millennials' heritage-country connections, the implications of such communication patterns are far-reaching: when communicating at the family level, children can have relationships with family friends in their home country whom neither they nor their parents have met in person. Communal ties to the heritage land can thus be strengthened.

Emotional Processes

Though ICT use does not necessarily increase an immigrant's longing for the presence of a faraway loved one, it does activate a desire for connection. In the documentary *Sin País*, the teenage daughter, who is visiting her parents and younger sister in Guatemala, and her mother video-chat with her teenage brother in the U.S. It is Christmas Eve, and the mother tells her son, "I hope to God that next year we are together," implying that somehow the Skype call is not enough—it allows her to see her son's face and hear his voice, but it still does not bring him fully to her. Sometime later, the girl tells her brother to listen for the fireworks, a family holiday tradition in Guatemala. Though sounds of fireworks in the distance can be heard on his end, the sound the brother hears in no way produces the excitement his sister is experiencing many miles away. In this instance, the technology seems to intensify the emotions felt, both positive and negative.

For immigrant youth and their families, the experience of longing is motivation for connecting via ICTs. In many families separated by distance, the behavioral manifestation of the desire to connect is their attempting virtual copresence, a phenomenon that emerging technologies greatly facilitate.[43] Technology use may attenuate the sense of distance experienced by many transnational families, so millennial youth may feel more closely tied to their heritage lands than ever before. Moreover, emerging technologies enable children who have never physically met family members in their heritage lands to conduct Internet-based activities before and after scheduled visits, thereby diminishing the awkwardness of initial physical meetings and ultimately decreasing anxiety.[44] Ultimately, it is important to remember that for children who leave their heritage lands, the quality of the premigration relationship will invariably affect the postmigration, and Internet-mediated, relationship established later.[45]

Developmental Considerations

Emerging technologies influence immigrant youth and children's development across a number of domains. Hamel discusses how their achievements in various developmental domains can be directly associated with the use or absence of emerging technologies.[46] He demonstrates the link between the 2009 ICT Development Index (IDI) and the Human Development Index (HDI), inferring that an important, albeit perhaps nuanced, relationship exists between international outcomes on the indexes. Migration is a critical transition point in many individuals' life histories; emerging technologies may help some immigrant youth bridge the gap between their daily routines in their sending and receiving countries by enabling them to learn about important events back home and to track everyday matters such as local politics.[47] Technologies thus help immigrant youth inhabiting the liminal space between sending and receiving countries to conduct their activities with minimal interference.

Language

Immigrant youth's ICT use encourages the development of multiple literacies and contributes to language maintenance of children born in the United States or those who left their heritage lands at a young age.[48] By frequently texting, e-mailing, and blogging in a combination of the heritage country's language and English, youth may develop the ability to switch rapidly between languages. A survey of 35 transnational youth found that "many of the literate functions" that youth "would carry out in their native language had been transferred to computer-mediated environments" and learned that the youth felt chatting online helped "improve their conversational fluency, vocabulary, and writing skills."[49] When immigrant children use emerging technologies to communicate with people back home, they generally communicate in the language spoken in the heritage land. These implications are especially important for reading and writing. While children who are English-language learners may speak and hear their native language when conversing with their parents at home, they less frequently have opportunities to read and write the family's language. E-mailing, text messaging, social networking, and blogging, among other forms of Internet-mediated communication, provide such opportunities.

Emotional and Cognitive Development

Millennial youth's use of Internet communication technology to connect with their heritage land benefits their emotional and cognitive development. Accessing online news in their home country may enable youth to better understand the circumstances of family members as well as those of same-age, or peer, youth living there.[50] Thus, immigrant youth's use of emerging technology may foster the development of empathy. Moreover, ready access to various perspectives online may serve to produce cognitive dissonance for them.[51] Viewing multiple perspectives may promote critical thinking skills, and confronting cognitive dissonance at an early age may help children learn to effectively integrate sometimes conflicting pieces of their stories to foster a coherent understanding. Madianou and Miller argue that understanding and recognizing the notion of ambivalence is critical to any understanding of migration. Emerging technologies may help youth resolve this ambivalence.[52]

Identity Development

The Internet provides immigrant youth with opportunities that extend beyond the mere transmission of information.[53] Emerging technologies give these youth additional occasions for "identity construction, performance, and transformation,"[54] serving as transnational social fields and loci for individual and collective identity formation.[55] Online collective identity construction may ameliorate the sense of disconnection that individuals experience after leaving their heritage lands. It might even change the connotation of dissolution altogether, rendering it neutral or even positive. Elias and Lemish explain, "The Internet seems to be playing a central role in the hybrid identity construction of immigrant youth. . . . It allows the concrete body to live in multiple cultures at the same time, to balance them one against the other, and to create individual combinations of their competing and complementary [realms]."[56]

Moreover, for many immigrant youth, emerging technologies provide access to positive role models from their native countries who do not correlate with popular stereotypes.[57] It may be that only those youth who already identify heavily with an ethnic community engage in Internet-mediated activities through which they relate or connect to their sending countries.[58] Thus, in some cases, emerging technology may be more of a mediator than a determinant in terms of youths' relationships to their heritage lands. While we know emerging technologies may serve to strengthen preexisting bonds between youth and their native countries, less is understood about ways in which these technologies might help youth construct relationships with their parents' homelands when little connection existed previously.

Immigrant millennials' use of emerging technology creates opportunities for the construction of new identities—individual and collective—that previously might not have been available to them. They can visit their homelands virtually, and these visits can help them confirm their internal perceptions of their native lands and perhaps validate their connection to them.[59] These "visits" may also enable youth to share their homelands with nonnatives and consequently develop confidence about their cultural heritage. Immigrant children, always "guests," now get to be hosts for their nonimmigrant friends, thereby changing the power dynamics in their peer relationships. Moreover, the testimonial dimension that social media outlets offer immigrant children may further validate identification with their heritage land.[60] Finally, helping migrant children and youth "retain their attachment to the original culture" is important since it can "reduce acculturation gaps" and ultimately "facilitate positive psychological adjustment by parents and children alike."[61]

Emerging technologies allow immigrant youth to write their own narratives and influence portrayals of their culture in cyberspace.[62] Online communication sites such as blogs and MySpace accounts serve as arenas for transnational "identity work" and enable "transformative literacy practices."[63] Immigrant youth use various social languages in their online spaces, depending on the audience they wish to target. For example, national pride and transnational pride are often communicated via text and images posted on personal sites, as are feelings of ambivalence about events occurring in heritage countries.[64] However, while many immigrant millennials do explore aspects of their heritage-country identities through technology, others, particularly those who feel that technology-mediated experiences of their family's original lands seem inauthentic, prefer to explore facets of their complex identities within the United States.[65] Therefore, the range of immigrant youth's emerging technology use in many ways mirrors the diversity of their personal experiences with their heritage countries in terms of their cultural identities and desires to connect with people back home.

Dilemmas in Emerging Media Engagement

Potential for Ambivalence

Just as the immigration process inexorably elicits feelings of ambivalence, the immigrant youth's adoption of emerging technology can also be the source of incongruity. Migration and the losses that accompany it are often spurred by emerging technologies. Hamel refers to media as a *lure*, suggesting that technology is sometimes a conveyor of false information or romanticized images of host countries.[66] Emerging technologies may make the concept of distance more manageable for adults, creating the illusion of feasibility of maintaining long-term relationships with people in distant lands. Moreover, Internet communication technologies themselves may constitute the reason for a family's, or an individual's, move.[67] The ICT job sector alone employs an unprecedented number of immigrants. Finally, emerging technologies play an integral role in helping potential migrants search for jobs that eventually require migration.[68] That some immigrant children would have troubled, or conflicted, relationships with emerging technologies is understandable in light of the fact that these technologies are often major factors precipitating the migration that takes children, and their parents, away from their heritage lands. Differences in generational attitudes toward adoption of emerging technologies are sometimes marked. A systematic ethnography of Filipino mothers living in England with children in the Philippines found that while mothers were largely *unequivocal* in praising the benefits of emerging technologies, nearly half of the children expressed ambivalence or outright negativity toward mediated communication via technology.[69]

The claim that emerging technologies are neutral tools has long been refuted; the use of technologies can serve to constrain as well as enable.[70] Their use can generate ambivalence, especially in the arenas of individual and collective identity creation. While some immigrants may use technologies to "preserve, develop, expand or celebrate their distinctiveness," technologies also serve as "means for dissolving cultural differences."[71] Immigrants can create the lived experience of forced transnationalism since the Internet and television provide a constant stream of information from the sending country, sometimes involving youth in "an unavoidable and involuntary engagement with the politics and affairs of the home country."[72] In describing Filipino women mothering from afar, Uy-Tioco captures the dual nature of emerging technologies: "Yet this same technology that empowers them to maintain their roles in the family also emphasizes the distance and reminds them that they are away and in many ways powerless."[73] Similarly, Haikkola describes how immigrant children communicating with their heritage lands via ICT often must work their way through "fields of relations" that linger beyond their "reach"; consequently, they experience "feelings of isolation, sadness and emotional distress."[74] Benítez has written of Salvadoran immigrants using video, "In consuming these images, immigrants may feel a sense of being rootless or being neither from here (host country) nor there (home country)," again highlighting the feelings of disconnection that emerging technologies might elicit.[75] Research with children and adolescents is needed to determine whether their accessing images from the family's home country has the same emotional resonance it has for adults. Hopkins counters this notion of irresolvable indeterminacy, arguing that communication over the Internet does occupy a *physical* locus, even if that place assumes novel and perhaps unfamiliar forms.[76]

The increased presence of emerging technologies may increase the expectations of relatives in heritage countries for more frequent communication with family members living abroad.[77] Additionally, constant contact can foster disagreement among family members, particularly parents engaging in long-distance parenting.[78] Moreover, the digital divide still persists: where there is access, there will also be exclusion, and those individuals who are excluded may struggle to build transnational connections that serve as a source of social capital.[79] Although children are using emerging technologies at increasingly younger ages, their parents and grandparents are unlikely to adopt the technologies as easily, and this generational divide might complicate children's relationships with relatives abroad.[80]

In transnational families, emerging technologies can underscore family members' differences in values, especially differences in degrees of assimilation and/or acculturation among generations.[81] In *Sin País*, teenager Helen returns to Guatemala to visit her parents, only to find that though she and they have connected via technology for months, difficult subjects—rarely breached during the copresence created via Skype or phone calls—quickly arise when she stands incarnate before them.[82] Only when Helen occupies the same geographical location as her parents does she learn of her mother Elida's frustration over her grades and her mother's strong desire for her to return to Guatemala permanently. This example illustrates how emerging technologies do little to resolve conflicts predating their utilization and how for some families technologies may postpone the inevitable confrontations that ultimately take place in person.

New technologies may also upset the balance of power in families—an effect with troublesome as well as positive implications. In *Sin País*, mother and daughter engage in an emotionally charged discussion about Helen's future. Having lived fairly autonomously for months in the physical absence of her parents, Helen strongly asserts herself and openly disagrees with her mother, perhaps revealing to Elida an unfamiliar side of her daughter. The mother-and-daughter power dynamics have effectively shifted, and mediated communication may have belied—or disguised the nature of—this confusing change. The literature substantiates how emerging media play a significant role in a family's power configuration. Cell-phone use alone has been shown to potentially strengthen, re-create, and/or disrupt existing power structures within a family.[83] Moreover, ICT use by children undercuts parental leadership in certain immigrant families, highlighting the crisis of patriarchy that children's ICT use has created for certain Latino men.[84] Similarly, citing Wilding, Hamel describes how emerging technologies can ultimately "circumvent traditional channels and hierarchies of communication and decision making, effectively displacing the seat of authority within a family and involving people who traditionally would not have been informed of decision making processes."[85] In immigrant children's lives, then, the decision-making process might be expanded via emerging media to include older relatives still residing in the heritage country. Should families struggle to accommodate the structural shifts that technologies create, they may experience instability.

Emerging Technologies: Not Enough

Although the adoption of technology may help protect against the utter loss that many transnational families feel when members emigrate, ICTs are frequently experienced as "not enough." They can be experienced as a *surrogate* for community but not as the real thing.[86] For children who have had a minimal relation to their parents' country of origin, emerging technologies alone may not allow for the development of strong transnational ties. Haikkola discusses the significance of a "face-to-face presence with people and places that a virtual presence cannot totally replace"[87] and suggests that emerging technologies may play a more important role in the maintenance of the transnational connections than in their creation. This is still, though, an open question that requires further research.

Emerging technologies can serve to intensify feelings. Joy can be more salient than ever before, but so can the experience of longing and the sense of loss. The "more effective the new media" is, the more it "can still be an unbearable reminder of an actual absence."[88] Rigby's documentary *Sin País* demonstrates to us the strength of technology as a connecting tissue among distant family members. The teenage children in the States rejoice in their ability to connect with their parents and younger sister back home via Skype. We witness a situation that is incredibly difficult yet is alleviated in some way by the availability of ICT and mediated copresence. The same technology, however, makes it obvious to us that there is still loss and pain. The parents' "presence" at their 14-year-old daughter's birthday party helps their children feel connected to them. At the same time, however, their online presence makes it clear that they occupy the background, rather than the foreground, of their children's lives. Therein lies the paradox of the technologically created connection: an ICT-mediated presence helps because it is *something*, but it also hurts because it illuminates the fact that it is not enough. Technology's ability to enable immigration has been extensively studied, but technology's emotional effect on children and their families is perhaps more nuanced and less understood.

Conclusion

Though we have sought to present a comprehensive view of immigrant children's relationships with technology, we recognize the need for future scholarship in this area, especially in light of the complexity, nuance, and ambivalence that characterize many of these children's experiences. Additionally, technological advances are intrinsically rapid and the pace of their adoption inherently fluid, making any concluding comments and predictions tentative. These millennials belonging to "Generation M" are migrants across both space and time, uniquely positioned to see both forward and backward. Like Janus, the Roman god of thresholds, these youth are accomplished dealers in ambiguity. While Internet communication technologies offer immigrant youth increased access to, and often control over, relationships with individuals in heritage countries and with the countries themselves, they also complicate those connections, often evoking feelings of ambivalence as youth struggle to negotiate transnational identities throughout their development. Emerging technologies enable these young people to establish and maintain bonds to their own and their parents' homelands that are qualitatively different from previous bonds. Still, youth are provided little scaffolding to help them navigate relational paths that are by no means clear-cut. Although emerging technologies help resolve some of the discontinuity experienced across time and place, they do not and cannot actually replace family members and friends left behind.

NOTES

1. Rigby, T., & New Day, F. (2010). *Sin País (Without Country)*. Harriman, NY: New Day Films.

2. Ito, M., Horst, H., Bittanti, M., Boyd, D., Herr-Stephenson, B., Lange, P. G., & Robinson, L. (2008). *Living and learning with new media: Summary of findings from the Digital Youth Project*. The John D. and Catherine T. MacArthur Foundation Reports on Digital Media and Learning.

3. McDevitt, M., & Butler, M. (2011). Latino youth as information leaders: Implications for family interaction and civic engagement in immigrant communities. *InterActions: UCLA Journal of Education and Information Studies, 7*(2).

4. Hamel, J. Y. (2009). *Information and communication technologies and migration*. Human Development Research Paper 2009/39. New York: United Nations Development Program, Human Development Report Office. (Quotation from p. 1.)

5. Bacigalupe, G., & Lambe, S. (2011). Virtualizing intimacy: Information communication technologies and transnational families in therapy. *Family Process, 50*(1), 12–26.

6. Madianou, M., & Miller, D. (2012). *Migration and new media.* New York: Routledge.

7. Ibid.

8. Bacigalupe, G., & Cámara, M. (2012). Transnational families and social technologies: Reassessing immigration psychology. *Journal of Ethnic and Migration Studies, 38*(9), 1425–1438.

9. Madianou & Miller. (2012).

10. Fong, E., Cao, X., & Chan, E. (2010). Out of sight, out of mind? Patterns of transnational contact among Chinese and Indian immigrants in Toronto. *Sociological Forum, 25*(3), 428–449.

11. McDevitt & Butler. (2011).

12. Gillwald, A., Milek, A., & Stork, C. (2010). Gender assessment of ICT access and usage in Africa. *Research ICT Africa, 1*(5), 1–44.

13. Lam, W. S. E., & Rosario-Ramos, E. (2009). Multilingual literacies in transnational digitally mediated contexts: An exploratory study of immigrant teens in the United States. *Language and Education, 23*(2), 171–190.

14. Gillwald et al. (2010).

15. Gardner, K. (2012). Transnational migration and the study of children: An introduction. *Journal of Ethnic and Migration Studies, 38*(6), 889–912.

16. Ibid., p. 890.

17. Ibid., p. 905.

18. Ibid.

19. Ibid.

20. Haikkola, L. (2011). Making connections: Second-generation children and the transnational field of relations. *Journal of Ethnic and Migration Studies, 37*(8), 1201–1217.

21. Ibid., p. 1202.

22. Elias, N., & Lemish, D. (2009). Spinning the web of identity: The roles of the Internet in the lives of immigrant adolescents. *New Media & Society, 11*(4), 533–551. (Quotation from p. 547.)

23. Haikkola. (2011), p. 1203.

24. McGinnis, T., Goodstein-Stolzenberg, A., & Saliani, E. C. (2007). "indnpride": Online spaces of transnational youth as sites of creative and sophisticated literacy and identity work. *Linguistics and Education, 18*(3–4), 283–304.

25. Gardner. (2012), p. 897.

26. Elias & Lemish. (2009), p. 534.

27. Uy-Tioco. (2007), Overseas Filipino workers and text messaging: Reinventing transnational mothering. *Continuum: Journal of Media & Cultural Studies, 21*(2), 253–265. (Quotation from p. 262.)

28. Alfred, M. V. (2010). Transnational migration, social capital and lifelong learning in the USA. *International Journal of Lifelong Education, 29*(2), 219–235.

29. Ito et al. (2008).

30. Benítez, J. L. (2006). Transnational dimensions of the digital divide among Salvadoran immigrants in the Washington DC metropolitan area. *Global Networks,* 6(2), 181–199.

31. McDevitt & Butler. (2011).

32. Uy-Tioco. (2007).

33. Sánchez, P., & Salazar, M. (2012). Transnational computer use in urban Latino immigrant communities. *Urban Education, 47*(1), 90–116.

34. McDevitt & Butler. (2011), p. 1.

35. Sánchez & Salazar. (2012).

36. McDevitt & Butler. (2011), p. 2.

37. Madianou & Miller. (2012), p. 142.

38. Uy-Tioco. (2007).

39. Ibid., p. 255.

40. McDevitt & Butler. (2011).

41. Sánchez & Salazar. (2012).

42. Ibid.

43. Baldassar, L. (2008). Missing kin and longing to be together: Emotions and the construction of co-presence in transnational relationships. *Journal of Intercultural Studies, 29*(3), 247–266.

44. Ibid.

45. Madianou & Miller. (2012).

46. Hamel. (2009).

47. Elias & Lemish. (2009).

48. Lam & Rosario-Ramos. (2009).

49. Ibid., p. 182.

50. Ibid.

51. Ibid.

52. Madianou & Miller. (2012).

53. Hopkins, L. (2009). Media and migration. *Australian Journal of Communication,* 36(2), 36.

54. McGinnis et al. (2007), p. 288.

55. Benítez. (2006).

56. Elias & Lemish (2009), p. 548.

57. Hamel. (2009).

58. Elias & Lemish. (2009).

59. Ibid.

60. Ibid.

61. Ibid., p. 1249.

62. Benítez. (2006).

63. McGinnis et al. (2007), p. 284.

64. Ibid.

65. Skop, E., & Adams, P. C. (2009). Creating and inhabiting virtual places: Indian immigrants in cyberspace. *National Identities, 11*(2), 127–147.

66. Hamel. (2009).

67. Ibid.

68. Ibid.

69. Madianou & Miller. (2012).

70. Benítez. (2006).

71. Skop & Adams. (2009), p. 128.

72. Haikkola. (2011), p. 1208.

73. Uy-Tioco. (2007), pp. 261–262.

74. Haikkola. (2011), p. 1210.

75. Benítez. (2006), p. 192.

76. Hopkins. (2009).

77. Hamel. (2009).

78. Madianou & Miller. (2012).

79. Benítez. (2006).

80. Panagakos, A. N., & Horst, H. A. (2006). Return to Cyberia: technology and the social worlds of transnational migrants. *Global Networks, 6*(2), 109–124.

81. McDevitt & Butler. (2011).

82. Rigby & New Day. (2010).

83. Uy-Tioco. (2007).

84. McDevitt & Butler. (2011).

85. Wilding, R. (2006). "Virtual" intimacies? Families communicating across transnational contexts. *Global Networks, 6*(2): 125–142. Cited in Hamel (2009), p. 29.

86. Skop & Adams. (2009).

87. Haikkola. (2011), p. 1212.

88. Madianou & Miller. (2012), p. 121.

4

Religion

MONA M. ABO-ZENA AND MEENAL RANA

Yarissa spends her afternoons volunteering in the Catholic early childhood program. Yarissa enjoys the spontaneity of the children and feels fulfilled when the children greet her with hugs. Plus, she wants to give back to the community that has invested so much in her. On Wednesdays, she attends Confraternity of Christian Doctrine (CCD) classes and is looking forward to being confirmed. God and the church community have always been a big part of her family and life, but there are certain faith questions she has that no one answers to her satisfaction, such as whether non-Catholics can go to heaven. Because her questions seem to make people uncomfortable, Yarissa has stopped asking.

In the context of youths' lives, religion is often part of the "wallpaper" of life and has been described as part of the background, something "lurking behind the normal."[1] The field of psychology is expanding its focus to better understand the direct and subtle ways religion, spirituality, and religious communities inform the development of children and adults.[2] The ways in which religion and religious spaces provide developmental contexts for immigrant-origin youth are both similar to and different from their nonimmigrant peers but are understudied for both groups.[3] In this chapter, we seek to describe how religion and religious communities are a context of development for immigrant-origin children and youth with implications both for processes (e.g., religious and cultural socialization) and for outcomes (e.g., identity, sexuality).

The Context of Religion in Child and Adolescent Development

Religion plays a prominent role in youth development,[4] but scholarly attention often focuses on issues related to ethnic or cultural influences, overlooking the particular role of religion in informing the cultural values and practices of individuals, parents, and communities.[5] Scholars acknowledge that religiousness and spirituality are multifaceted with few clear and widely agreed-on definitions.[6] Overly broad definitions are difficult to apply, and overly narrow definitions fail to capture the richness and complexity of the subject.[7] Thus, we define *spirituality* as searching for the sacred,[8] while *religiousness* characterizes this search when it is undertaken within an institution established to promote spirituality.[9]

Religious and spiritual development are central to understanding the positive development of individuals within society.[10] In the embedded context of home, families provide children a context for socialization that is informed by a range of cultural values, including religious and spiritual ones.[11] The family context may include practices that draw from multiple faith traditions and types of religious socialization (e.g., attending religious school, membership in a church choir). Families may provide religious and spiritual contexts that contribute to a moral system that promotes charity, compassion, and justice.[12] A meta-analysis studying the relationship between spirituality and religiosity and psychological outcomes in adolescents and emerging adults (i.e., ages 18 to 29) found that religion and spirituality predicted well-being and self-esteem but were negatively associated with risk behavior and depression. The results varied by race, age, and how spirituality and religiosity were measured.[13]

Despite these findings, there is little known about the mechanisms through which religion and spirituality influence youth's development.[14] Drawing on their interpretations of experiences earlier in their childhood, youth may explore religion/spirituality in their general search for meaning.[15] Cognitive development, fueled by an interaction between the maturing brain and lived experiences, allows adolescents to engage in more advanced levels of metacognition and perspective taking,[16] including thinking abstractly about the meaning of life and death, the existence of God, and other existential questions. For some, identity and faith are inseparably linked through beliefs, actions, morals, and community.[17] That is, they provide a structure for transcending ourselves, furnishing meaning and direction, and helping us integrate values, beliefs, and commitments. As individuals navigate sometimes conflicting messages and demands, the "boundaries between what is cognitive, emotional, academic, or moral in one's developmental experiences basically disappear."[18]

Beyond the contributions of religion and spirituality to meaning making, they provide a social context that may inform developmental processes and outcomes. For some children and adolescents, religious communities are central and provide comfort and grounding amid the instability of this developmental period.[19] Religious and spiritual communities and the religious doctrines that guide them often promote social justice and contributions beyond self, such as volunteering. However, issues associated with religion are not unequivocally experienced as positive. For example, religious-group membership may highlight differences between and across groups.

The Religious Dimension of Person-Context Fit for Immigrant-Origin Youth

Figure 4.1 presents a dynamic, person-context life-span model of the influential relationships between the individual and the social, cultural, and structural levels of society.[20] Critical within this framework is a consideration of coping with developmental challenges, such as discrimination.[21] Discrimination based on one's religion and culture creates dissonance between *private regard* (i.e., a feeling about one's own affiliation and beliefs) and *public regard* (i.e., what an individual thinks about other people's perception of their religious group).[22] The model considers the intersection of religion and ethnicity, race, culture, and other social-address variables that inform person-context fit.[23] The goodness of fit between the individual and their setting has critical implications for well-being.[24] Religious beliefs and practices are coupled with social experiences and contribute to the multifaceted role of religion in the development of immigrant youth.[25]

Religion and the Development of Immigrant-Origin Children and Youth

The need to study religion and spirituality in relation to immigrant-origin youth represents a perfect storm of personal and social factors.

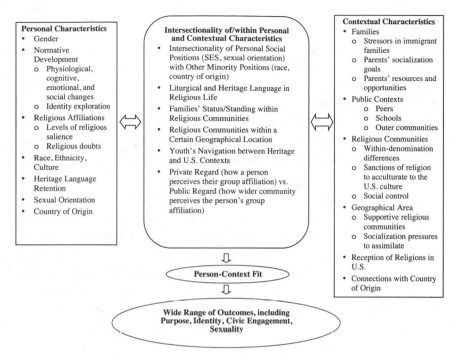

Figure 4.1. Person-context characteristics in studying religious development in immigrant-origin youth

As noted, religion and spirituality are relevant to human development generally but particularly throughout the formative periods from early childhood to emerging adulthood, given how socialization messages inform socioemotional, physical, and cognitive development (e.g., setting up a Buddhist shrine or arranging a weekly Seder, with varying levels of enthusiasm among youth). Further, a particular focus on immigrant-origin youth is needed for multiple reasons. Religious values and beliefs (i.e., belief in God and a divine purpose) provide a supportive bridge between the heritage context and the United States that may mediate acculturative stress.[26] Involvement in religious communities provides one with concrete, adaptive strategies for assimilating into "mainstream" communities, through participation in interfaith groups that join together for events such as a Walk for Hunger.[27] Religious communities create economic enclaves that provide material support and networks for their members.[28] For example, in addition to job leads, immigrants may pool money for a large purchase (e.g., house down payment, taxi medallion) and then pay each other back, thus navigating obstacles by formal lenders. Faith communities can provide fellowship and serve as a surrogate family that is coethnic and coreligious,[29] thus giving both religious and cultural socialization and support. Post-1965 immigration laws have contributed to increased religious and cultural diversity in the United States and a changing religious landscape that reflects Muslims, Hindus, Buddhists, Zoroastrians, and Christians from around the world whose new homes are in rural, urban, and suburban areas.[30]

Despite the surge in immigration and the waves of religious influences accompanying it, the tide of developmental science scholarship reflecting such changes has been slow to arrive. Early immigration scholarship analyzing post-1965 immigrant groups was largely from a sociological perspective that focused mostly on assimilation and acculturation, making no mention of the role of religion.[31] As political science and economics researchers and practitioners tracked the civic and economic participation of immigrant groups, religion emerged as an important dimension for understanding immigrant communities.[32] Integrating anthropological and sociological approaches, Leonard and colleagues focus on immigrant families in particular communities (e.g., Indian Hindus, Korean Protestants) and describe how immigrants' religious practices became cultural hybrids and also how immigrants introduced practices within the United States resulting in different religious trends (e.g., a Bu-Jew).[33]

Through varied samples and measures, developmental scholars have begun describing the myriad ways in which religion and spirituality may relate to the developmental processes, contexts, and outcomes of immigrant-origin youth. For example, a longitudinal, qualitative study of predominantly low-income Chinese, Dominican, and Mexican first-generation immigrant mothers of young children showed how spiritual capital (i.e., quantifying spiritual or moral beliefs or practices) helps to shape developmental goals. Spiritual capital was also associated with outcomes related to learning, health, and behavior.[34] For example, faith traditions that value learning and literacy may lead children socialized in those traditions to develop text-based study habits and to higher educational outcomes. Given variations by religious tradition of what constitutes spiritual capital, two issues relating to person-context fit warrant attention as we examine how the context of religion and religious communities affects the developmental processes and outcomes of immigrant youth: (1) assumptions that regard religious influences as strictly positive, Christian, and within "traditional" congregations need to be expanded to consider how religion may both support and challenge developmental outcomes and consider a range of theistic and non-theistic perspectives and practices;[35] (2) findings related to main effects for religion may be interpreted to account for the relative compatibility between the norms prevalent in the culture of origin and those prevalent in "mainstream" U.S. society.[36]

Purpose. Religion and religious institutions may facilitate youth's development of a sense of purpose.[37] While religion's relative contribution to an individual's sense of purpose may be a widely accepted potential developmental pathway, the specific processes and the understanding of what constitutes purpose may vary in manners not accounted for in the scholarly literature. For example, within Christianity, individuals with different denominations have consistently reported different levels of life satisfaction.[38] Alternately, clinical psychologists have documented how the Buddhist tradition has cultivated mental balance and well-being for thousands of years by promoting a contemplative lifestyle.[39] The diversity represented in the religious lives of contemporary immigrants has been reflected in broader definitions of what constitutes ultimate purpose to include representations beyond those of Christian faith traditions (e.g., peace by submission to God, noble living, enlightenment).

In addition to having different conceptions of life's purpose, immigrant youth may have different pathways for meaning making. World faith traditions are often nurtured and maintained by spiritual guides, some dead (e.g., prophets, familial ancestors, saints, gurus) and some living (e.g., gurus, elders, priests, rabbis, imams), many of whom need to meet guidelines to acquire special visa status (e.g., R-1, Religious Worker) before entering the United States. Although these spiritual guides may have the requisite religious knowledge, immigrant-origin youth may not believe that these guides have the necessary cross-cultural knowledge to help them develop religious commitment in a new land where the guides' practices and beliefs seem foreign. Immigrant-origin youth, then, may regard their parents and the religious guides as well intentioned in their efforts to support the youth's spiritual development but unable to provide relevant support.[40] While youth-mentoring models are integral in many faith communities, the identification and training of religiously committed older teens and young adults who are familiar with the cultural landscape and the building of youth-friendly religious communities are particularly important for immigrant-origin youth for a combination of personal and social reasons (i.e., a practicing Muslim student-athlete who models for younger students how she maintains religious dress within her athletic competitions).[41]

For many immigrant-origin youth, the ultimate guide "needs no passport."[42] The belief in God (i.e., an ultimate power or higher order) provides many adults and youth with a sense of purpose. Religious values and a belief in God and participation in worship communities is a prominent feature of immigrant-origin youth's home and community lives; moreover, this participation is associated with positive outcomes, including a sense of purpose.[43] Similarly, a study of Puerto Rican high school students revealed the multifaceted role of religiousness in the academic experience of academically and socially vulnerable students.[44] On a social level, relationships with adults from church provided social capital, support, and mentoring generally and during crisis times. On a personal level, students' religious beliefs included a sense that God was within them and highlighted an internal locus of control, which was associated with higher expectations of oneself and a sense of effectiveness. Future scholarship should study the varied ways religion and religious communities promote a sense of purpose among immigrant and nonimmigrant youth.

Identity. While identity development is considered an integrated, fluid construct, the intersecting nature of religious, ethnic, and gender identities of immigrant-origin families is particularly worth examining.[45] Early in U.S. history, the study of religious institutions necessarily included the study of the particular ethnic or national group (e.g., Greek Orthodox, Irish Catholic).[46] Contemporary immigrants who worship in a religious community often simultaneously experience socialization into their coethnic communities. Particularly for young children and families, such contexts may help reinforce heritage language, cultural dress, and practices (e.g., a church cricket tournament or collective viewing of presidential debates). Parents may find that this ethnic-religious enclave provides an important respite and a context to identify future marriage prospects for their children or business partners for themselves. However, children may respond to interactions with others of their ethnicity or religion in a variety of ways ranging from feeling highly affirmed and included to feeling disdain for the "backward" environment that is too different from their "real" life (e.g., religious events or programs that seem poorly organized and predictably start late).

As children develop additional cognitive, personal, and social awareness, they may examine the relationship between aspects of their identity and religion more critically. Immersion in a coethnic or coracial congregation may contribute to an overlap, or perhaps conflation, of culture and religion. For example, in a qualitative study of Indian American Hindu and Muslim emerging adults, participants described entering college as an important beginning of self- and religious discovery.[47] Before being in a college setting, many participants had difficulty distinguishing religious practices from their ethnic cultural practices. However, exposure to other observant religious groups or nonreligious cultural groups allowed them to separate religion and culture. Instead of praying because it is something a family "always did," individuals learn the meaning of prayers and develop a fuller understanding of and commitment to prayer. Culture itself can serve as a de facto "religion," in which cultural practices are codified even though they may not be grounded in the religion. Some young adults may consider culture as influencing religion in ways that are not theologically grounded and have sought to purge cultural innovations (e.g., culturally popular prayers that are without theological foundations) from religion in order to return to a purer, fundamental form of religious practice.[48] Such examinations triggered by immigrant youth may be associated with parental conversion from their family-of-origin religion, which was notably 25.4 percent of the urban sample of immigrant Dominican-, Central American–, Mexican-, Haitian-, and Chinese-origin families.[49]

While there are many ways to measure ethnic identity, for immigrant-origin youth, the figurative and literal translation between worlds and words is an integral feature of becoming bicultural or multicultural, with implications for religious identity. Consider the language and identity demands on Muslim, Sikh, and Hindu South Asian immigrant-origin adolescents in Britain who speak a combination of languages and dialects based on their region of origin and religious affiliation (e.g.,

Punjabi/Urdu, Arabic, Mirpuri, and Gujarati) in addition to English.[50] Describing their ability to recite but not understand Arabic as "pretended bilingualism," participants had to negotiate their ethnic, religious, and linguistic identities (and loyalties) based on the barriers and demands of a particular context.[51]

Immigrant-origin children's home and community environments may vary in language practices and the cultural messages and materials to promote their heritage-language acquisition and maintenance. Many immigrant-origin and religious-minority children spend numerous nonleisure hours in a language school learning to read Arabic, Hebrew, Chinese, or other languages through a wide variety of incentives, coercion, and personal agency. Their development of heritage-language proficiency (or its stagnation) can be an important dimension of their heritage-country and family identity that connects them to grandparents and elders within their family and faith tradition. Although children may be encouraged to, and in fact do, struggle to learn the language of prayer within their faith communities, these efforts can result in varying levels of proficiency: some may understand or recognize the language but may not be able to verbalize their thoughts; others may memorize prayers or chants but not understand their meaning; still others may develop considerable language skills. While the lack of heritage-language proficiency may limit one's sense of ethnic identity or affect others' assessment of the person as a group member, limited heritage- or liturgical-language literacy may also limit the person's religious socialization and development. A female Chinese Buddhist young adult explained why she primarily spent her time at the temple volunteering in the kitchen rather than in the areas dedicated to prayer: "And because we [participant and other immigrant-origin peers] don't go in for the mass and the chanting and everything because, I don't know . . . we feel that we shouldn't be doing something if we don't really know it very well. Because you have to chant it from a book, and we're not very fluent in reading the whole thing. And it feels embarrassing to make a mistake because people are doing it right."[52] Since the language is integral to the prayers, a lack of proficiency may prohibit a person's participation in certain practices altogether or limit access to or understanding of particular services and religious texts. Ultimately, the loss of the heritage language or diminished proficiency in it may limit a person's religious experience and exploration. Further, the loss may adversely affect a person's sense of efficacy on personal and social levels, reducing ability to converse and bond with friends and family.

Civic Engagement. Participating in a religious community can serve as a bonding experience for immigrants as well as a bridging resource that may serve as an acculturation pathway. A substantial body of research maintains that for the children of immigrants—particularly the second generation and beyond—religion has served the function of "turn[ing] immigrants into Americans and giv[ing] them a sense of belonging and membership."[53] Many immigrant-origin families and their children receive applied civics lessons in a religious context through workshops (that start on time and model multiple levels of successful business behaviors in the United States) on how to apply for a home loan, know one's rights when visited by the FBI, or organize around an issue relevant to the health or educational needs of immigrants.

Religious communities are often spaces that house or promote volunteerism and civic engagement (e.g., soup kitchens, SAT preparation programs). However, there are variations in the nature and frequency of volunteering both across and within immigrant and nonimmigrant groups. Analysts of civic engagement do not agree on whether religiosity is a major incentive for youth civic engagement. Some researchers maintain that youth's civic engagement is enhanced by their religious involvement.[54] Others see political rather than religious socialization as the primary motivation for civic engagement.[55] Further, variations in individual and group involvement may be related to one's needs and other aspects of the ecological context (e.g., gender, race, and socioeconomic status), including views about helping oneself and others. Involvement in religious institutions generally may encourage civic engagement, but the levels of and motivations for a person's involvement remain unclear.[56] While there has been research on religious congregations and civic engagement, to the best of our knowledge there has been no focus on this intersection with immigrant-origin youth.[57] The multiple types of and motivations for civic engagement suggest the need for additional research in this area.

Sexuality. A review of the scholarly research on adolescent sexuality posits that young people explore their sexuality as a normative developmental phenomenon but does not advocate for normative time lines or benchmarks.[58] This caveat acknowledges the tremendous personal nature of and variation in youth's exploration, including cultural and religious values with outright prohibitions of sex. While values within the United States seem to normalize sexual behavior outside marriage and heterosexual boundaries, it is important to note that the cultures from which the current waves of immigrants are coming are those in which children and adolescents generally have less freedom and autonomy than do U.S. adolescents and in which family traditions are stronger.[59] Findings from a large-scale school-based study of nearly 10,000 students in midadolescence, focusing on romantic relationships, suggest the importance of both family and peer context in predicting romantic relations, particularly when considering interactions involving acculturation and gender.[60] Parents were more effective in monitoring girls than boys, and immigrant parents were less effective in monitoring their adolescents than nonimmigrant parents perhaps because of their lack of knowledge of adolescent dating norms and practices in the United States as well as their adolescents' desires to fit in. Further, friendship groups predominantly composed of first-generation adolescents were associated with more conservative levels of sex-related activities for individual adolescents. Among males involved in romantic relationships, the main influence on sex-related activities is their personal level of religiosity.

A six-year longitudinal study of 4,535 females and 3,759 males beginning in the eighth grade examined the joint effects of race/ethnicity and immigrant status on adolescents' loss of virginity.[61] Findings suggest that the influence of generational status depends on gender, and the expression of the gender difference varies across race/ethnic groups, perhaps because of gendered social messages (e.g., media portrayals of sexuality for girls versus boys). Although gendered messages may also be religious, the study did not consider religious beliefs or practices within the model.

Adolescents and emerging adults navigate the way in which their specific religious affiliation, if any, combine with cultural influences to guide their sexuality. This process may include exploring romantic relationships and intimacy and addressing sexual desire such as masturbation and partnered heterosexual or homosexual activities. Further, religious values and groups may influence countless private and public decisions with important personal, familial, and societal implications that include resolving issues about where to hold a wedding (e.g., church, synagogue, social hall, outdoors) and the timing and nature of beginning a family (e.g., adoption, types of assisted fertilization).[62] Future research may utilize measures that incorporate religious values surrounding romantic relationships and adolescents' heterosexual and homosexual activity in order to elucidate the distinct role of religiosity in predicting romantic relationships among immigrant adolescents.

Conclusions, Implications, Limitations, and Future Research Directions

The research and theory about the role of religion in child and adolescent development is growing and needs to include the journeys of immigrant-origin youth. Theories of religious and spiritual development should seek to determine what may be generalized across religious traditions and across the population and also what must be specified within a religious tradition, within a community, and within an individual. Toward this end, scholars need to draw from interdisciplinary and multiple research methods and develop measures and research designs that represent the tremendous variations within and among religious groups and the immigrant population. Research should attend to issues important to children and young adults and their care providers and capture the contradictions and simplicity of their real-world experiences (e.g., religious practices at home, at school or work, in public, and in places of worship).

Implications. Issues related to religion and spirituality have implications for developing culturally appropriate interventions and are an important aspect of developing authentic rapport in the service relationship. While the task may seem daunting, a multitude of resources exist to help support practitioners in general terms and from field-specific approaches. For example, while practitioners may group all Catholic immigrants or all Latino/a immigrants together, Lujan and Campbell provide a semianthropological portrayal of the role of religion on the health practices of Mexican Americans in order to reduce health disparities and promote holistic care.[63] A sociohistorical overview discusses the specific way in which Catholicism was introduced in Mexico and mixed with traditions of native people, creating a unique form of folk Catholicism with variations related to ethnic, historical, and other factors. Failing to adequately account for this history and how it is manifested in contemporary contexts may be an underlying cause of health disparities (e.g., diabetes, infant mortality). While a prescriptive guide to practice would be incongruent with a person-centered, culturally sensitive approach, such a portrait provides practitioners a useful reference and framework to build rapport.

Future Research. Future research in the study of religion in immigrant-origin communities may draw from a close study of the salience, function, and form of the Black Church within the lives of African Americans, given its role in mediating the challenges of the broader social environment. While a study of religion and spirituality in the lives of African Americans, Caribbean Blacks, and non-Hispanic Whites found differences in affiliation, it also found differences in their endorsement of religiosity and spirituality as constructs, suggesting that measures that tap public behavior do not capture dimensions of religious life important to minority participants.[64] An authentic conceptualization of religion and spirituality may include cross-cultural approaches that explore science, sociology, history, theology, and philosophy in order to identify the connections between religion and spirituality in an interdisciplinary fashion as well as to ground the analysis contextually. Finally, a sustained focus on studying the role of religion and religious communities in the lives of immigrant children and adolescents, embedded in their families and communities and located within a quest to understand the development of faith more broadly, may help promote the development of youth, irrespective of their generational status and whatever gaps in meaning making, identity, engagement in family and society, and relational intimacy. Ultimately, the hope is for Yarissa and all in her generation and the generations to come to fulfill their potential, avoiding getting lost in translation or transition.[65]

NOTES
1. Marty, M. (1997). *The one and the many: America's struggle for the common good.* Cambridge: Cambridge University Press.
2. Roehlkepartain, E. C., King, P. E., Wagener, L. M. & Benson, P. L. (Eds.). (2006). *The handbook of spiritual development in childhood and adolescence.* Thousand Oaks, CA: Sage.

3. Suárez-Orozco, C., Singh, S., Abo-Zena, M. M., Du, D. & Roeser, R. W. (2011). The role of religion and religious organizations in the positive youth development of immigrant youth. In A. E. A. Warren, R. M. Lerner, & E. Phelps (Eds.), *Thriving and spirituality among youth: Research perspectives and future possibilities* (pp. 255–288). Hoboken, NJ: Wiley.

4. Holden, G. W., & Vittrup, B. (2009). Religion. In M. H. Bornstein (Ed.), *Handbook of cultural developmental science* (pp. 279–295). New York: Routledge.

5. Tarakeshwar, N., Stanton, J., & Pargament, K. I. (2003). Religion: An overlooked dimension in cross-cultural psychology. *Journal of Cross-Cultural Psychology, 34*(4), 377–394.

6. Hill, P. C., Pargament, K. I., Hood, R. W., McCullough, M. E., Swyers, J. P., Larson, D. B., & Zinnbauer, B. J. (2000). Conceptualizing religion and spirituality: Points of commonality, points of departure. *Journal for the Theory of Social Behavior, 30*(1), 51–77.

7. Benson, P. L., Roehlkepartain, E. C., & Rude, S. P. (2003). Spiritual development in childhood and adolescence: Toward a field of inquiry. *Applied Developmental Science, 7*(3), 205–213.

8. Pargament, K. I. (1999). The psychology of religion and spirituality? Yes and no. *International Journal for the Psychology of Religion, 9*(1), 3–16.

9. Pargament, K. I., Mahoney, A., Exline, J. J., Jones, J. W., & Shafranske, E. P. (2013). Envisioning an integrative paradigm for the psychology of religion and spirituality. In K. I. Pargament (Ed.), *APA handbook of psychology, religion, and spirituality: Vol. 1, Context, theory, and research* (pp. 3–19).

10. King, P. E., & Furrow, J. L. (2004). Religion as a resource for positive youth development: Religion, social capital, and moral outcomes. *Developmental Psychology, 40*(5), 703–713.

11. Boyatzis, C. J., Dollahite, D. C., & Marks, L. D. (2006). The family as a context for religious and spiritual development in children and youth. In E. C. Roehlkepartain, P. E. King, L. Wagener, & P. L. Benson (Eds.), *The handbook of spiritual development in childhood and adolescence* (pp. 297–303). Thousand Oaks, CA: Sage.

12. Furrow, J. L., King, P. E., & White, K. (2004). Religion and positive youth development: Identity, meaning, and prosocial concerns. *Applied Developmental Science, 8*(1), 17–26.

13. Yonker, J. E., Schnabelrauch, C. A., & De Haan, L. G. (2012). The relationship between spirituality and religiosity on psychological outcomes in adolescents and emerging adults: A meta-analytic review. *Journal of Adolescence, 35*(2), 299–314.

14. King, P. E. (2008). Spirituality as fertile ground for positive youth development. In R. M. Lerner, R. W. Roeser, & E. Phelps (Eds.), *Positive youth development and spirituality: From theory to research* (pp. 55–73). West Conshohocken, PA: Templeton Foundation Press.

15. Erikson, E. (1968). *Identity, youth, and crisis.* New York: Norton.

16. Piaget, J. (with Inhelder, B.). (1958). *The growth of logical thinking from childhood to adolescence.* New York: Basic Books.

17. Nakkula, M. J., & Toshalis, E. (2010). *Understanding youth: Adolescent development for educators.* Cambridge: Harvard Education Press.

18. Ibid., p. 207.

19. Roehlkepartain, E. C., & Patel, E. (2006). Congregations: Unexamined crucibles for spiritual development. In E. C. Roehlkepartain, P. E. King, L. Wagener, & P. L. Benson (Eds.), *The handbook of spiritual development in childhood and adolescence* (pp. 324–336). Thousand Oaks, CA: Sage.

20. Lerner, R. M., & Overton, W. F. (2008). Exemplifying the integrations of the relational developmental system: Synthesizing theory, research, and application to promote positive development and social justice. *Journal of Adolescent Research, 23*(3), 245–255.

21. Spencer, M. B. (2006). Phenomenology and ecological systems theory: Development of diverse groups. In W. Damon & R. M. Lerner (Eds.). *Handbook of child psychology: An advanced textbook* (pp. 829–893). Hoboken, NJ: Wiley.

22. Rivas-Drake, D., Hughes, D., & Way, N. (2009). A preliminary analysis of associations among ethnic-racial socialization, ethnic discrimination, and ethnic identity among urban sixth graders. *Journal of Research on Adolescence, 19*(3), 558–584; Sellers, R. M., Rowley, S. A., Chavous, T. M., Shelton, J. N., & Smith, M. A. (1997). Multidimensional Inventory of Black Identity: A preliminary investigation of reliability and construct validity. *Journal of Personality and Social Psychology, 73*(4), 805.

23. Mattis, J. S., Ahluwalia, M. K., Cowie, S. E., & Kirkland-Harris, A. M. (2006). Ethnicity, culture, and spiritual development. In E. C. Roehlkepartain, P. E. King, L. Wagener, & P. L. Benson (Eds.), *The handbook of spiritual development in childhood and adolescence* (pp. 283–296). Thousand Oaks, CA: Sage.

24. Lerner & Overton. (2008).

25. Pargament et al. (2013).

26. Levitt, P. (2007). *God needs no passport: Immigrants and the changing American religious landscape.* New York: New Press.

27. Rumbaut, R. G. (1994). The crucible within: Ethnic identity, self-esteem, and segmented assimilation among children of immigrants. *International Migration Review, 28*(4), 748–794.

28. Kwon, V. H. (1997). *Entrepreneurship and religion: Korean immigrants in Houston, Texas.* New York: Garland.

29. Cao, N. (2005). The church as a surrogate family for working class immigrant Chinese youth: An ethnography of segmented assimilation. *Sociology of Religion, 66*(2), 183–200.

30. Eck, D. L. (2002). *A new religious America: How a "Christian country" has become the world's most religiously diverse nation.* San Francisco: Harper.

31. Leonard, K., Stepick, A., Vasquez, M., Holdaway, J. (Eds.). (2005). *Immigrant faiths: transforming religious life in America.* Walnut Creek, CA: AltaMira.

32. Cadge, W., & Ecklund, E. H. (2007). Immigration and religion. *Annual Review of Sociology, 33,* 359–379.

33. Leonard et al. (2005).

34. Oh, S. S., & Yoshikawa, H. (2012). Examining spiritual capital and acculturation across ecological systems: Developmental implications for children and adolescents in diverse immigrant families. In L. Nucci (Series Ed.) & C. García Coll (Vol. Ed.), *Contributions to Human Development: Vol. 24, The impact of immigration on children's development* (pp. 77–98). New York: Karger.

35. Bender, C., Cadge, W., Levitt, P., & Smilde, D. (Eds.) (2012). *Religion on the edge: De-centering and re-centering the sociology of religion.* New York: Oxford University Press.

36. Portes, A., & Rumbaut, R. G. (2001). *Legacies: The story of the immigrant second generation.* Berkeley: University of California Press.

37. Roehlkepartain & Patel. (2006).

38. Ellison, C. G. (1991). Religious involvement and subjective well-being. *Journal of Health and Social Behavior, 32*(1), 80–99.

39. Wallace, B. A., & Shapiro, S. L. (2006). Mental balance and well-being: Building bridges between Buddhism and Western psychology. *American Psychologist, 61*(7), 690–701.

40. Suárez-Orozco et al. 2011.

41. Abo-Zena, M. M., & Ahmed, S. (2014). Religion and spirituality of emerging adults: Processing meaning through culture, context and social position. In C. M. Barry, & M. M. Abo-Zena (Eds.), *Emerging adults' religiousness and spirituality: Meaning-making in an age of transition* (pp. 220–236). New York: Oxford University Press.

42. Levitt. (2007).

43. Suárez-Orozco et al. (2011).

44. Antrop-González, R., Vélez, W., & Garrett, T. (2007). Religion and high academic achievement in Puerto Rican high school students. *Religion and Education, 34*(1), 63–75.

45. Juang, L., & Syed, M. (2008). Ethnic identity and spirituality. In R. M. Lerner, R. W. Roeser, & E. Phelps (Eds.). *Positive youth development and spirituality: From theory to research* (pp. 262–284). West Conshohocken, PA: Templeton Foundation Press.

46. Pozzetta, G. E. (Ed.) (1991). *American immigration and ethnicity: The immigrant religious experience.* New York: Garland.

47. Levitt, P., Barnett, M., & Khalil, N. A. (2011). Learning to pray: Religious socialization across generations and borders. In K. F. Olwig & M. Rytter (Eds.), *Mobile bodies, mobile souls* (pp. 139–159). Aarhus, Denmark: Aarhus University Press.

48. Ibid.

49. Suárez-Orozco et al. (2011).

50. Jaspal, R., & Coyle, A. (2010). "Arabic is the language of the Muslims—that's how it was supposed to be": Exploring language and religious identity through reflective accounts from young British-born South Asians. *Mental Health, Religion and Culture, 13*(1), 17–36.

51. Jaspal & Coyle. (2010).

52. Abo-Zena, M. M., & Barry, C. M. (2013). Religion and immigrant-origin youth: A resource and a challenge. *Research in Human Development, 10*(4), 353–371. (Quotation from p. 362.)

53. Foner, N., & Alba, R. (2008). Immigrant religion in the U.S. and western Europe: Bridge or barrier to inclusion? *International Migration Research, 42*(2), 360–392. (Quotation from p. 365.)

54. Youniss, J., & Yates, M. (1999). Youth service and moral-civic identity: A case for everyday morality. *Educational Psychology Review, 11*(4), 361–376.

55. Youniss, J., & Levine, P. (Eds.) (2009). *Engaging young people in civic life.* Nashville: Vanderbilt University Press.

56. Jensen, L. A. (2008). Immigrants' cultural identities as sources of civic engagement. *Applied Developmental Science, 12*(2), 74–83.

57. Kniss, F., & Numrich, P. D. (2007). *Sacred assemblies and civic engagement: How religion matters for America's newest immigrants.* New Brunswick: Rutgers University Press.

58. Tolman, D. L., & McClelland, S. I. (2011). Normative sexuality development in adolescence: A decade in review, 2000–2009. *Journal of Research on Adolescence, 21*(1), 242–255.

59. King, R. B., & Harris, K. M. (2007). Romantic relationships among immigrant adolescents. *International Migration Review, 41*(2), 344–370.

60. Ibid.

61. Spence, N. J., & Brewster, K. L. (2010). Adolescents' sexual initiation: The interaction of race/ethnicity and immigrant status. *Population Research and Policy Review, 29*(3), 339–362.

62. Magyar-Russel, G., Deal, P. J., & Brown, I. T. (2014). Potential benefits and detriments of religiousness and spirituality to emerging adults. In C. M. Barry, & M. M. Abo-Zena (Eds.), *Emerging adults' religiousness and spirituality: Meaning-making in an age of transition* (pp. 39–55). New York: Oxford University Press.

63. Lujan, J., & Campbell, H. B. (2006). The role of religion on the health practices of Mexican Americans. *Journal of Religion and Health, 45*(2), 183–195.

64. Taylor, R. J., & Chatters, L. M. (2010). Importance of religion and spirituality in the lives of African Americans, Caribbean Blacks and non-Hispanic whites. *Journal of Negro Education, 79*(3), 280–294.

65. Smith, C. (with Snell, P.). (2009). *Souls in transition: The religious and spiritual lives of emerging adults.* New York: Oxford University Press.

5

The Shadow of Undocumented Status

CAROLA SUÁREZ-OROZCO AND HIROKAZU YOSHIKAWA

At age eight, Lucia came to the United States with her parents from El Salvador during the height of civil unrest. Her family was granted temporary refugee status and settled in rural Texas. Her father, who had been a doctor in his homeland, took a job as a lab assistant while her mother stayed home caring for Lucia and her younger brother and sister, who were born after the family had immigrated. After an initial period of transition, quiet and studious Lucia began to thrive in school. She loved science and set her heart on becoming a doctor so she could "help people." Her parents petitioned for asylum with an attorney they had seen advertised on a local billboard, but he absconded with their fees, so their file went to the end of the queue. Lucia graduated as valedictorian of her high school and was accepted with scholarships by several colleges. Shortly after turning 18, she accompanied her parents for a hearing at the United States Citizenship and Immigration Services offices, where she served as the translator. At that time she learned the good news—her parents had been granted asylum. Lamentably, however, she was also told that since she was now an adult, she would not be covered by the asylum application—deportation proceedings would begin shortly.[1]

During the boom economic years of the last decade of the 20th century, the undocumented population grew dramatically from under a million (in 1980), peaked at nearly 12 million (in 1996), and is currently estimated to have dropped to approximately 11 million.[2] The majority arrive through the borders "uninspected," though a substantial number are visa overstayers.[3] All told, undocumented adult immigrants constitute approximately 4 percent of the total U.S. population.[4] Many exist in a state of "liminal legality"[5] with ambiguous documentation, patiently waiting in broken queues.[6] Across the nation, immigrants have become the subject of negative media coverage,[7] hate crimes,[8] and exclusionary political legislation.[9]

The focus of the immigration debate is on adults, with little or no consideration given to children. In this chapter, we reflect on two groups of children and youth who contend with undocumented status. The first consists of those brought into this country during their childhoods who are themselves undocumented (approximately 1.5 million); the other consists of *citizen-children*, legal citizens because they were born here to undocumented parents (an additional estimated 4.5 million).[10] Because undocumented immigrants are disproportionately young and in prime childbearing years, their children make up a large share of both the U.S. newborn (8 percent) and school-age (7 percent) populations.[11] Approximately 79 percent of the children of undocumented immigrants are citizen-children.[12]

As in the case of Lucia, an estimated 14.6 million individuals live in some sort of mixed-status home[13] where at least one member of the family is undocumented.[14] Currently, *one in 10 children* living in the United States is growing up in such a household.[15] There are multiple patterns of mixed authorization: 41 percent have one documented and one undocumented parent, 39 percent have two undocumented parents, and 20 percent live in households headed by a single undocumented parent.[16] Within these mixed-status households, there is also a range of documentation patterns involving siblings: some born in the United States with birthright citizenship, some in the process of attempting to obtain documentation, and some completely undocumented.[17]

Long backlogs, a byzantine bureaucracy, and increasing rates of denials of legal status are cementing growing numbers of immigrants as transnationally separated mixed-status families.[18] Many find themselves living apart not only from their extended families but also from parents and some siblings, split between the United States and the country of origin.[19] These family separations result for a host of reasons. A father may immigrate first, planning to find a job and send for his wife and children later. A widowed mother may be forced to leave her children behind with her mother while earning enough to support them and save for their transport. Both parents may be paying off their passage fees and may decide that their U.S.-citizen infant will get more consistent care from a grandmother than in an overcrowded day-care center. As in Lucia's case, the asylum application may take more than half a childhood to be approved. Some parents, facing long delays and realizing that they are missing their offspring's childhood, make the always-difficult decision to bring their children to the United States without papers.

In 2014, for example, the number of unaccompanied children in the U.S. increased dramatically—most of these children were Central American.[20] Fueling this growth was a violence epidemic in the region; in 2013, the United Nations identified Honduras as the most violent country in the world, El Salvador as the fourth most violent, and Guatemala as the fifth. Children and young adults were particularly targeted in the violence. Frightened children, longing for their parents, began the long, arduous passage often with nothing more than a piece of paper and their parents' contact information in hand.[21] Parents who had migrated ahead, after failed asylum requests, hearing rumors that the Trafficking Victims Protection Reauthorization Act might provide their children entry, sent for them.[22] The number of unauthorized and unaccompanied children at the border surged, creating a humanitarian crisis, launching a media frenzy, drawing attention as far as the Vatican, but resulting in a continued political stalemate in Washington.

In some families, older siblings enter with their undocumented parents, while younger siblings were born as U.S. citizens. In many families in which the children are citizens, the parents remain at high risk for deportation during the course of their offspring's childhood. Heidi, for example, described at a congressional hearing her experience, one repeated in hundreds of thousands of families every year: "At only 10 years of age . . . I woke up and found out that my mother had been arrested."[23] Soon thereafter, her mother was deported. A year and a half later, Heidi had not seen her mother again, and the prospects for reunification are slim.

What Are the Implications of Such Contexts for Child Development?

Through an Ecological Lens

Undocumented families strive to support and enhance developmental outcomes for their children; there are specific vulnerabilities, however, associated with growing up in an undocumented family.[24] An ecological lens provides a useful framework for systematically considering these risks.[25]

The Macrosystem

The global economy, emigration policies, social and cultural conditions in countries of origin, and immigration policies in the United States influence individuals' decisions of whether to migrate or overstay visas.[26] Since 1988, when the amnesty provisions of the Immigration Reform and Control Act largely ended, U.S. immigration policy has increasingly restricted access and pathways to citizenship for the undocumented.[27] Today, there is no pathway to citizenship for the undocumented, not even for the restricted population targeted by the Development, Relief, and Education for Alien Minors (DREAM) Act (S. 1291).

Attitudes toward undocumented immigrants have become increasingly harsh in recent years, as reflected in the flurry of state and local legislation aimed at curbing undocumented immigration.[28] Beginning in 2010, a number of draconian laws targeting undocumented immigrants were passed in Arizona, Georgia, Alabama, and South Carolina. Bias crimes against Latinos have risen steadily since 2003, even in the midst of overall decreases in violent crime.[29] A deep body of developmental research demonstrates the negative health and developmental outcomes associated with growing up in a social environment marked by prejudice, stereotyping, and limited access to essential social services.[30] Thus, the macrosystemic context for undocumented families and those who are associated with them is far from optimal.

The Exosystem

Beyond the social and cultural belief systems embodied in the spate of legislation and new patterns of discrimination, multiple variables at the neighborhood and community levels also affect children and youth in undocumented families. Above and beyond undocumented parents' relative disadvantages due to their lower levels of education, evidence that a range of everyday experiences—from interactions with authorities to characteristics of their social networks and work conditions—prohibits them from obtaining resources to help their children's development. The threat of deportation results in lower levels of enrollment of citizen-children in programs for which they are eligible—including child-care subsidies, public preschool, and food stamps—and in the undocumenteds' limited interaction and engagement with public institutions such as schools. Their fear of authorities in public institutions can extend to timidity in reporting crimes to police and in reporting housing problems and violations to landlords as well as lower use of resources such as public libraries.

The poor working conditions of the undocumented contribute substantially to the lower cognitive skills of children in their families, whether these children are citizens or not. As two recent studies show, 30 to 40 percent of undocumented parents earn illegally low wages, a rate much higher than that of their authorized low-wage counterparts.[31] The combustive combination of exploitation and indebtedness forces many undocumented parents to work 12-hour days, six days a week, for years at jobs with the lowest levels of autonomy or very basic protections afforded by a democracy. Having undocumented status means these workers typically do not dare ask for a raise or report unacceptable working conditions; many live in constant fear of being fired. Without recourse to unions or public safeguards, the undocumented endure working conditions that are not only poor but also chronic. These have harmful effects on their children's development by creating increased economic hardship and psychological distress and by blocking access to resources that require proof of employment, such as childcare subsidies.

Microsystems

Neighborhoods. Although immigrants reside in virtually every type of social and geographical setting, from the inner city to suburbs and rural outskirts, the majority of individuals who migrated to the United States after 1965 are concentrated in cities with large ethnic populations.[32] These neighborhoods are typically segregated across multiple dimensions, including class, race and ethnicity, and language.[33] Immigrants are disproportionately likely to live in poverty.[34] While some are able to extract valuable social capital from their ethnic enclaves,[35] others have minimal engagement with institutions in their communities.[36] For very recent undocumented immigrants, the economic and social-capital benefits of ethnic enclaves are often elusive. For such families, the majority in their social network may be undocumented themselves, thus only able to share a limited quantity and quality of information about community and public resources.

Schools. The children of new arrivals most often find themselves in underresourced schools. These typically are highly segregated[37] and provide few opportunities for students to engage with school.[38] Racially and linguistically isolated schools put students at academic risk and can have a variety of negative characteristics, including overcrowding, inadequate resources, teachers' low expectations of students, poor student achievement test scores, high dropout rates, and limited availability of information about ways to access college.[39] These factors are also associated with negative school climates and increased school violence.[40] Further, because undocumented families are often in tenuous financial circumstances, they frequently move, so children must change schools. School mobility, not surprisingly, has been linked to negative school performance.[41] The children of the undocumented, in sum, find themselves in the most transitory spaces of the United States' dystopian schools.

Family Processes. Undocumented parents are as dedicated to their children's learning as parents with authorized or citizenship status are.[42] Parents of different status do not differ, for example, in their rates of reading books, telling stories, or engaging in other cognitively stimulating activities with their young children. Undocumented fathers, despite working significantly more hours than those worked by the authorized, display high levels of engagement in social and caregiving activities. Despite these family strengths, children growing up in undocumented homes face a number of uniquely complicated family dynamics.[43] Many endure long family separations and complicated reunifications following protracted times apart mandated by parents' undocumented status.[44] Parents with liminal authorized status will often spend years attempting to attain legal status before sending for their children. In many cases, children spend half or more of their childhood raised apart from their biological parents.[45]

Children and youth in households with undocumented individuals live in fear of being separated from parents or other family members should any member be apprehended or deported.[46] As Mateo, an 11-year-old, U.S.-born, Mexican-origin boy, explained in his testimony to members of Congress, "I am always worried when my family leaves the house that something might happen to them. I think about it when my dad goes to work that he might not come back or when I go to school that there might not be someone to pick me up when I get out."[47] To prepare children, some parents may discuss a contingency plan in the event of detention or deportation; a survey of Latino parents found that among the undocumented, 58 percent had a plan for the care of their children if they were detained, and 40 percent reported that they had discussed that plan with their children.[48] Having a contingency plan is an example of unique parental ethnic-racial socialization[49] to the realities of a shadowed existence. Other parents, perhaps because they believe their children are less likely to be detained or because they wish to protect them from harsh realities as long as possible, do not tell their children about their own status until children reach mid to late adolescence, only postponing a difficult and alienating conversation. These family socialization practices likely impact the developing children's sense of belonging in their communities, their growing ethnic-racial identities, and other psychological processes. Research is needed to fully explore and understand these unique immigration-status socialization experiences.

In addition to these family dynamics, a number of factors appear to contribute to uneven family investments in children who live in homes of the undocumented.[50] Although there is no evidence of differences in educational goals or psychological investments among groups with high, moderate, and low proportions of undocumented populations, there is some evidence of differences in economic investments, including the purchase of books, toys, and learning materials.[51] These can be attributed to lower rates of parental education as well as to the financial precariousness of many family situations. When a parent owes money to a human smuggler (aka a *coyote* or *snakehead*), has unpredictable low-wage work, is sending funds home, and has many dependents, purchasing books and educational toys may be an unaffordable luxury. Home space where children can study is often extremely limited as undocumented families often pool resources, sharing space with other families or taking boarders into already tight quarters.[52] While parents work long hours, older siblings often take on the responsibilities of child care, elder care, cooking, and translation.[53] These circumstances have been linked to high levels of stress; though well intentioned, undocumented parents may have difficulty being fully physically or psychologically available to their children.[54]

The Individual Experience

At the individual level, children growing up in the shadow of undocumented status take the body blows of both distal and proximal contexts. In addition to children's lived experiences within neighborhoods, schools, and families, their daily lives may reflect food and housing insecurities and, above all, the ever-present threat of a loved one's deportation—or their own.[55] A dawning awareness of their own legal status includes concerns about their future. These worries include limited access to educational and work opportunities, negative experiences with the authorities, and a barrage of derogatory social reflections of immigrants[56] (particularly of the undocumented). Such experiences shape critical developmental outcomes for these children and youth.

Developmental Implications

Health

Undocumented parents are currently ineligible for all health care except perinatal and emergency-room care. Although citizen-children of the undocumented are eligible for all government health benefits, undocumented children are not. The effects of these limitations on the health of adults and children in undocumented families have not been well established. On the one hand, research on the *immigrant health paradox* (see Suárez-Orozco, Marks, and Abo-Zena, introduction to this volume) shows that groups with high rates of undocumented immigrants, such as lower-income Mexicans, have better perinatal and postnatal outcomes than do their U.S.-born counterparts with roughly equal economic conditions.[57] On the other hand, the effects of disparate health-care access on lifelong health outcomes are largely unknown since the large increases in undocumented migration (starting in the early 1990s) have been of adults and children during the relatively more protected developmental periods of childhood and young adulthood. The cumulative consequences of social disadvantage for lifelong health and mental health problems such as heart disease, diabetes, and depression are well established;[58] they suggest that the costliest consequences of undocumented status will emerge later in life as current generations of undocumented parents, children, and youth move into midlife and older ages.

Cognitive Development

Early childhood is the foundational period for later cognitive and social skills.[59] When compared with children of the authorized, children of undocumented parents are disadvantaged in school readiness.[60] Moreover, such disparities are evident earlier than age five—as early as 24 and 36 months. A number of factors appear to contribute to these patterns, including greater parental economic hardship, adverse working conditions, and psychological distress combined with less available help with infant child care and less access to information about community and public resources that could help children's development.[61]

Educational Trajectories

The size, growth, and heterogeneity of the population of children growing up in undocumented households warrant particular attention in the context of education as these youngsters enter formal schooling. These millions of children and youth in undocumented households face varying degrees of academic challenges. While some enter the U.S. educational system as young children and are quite acculturated and speak English as a primary language, more arrive sometime during the midway point of their educational trajectory with many language and academic hurdles to overcome. Many immigrant parents have not been educated in their home countries and are unfamiliar with the U.S. educational system, factors that hinder not only their access to information and resources that can help them navigate the system but also their ability to facilitate their children's educational mobility.[62] Although immigrant parents have high educational aspirations and expectations for their children, many arrive in the United States with few resources and opportunities to realize these goals.[63]

Parental engagement with children's school—a positive predictor of academic achievement, high self-esteem, high school completion, and college enrollment[64]—is often a challenge for immigrant parents.[65] In some cases, language is a significant barrier that prevents meaningful contact between immigrant families and schools. The use of interpreters in family-school correspondence often makes communication difficult, so students themselves are often called on to translate (see Orellana and

Guan, "Child Language Brokering," chapter 9 in this volume). Aside from apprehension about navigating language barriers, immigrant parents have reported feeling intimidated by schools, particularly if they are undocumented and fear deportation if their status is recorded in any way by a school.[66]

Schools in areas where many unauthorized families live are often characterized by high dropout rates, inadequate preparation of students for postsecondary education, and low rates of college matriculation.[67] In fact, many immigrant youth who pursue postsecondary education may not have the academic skills or background necessary for college coursework. Too many must complete remedial courses before being allowed to enroll in credit-bearing courses. Moreover, more than half (53 percent) of immigrant college students are over the age of 24, and a sizeable proportion (60 percent) are classified as *independent* for financial aid purposes. They are also more likely to attend college as part-time students while working either a part-time or full-time job,[68] a situation that correlates with low persistence for completing studies and attaining a degree.

In addition, affordability is a significant factor in a student's decision to attend college. Research has shown that immigrant students lack information about ways to finance college and are less likely to apply for and obtain student loans, borrow less money, and pay for more of their college costs with their own finances than other students do.[69] While naturalized citizens and legal permanent residents typically are eligible to pay in-state tuition, nonpermanent residents and undocumented students are treated differently from one state to the next. Additionally, undocumented students and nonpermanent residents are not eligible for federal aid and most forms of state aid.[70] In combination, these factors relegate undocumented youth to community colleges because of their lower tuition costs or discourage college attendance altogether.[71] And in at least one state (Alabama), legislation was passed barring undocumented students from attending any public college.[72]

Socioemotional Development

Limited research has been done on the psychosocial implications of growing up undocumented or in an undocumented household,[73] an issue about which the field of psychology has only recently become aware. Although more research is needed to better inform service providers working with these children and youth about this condition,[74] there are several areas in which there is emerging data or about which we can make educated guesses.

The duress of living in limbo[75] takes a heavy toll on the socioemotional development of undocumented children and youth. Previous research has demonstrated that stressed and depressed parents have compromised parenting abilities.[76] Obviously, a larger than average percentage of undocumented parents may be at risk for stress or depression. The negative consequences of having a parent who has been detained are well documented in an Urban Institute study of children across a range of ages; these include a high incidence of reported depressive, anxiety, and posttraumatic stress disorder (PTSD) symptoms.[77] Living in a community in which family members or friends' parents have been detained or deported likely heightens insecurity and may undermine a sense of belonging and trust. If the child is a citizen, their sense of belonging to the United States could be undermined as its authorities actively seek to expel their parents, siblings, or other loved ones.[78] And if the child is themselves undocumented, belonging can be elusive because they will be encircled by the hard boundaries of this liminal state and unable to participate in the social rituals that define personhood in early adulthood (e.g., obtaining a driver's license). Although the child may strongly aspire to belong, doing so will remain a frustrated ambition. Identity formation, already a complicated task for immigrant youth,[79] will be particularly stymied under these conditions and in the face of hostile and disparaging social, political, and media representations,[80] creating a perfect storm of "perpetual outsider-hood."[81] The inability to participate in rites of passage, along with legal and social exclusions, can lead to deep social isolation.

Significant increases in stress levels during adolescence have far-reaching neurobiological and psychological consequences, including structural changes in stress and emotion reactive systems.[82] The myriad of stresses to which children of unauthorized immigrants are exposed have been linked to both externalizing and internalizing symptoms. For some, they lead to externalizing and acting-out behaviors such as substance abuse or sexual activities that are especially relevant during adolescence and emerging adulthood.[83] For many others, however, the pattern is one of internalizing, or turning distress inward. Typical complaints include feeling shame, anxiety, or chronic sadness; overeating or undereating; having difficulty sleeping; and never wanting to get out of bed.[84] Also common are somatic complaints such as high blood pressure, chronic headaches, toothaches, stomachaches, and backaches.[85] Some may abandon hope and be unable to visualize their future, leading to thoughts, gestures, or acts of suicide.[86]

Civic Engagement

To date, research on the civic engagement of immigrant-origin youth has been sparse. Historically, civic engagement has been defined by the gold standard of voting, though more recently it has been conceived more broadly to include commitment to society, activities to help the needy, and collective action to fight for social justice.[87] Since voting is a blocked pathway for both permanent lawful residents and the undocumented, broader definitions of civic engagement should be considered for immigrants and their children to realize the promise of their integration into the life of the country.[88] Some scholars have claimed that immigrants represent a threat to U.S. civil society because of their alleged divided loyalties.[89] However, the few existing studies of civic engagement suggest that this fear may be misplaced. In fact, when a broader definition of civic participation was applied, immigrant-origin youth were found to be actively engaged civically, especially in immigrant-specific activities such as interpreting, translating, advocating, filling out official documents, and other forms of civic engagement often overlooked in traditional measures.[90]

When studying immigrants, it is wise to distinguish civic incorporation from political incorporation.[91] Although greater civic *and* political participation come with citizenship and second-generation status, nonnaturalized immigrants can be involved in an array of civic projects even though they cannot vote.[92] Additionally, although not speaking English can block participation in some activities for the first generation, bilingual competencies can serve as tools for civic engagement among the children of immigrants.[93] For the 1.5 and second generations, bilingualism acts as a vector of engagement.[94] Further, immigrants tend to be highly religious, and religious involvement and religious organizations can generate multiple pathways to civic involvement.[95] Religious institutions socialize youth into participating in collective efforts and traditionally have been places where members exchange political information and discuss public issues. For many immigrants, religious institutions and spiritual communities provide ready-made social ties for fostering civic participation. Additionally, there is growing evidence that among emerging adults, civic responsibility and civic mindedness may lead to conscious decisions to enter professions that "give back" to the community—such as being a teacher, a police officer, or a firefighter.[96] Finally, immigration-related controversies can serve as catalysts for civic engagement by mobilizing some immigrants to participate in a variety of political activities, a phenomenon called *reactive ethnicity*.[97] Young people on campus who are "coming out illegal"[98] and those who march, sign petitions, participate in sit-ins, and organize letter-writing campaigns in support of the DREAM Act are recent examples.

Labor-Market Access

Nationally, almost 30 percent of young adults (those between the ages of 18 and 34) are of immigrant origin.[99] Strikingly, nearly half of the foreign-born in this age group are undocumented, having "entered without inspection," overstayed their visas as young adults, or reached early adulthood after having been brought over as children.[100] Undocumented status has distinct implications for their participation in the labor market as well as for the developmental opportunities of the next generation as these individuals begin having children of their own. Since immigrants and their children constitute a growing portion of the U.S. population, it is important to examine their access to the labor market, particularly as it pertains to occupations, wages, and opportunities for mobility. Adult immigrants tend to have high rates of labor-force participation, lower rates of unemployment, and lower wages.[101] However, it is important to consider the trajectory of children of immigrants entering the labor force and the factors that shape their work opportunities. Research on the intergenerational mobility of immigrant youth has yielded important insights into the success rates of children of immigrants. U.S.-born youth of immigrant parents and immigrant youth who arrived at a young age have made significant gains in upward mobility: they are more educated, earn higher wages, and work in occupations with more job security than their parents.[102] By the second generation, children of immigrants are experiencing labor-force outcomes that are equal to or greater than the national average.

However, for undocumented youth, there is a very different trajectory into the labor force. When undocumented young adults are in the midst of their high school education and contemplating their college or career aspirations, many discover that they do not have a Social Security card and will not be able to apply for jobs.[103] In a study of undocumented youth, Gonzales found that it is while filling out job applications or navigating the college admissions process that many come to learn of their illegal status. Consequently, a sizeable proportion of undocumented youth ultimately drop out of school and end up in low-skilled jobs with low wages, little or no job security, no benefits, and limited opportunities for mobility. A generation later, they find themselves where their parents started. In some cases, undocumented youth pursue college and earn a degree. However, despite their skills and credentials, without a means to change their immigration status, they face barriers to employment. Ultimately, many undocumented youth are forced deeper and deeper into an underground workforce in which they will be vulnerable to depressed wages, a lack of benefits, and other forms of exploitation.[104]

Implications

The sheer number of children of immigrants presents a large-scale national concern that will continue well into the future. The experience of being undocumented involves broad swatches of the U.S. fabric and is not restricted to populations in a few states or limited to Latinos. Relatively large portions of certain Asian immigrant groups are also represented among the undocumented, and these groups are particularly vulnerable to long periods of parent-child separation, with the consequent socioemotional problems discussed earlier.[105] Finally, the impact of undocumented status is not only evident in educational outcomes or access to college and the military, the foci of the proposed DREAM Act. The implications of growing up in an undocumented family span a variety of developmental contexts that shape multiple outcomes.

Undocumented status casts a shadow, placing many youth at risk for an array of negative outcomes such as compromised socioemotional well-being, cognitive delays, low educational performance, economic stagnation, blocked mobility, and ambiguous social belonging.

An individual's undocumented status harms their development from the beginning of life through adolescence and young adulthood by restricting access to some of the most important pathways to adult well-being and productivity: early learning opportunities provided through quality child care, preschool, and school as well as higher education and formal entry into the working world. For millions of children and youth growing up in undocumented families, the American Dream and the promise of a better tomorrow have become an elusive mirage. Though undocumented parents exhibit strength and resilience and are as dedicated and committed to their children's learning as more privileged, authorized parents are,[106] their undocumented status represents a measurable risk threatening the well-being of their children.

There is still a lot we do not know about the ways that undocumented status affects developmental outcomes across domains, life stages, and contexts. Forthcoming large-scale and longitudinal studies with direct information on undocumented status (e.g., the L.A. Family and Neighborhood Study and work by K. Perreira and by R. Smith) will help fill in the picture. However, the vast majority of developmental and policy studies of children and youth do not collect any information on undocumented status. With the appropriate protections for anonymity and confidentiality, such data can be collected. A variety of methods ranging from ethnography and in-depth interviews to survey and observational methods can be used to study this phenomenon.[107] Research on health and socioemotional development is particularly needed, as are studies of the middle childhood period and of young and older adults in higher education, adult education, employment, and other settings.

Another important area is the study of the effects that high levels of protracted undocumented immigration have on democratic practices at the local, state, and federal levels. Further studies should explore the ethics of systems—health, education, justice—that de facto punish children and youth for embodying a condition not of their own making. Educational, developmental, and legal research as well as practice in schools and community centers should focus on the lives of the millions of children who, day in and day out, simply grow up in the shadow of their undocumented status. The developmental and societal importance of these issues is unquestionable.

NOTES

An extended version of this chapter was first published in Suárez-Orozco, C., Yoshikawa, H., Teranishi, T., & Suárez-Orozco, M. (2011), Living in the shadows: The developmental implications of unauthorized status, in special issue on immigrant students in education, *Harvard Education Review, 81*(3), 438–472.

1. Lucia's case turned out well. After multiple appeals and a public outcry, a media campaign, and a significant legal battle, she was granted asylum, attained her college degree, and went on to graduate school.

2. Hoefer, M., Rytina, N., & Baker, B. C. (2009). Estimates of the undocumented immigrant population residing in the United States: January 2008. Population Estimates. Washington, DC: U.S. Department of Health and Human Services; Passel, J. S., & Cohn, D. (2010). *Undocumented immigrant population: National and state trends.* Washington, DC: Pew Hispanic Center. Retrieved from http://pewhispanic.org/reports/report.php?ReportID=133.

3. Hoefer et al. (2009).

4. Passel, J. S., & Taylor, P. (2010). *Undocumented immigrants and their U.S.-born children.* Washington, DC: Pew Research Center. Retrieved from http://pewhispanic.org/reports/report.php?ReportID=125.

5. Menjívar, C. (2006). Liminal legality: Salvadorian and Guatemalan immigrants' lives in the United States. *American Journal of Sociology, 111*(4), 999–1037.

6. Anderson, S. (2009). *Employment-based green card projections point to decade-long waits.* Arlington, VA: National Foundation for American Policy. Retrieved from http://www.nfap.com; Anderson, S. (2010). *Family immigration: The long wait to immigrate.* Arlington, VA: National Foundation for American Policy. Retrieved from http://www.nfap.com.

7. Massey, D. S. (2010). *New faces in new places: The changing geography of American immigration.* New York: Russell Sage Foundation; Suro, R. (2011). Preface. In M. Suárez-Orozco & V. Louie (Eds.), *Writing immigration: Academics and journalists in dialogue.* Berkeley: University of California Press.

8. Leadership Conference on Civil Rights Education Fund. (2009). *Confronting the new faces of hate: Hate crimes in America—2009.* Washington, DC: Author. Retrieved from http://www.civilrights.org/publications/hatecrimes/lccref_hate_crimes_report.pdf.

9. Carter, A., Lawrence, M., & Morse, A. (2011). *2011 immigration-related laws, bills, and resolutions in the states: Jan. 1–March 31, 2011.* Washington, DC: National Conference of State Legislatures. Retrieved from http://www.ncsl.org/default.aspx?tabid=13114.

10. Passel & Cohn. (2010).

11. Passel & Taylor. (2010).

12. Ibid.

13. Passel, J. S. (2006). *The size and characteristics of the undocumented migrant population in the U.S.: Estimates based on the March 2005 current population survey.* Washington, DC: Pew Hispanic Center. Retrieved from http://pewhispanic.org/files/reports/61.pdf.

14. Fix, M., & Zimmerman, W. (2001). All under one roof: Mixed-status families in an era of reform. *International Migration Review, 35*(2), 397–419.

15. Ibid.

16. Ibid.

17. Ibid.

18. Suárez-Orozco, C., Bang, H. J., & Kim, H. Y. (2011). "I felt like my heart was staying behind": Psychological implications of immigrant family separations and reunifications. *Journal of Adolescent Research, 26*(1), 222–257.

19. Suárez-Orozco, C., Yoshikawa, H., Teranishi, T., & Suárez-Orozco. M. (2011). Living in the shadows: The developmental implications of undocumented status. In Immigrant students in education. Special issue of *Harvard Education Review, 81*(3) 438–472.

20. Krogstad, J. M., Gonzalez-Barrera, A., & Lopez, M. H. (2014). Children under 12 are the fastest growing group of unaccompanied minors at the U.S. border. Washington, DC: Pew Hispanic Foundation. Retrieved from http://www.pewresearch.org/fact-tank/2014/07/22/children-12-and-under-are-fastest-growing-group-of-unaccompanied-minors-at-u-s-border/.

21. Nazzario, S. (2007). *Enrique's journey.* New York: Random House.

22. Martínez, O. Why the children from Central America will not stop fleeing. *Nation.* August 18. Retrieved from http://www.thenation.com/article/180837/why-children-fleeing-central-america-will-not-stop-coming#; Krogstad et al. (2014).

23. U.S. Congress. (2010, July 15). *In the best interest of our children: Examining our immigration enforcement policy* (Ad hoc hearing). U.S. House of Representatives, Washington, DC. Retrieved from http://www.apa.org/about/gr/issues/cyf/immigration-enforcement.aspx.

24. Wagmiller, R. L., Lennon, M. C., Kuang, L., Alberti, P. M., & Aber, L. (2006). The dynamics of economic disadvantage and children's life chances. *American Sociological Review, 71*(5), 847–866.

25. Bronfenbrenner, U., & Morris, P. A. (2006). The bioecological model of human development. In W. Damon, & R. M. Lerner (Eds.), *Handbook of child psychology: Vol. 1, Theoretical models of human development* (6th ed., pp. 993–1023). Hoboken, NJ: Wiley.

26. Ngai, M. (2004). *Impossible subjects: Illegal aliens and the making of America.* Princeton: Princeton University Press.

27. Motomura, H. (2008). Immigration outside the law. *Columbia Law Review, 108*(8). UCLA School of Law Research Paper No. 09-01. Retrieved from http://ssrn.com/abstract=1323914.

28. Preston, J. (2011, June 4). Immigrants are focus of harsh bill in Alabama. *New York Times*, p. A10.

29. Keller, L. (2010, August 23). Anti-Latino hate crimes seen from Baltimore to Arizona. *Hatewatch* (blog), Southern Poverty Law Center. Retrieved from http://www. splcenter.org/blog/2010/08/23/ anti-latino-hate-crimes-seen-from-baltimore-to-arizona/.

30. García Coll, C., Lamberty, G., Jenkins, R., McAdoo, H. P., Crnic, K., Wasik, B. H., & Vázquez García, H. (1996). An integrative model for the study of developmental competencies in minority children. *Child Development, 67*(5), 1891–1914.

31. Bernhardt, A., Milkman, R., Theodore, N., Heckathorn, D., Auer, M., DeFilippis, J., Gonzales, A., Narro, V., Perelshteyn, J., Polson, D., & Spiller, M. (2009). *Broken laws, unprotected workers: Violations of employment and labor laws in America's cities*. New York: National Employment Law Project.

32. Bartel, A. P. (1989). Where do the new U.S. immigrants live? *Journal of Labor Economics, 7*(4), 371–391.

33. Orfield, G., & Lee, C. (2006). *Racial transformation and the changing nature of segregation*. Cambridge: Civil Rights Project at Harvard University.

34. U.S. Census. (2007). Selected characteristics of the native and foreign-born populations. American Community Survey. Retrieved from http://factfinder.census. gov/servlet/ STTable?_bm=y&-geo_id=01000US&-qr_name=ACS_2007_1YR_G00_S0501&-ds_ name=ACS_2007_1YR_G00_&-_lang=en&-redoLog=false.

35. Louie, V. S. (2004). *Compelled to excel: Immigration, education, and opportunity among Chinese Americans*. Stanford: Stanford University Press.

36. Stanton-Salazar, R. D., & Dornbusch, S. M. (1995). Social capital and the reproduction of inequality: Information networks among Mexican-origin high school students. *Sociology of Education, 68*(2), 116–135.

37. Orfield & Lee. (2006).

38. Noguera, P. (2003). City schools and the American dream: Reclaiming the promise of public education. New York: Teachers College Press; Suárez-Orozco, C., Suárez-Orozco, M., & Todorova, I. (2008). *Learning a new land: Immigrant students in American society*. Cambridge: Harvard University Press.

39. Gándara, P., & Contrera, F. (2008). *The Latino educational crisis: The consequences of failed policies*. Cambridge: Harvard University Press.

40. Goldstein, A. P., & Conoley, J. C. (Eds.). (1997). *School violence intervention: A practical handbook*. New York: Guilford.

41. Rumberger, R. W., & Larsen, K. A. (1998). Student mobility and the increased risk of high school dropout. *American Journal of Education, 107*(1), 1–35; Suárez-Orozco, C., Gaytan, F. X., Bang, H. J., Pakes, J., O'Connor, E., & Rhodes, J. (2010). Academic trajectories of newcomer youth. *Developmental Psychology, 43*(3), 602–618.

42. Yoshikawa, H. (2011). *Immigrants raising citizens: Undocumented parents and their young children*. New York: Russell Sage Foundation.

43. Yoshikawa, H., & Kalil, A. (2011). The effects of parental undocumented status on the developmental contexts of young children in immigrant families. *Child Development Perspectives, 5*(4), 291–297.

44. Suárez-Orozco, Bang, & Kim, 2011.

45. Abrego, L. J. (2006). I can't go to college because I don't have papers: Incorporation patterns of Latino undocumented youth. *Latino Studies, 4*(3), 212–231.

46. Capps, R., Castañeda, R. M., Chaudry, A., & Santos, R. (2007). *Paying the price: The impact of immigration raids on America's children.* Retrieved from http://www. urban.org/publications/411566.html; Chaudry, A., Capps, R., Pedroza, J., Castañeda, R. M., Santos, R., & Scott, M. M. (2010). *Facing our future: Children in the aftermath of immigration enforcement.* Washington, DC: Urban Institute. Retrieved from http:// www.urban.org/publications/412020.html.

47. U.S. Congress. (2010).

48. Brabeck, K., & Xu, Q. (2010). The impact of detention and deportation on Latino immigrant children and families: A quantitative exploration. *Hispanic Journal of Behavioral Sciences, 32*(3), 341–361.

49. Hughes, D., Rodriguez, J., Smith, E. P., Johnson, D. J., Stevenson, H. C., & Spicer, P. (2006). Parents' ethnic-racial socialization practices: A review of research and directions for future study. *Developmental Psychology, 42*(5), 747–770.

50. Yoshikawa. (2011).

51. Ng, F. F., Godfrey, E. B., Hunter, C. J., Tamis-LeMonda, C. S., Yoshikawa, H., & Kahnana-Kalman, R. (2009). Mothers' socializing goals for children in the first years of life: Developmental, ethnic, and economic differences. Paper presented in *Parental goals for children: The role of cultural and social context* (paper symposium) at the biennial meeting of the Society for Research in Child Development, Denver, CO; Yoshikawa. (2011).

52. Ng et al. (2009); Yoshikawa. (2011).

53. Faulstich-Orellana, M. (2009). *Translating childhoods: Immigrant youth, language, and culture.* New Brunswick: Rutgers University Press; Fuligni, A. J. (2010). Social identity, motivation, and well-being among adolescents from Asian and Latin American backgrounds. In G. Carlo, N. J. Crockett, & M. A. Carranza (Eds.), *Health disparities in youth and families: Research and applications.* Nebraska Symposium on Motivation (Vol. 57, pp. 97–120). New York: Springer Science.

54. Suárez-Orozco, M., & Suárez-Orozco, C. (2001). *Children of immigration.* Cambridge: Harvard University Press.

55. Chaudry et al. (2010).

56. Suárez-Orozco, C. (2001). Identities under siege: Immigration stress and social mirroring among the children of immigrants. In A. Robben & M. Suárez-Orozco (Eds.), *Cultures under siege: Social violence and trauma* (pp. 194–206). Cambridge: Cambridge University Press.

57. Hu-DeHart, E., & García Coll, C. (2010). *The immigrant paradox in children's education and behavior: Evidence from new research.* Providence, RI: Brown University.

58. Center on the Developing Child. (2010). *The foundations of lifelong health are built in early childhood.* Cambridge, MA: Author.

59. Knudsen, E. I., Heckman, J. J., Cameron, J. L., & Shonkoff, J. P. (2006). Economic, neurobiological, and behavioral perspectives on building America's future workforce. *Proceedings of the National Academy of Sciences, 103*(27), 10155–10162.

60. Crosnoe, R. (2007). Early child care and the school readiness of children from Mexican immigrant families. *International Migration Review, 41*(1), 152–181; Han, W. (2006). Academic achievements of children in immigrant families. *Educational Research and Reviews, 1*(8), 286–318.

61. Yoshikawa. (2011).

62. Teranishi, R. T. (2010). *Asians in the ivory tower: Dilemmas of racial inequality in American higher education.* New York: Teachers College Press.

63. Ruiz-de-Velasco, J., & Fix, M. (2000). *Overlooked and underserved: Immigrant students in U.S. secondary schools.* Washington, DC: Urban Institute.

64. Hill, N. E., & Taylor, L. C. (2004). Parental school involvement and children's academic achievement. *Current Directions in Psychological Science, 13*(4), 61–164.

65. Hill, N. E., & Torres, K. (2010). Negotiating the American dream: The paradox of aspirations and achievement among Latino students and engagement between their families and schools. *Journal of Social Issues, 66*(1), 5–112.

66. Advocates for Children of New York. (2009). *Our children, our schools: A blueprint for creating partnerships between immigrant families and New York City public schools.* New York: Author.

67. Teranishi, R. T., Allen, W. R., & Solorzano, D. G. (2004). Opportunities at the crossroads: Racial inequality, school segregation, and higher education in California. *Teachers College Record, 106*(11), 2224–2245.

68. Teranishi, R. T., Suárez-Orozco, C., & Suárez-Orozco, M. (2011). Immigrants in community college: Toward greater knowledge and awareness. *Future of Children, 21*(1), 153–169.

69. National Center for Education Statistics (NCES). (2006). *Profile of undergraduates in U.S. postsecondary education institutions 2003–04 with a special analysis of community college students.* Washington DC: U.S. Department of Education.

70. Gonzales, R. G. (2009). *Young lives on hold: The college dream of undocumented students.* Washington, DC: College Board. Retrieved from http://professionals.collegeboard.com/profdownload/young-lives-on-hold-college-board.pdf.

71. Dougherty, K. J., Nienhusser, H. K., & Vega, B. E. (2010). Undocumented immigrants and state higher education policy: The politics of in-state tuition eligibility in Texas and Arizona. *Review of Higher Education, 34*(1), 123–173.

72. Preston. (2011).

73. Gonzales, R., Suárez-Orozco, C., & Dedios-Sanguineti, M. C. (2013). No place to belong: Contextualizing concepts of mental health among undocumented immigrant youth in the United States. *American Behavioral Scientist, 57*(8) 1174–1199.

74. American Psychological Association, *APA Crossroads: The psychology of immigration in the new century—The report of the Presidential Task Force on Immigration.* (2012). Washington, DC: Author.

75. Suárez-Orozco, Yoshikawa, Teranishi, & Suárez-Orozco. (2011).

76. Ashman, S. B., Dawson, G., Panagiotides, H., Yamada, E., & Wilkins, C. W. (2002). Stress hormone levels of children of depressed mothers. *Development and Psychopathology, 14*(2), 333–349; Athey, J. L., & Ahearn, F. L. (1991). *Refugee children: Theory, research, and services.* Baltimore: Johns Hopkins University Press.

77. Chaudry et al. (2010).

78. Ibid.

79. Fuligni. (2010); Suárez-Orozco, C. (2004). Formulating identity in a globalized world. In M. Suárez-Orozco & D. B. Qin-Hilliard (Eds.), *Globalization: Culture and education in the new millennium* (pp. 173–202). Berkeley: University of California Press.

80. Fuligni. (2010); Suárez-Orozco. (2004).

81. Fuligni. (2010); Suárez-Orozco. (2004); Suárez-Orozco, Yoshikawa, Teranishi, & Suárez-Orozco. (2011).

82. Srortelder, F., & Ploegmaker-Burg (2010). Adolescence and the reorganization of infant development: A neuropsychoanalytic model. *Journal of the American Academy of Psychoanalysis and Dynamic Psychiatry, 38*(3), 503–531.

83. Gonzales et al. (2013).

84. Ibid.

85. Bui, Q., Doescher, M., Takeuchi, D., & Taylor. (2011). Immigration, acculturation and chronic back and neck problems among Latino-Americans. *Journal of Immigrant and Minority Health, 13*(2), 194–201; Gonzales et al. (2013).

86. Bui et al. (2011); Gonzales et al. (2013).

87. Flanagan, C. A., Gallay, L. S., Gill, S., Gallay, E. E., & Nti, N. (2005). What does democracy mean? Correlates of adolescents' views. *Journal of Adolescent Research, 20*(2), 193–218; Morsillo, J., & Prilleltensky, I. (2007). Social action with youth: Interventions, evaluation, and psychopolitical validity. *Journal of Community Psychology, 35*(6), 725–740.

88. Jensen, L. A., & Flanagan, C. A. (2008). Immigrant civic engagement: New translations. *Applied Developmental Science, 12*(2), 55–56.

89. Huntington, S. P. (2004). *Who are we? The challenges of America's national identity.* New York: Simon and Schuster.

90. Jensen & Flanagan. (2008); Stepick, A., Stepick, C. D., & Labissiere, Y. (2008). South Florida's immigrant youth and civic engagement: Major engagement minor differences. *Applied Developmental Science, 12*(2), 57–65.

91. Waters, M. C. (2008). The challenges of studying political and civic incorporation. *Applied Developmental Science, 12*(2), 105–107.

92. Stoll, M. A., & Wong, J. S. (2007). Immigration and civic participation in a multiracial and multiethnic context. *International Migration Review, 41*(4), 880–908; Lopez, M. H., & Marcelo, K. B. (2008). The civic engagement of immigrant youth: New

evidence from the 2006 Civic and Political Health of the Nation Survey. *Applied Developmental Science, 12*(2), 66–73.

93. Ramakrishnan, S. K., & Baldasarre, M. (2004). *The ties that bind: Changing demographics and civic engagement in California.* San Francisco: Public Policy of California.

94. Jensen & Flanagan. (2008); Stepick et al. (2008).

95. Levitt, P. (2008). Religion as a path to civic engagement. *Ethnic and Racial Studies, 31*(4), 766–791; Stepick, A. (2005). God is apparently not dead: The obvious, the emergent, and the still unknown in immigration and religion. In K. Leonard, A. Stepick, M. A. Vasquez, & J. Holdaway (Eds.), *Immigrant faiths: Transforming religious life in America* (pp. 11–38). Lanham, MD: AltaMira.

96. Suárez-Orozco, C., Hernandez, M. G., & Casanova, S. (Forthcoming). "It's sort of my calling": The civic participation and social responsibility of immigrant origin emerging adults. *Journal of Research in Human Development.*

97. Rumbaut, R. G. (2008). Reaping what you sow: Immigration, youth, and reactive ethnicity. *Applied Developmental Science, 12*(2), 108–111.

98. Jones, M. (2010, October 24). Coming out illegal. *New York Times Magazine,* pp. 36–39.

99. Rumbaut, R., & Komaie, G. (2010). Immigration and adult transitions. *Future of Children, 20*(1), 43–66.

100. Hoefer et al. (2009).

101. Bureau of Labor Statistics. (2008). Labor force statistics from the current population survey: Unemployment rates by education for those 25 and over. Retrieved from www.bls.gov/cps/.

102. Haskins, R. (2010). *Economic mobility of immigrants in the United States.* Washington, DC: Pew Charitable Trust.

103. Gonzales, R. G. (2011). Learning to be illegal: Undocumented youth and shifting legal contexts in the transition to adulthood. *American Sociological Review, 76*(4), 602–619; Perez, W. (2009). *We ARE Americans: Undocumented students pursuing the American dream.* Sterling, VA: Stylus.

104. Gonzales. (2011); Perez. (2009).

105. Suárez-Orozco, Bang, & Kim. (2011).

106. Yoshikawa. (2011).

107. Yoshikawa, H., Weisner, T. S., Kalil, A., & Way, N. (2008). Mixing qualitative and quantitative methods in developmental science: Uses and methodological choices. *Developmental Psychology, 44,* 344–354.

PART II

Processes of Development

AMY K. MARKS AND MONA M. ABO-ZENA

Having examined in the initial section of this book how immigrant children and their families shape and are shaped by unique developmental contexts, we turn in this section to address critical *developmental processes*. We consider developmental processes that are particularly relevant for children and youth of immigrant origin, such as acculturation, identity development, and being bilingual. In doing so, we are able to more closely examine the ways in which cultural contexts shape developmental processes more broadly. As all children develop in shared social and physical environments, the study of immigrant youth helps us focus on *how* such developmental processes occur across cultures. Understanding, for instance, the unique ways many immigrant youth shape new ethnic identities can provide tangible understanding of how identity development is generally of central importance in adolescence. By observing the influences of social settings, parents, teachers, and peers on the pride or satisfaction with an immigrant's sense of self as an "American," we are given a window to observe the inner workings of adaptation, social mirroring, and identity formation as occurs with all humans.

A process-oriented approach to development takes several perspectives. It focuses on aspects of development that are most dynamic and subject to change over time. This approach also emphasizes the variations that exist for individuals across time as well as across and within groups, examining factors that contribute to dynamic change, such as socioeconomic statuses and conditions, cultures of origin, and characteristics of the receiving community. In this section, we address the most salient and timely developmental processes central to developing immigrant children, considering the variations of these processes observed across the life span, with a central goal of understanding how everyday ecological contexts such as families, peers, schools, and neighborhoods shape these children.

Long at the crux of efforts to understand the development of immigrant-origin youth, Dina Birman and Dorothy Addae provide an overview of acculturation theory, research, and measurement strategies in chapter 6. Rooted in a developmental perspective, the chapter also incorporates social, psychological, cognitive, and linguistic orientations to explore acculturation processes. This chapter describes how acculturation processes and domains in turn shape developmental processes such as cognitive development and social skills and how they vary within ethnic and racial groups.

In chapter 7, Seth J. Schwartz, Miguel Ángel Cano, and Byron L. Zamboanga discuss how the acculturation process is closely associated with immigrant adolescents' and emerging adults' complex and dynamic identity development processes. Once thought to be pertinent only to immigrant adolescents, ethnic identity has now also been documented in children of immigrant families. This chapter reviews the current state of research on ethnic identity among both children and adolescents from immigrant families and its relationship to their development of a U.S. identity. In addition, the authors discuss other aspects of the development of immigrant-origin youth's ethnic identity and examine ways in which it may not always be protective. This chapter also focuses on peer relationships and the development of sexual identity.

For many immigrant-origin youth, an integral aspect of acculturation and ethnic identity development is bilingualism. In chapter 8, Mariela M. Páez and Cristina J. Hunter describe the language learning of the approximately 20 percent of families in the United States who speak a second language or multiple languages at home. These families employ a variety of strategies to develop and maintain their children's competence in their heritage language, with a range of goals regarding proficiency. Given competing academic, linguistic, cultural, familial, and societal demands, families often place great importance on both heritage-language learning and bilingualism. This chapter discusses the effects of heritage-language proficiency and bilingualism on various aspects of immigrant-origin children's and youth's development and socialization, including family and community interactions, academic achievement, ethnic identity formation, religious development, and social development. The authors also address issues surrounding language status and school policies regarding language instruction.

Sometimes the language proficiency of immigrant children and adolescents can qualify them as language brokers who support their family's settlement practices. In chapter 9, Marjorie Faulstich Orellana and Shu-Sha Angie Guan examine the acculturative and other stressors inherent in the immigration process and the ways in which immigrant-origin children and youth are often obligated to provide emotional, financial, and technical support services for other (often older) family members. This chapter discusses various family processes and functions in which immigrant-origin children and youth are called on to assist, focusing particularly on employment of their language-brokering skills. The authors provide empirical evidence when exploring whether fulfilling such family obligations contributes to the children's well-being, creates stress for them, or does both. In addition, the authors study the connections among immigrant-origin children's and youth's family obligations and their academic achievement, civic engagement, and peer relations.

6

Acculturation

DINA BIRMAN AND DOROTHY ADDAE

Two years ago, when Andre was 10 years old, he was excited about coming to the United States from Haiti. Because he did not speak English initially, he struggled at school and was very isolated, going straight home after school to watch his younger sister while his mom went to work. During the first year, the family joined a Haitian church and got to know other families, and Andre made friends with some of the other kids. Now he spends a lot of time hanging out with them, speaks fluent English, listens to American music, and plays basketball. In fact, he admires rappers and basketball players so much that he wonders if he can become one. But he is concerned because his mother, Laurette, does not approve of these new interests. She thinks Andre is becoming "too American." Andre is also concerned about his 17-year-old sister, Nadege, who is having even more arguments with their mother than he does. Nadege wants to go to college and become a professional, a task she is handling independently since Laurette does not know enough about the U.S. college admissions process to help her. At the same time, Laurette argues that Nadege is too young to decide for herself how much time to spend with her friends and when to start dating; besides, Nadege's social life is taking time away from her studies. Andre's younger sister, Marriette, just started school and loves it. She picked up English quickly and no longer speaks Creole, a source of more worry for Andre's mother. Laurette had believed that moving to the U.S. would change her children's lives for the better, but she had not anticipated how much the U.S. would change them.

Acculturation research and theory have long been at the heart of understanding the development of immigrant-origin youth. In this chapter, we consider the particular ways that acculturation can be conceptualized within a developmental framework. The description of Andre's family depicts individuals at different developmental stages as they experience the process of acculturation. Educational experiences, peer relationships, and language development represent some of the issues immigrant youth encounter as they navigate life in a new country.

Culture and Development

An increasing number of researchers are recognizing the critical role of culture in shaping all psychological processes,[1] including children's cognitive and social development. Human development is a cultural process, and "the goals of human development—what is regarded as mature or desirable—vary considerably according to the cultural traditions and circumstances of different communities."[2] The transmission of culture to children occurs through the related processes of enculturation and socialization.[3]

Socialization refers to a deliberate shaping of the developing child as done through child rearing by parents or through formal educational practices by schools.[4] In today's societies, teachers and textbooks impart cultural values and perspectives through content taught in the classroom and socialize the child into the role of student.[5] *Enculturation*, on the other hand, is considered to be a more tacit and implicit "process of learning a culture in all of its uniqueness and particularity."[6] The process of enculturation occurs through subtle messages[7] that children receive from the surrounding culture from parents, other adults, and peers as well as from the media that increasingly enter homes in all societies.[8]

These dual processes of socialization and enculturation are influenced by developmental changes. For example, in adolescence children undergo profound changes cognitively, socially, physically, and emotionally[9] while continuing the process of development and learning about the culture that surrounds them. As children's cognitive abilities mature, through socialization at school they come to comprehend increasingly complex and abstract concepts and to learn vocabulary that reflects this complexity. Socially and emotionally, during this period peers become increasingly important, romantic interests develop, and adolescents face important choices about how to negotiate various social circles and construct their own network of relationships. They also begin to consider future careers and to have academic aspirations. In the U.S. context, generally adolescents are expected to discover their identity as they separate from parents, and some intergenerational conflict or even adolescent rebellion is considered natural.[10] Whether adolescents' development across these life spheres is consistent with their parents' expectations or is in opposition to them, it is still shaped by the surrounding culture that guides adolescents' options and decisions. Young adults are guided by perceptions and assumptions deeply embedded in their emergent understanding of the world, often without reflecting on the extent to which it is cultural. As a result, as Jessica Scheer notes, "whatever in a culture is stated as if it were *natural* is precisely what is *cultural*."[11]

Children of immigrants, however, may not experience the process of enculturation as natural because their development occurs within overlapping cultural systems and worldviews. Their process of enculturation is much more complex as they absorb their heritage culture at home while being socialized to the U.S. culture in school. At the same time, immigrant families are also embedded within the larger U.S. society, which plays a role in how the heritage culture is expressed and passed down to the children at home. In addition, for them cultural transmission occurs through a third mechanism—*acculturation*, or the acquisition of the culture of the resettlement country through both tacit absorption and deliberate teaching such as that occurring at school.[12] This bricolage of cultural influences is so complex for children of immigrants because *en*culturation becomes intertwined with *ac*culturation.

Acculturation Theory

Acculturation, an important construct articulated across several disciplines, refers to cultural change that occurs as a result of contact with the new culture. In sociology, for example, it refers to the process by which immigrant groups are incorporated into the larger society over the course of generations.[13] In psychology, emphasis has been placed on understanding the ways in which individuals change as a result of cultural contact with respect to their attitudes, behaviors, and cultural identities.[14] Psychological research has questioned what is more adaptive for immigrants—maintaining their heritage culture, adopting U.S. culture, or doing both.

Psychological theories of acculturation have largely been developed with adults in mind, without taking into account the special developmental issues faced by children. For example, *acculturation* has been defined as a strategy or choice,[15] suggesting that the extent to which immigrant individuals balance their heritage and new cultures in their lives is a choice. However, this notion of acculturation as a strategy does not readily apply to children. For them, acculturation is both a result of subtle influences similar to enculturation and a deliberate process by which parents, schools in the new country, and others transmit cultural practices, beliefs, and values as well as attitudes about which culture(s) is/are more desirable to adopt. Thus, while children have agency with respect to these opportunities and pressures, these contextual factors, including the decision to immigrate itself, are shaped by the adults in their lives.

The conversation in psychology has shifted away from assimilation as the inevitable and desirable outcome of the acculturation process to the possibility of biculturalism. Early theories of acculturation assumed that assimilation was the only possible and desirable outcome for immigrants.[16] This view has been called "subtractive" acculturation,[17] in that as newly arriving immigrants learn the new language and culture, they are assumed to simultaneously let go of their attachments to their native country. However, this either/or conceptualization of acculturation does not adequately describe the range of immigrant experiences. Instead, for many of today's immigrants, acculturation can also be "additive"[18]—that is, as new immigrants adopt aspects of the new culture, they also maintain their connection with their culture of origin, integrating the two. Research suggests there may be advantages to such an additive acculturation process, or *biculturalism*.[19] Biculturalism may be increasingly adaptive with transnationalism since in today's global context most immigrants do not sever their connections to their native country.

Implicit in this model of acculturation is the assumption that bicultural individuals are better adjusted psychologically than are those immigrants choosing any of the other acculturation strategies.[20] However, another way to think about the benefits of acculturation to both the new and the native culture is not in purely psychological terms but from the perspective that both cultures are useful because they provide access to different kinds of resources.[21] The cultural repertoire that enables one to function within one's immigrant group provides access to ethnic resources such as social support from coethnic friends and family.[22] Acculturation to the host culture provides access to resources such as social support from its members.[23] For these reasons, acculturation can be seen as a way for immigrants to cope with living in the context of two cultural worlds.

Contextual Issues in Acculturation

The context-free assumption that acculturation is an individual strategy or choice does not apply well to children, and it also ignores the presence of structural issues in different societies that may prevent immigrant groups from being able to choose assimilation or biculturalism.[24] Urie Bronfenbrenner's influential framework that views the developing person as nested within systems is useful in conceptualizing the acculturation and development of immigrant children.[25] The microsystems (e.g., family, school, neighborhood) are the most immediate contexts within which the child participates directly. The mesosystem, involving the relationships among the microsystems, and the exosystem, representing laws and regulations, also have an indirect influence on the child. The macrosystem represents the larger cultural and societal context that influences the child indirectly through all the other levels down to the microsystem. However, for *immigrant* children, this framework needs to be expanded to represent how the varied microsystems in their lives are influenced not only by the macrosystem of their new country but also by the culture of their country of origin.[26]

For immigrants, each of the microsystems reflects and requires knowledge of different cultural repertoires and exerts an *acculturative press*[27] on immigrant children. For example, during the previous century, immigrant families in the United States favored assimilation and insisted that their children speak only English. Today many immigrant parents expect their children to preserve their heritage cultural and religious traditions and values, thus exerting a traditionalist acculturative press. In many immigrant cultures, such expectations are particularly strict for girls,[28] who are expected to maintain traditional gender roles. Schools are more likely to exert an assimilationist press since teachers are inclined to view the children's heritage culture as a barrier to learning and to encourage success through assimilation.[29]

At the mesosystem level, there is often poor communication between immigrant parents and schools.[30] As a result, immigrant children struggle with a lack of alignment of goals and values originating from these two important settings in their lives. In fact, some school staff may regard immigrant parents as inhibiting their children's progress, while parents feel too uncomfortable to become involved in their children's schools.[31] The resulting discontinuity between these settings can negatively impact the children.

Neighborhoods where immigrants settle also exert acculturative press and have different consequences for psychological adjustment,[32] though research on these effects is only beginning to emerge. Neighborhoods where immigrants have a visible and growing presence and are viewed as a threat to the dominant culture are likely to exert an assimilationist press. In contrast, ethnic enclaves exert little pressure on immigrants to acculturate to the host culture if the community has a critical mass large enough to provide resources within itself.[33]

For immigrants, the macrosystem level of analysis encompasses the cultural influences of both the culture of origin and the culture of the host society. The cultural macrosystem of the country of origin continues to influence how immigrant parents transmit cultural repertoires to their children. At the macrosystem level, immigrants' culture, ethnicity, and race are redefined to be consistent with U.S. constructions of these concepts and identities. Continued racial discrimination in the United States creates difficulties in acculturation experiences for immigrants who are defined as non-White.[34] Further, children of immigrants whose cultural and educational traditions and values align with U.S. norms have an easier adaptation process than do children from societies that are more culturally distant from the United States.

In sum, the kinds of acculturation that are adaptive depend on the characteristics of the contexts, the background of immigrants, and the outcomes considered.[35] For example, for children of immigrants from traditional societies, maintaining their heritage culture may keep peace in the family but compromise a young woman's desire to gain more independence. White immigrants in settings with assimilationist press may adapt well academically by assimilating to gain connections with teachers and blending in with majority students but do so at the cost of disconnecting from coethnic peers who can provide emotional support given similar experiences. Although biculturalism seemingly has advantages, it may not be an option if immigrants are discriminated against for continuing their cultural practices. Even when they assimilate and adopt U.S. culture, immigrants of color may continue to be viewed as "perpetual foreigners,"[36] as is the case for Asian Americans. Under conditions of discrimination, immigrant youth may develop a reactive stance toward the dominant culture, finding comfort with coethnic friends. Thus, it is important to consider the ways in which contexts at multiple levels of analysis shape acculturative options for children of immigrants.

Measurement of Acculturation

Criticism of the measurement of acculturation has been prominent in the psychological literature since various studies have found acculturation to be positively, negatively, or not at all related to psychological adjustment.[37] One source of confusion in existing research is that most studies have continued to measure immigrants' assimilation rather than their involvement with both heritage and host cultures.

If a study finds that assimilation is related to more distress for immigrants, it is not clear whether this result occurs because losing their connection to their heritage culture is harmful, because becoming more acculturated to U.S. culture is harmful, or both.[38] Without using separate measures of acculturation to the new and old cultures, it is impossible to discern predictors of positive or negative effects. For this reason, studies are increasingly using *bilinear* or separate measures of acculturation to the heritage and host cultures to better discern acculturation patterns that are adaptive in varied situations.[39]

Another criticism is that acculturation measures have not distinguished among different aspects of the acculturation experience. In the sociological and medical literature, acculturation is generally approximated through indicators such as language use or the language in which study participants preferred to be interviewed.[40] In psychological literature, acculturation has been measured primarily as behavior such as the extent to which immigrants use their native language; frequent ethnic grocery stores, doctors, and entertainment venues; maintain relationships with their coethnic friends; listen to native music; watch native television programs; and read native-language publications.[41] A somewhat separate line of research, ethnic identity, deemed important for ethnic minorities, has also been highlighted as an important component of immigrants' acculturation.[42] However, few studies assess these different aspects of acculturation, language, behavior, and identity together in a bicultural framework. As a result, we continue to have questions about acculturation, and there appears to be no simple answer to the question of which way of acculturating is most adaptive for immigrant children.

Developmental Differences in Acculturation

Psychological acculturation to both the new and heritage cultures occurs differently for immigrants across the life span, including first-generation immigrants who arrive as adults, the 1.5 generation who arrive before or during their teens, and second-generation children born in the United States.

Acculturation of Adult Immigrants

Existing acculturation models more readily capture the process of acculturation for adults than for children. Having been enculturated within the heritage culture, adults come to the new society with their existing cultural repertoires. Learning the new language is a primary, though often difficult, task for adult immigrants.[43] They often must engage with the new culture behaviorally to enter the labor force.[44] At the same time, maintaining relationships with coethnic friends and participating in the immigrant community are important ways of getting social support and creating a social world with those who share similar values and customs. The question of whether adult immigrants come to identify themselves as American, as part of a U.S. ethnic or racial group, and/or as members of their native culture has not been studied extensively. Developmentally, identity is much more important for children and adolescents than it is for adults.

Acculturation of Children of Immigrants

For children of immigrants, the complexity of the process of acculturation that is intertwined with enculturation has not been sufficiently theorized. Since they have not completed their socialization or enculturation within their birth culture, their contact with the new culture not only results in cultural change but also has a profound impact on their continued development.[45]

Language Acculturation

Second-language development is a very different process for children than it is for adults. Research suggests that the "critical" or "sensitive" period that is the optimal time for learning language is between the ages of two and 12.[46] School-age immigrant children pick up the new language quickly, becoming conversationally fluent at the age-appropriate level within approximately two years after coming to this country.[47] U.S.-born children of immigrants who are socialized in their heritage language at home also become fluent in English after they start school. However, achieving cognitive-academic language proficiency may take much longer, typically about five years.[48]

For younger children, learning the new language occurs simultaneously with cognitive maturation and socialization. Once children start school, they begin to learn increasingly complex concepts and vocabulary in the new language. While for adults second-language acquisition involves learning new words for concepts they already know, without bilingual education children do not learn words for these concepts in their native language. As a result, their native language atrophies, not because they are forgetting how to speak it but because they do not continue to acquire age-appropriate native-language skills. Even if they continue to use their native language at home, their fluency remains at the level of "kitchen language"[49]—that is, being able to describe household objects and maintain simple conversations but unable to express more complex thoughts and emotions as they develop. Those who arrive as adolescents are better able to maintain their heritage language because their knowledge of it was established when they were young. Having learned to read and write in the language gives them a broader range of native-language skills.

Contrary to assimilationist views prevalent in U.S. society, transitioning to English as quickly as possible may not be the best path for immigrant children. Research suggests that maintaining and continuing to develop their native language can improve immigrant children's academic performance *in English*.[50] Studies have found academic advantages for children who maintain their native language.[51] There are several explanations for this phenomenon. One is that knowledge of the native language provides access to people, materials, and media within children's ethnic community that can provide cultural enrichment and facilitate learning. Particularly while making the linguistic transition to academic English, children may find it easier to learn new concepts and content in their native language, and they can transfer this knowledge into English as they become more fluent in it.[52] Second, immigrant children who maintain their native language have also been found to have less conflict with their parents.[53] It is perhaps this better communication that allows parents to be involved in their children's schooling. In addition, bilingualism is associated with cognitive advantages,[54] making it a valuable asset for immigrant children.

Behavioral Acculturation

With globalization and the spread of U.S. culture worldwide,[55] immigrant children and adolescents may be exposed to the culture even before arriving in the United States through movies, music, television programs, and other increasingly available media. The degree of freedom that U.S. culture provides to its youth can be very enticing for adolescents used to strict parental control.

Behavioral participation in the U.S. youth culture can involve exploration of sexual activity, alcohol, and drugs,[56] behaviors regarded as normal to some degree for U.S. adolescents.[57] Given these norms, behaviorally participating in the heritage culture can serve a protective function for immigrant youth.[58] Children who are engaged with their ethnic communities receive more parental monitoring[59] and in collectivistic cultures are known and accountable to an entire community of adults rather than only to their nuclear families. As a result, U.S. acculturation may be a risk factor and acculturation to the heritage culture a protective factor with respect to high-risk behavior in adolescence.

On the other hand, in peer relationships both types of acculturation have been shown to be positive effects. Developing and participating in peer networks are important tasks for adolescents. For immigrant adolescents, potential peers include coethnic and U.S. peers. Coethnic peers can provide much-needed social support, particularly when individuals feel alienated from the new society. Acculturation to the heritage culture has been found to predict satisfying relationships with coethnic peers. Engaging with U.S. peers can also result in less alienation and allow children of immigrants to feel integrated into the larger social world. Acculturation to the host culture has been associated with support from dominant-culture peers.[60]

Identity Acculturation

Identity exploration in adolescence is particularly complex for immigrants. As children become socialized to develop their educational, career, gender, and other identities, they negotiate cultural expectations from both the U.S. culture and their heritage culture. When seen as an aspect of a bilinear[61] process of acculturation occurring simultaneously with respect to both cultures, adolescents balance their developing heritage identity with feeling a part of the new society—called *national identity*.[62] Immigrant youth may *assimilate* (give up their native cultural identity and consider themselves American), identify themselves only with their native culture, or develop an additive, hyphenated "bicultural" identity.

The topic of immigrant "ethnic" identity is complex since it involves cultural, ethnic, and racial identities, and the social construction of these concepts is different in the United States than it is in the immigrant-sending societies. In the U.S. context, *cultural identity* involves a sense of belonging to, positive regard for, and pride in one's native culture.[63] *Ethnic identity* is a more complicated construct. Phinney defines *ethnicity* as broad groupings in the United States based on both race and culture of origin and considers ethnic and racial identity to be overlapping constructs.[64] On the other hand, Helms and Talleyrand argue that "race is not ethnicity"[65] and suggest that the term *ethnicity* is often used as a euphemism to highlight cultural differences but to obscure the salience of race and racial disparities in the United States. Thus, *racial identity* is closely related to negotiating the impact of racism in society. To complicate matters, the construct of racial identity applies to Hispanics in the United States because their ethnicity is perceived as race; that is, it has been racialized.[66]

For these reasons, most authors use the terms *race* and *ethnicity* somewhat interchangeably or together to distinguish groups that are visibly different from the White U.S. majority. Regardless of the specific definitions used by particular researchers, immigrants' culture, ethnicity, and race are important social identities and are defined in a particular way in the U.S. context. For example, immigrants from China may identify with their native *culture* (Chinese or perhaps Tibetan or Uyghur if they were ethnic minorities in China), with the larger *ethnic group* within the United States (Chinese American), and with the U.S. Census *racial category* (Asian). However, this complexity of immigrants' cultural/ethnic/racial identities has not been sufficiently captured in theory and research, making it difficult to summarize findings across studies of larger ethnic groups (Hispanic, Asian) and specific cultural groups (Chinese, Mexican).

In response to discrimination, immigrants may adopt *reactive identification*, rejecting the U.S. culture[67] and developing a strong ethnic and racial identity as a member of an oppressed group. Generally, however, research suggests that a strong ethnic identity may buffer the negative impact of discrimination experienced by immigrants of color.[68] At the same time, if the larger society expects immigrants to assimilate, becoming more "ethnic" can elicit even further discrimination and marginalization. This consequence may be one reason that a few recent studies with Asian American college students[69] and Americans of Chinese descent[70] found that ethnic identity did not have a protective effect or may even exacerbate the impact of discrimination on mental health.[71] Thus, while assimilation may be a more adaptive strategy for Asian immigrants, orientation toward the heritage culture may be more adaptive for Latinos.[72]

Acculturation Gaps

As noted, the process of acculturation unfolds differently for immigrant children than it does for adults. As a result, acculturation "gaps" develop between parents and children in immigrant families and create conflicts that are more pronounced than those in nonimmigrant families.[73] Family separations resulting from sequential migration or deportation[74] create additional cultural distance between the generations. Research with a variety of immigrant groups has documented that acculturation gaps have been linked to child maladjustment and family conflict in

Chinese,[75] Asian Indian,[76] Asian American,[77] Vietnamese,[78] Mexican American,[79] and former Soviet immigrant families.[80]

Immigrant parents often know little of their children's lives outside the home. Not having themselves grown up in the society, they are unfamiliar with how U.S. schools operate. They may not be able to provide advice for children choosing among multiple after-school activities, high school options and tracking systems, and preparations for college.[81] Children may not turn to their parents with problems and concerns, believing that they do not know the culture and its institutions well enough to provide children with good advice or assistance. Additionally, they may regard their parents as already burdened with the multiple stresses of resettlement and more generally as psychologically unavailable.

The less parents know about their children's lives, the less they can monitor the children's activities. Adolescents may have ambivalent feelings about their parents' inability to fully understand their experiences. On one hand, having parents less involved in their lives can provide greater freedom. On the other, parents cannot offer them the guidance and advice they need. One potential implication of this situation is that parents' and children's discussion of these cultural differences can reduce acculturation gaps, as found in studies of several interventions with Latino adolescents.[82]

Culture Brokering

One consequence of acculturation gaps is that children of immigrants are often asked to be culture and language brokers for their parents. Immigrant parents with insufficient English- language skills rely on their children to help in situations such as doctors' appointments and parent-teacher conferences and with financial and legal documents. In addition to *language brokering*—that is, direct *translation* of documents and conversations—parents may rely on children to be *culture* brokers and to *interpret* cultural meanings in these situations.[83]

Culture brokering can affect children and families in both negative and positive ways.[84] For younger children, using two languages while brokering may contribute to cognitive development.[85] At the same time, studies with adolescents suggest that brokering can be burdensome, causing stress, interfering with children's success, making it difficult for children to establish autonomy from their parents and control their own time,[86] and contributing to family conflict.

However, research also posits the importance of understanding the larger context surrounding brokering. For example, the need to rely on children as brokers may be caused not only by parental characteristics (such as inadequate English-language skills) but also by external pressures experienced by the entire family. One recent study found that immigrant children living in economically disadvantaged communities were more likely than those in economically privileged contexts to broker for their parents,[87] perhaps because their parents were more likely to be unemployed and to lack access to resources. Furthermore, while brokering was linked to family conflict, it functioned as a mediator of neighborhood economic conditions in predicting family conflict. Thus, in this study the characteristics of the surrounding community were responsible for placing immigrant children in the position of having to broker for their parents. The burden on children of immigrants and conflict in immigrant families can be reduced if communities and institutions provide interpreters and other resources to relieve children of this responsibility.

Conclusion and Future Directions

Acculturation is an important process in the lives of immigrant children that interacts with their development. Different aspects of the acculturation experience play out differently for children than they do for adults. Even within the younger age group, developmental differences play a role in how acculturation unfolds. Behavioral acculturation and identity become more salient in adolescence, whereas language acculturation and development are particularly important for younger children. This differentiated view of acculturation as composed of distinct but interrelated dimensions allows for a more nuanced description of acculturation and enculturation processes. An important issue warranting more attention is determining how to conceptualize the varied meanings of culture, ethnicity, and race as they relate to immigrant children, particularly in the increasingly transnational context. A related matter is how to categorize immigrant groups and whether collapsing varied immigrant classifications such as Latino, Asian, or African without drawing specific distinctions among their cultural groupings makes sense. There may be practical reasons to do so in studies, but some groupings may be better suited for studying culture, some for ethnicity, and others for race.

Acculturation unfolds differently in different contexts such as neighborhoods and schools. Immigrant children growing up in different neighborhoods experience different processes of acculturation and enculturation. Settings such as schools need to examine the acculturative press exerted on students and consider ways of offering a broader range of options to children of immigrants to maintain their heritage culture while they are learning to function adaptively in U.S. contexts. Research suggests some important ways to enhance the acculturation of children's development by helping them retain their heritage culture. For example, there are important costs to pressuring children to transition quickly into English, particularly when they do so at the expense of maintaining their heritage cultural repertoire.[88] Empowering parents to learn about and monitor their adolescents' lives outside the home can prevent high-risk behavior, but doing so is easier if children are encouraged to maintain their heritage culture, an activity that facilitates mutual understanding and better communication with parents. Family conflict resulting from putting adolescents in positions of culture brokering can be reduced by providing immigrants with access to interpreters in medical, educational, and financial settings.

As the world becomes more interconnected, there is a need for better theorizing about the interrelated constructs of acculturation, enculturation, and socialization for children and adolescents growing up in multicultural societies. Development is a cultural process that increasingly involves enculturation and socialization not simply into a given culture but also into a multicultural society. Acculturation was initially conceptualized as culture *change*, a definition that fits the experience of adult immigrants as they transition to life in a new country. However, for children and adolescents, acculturation is not so much a process of culture change as one of cultural adoption and of learning about more than one culture. As cultural boundaries become more permeable, it is important to reconsider these constructs and to develop a theory that captures the increasing cultural complexity[89] for all children and youth, including immigrants.

NOTES

1. Kitayama, S. (2002). Culture and basic psychological processes—Toward a system view of culture: Comment on Oyserman. *Psychological Bulletin, 128*, 89.

2. Rogoff, B. (2003). *The cultural nature of human development.* Oxford: Oxford University Press. (Quotation from p. 434.)

3. Berry, J., & Georgas, J. (2009). The ecocultural perspective on cultural transmission: The family across cultures. In U. Schönpflug (Ed.), *Cultural transmission: Psychological, developmental, social, and methodological aspects* (pp. 95–125). New York: Cambridge University Press.

4. Ibid., p. 95.

5. Rogoff. (2003).

6. Mead, M. (1963). Socialization and enculturation. *Current Anthropology, 4,* 184–188. (Quotation from p. 187.)

7. Kitayama. (2002).

8. Berry & Georgas. (2009).

9. Zarrett, N., & Eccles, J. (2006). The passage to adulthood: Challenges of late adolescence. *New Directions for Youth Development, 111,* 13–28.

10. Luthar, S. S., & Ansary, N. S. (2005). Dimensions of adolescent rebellion: Risks for academic failure among high- and low-income youth. *Development and Psychopathology, 17*(1), 231–250.

11. Scheer, J. (1994). Is there a culture of disability? In E. J. Trickett, R. J. Watts, and D. Birman (Eds.), *Human diversity: Perspectives on people in context* (pp. 244–260). San Francisco: Jossey-Bass. (Quotation from p. 248.)

12. Berry & Georgas. (2009).

13. For example, see Portes, A., & Zhou, M. (1993). The new second generation: Segmented assimilation and its variants. *Annals of the American academy of political and social science, 530*(1), 74–96.

14. Berry, J. (2001). A psychology of immigration. *Journal of Social Issues, 57*(3), 615–631.

15. Berry, J. W. (1980). Acculturation as varieties of adaptation. In A. M. Padilla (Ed.), *Acculturation: Theory, models and some new findings* (pp. 9–25). Boulder, CO: Westview.

16. Stonequist, E. V. (1937). *The marginal man: A study in personality and culture conflict.* New York: Scribner / Simon and Schuster.

17. Berry, J. W., & Kim, U. (1988). Acculturation and mental health. In P. R. Dasen, J. W. Berry, & N. Sartorius (Eds.), *Health and cross-cultural psychology* (pp. 207–236). Newbury Park, CA: Sage. Berry and Kim use *subtractive acculturation* to refer only to the marginalization category, although using the same logic, when acculturation to the host culture is greater than that to the heritage culture, the subtraction would result in assimilation, as suggested by Gibson (2005). When acculturation to the heritage culture is greater than that to the host culture, it would result in separation, also a "subtractive" way of acculturating. Gibson, M. A. (2005). Promoting academic engagement among minority youth: Implications from John Ogbu's Shaker Heights ethnography. *International Journal of Qualitative Studies in Education, 18*(5), 581–603.

18. Berry & Kim. (1988).

19. Minh, A., Nguyen, T. D., & Benet-Martínez, V. (2013). Biculturalism and adjustment: A meta-analysis. *Journal of Cross-Cultural Psychology, 44*(1), 122–159.

20. Berry. (2001).

21. Oppedal, B., Røysamb, E., & Sam, D. L. (2004). The effect of acculturation and social support on change in mental health among young immigrants. *International Journal of Behavioral Development, 28*(6), 481–494.

22. Birman, D., & Taylor-Ritzler, T. (2007). Acculturation and psychological distress among adolescent immigrants from the former Soviet Union: Exploring the mediating effect of family relationships. *Cultural Diversity and Ethnic Minority Psychology, 13*(4), 337–346.

23. Oppedal et al. (2004).

24. Cabassa, L. J. (2003). Measuring acculturation: Where we are and where we need to go. *Hispanic Journal of Behavioral Sciences, 25*(2), 127–146.

25. Bronfenbrenner, U. (1977). Toward an experimental ecology of human development. *American Psychologist, 32*(7). 513–531.

26. Birman, D. (2011). Migration and well-being: Beyond the macrosystem. *Psychosocial Intervention, 20*(3), 339–342.

27. Trickett, E. J., & Birman, D. (2005). Acculturation, school context, and school outcomes: Adaptation of refugee adolescents from the former Soviet Union. *Psychology in the Schools, 42*(1), 27–38.

28. Rosenthal, D., Ranieri, N., & Klimdis, S. (1996). Vietnamese adolescents in Australia: Relationships between perceptions of self and parental values, intergenerational conflict, and gender dissatisfaction. *International Journal of Psychology, 31*(2), 81–92.

29. Horenczyk, G., & Tatar, M. (2002). Teachers' attitudes toward multiculturalism and their perceptions of the school organizational culture. *Teaching and Teacher Education, 18*(4), 435–445.

30. Delgado-Gaitan, C. (2007). Fostering Latino parent involvement in the schools: Practices and partnership. In S. J. Paik and H. J. Walberg (Eds.), *Narrowing the achievement gap: Strategies for educating Latino, Black, and Asian students* (pp. 17–32). New York: Springer.

31. Huss-Keeler, R. L. (1997). Teacher perception of ethnic and linguistic minority parental involvement and its relationships to children's language and literacy learning: A case study. *Teaching and Teacher Education, 13*(2), 171–182.

32. Miller, A. M., Birman, D., Zenk, S., Wang, E., Sorokin, O., & Connor, J. (2009). Neighborhood immigrant concentration, acculturation, and cultural alienation in former Soviet immigrant women. *Journal of Community Psychology, 37*(1), 88–105.

33. Ibid.

34. Portes & Zhou. (1993).

35. Birman, D., & Simon, C. D. (2014). Acculturation research: Challenges, complexities, and possibilities. In F. T. L. Long, L. Comas-Díaz, G. C. Nagayama Hall, V. C. McLoyd, & J. E. Trimble (Eds.), *American Psychological Association handbook of*

multicultural psychology: Vol. 1: Theory and research. Washington, DC: American Psychological Association.

36. Sue, S., & Okazaki, S. (2009). Asian-American educational achievements: A phenomenon in search of an explanation. *Asian American Journal of Psychology, 1,* 45–55.

37. Escobar, J. I., & Vega, W. A. (2000). Mental health and immigration's AAAs: Where are we and where do we go from here? *Journal of Nervous and Mental Disease, 188*(11), 736–740.

38. García Coll, C., & Marks, A. K. (Eds.). (2012). *The immigrant paradox in children and adolescents: Is becoming American a developmental risk?* Washington, DC: American Psychological Association.

39. Birman, D., Trickett, E. J., & Buchanan, R. M. (2005). A tale of two cities: Replication of a study on the acculturation and adaptation of immigrant adolescents from the former Soviet Union in a different community context. *American Journal of Community Psychology, 35*(1–2), 83–101.

40. Escobar & Vega. (2000).

41. Marin, G., Organista, P. E. B., & Chun, K. M. (2002). Acculturation research. In G. Bernal, J. E. Trimble, A. K. Burlew, & F. T. L. Leong (Eds.), *Handbook of racial and ethnic minority psychology* (Vol. 4, pp. 208–219). Thousand Oaks, CA: Sage.

42. Phinney, J. S., Horenczyk, G., Liebkind, K., & Vedder, P. (2001). Ethnic identity, immigration, and well-being: An interactional perspective. *Journal of Social Issues, 57*(3), 493–510.

43. Brown, D. H. (2000). *Principles of language learning and teaching* (4th ed.). New York: Addison Wesley Longman.

44. Nekby, L., & Rödin, M. (2010). Acculturation identity and employment among second and middle generation immigrants. *Journal of Economic Psychology, 31*(1), 35–50.

45. Oppedal, B. (2006). Development and acculturation. In D. L. Sam and J. W. Berry (Eds.), *The Cambridge handbook of acculturation psychology* (pp. 97–112). New York: Cambridge University Press.

46. Brown. (2000).

47. Goldenberg, C. (2008). Teaching English language learners: What the research does—and does not—say. *American Educator, 32*(2), 8–23, 42–44.

48. Ibid.

49. Pavlenko, A., & Malt, B. C. (2011). Kitchen Russian: Cross-linguistic differences and first-language object naming by Russian-English bilinguals. *Bilingualism: Language and Cognition, 14*(1), 19–45.

50. Goldenberg. (2008).

51. Bankston, C. L., & Zhou, M. (1995). Effects of minority-language literacy on the academic achievement of Vietnamese youths in New Orleans. *Sociology of Education, 68*(1), 1–17.

52. Goldenberg. (2008).

53. Birman, D. (2006). Acculturation gap and family adjustment findings with Soviet Jewish refugees in the United States and implications for measurement. *Journal of Cross-Cultural Psychology, 37*(5), 568–589.

54. Bialystok, E. (2009). Bilingualism: The good, the bad, and the indifferent. *Bilingualism: Language and Cognition, 12*(1), 3–11.

55. Watters, E. (2010, January 10). The Americanization of mental illness. *New York Times*. Retrieved from http://www.nytimes.com/2010/01/10/magazine/10psyche-t.html?pagewanted=all&_r=0.

56. Afable-Munsuz, A., & Brindis, C. D. (2006). Acculturation and the sexual and reproductive health of Latino youth in the United States: A literature review. *Perspectives on Sexual and Reproductive Health, 38*(4), 208–219.

57. Luthar & Ansary. (2005).

58. Afable-Munsuz & Brindis. (2006).

59. Coatsworth, J. D., Maldonado-Molina, M., Pantin, H., & Szapocznik, J. (2005). A person-centered and ecological investigation of acculturation strategies in Hispanic immigrant youth. *Journal of Community Psychology, 33*(2), 157–174.

60. Birman, D. (1998). Biculturalism and perceived competence of Latino immigrant adolescents. *American Journal of Community Psychology, 26*(3), 335–354.

61. Birman et al. (2005).

62. Phinney, J. S., Horenczyk, G., Liebkind, K., & Vedder, P. (2001). Ethnic identity, immigration, and well-being: An interactional perspective. *Journal of Social Issues, 57*(3), 493–510.

63. Birman, D., Persky, I., & Chan, W. Y. (2010). Multiple identities of Jewish immigrant adolescents from the former Soviet Union: An exploration of salience and impact of ethnic identity. *International Journal of Behavioral Development, 34*(3), 193–205.

64. Phinney, J. S. (1996). When we talk about American ethnic groups, what do we mean? *American Psychologist, 51*(9), 918.

65. Helms, J. E., & Talleyrand, R. M. (1997). Race is not ethnicity. *American Psychologist, 52*(11), 1246–1247.

66. Golash-Boza, T. (2006). Dropping the hyphen? Becoming Latino(a)-American through racialized assimilation. *Social Forces, 85*(1), 27–55.

67. Portes & Zhou. (1993).

68. Banks, K. H., & Kohn-Wood, L. P. (2007). The influence of racial identity profiles on the relationship between racial discrimination and depressive symptom. *Journal of Black Psychology, 33*(3), 331–354.

69. Lee, R. M. (2003). Do ethnic identity and other-group orientation protect against discrimination for Asian Americans? *Journal of Counseling Psychology, 50*(2), 133–141.

70. Yip, T., Gee, G. C., & Takeuchi, D. T. (2008). Racial discrimination and psychological distress: The impact of ethnic identity and age among immigrant and United States–born Asian adults. *Developmental Psychology, 44*(3), 787–800.

71. Ibid.

72. Sue, S., & Chu, J. Y. (2003). The mental health of ethnic minority groups: Challenges posed by the supplement to the surgeon general's report on mental health. *Culture, Medicine and Psychiatry, 27*(4), 447–465.

73. Dinh, K. T., & Nguyen, H. H. (2006). The effects of acculturative variables on Asian American parent-child relationships. *Journal of Social and Personal Relationships, 23*(3), 407–426.

74. Suárez-Orozco, C., Yoshikawa, H., Teranishi, R. T., & Suárez-Orozco, M. M. (2011). Growing up in the shadows: The developmental implications of unauthorized status. *Harvard Educational Review, 81*(3), 438–473.

75. Buki, L. P., Ma, T., Strom, R. D., & Strom, S. K. (2003). Chinese immigrant mothers of adolescents: Self-perceptions of acculturation effects on parenting. *Cultural Diversity and Ethnic Minority Psychology, 9*(2), 127–140.

76. Farver, J. M., Narang, S. K., & Bhadha, B. R. (2002). East meets West: Ethnic identity, acculturation, and conflict in Asian Indian families. *Journal of Family Psychology, 16*(3), 338–350.

77. Lee, R. M., Choe, J., Kim, G., & Ngo, V. (2000). Construction of the Asian American Family Conflicts Scale. *Journal of Counseling Psychology, 47*(2), 211–222.

78. Ho, J., & Birman, B. (2010). Acculturation gap in Vietnamese refugee families: Impact on family adjustment. *International Journal of Intercultural Relations, 34*(1), 22–33.

79. Martinez, C. R. (2006). Effects of differential family acculturation on Latino adolescent substance abuse. *Family Relations, 55*(3), 306–317.

80. Birman. (2006).

81. Birman, D., & Espino, S. R. (2007). The relationship of parental practices and knowledge to school adaptation for immigrant and nonimmigrant high school students. *Canadian Journal of School Psychology, 22*(2), 152–166.

82. Pantin, H., Schwartz, S. J., Sullivan, S., Coatsworth, J. D., & Szapocznik, J. (2003). Preventing substance abuse in Hispanic immigrant adolescents: An ecodevelopmental, parent-centered approach. *Hispanic Journal of Behavioral Sciences, 25*(4), 469–500.

83. Jones, C. J., Trickett, E. J., & Birman, D. (2012). Determinants and consequences of child culture brokering in families from the former Soviet Union. *American Journal of Community Psychology, 50*(1–2), 182–196.

84. Orellana, M. F., Dorner, L., & Pulido, L. (2003). Accessing assets: Immigrant youth's work as family translators or "para-phrasers." *Social Problems, 50*(4), 505–524.

85. Raschke, V. (2013). *Processes underlying syntactic control: Evaluating linguistically diverse children.* Ph.D. dissertation, Loyola University.

86. Sy, S. R. (2006). Family and work influences on the transition to college among Latina adolescents. *Hispanic Journal of Behavioral Sciences, 28*(3), 368–386.

87. Jones et al. (2012).

88. Goldenberg. (2008).

89. Ferguson, G. M., & Bornstein, M. H. (2012). Remote acculturation: The "Americanization" of Jamaican Islanders. *International Journal of Behavioral Development, 36*(3),167–177.

7

Identity Development

SETH J. SCHWARTZ, MIGUEL ÁNGEL CANO, AND
BYRON L. ZAMBOANGA

Nineteen-year-old Yuliana, a second-generation Dominican American who had grown up in New York City, recently moved to a small Ohio college town to pursue her studies. In NYC, she rarely thought about her ethnicity. The Washington Heights neighborhood where she had lived is a densely populated, largely Dominican neighborhood. During early and middle childhood, when she attended a neighborhood school, most of her friends were other Dominican Americans from the area. When asked as a child where she was from, she had always responded, "Dominican." Although she was born in the United States and barely speaks Spanish, the Dominican Republic is where all her family and friends are from. When she later attended a commuter high school in Lower Manhattan with students from all over the Caribbean and the rest of the world, she made a more diverse group of friends. During midadolescence, if pressed, she would usually respond that she was a New Yorker and sometimes that she was Dominican, depending on who was asking. Then she left for college and became one of only a few students of color on campus. There she found people asking every day, "Where are you really from?" "New York" did not seem to satisfy them. She joined the La Raza Student Association, in which most members are from the Southwest and of Mexican origin. But even here she does not seem to belong. Is she Black? Is she Latina? Is she American? Dominican? A New Yorker? For the first time, Yuliana finds herself daily questioning her identity and place.

Stories like Yuliana's have become increasingly common in the United States during the past 50 years. The country has been undergoing an unprecedented wave of immigration since 1965, when the restrictive immigration laws passed in 1924 were repealed. Although the reason for lifting the strict immigration quotas was to permit European immigrants to reunite with their families, the end result was that the primary immigrant-sending countries shifted from Europe to Latin America, Asia, and the Caribbean.[1]

Although ethnic minorities constitute a rapidly increasing segment of the U.S. population, their share of the country's political and economic power has increased more slowly. Research indicates that Whites are more likely to be considered "American" than individuals from other ethnic groups are.[2] In a series of experimental studies in which respondents were instructed to answer as quickly as possible without thinking first, U.S.-born celebrities from ethnic minority groups, such as George Lopez and Lucy Liu, were less likely to be characterized as American than were White celebrities from other countries, such as Kate Winslet and Gérard Depardieu.[3] Some writers have referred to this phenomenon as *perpetual foreigner syndrome*.[4] It is one of the primary dynamics distinguishing the current wave of immigrants from the primarily European immigrants who arrived earlier. For example, Jewish and Italian immigrants who entered between 1880 and 1924 were often discriminated against and cast as separate "races" distinct from the White population.[5] However, the U.S.-born children of these immigrants were indistinguishable from other Americans in terms of physical appearance and spoken English. Ethnicity, then, was most important during the first generation and became far less important for second-generation European immigrants.

The situation is quite different for contemporary immigrants and their children largely because the majority of today's immigrants are from ethnic minority groups. Children from immigrant families, including those born in the United States (second generation) or those who arrived as young children (1.5 generation)[6]—many of whom speak unaccented English—are nonetheless faced with perpetual foreigner syndrome. In *Yellow: Race in America beyond Black and White*, Wu tells of being asked where he was from and what life in China was like— even though he was born in the United States and has never set foot in China.[7] Perpetual foreigner syndrome is a form of discrimination—a "microaggression."[8] Such remarks remind the person that he or she is not considered an integrated member of the larger society.[9] Comments such as "Where are you *really* from?" or "Your English is so good!" can motivate contemporary young immigrants to explore their cultural heritage and what it means to be a member of their ethnic group.

Perpetual foreigner syndrome is one of a number of contextual processes that help maintain a sense of separateness between many immigrant-origin children and the White American "mainstream." *Context* can be framed in terms of a set of interlocking systems that are more rather than less proximal to the person.[10] These levels include interpersonal relationships (microsystems), the social ecologies of family members (exosystems), and larger contextual forces that operate at the community or societal level (macrosystems). For example, microsystems include adolescents' relationships with friends, parents, and teachers; mesosystems include parental monitoring of adolescents' peer activities; exosystems include parents' own life stressors (immigration related and otherwise); and macrosystems include economic conditions, immigration policies, and social norms regarding the acceptability of foreign language use in public places. The processes highlighted in this chapter operate simultaneously at all of these levels. For example, perpetual foreigner syndrome is a macrosystemic phenomenon present in many countries that receive immigrants in which a specific ethnic group (generally Whites in Western countries) is most closely associated with the country in general, and other ethnic groups are likely to be perceived as foreigners. However, perpetual foreigner syndrome also operates within interpersonal interactions and relationships when people make insensitive remarks that are regarded as discriminatory (even if not intended that way) by the person toward whom the remark was directed.

Similarly, self-categorization into ethnic groups operates at the macrosystemic level, but it can also manifest itself through interpersonal relationships—as in people's attitudes toward interethnic friendships, dating relationships, and marriages. We will examine three additional contextual processes that operate at various levels and contribute to the development and maintenance of ethnic identity.

First, many immigrant-origin children, especially Black and Hispanic, are often geographically segregated from White Americans.[11] In such cases, immigrant-origin children usually interact primarily with other minority group members, and their exposure to White Americans mainly occurs through the media and other distant sources.[12] Many immigrant children therefore acculturate primarily toward the segment of U.S. society to which they are most frequently exposed, a phenomenon known as *segmented assimilation*.[13] For example, many Caribbean and

African adolescents and emerging adults are linked with African American culture (willingly or otherwise) because of their skin tone and may find themselves gravitating toward that cultural stream.[14] Second, immigrant families often *choose* to maintain at least some of the customs and values of their cultural heritage and discourage their children from fully assimilating into the U.S. mainstream.[15] This process of *selective acculturation* involves immigrants choosing, and encouraging their children, to retain specific aspects of their heritage culture and to incorporate only selected aspects of U.S. culture into their lives. The principle of ethnic identity represents an instance of selective acculturation. Third, the concept of *self-categorization* refers to people thinking of themselves as group members rather than as individuals when their group is compared with other relevant groups perceived as having higher or lower status.[16] Identifying with one's ethnic group—which is essentially what ethnic identity is—helps immigrants identify and highlight positive attributes of their cultural groups. For example, although some Caribbean Black immigrants may gravitate toward African American culture, they also attempt to assert themselves as different from African Americans by developing ethnic identities centered around their cultures of origin.[17] Nonetheless, Caribbean immigrants are often mistaken for African Americans and are often treated accordingly.[18] Generally speaking, immigrant groups are likely to identify with their native U.S. counterparts in cases in which the superordinate panethnic group is evaluated favorably but to identify with their specific national or regional origin group in cases in which the superordinate panethnic group is regarded less favorably.[19]

Ethnic Identity: A Challenge for Immigrant-Origin Children

The sense of being different from others introduces important identity challenges for immigrant-origin children. These challenges are often salient for both children born outside the United States (first generation) and those born in the United States (second generation). In addition to developing a sense of self in areas such as career aspirations, religious beliefs, and friendships, these children, especially those from ethnic minority backgrounds, must make sense of themselves both as members of the larger U.S. culture and as members of a specific ethnic or cultural group.[20] One way of thinking about ethnic identity is to view it as a person's beliefs, attitudes, and feelings about the meaning of their ethnicity.

Ethnic identity generally (but not always) serves important protective and developmental functions for immigrant-origin youth. For example, research on ethnic identity among immigrant children and adolescents has found modest positive associations between ethnic identity and various forms of well-being.[21] Some studies have found that ethnic minority individuals with stronger ethnic identities report lower levels of anxiety,[22] depressive symptoms,[23] conduct problems,[24] and substance use.[25] But what exactly is ethnic identity? Various research groups have defined *ethnic identity* differently, but from a developmental and social psychological perspective, ethnic identity represents the confluence of (a) having explored the subjective meaning of one's ethnic group and (b) regarding one's ethnic group positively.[26] These two components were integrated from the neo-Eriksonian personal identity literature (exploration) and social identity theory (affirmation/commitment). The neo-Eriksonian view focuses on ways young people explore and make choices in areas such as career, values, friendships, and dating relationships.[27] Social identity theory focuses on the positive feelings that individuals derive from group memberships that are important to them.[28] Integrating these two perspectives provides both developmental and social psychological lenses for viewing the ways in which young people become attached to their ethnic backgrounds—and the consequences of these attachments for a person's psychosocial and physical health.

It is important to note that ethnic identity is a subjective phenomenon and can be claimed by any individual, regardless of the specific ethnic group to which the individual views themselves as belonging.[29] For example, multiethnic individuals, who are the fastest growing demographic group in the United States, often identify with a superordinate "biracial-multiracial" group that is distinct from any of the standard U.S. ethnic groupings such as White, Black, Hispanic, or Asian.[30] Indeed, the prominence of multiethnic individuals such as Barack Obama and Tiger Woods has helped other multiethnic people take pride in their ethnicity.

Experiences with discrimination, social exclusion, or "feeling different" can set the process of ethnic identity development in motion.[31] For example, finding that one looks or sounds different from one's friends or hearing derogatory remarks about one's ethnic or cultural group can motivate a person to explore more deeply what it means to be a member of that group. The very experience of growing up in an immigrant family and living in two worlds may also prompt individuals to consider what their ethnic or cultural group means to them.[32]

Results from a number of studies provide a picture of how ethnic identity develops between early adolescence and emerging adulthood (i.e., roughly ages 12 to 25). During early and middle adolescence (ages 12 to 14),[33] late adolescence (ages 14 to 17),[34] and the early part of emerging adulthood (ages 18 to 21),[35] youth from ethnic minority groups tend to increase their ethnic identity exploration and affirmation, whereas White youth appear to be less invested in their ethnic group membership. Ethnic identity exploration seems to level off in late adolescence, although for adolescents who experience discrimination, levels of ethnic identity exploration tend to remain somewhat high. For ethnic minority individuals attending postsecondary institutions, ethnic identity exploration often resumes in emerging adulthood—probably due to exposure to new ideas, peers (coethnic and others), and college relationships.

Research on ethnic identity has furthered the study of immigrant adolescents in some ways but has also created confusion. Most research has focused primarily on panethnic groups (e.g., Blacks, Hispanics, Asians) or on specific national groups (e.g., Mexican Americans).[36] However, the groups surveyed have been a "mixed bag," including some first- and second-generation individuals but also third- or later-generation participants with U.S.-born parents. Such studies provide information about the experiences of members of *ethnic groups*, but only some of it tells of the experiences of *immigrants*. In particular, it is not clear whether immigrants—especially first-generation immigrants—understand the concept of ethnicity in the same way that second- and later-generation individuals do. In particular, panethnic classifications such as *Hispanic* and *Asian* used in the United States do not carry much meaning in immigrants' heritage countries. Self-categorization theory holds that ethnic identities are context dependent,[37] so members of ethnic groups within a given national context would evaluate themselves with that context in mind. Individuals residing in separate countries likely do not have such a common frame of reference. For example, Dominicans, Nicaraguans, and Venezuelans are all grouped under the heading of *Hispanic* in the

United States, but individuals living in these countries would probably not find much in common with each other.

First-generation immigrants, especially those who arrived when they were old enough to remember life in their countries of origin, are in a state of transition between being residents of another country and being members of an ethnic group in the United States. It is not clear when the concept of ethnicity becomes relevant for first-generation immigrants, so more research is needed in this area. Further, first- and second-generation immigrants appear to understand ethnicity differently. Because ethnic identity is grounded within one's understanding of ethnicity, it may be problematic to aggregate participants in studies of ethnic identity and other cultural constructs across immigrant generations (or to combine recent and longer-term immigrants).[38]

Ethnic and U.S. Identity as Separate Dimensions. Although research on the ethnic identity of immigrant and ethnic minority individuals has been ongoing for more than two decades, there has not been much research on their identification with the United States. Indeed, within a bidimensional model of cultural identifications,[39] individuals can identify with a number of groups to which they belong—including the United States, an ethnic background, a religious faith, a political party or movement, or a peer group. The omission of the category of "U.S. identity" from contemporary research on ethnic identity is important to rectify because identifying as a member of the U.S. community and becoming civically involved are critical to immigrant youth's incorporation into the country.[40] Demographers such as Jiménez have illustrated that according to demographic markers such as English-language proficiency, postsecondary education, and upward economic mobility, post-1965 immigrants are integrating into the U.S. cultural fabric.[41] However, these markers do not tell us (a) the extent to which immigrants consider themselves "American," (b) whether they have considered what being "American" means to them, and (c) the extent to which they feel attached to the United States. Moreover, because many demographers, sociologists, and political scientists use national surveys of immigrants of varying ages, we are limited in terms of what we can learn about immigrant-origin children, adolescents, and emerging adults from these surveys. Also, demographic data on immigrants generally provide information about the first generation but not the U.S.-born second generation.[42] To learn how immigrant-origin children and adolescents think of themselves as members of U.S. society, we must ask them specifically.

When we consider ethnic and U.S. identity together, we can extract a form of *biculturalism*, which includes identifying with one's cultural heritage as well as with the United States. Biculturalism has been found to strongly promote well-being, especially when the person is equally comfortable with the two cultural streams and is able to integrate them into an individualized and creative cultural mosaic.[43] However, the perceived difference between a person's heritage culture and U.S. culture may serve as an important mitigating factor in the ease versus difficulty involved in integrating the two cultural streams.[44] For example, consider a Chinese American adolescent who believes that the collectivist and family-oriented value system underlying Chinese culture is fundamentally incompatible with the individualistic and competitive value system underlying U.S. culture. This adolescent may regard her two cultural backgrounds as irreconcilable. However, another Chinese American adolescent may view the situation differently, adopting a largely collectivist mind-set while at home with family members but a largely individualistic one while at school. These two adolescents, despite being from the same cultural background, may approach (or avoid) integrating their Chinese and American cultural streams in very different ways. The first adolescent may "compartmentalize" her two cultural streams and may experience switching between them as requiring a great deal of psychological energy. The second adolescent may integrate her two cultural streams (although there may be some situations in which they will be kept separate, such as when spending time with family elders) and may find that switching between these streams does not require much effort.

Ethnic Identity and Panethnic Labels. Prominent ethnic identity theories are explicitly intended to apply to anyone, regardless of the person's ethnic background. As such, these theories and the measures associated with them generally do not attend to the *content* of the person's ethnic identity—that is, the specific groups with whom the person is identifying—or the *context* in which the ethnic identity is being developed. As noted previously, today's immigrants, many of whom come from non-White ethnic groups, are often lumped into panethnic groups in the United States. Because these groupings are generally not used in heritage countries, when immigrant children and adolescents come to (or are socialized in) the United States, they must make sense of what it means to be classified in a panethnic category with people from quite different backgrounds.[45] Even if immigrants of color do not embrace a panethnic label, it may be imposed on them by others, so they may still need to consider what it means to them. Indeed, a longitudinal study tracking inner-city adolescents' ethnic self-categorizations between sixth and eighth grade found that as many as 27 percent of adolescents changed their ethnic self-identification during that time period.[46] For Hispanics, these shifts were most common in schools that were primarily African American and less common in schools that were primarily Hispanic or multicultural. Panethnic labels ("Hispanic" or "Latino") were more likely to be switched to identifications with specific countries of origin, whereas the reverse was less likely. Asian American students' self-categorizations were similarly consistent across school types, and the stability of their self-chosen labels did not differ between panethnic and national labels.

Ethnic Identity as a Dimension of Acculturation. Ethnic identity has been posited as a subjective domain of acculturation.[47] That is, whereas acculturation has been studied as a primary behavioral process—indexed by practices such as language use, choice of foods and friends, and media preferences (see Birman and Addae, "Acculturation," chapter 6 in this volume)—ethnic identity is conceptualized as the extent to which one is attached to one's ethnic or cultural group.

A number of writers have proposed more integrative definitions of acculturation that *include* ethnic identity as a domain of acculturation. Specifically, cultural identifications would represent one domain of acculturation, with ethnic and U.S. identities situated within this domain. The development of ethnic identity, which has often been studied separately from other domains of acculturation, may or may not parallel the development of other dimensions of heritage-culture retention such as the origin country's cultural practices and values. For example, Knight and colleagues found that among a sample of Mexican American adolescent offenders, those with high or increasing ethnic identity scores over a three-year period also tended to maintain Spanish fluency and to affiliate primarily with Mexican American friends.[48] On the contrary, those adolescents with moderate trajectories of ethnic identity tended to be monolingual English speakers and to affiliate primarily with friends from other ethnic groups. In this sample, the longitudinal trajectories of ethnic identity and cultural practices tended to overlap considerably. This finding suggests that immigrant adolescents may develop a sense of themselves as members of an ethnic group in a way similar to the manner in which they retain (or do not retain) language and social relationships characteristic of their cultural heritage. However, this study focused on adolescent offenders, so different results might have emerged with non-offenders.

In addition, the local context—for example, availability of same-ethnic peers and opportunities to engage in heritage-culture practices—may significantly influence the extent to which ethnic identity and heritage-culture practices converge as indices of acculturation. The Knight study was conducted in Phoenix, Arizona, which has a large Mexican American population and where one is likely to interact with peers from various ethnic backgrounds. A similar study conducted in the rural Midwest or New England might yield much different results. In communities there, individuals who remained high in Mexican ethnic identity might have scored low on Mexican cultural practices simply because Mexican food, media, and friends may be more difficult to find. Further, the political context of the local community must be considered. For example, the Arizona state legislature passed laws in 2009 that were intended to discourage unauthorized immigration but that the Hispanic community interpreted as hostile and discriminatory.[49] A study conducted in New York City, which is generally receptive to immigrants from many different backgrounds,[50] might produce quite different findings.

Unlike studying other aspects of acculturation, studying ethnic and U.S. identity in children and adolescents requires an understanding of the developmental periods during which children become capable of recognizing ethnic differences, understanding themselves as ethnic beings, and reflecting on the personal meaning of their ethnicity. Whereas visible behaviors such as language use and friendships can be observed beginning in early childhood, subjective dimensions of acculturation such as cultural identifications require specific skills on the part of the child. Generally, children as young as age three or four are able to group people according to their skin color and other physical features associated with ethnicity.[51] At age five or six, children begin to understand the difference between socially constructed groups such as "Americans" and "immigrants."[52] Understanding of *ethnic constancy*—that one belongs to the same ethnic group across time—emerges around age eight.[53] Finally, the ability to think about oneself abstractly, such as considering the subjective meaning of one's ethnicity, begins to emerge during the middle-school years.[54] Of course, these competencies may be shaped and mobilized by familial socialization such as the expectation that a child will seek out friends from their own ethnic or cultural group.

Ethnic Identity as a Dimension of Personal Identity. For much of the history of ethnic identity literature, it was not integrated with literatures on other dimensions of identity.[55] Personal identity, especially within the neo-Eriksonian tradition, was primarily studied in White samples, whereas ethnic identity was mainly studied in ethnic minority samples.[56] This situation has begun to change in recent years, however, as the study of personal identity has been extended to more ethnically diverse samples and as personal and ethnic identity have increasingly been studied together.

Three central themes have emerged from this simultaneous consideration. First, among first- and second-generation emerging adults across ethnic groups, individuals who were exploring (or had committed to) personal identity alternatives were also considering ethnic identity alternatives and were positively attached to their ethnic group.[57] Second, when both personal and ethnic identity were modeled as predictors of psychosocial or risk-behavior outcomes, personal identity tended to emerge as a far stronger predictor of these outcomes.[58] Third, evidence demonstrates that personal identity may mediate the links between ethnic identity and adjustment outcomes.[59] That is, from a developmental perspective, immigrants' developing a *cultural* sense of self can contribute to the development of a *personal* sense of self. Understanding oneself in relation to one's ethnic group allows a person to make firm choices in areas such as career goals, personal values, friendships, dating relationships, and family obligations. Such cultural self-understanding includes the possibility of deciding not to engage with one's ethnic or cultural group—that is, considering what one's ethnicity means to oneself does not imply or require that a person will eventually regard the ethnic group positively.[60] The eventual outcome of the process of ethnic identity development may therefore fall into one of three general categories—affirming one's ethnicity, rejecting one's ethnic group, or concluding that ethnicity is not important.

Regardless of how any given individual ultimately addresses the issue of ethnicity, a general conclusion one can draw is that for immigrant and minority individuals ethnicity represents an additional domain in which personal identity development takes place.[61] Ethnicity is likely an "optional" identity domain for Whites from nonimmigrant families, and the majority of Whites do not consider ethnicity important. A likely explanation for this phenomenon lies within the concept of *cultural scripts*,[62] the assumptions and values underlying a specific cultural group or context. The cultural script most often associated with the United States—individualism and competition—is more or less the cultural script attributed to White Americans. The cultural script assigned to the United States is also one of Whiteness; Devos and colleagues have found that the idea of *American* is most closely associated with Whites.[63] Thus, one could argue that White Americans do not need the concept of ethnic identity to distinguish their cultural script from that of the larger society in which they live. However, ethnic minority groups are generally not inherently associated with being American, so their cultural scripts are often quite different from those endorsed by many White Americans. Therefore, ethnic identity serves a number of functions for ethnic minority groups that may not be shared by Whites.

This is not to say that Whites never engage with ethnic identity. For example, some White Americans of Greek, Italian, or Jewish descent do choose to retain aspects of their cultural heritage such as foods and holiday celebrations. However, these ethnic identifications tend to be less prevalent than those maintained by ethnic/racial minority group members.[64] The kinds of experiences reported by participants in Syed and Azmitia's study—such as witnessing or being subjected to discrimination, feeling different from others, and embracing cultural values that vary from the dominant cultural script—may be more common for ethnic minorities than for Whites.[65] This result may be one reason that ethnicity is more apt to serve as a domain of identity work for minority groups than for White Americans. However, ethnic identity may be more relevant or central for Whites who live in heavily minority areas or whose social networks include many minority group members.

Ethnic Identity Centrality. A primary difference between majority and minority ethnic group members appears to be the extent to which ethnicity is *central* to a person's sense of self. As defined by Vignoles and colleagues,[66] *identity centrality* refers to the extent to which a specific component or domain is an integral part of one's self-definition. Indeed, Sellers and colleagues have identified centrality as a component of ethnic identity.[67] Individuals for whom ethnic identity is central are likely to interpret their experiences through the lens of their ethnicity, such as interpreting ambiguous events (like a neighbor's not saying hello) as discriminatory. Someone for whom ethnicity is not central may interpret the same events quite differently. Centrality can also promote well-being. Brittian and colleagues found that among ethnic minority college students, ethnic identity served more strongly as a protection against anxiety and depression for those for whom ethnicity was a central component of their sense of self.[68] Therefore, ethnic minority individuals differ in the extent to which ethnicity is regarded as an essential domain for identity work, and these individual differences carry important implications for positive and negative psychosocial functioning.

Ethnic identity can be central for various reasons, including a tendency to regard ethnicity as important as well as specific events that can increase the importance of one's ethnicity. For Mexican Americans, various initiatives to curb unauthorized immigration (including the Arizona racial profiling law) have increased the salience of ethnic identity. For Cuban Americans, a similar increase in ethnic identity centrality occurred in 2000 when the U.S. government decided to return Elián González, a young Cuban boy who had been rescued off the coast of Florida and had become a cause célèbre among Miami's Cuban community, to Cuba to live with his father. In both cases, members of the ethnic community conducted protests and waved the flag of their heritage country, and in some cases U.S. flags were desecrated.[69] These examples illustrate how reactive ethnicity can increase the extent to which one's ethnic group is central to an individual's sense of self. *Reactive ethnicity* refers to a defensive strengthening of one's ethnic identification following a perceived threat to one's ethnic group.[70]

A related but infrequently examined issue is the extent to which *belonging to the larger society* is considered an essential domain for identity work. In the United States, for example, being American is more central to some people's identities and less central to those of others.[71] In the weeks and months after the September 11, 2001, terrorist attacks, however, the United States witnessed a wave of patriotism that had rarely been observed previously. There might therefore be a phenomenon called *reactive patriotism* that would increase people's identification with their country of residence following a physical or symbolic attack on that country.

Ethnic and U.S. identity centrality, reactive ethnicity, and reactive patriotism have several implications for immigrant-origin children. In some cases, children and adolescents who are teased about their ethnic background may respond by identifying even more strongly with their ethnicity. We know that ethnic identity in adolescents tends to be strongly related to the extent to which their parents teach them about their ethnic background and expose them to role models and historical figures from their cultural heritage.[72] However, the effects of such socialization on the *centrality* of ethnicity have not received much attention. Moreover, what do parents do to socialize their children to identify with the United States? Some studies suggest that familial ethnic socialization may be positively related to U.S. practices, but links between familial socialization processes and young people's identification with the United States have not been reported.[73] This area remains a direction for future research.

Is Ethnic Identity Always Protective?

In most cases, ethnic identity promotes well-being and protects against anxiety, depression, behavior problems, and substance use. Moreover, in some cases, ethnic identity might *offset* the effects of discrimination on delinquent behavior[74] and on internalizing symptoms.[75] Social identity theory suggests that an individual with a strong sense of ethnic identity might be able to reframe discrimination as coming from outside one's ethnic group and therefore reduce its impact on one's functioning. Indeed, from a self-categorization perspective, one of the functions of ethnic identity is to reframe comparisons of one's ethnic group with other groups so that one's group is evaluated more favorably. For example, members of some ethnic groups may focus on specific forms of achievement in which the group has performed well rather than on other forms of achievement in which it has not.

Another question is whether ethnic identity may actually represent a *risk* for producing certain outcomes in some groups. One study found that, once cultural practices had been accounted for, ethnic identity was *positively* associated with hazardous alcohol use, illicit drug use, and unsafe sexual behavior among Hispanic adolescents and emerging adults.[76] There are at least three explanations for this counterintuitive effect. The first draws on the notion that ethnic identity exploration and affirmation may consist of multiple domains. For example, using two prominent measures of ethnic identity exploration, Syed and colleagues empirically extracted two dimensions of ethnic identity exploration—search and participation. *Search* refers to thinking and talking to others about the meaning of one's ethnic group.[77] *Participation* refers to engaging in activities typical of one's ethnic group, such as attending celebrations. The researchers found that participation was positively linked with well-being for Blacks, Hispanics, and Asians, but that search was negatively linked with well-being across these same groups. This finding is consistent with the personal identity literature, in which exploring multiple alternatives is associated with anxiety, depression, and low levels of self-esteem and life satisfaction.[78] Controlling for cultural practices removes the participation component from ethnic identity exploration, leaving only the search component. In turn, searching for an ethnic identity may be linked with risky behavior, possibly through low levels of well-being.

A second explanation involves the concept of *reactive ethnicity*.[79] For example, exposure to discrimination—either toward oneself or toward others belonging to one's ethnic group—can increase the importance of one's ethnic identification.[80] Sensitivity to discrimination may be especially heightened among Hispanics, who are at the center of immigration, language, and cultural debates in the United States.[81]

Third, ethnic identity may be more important for some individuals than for others.[82] For example, Yoo and Lee[83] found that Asian Americans for whom ethnic identity was most important rated thinking about discriminatory events as highly stressful, whereas individuals who placed the least importance on ethnic identity rated thinking about such events as not stressful. Similarly, Brittian and colleagues found that ethnic identity was most protective against anxiety and depression for individuals for whom ethnicity was most central.[84] Similar moderating effects may operate for other culturally based stressors, such that youth who invest most strongly in their ethnicity may be most at risk for negative psychosocial or health outcomes. This pattern may be further moderated by the ethnic group to which a specific immigrant youth belongs. For example, immigrants from certain countries may be viewed as more devalued than others, so identifying with an ethnic group perceived as such may have adverse psychosocial and health-related consequences. For example, some groups may be discriminated against because a large proportion of members live in poverty, enter the country on an undocumented basis, and send much of their earnings back to their countries of origin.[85] Moreover, the effects of identifying with a stigmatized ethnic group are likely moderated by the extent to which one is successful in reframing the intergroup comparison to focus on positive aspects of the group.

Conclusion

This chapter has reviewed much of what is known about ethnic identity among immigrant-origin youth and its importance for immigrant-origin children. Ethnic identity is generally promoted through parents' efforts to teach children about the family's cultural heritage, although the behavioral expression of ethnic identity is at least to some extent dependent on the availability of resources (e.g., peers, food, media) from one's heritage group. More work is needed to determine the precise role of context in the functions of ethnic identity. Specifically, does ethnic identity promote well-being and protect against health risks to a greater extent in multicultural contexts than it does in less supportive contexts?

The present wave of immigration is expected to continue for at least the foreseeable future, and the U.S.-born second generation is rapidly increasing, indicating that ethnic identity will remain important. Understanding ethnic identity in immigrant-origin children will also continue to be an important research inquiry.

NOTES

1. Portes, A., & Rumbaut, R. G. (2006). *Immigrant America: A portrait* (3rd ed.). Berkeley: University of California Press.

2. Devos, T., & Heng, L. (2009). Whites are granted the American identity more swiftly than Asians: Disentangling the role of automatic and controlled processes. *Social Psychology, 40*(4), 192–201.

3. Ibid.; Devos, T., & Ma, D. S. (2006). Is Kate Winslet more American than Lucy Liu? The impact of construal processes on the implicit ascription of a national identity. *British Journal of Social Psychology, 47*(2), 191–215.

4. Armenta, B. E., Lee, R. M., Pituc, S. T., Kyoung-Rae, J., Park, I. J. K., Soto, J. A., Kim, S. Y., & Schwartz, S. J. (2013). Where are you from? A validation of the Foreigner Objectification Scale (FOBS) and the psychological correlates of foreigner objectification among Asian Americans and Latinos. *Cultural Diversity and Ethnic Minority Psychology, 19*(2), 131–142; Huynh, Q.-L., Devos, T., & Smalarz, L. (2011). Perpetual foreigner in one's own land: Potential implications for identity and psychological adjustment. *Journal of Social and Clinical Psychology, 30*(2), 133–162.

5. Sterba, C. M. (2003). *Good Americans: Italian and Jewish immigrants during the First World War*. New York: Oxford University Press.

6. Portes, A., & Rumbaut, R. G. (2001). *Ethnicities: The story of the immigrant second generation*. Berkeley: University of California Press.

7. Wu, F. H. (2001). *Yellow: Race in America beyond Black and White*. New York: Basic Books.

8. Sue, D. W., Capodilupo, C. M., Torino, G. C., Bucceri, J. M., Holder, A. M. B., Nadal, K. L., & Esquilin, M. (2007). Racial microaggressions in daily life: Implications for clinical practice. *American Psychologist, 62*(4), 271–286.

9. Lee, R. M. (2005). Resilience against discrimination: Ethnic identity and other-group orientation as protective factors for Korean Americans. *Journal of Counseling Psychology, 52*(1), 36–44.

10. Bronfenbrenner, U. (1979). *The ecology of human development: Experiments by nature and design*. Cambridge: Harvard University Press.

11. Lichter, D. T., Parisi, D., Taquino, M. C., & Grice, S. M. (2010). Residential segregation in new Hispanic destinations: Cities, suburbs, and rural communities compared. *Social Science Research, 39*(2), 215–230.

12. Alba, R. D., & Nee, V. (2006). *Remaking the American mainstream: Assimilation and contemporary immigration*. Cambridge: Harvard University Press.

13. Ibid.

14. Waters, M. C. (1999). *Black identities: West Indian immigrant dreams and American realities*. New York: Russell Sage Foundation.

15. Portes, A., & Hao, L. (2002). The price of uniformity: Language, family, and personality adjustment in the immigrant second generation. *Ethnic and Racial Studies, 25*(6), 889–912.

16. Turner, J. C., Hogg, M. A., Oakes, P. J., Reicher, S. D., & Wetherell, M. S. (1987). *Rediscovering the social group: A self-categorization theory.* Oxford, UK: Blackwell.

17. Ferguson, G. M., Bornstein, M. H., & Pottinger, A. M. (2012). Tridimensional acculturation and adaptation among Jamaican adolescent-mother dyads in the United States. *Child Development, 83*(5), 1486–1493.

18. Waldinger, R. D., & Feliciano, F. (2004). Will the new second-generation assimilate downward? Segmented assimilation re-assessed. *Ethnic and Racial Studies, 27*, 376–402.

19. Joseph, N., Watson, N. N., Wang, Z., Case, A. D., & Hunter, C. D. (2013). Rules of engagement: Predictors of black Caribbean immigrants' engagement with African American culture. *Cultural Diversity and Ethnic Minority Psychology, 19*(4), 414–423.

20. Phinney, J. S., & Ong, A. D. (2007). Conceptualization and measurement of ethnic identity: Current status and future directions. *Journal of Counseling Psychology, 54*(3), 271–281.

21. Chae, M. H., & Foley, P. F. (2010). Relationship of ethnic identity, acculturation, and psychological well-being among Chinese, Japanese, and Korean Americans. *Journal of Counseling and Development, 88*(4), 466–476; Umaña-Taylor, A. J., & Updegraff, K. A. (2007). Latino adolescents' mental health: Exploring the interrelations among discrimination, ethnic identity, cultural orientation, self esteem, and depressive symptoms. *Journal of Adolescence, 30*(4), 549–567.

22. Hovey, J. D., Kim, S. E., & Seligman, L. D. (2006). The influences of cultural values, ethnic identity, and language use on the mental health of Korean American college students. *Journal of Psychology, 140*(5), 499–511.

23. St. Louis, G. R., & Liem, J. H. (2005). Ego identity, ethnic identity, and the psychosocial well-being of ethnic minority and majority college students. *Identity: An International Journal of Theory and Research, 5*(3), 227–246.

24. Schwartz, S. J., Zamboanga, B. L., & Jarvis, L. H. (2007). Ethnic identity and acculturation in Hispanic early adolescents: Mediated relationships to academic grades, prosocial behavior, and externalizing symptoms. *Cultural Diversity and Ethnic Minority Psychology, 13*, 364–373.

25. Marsiglia, F. F., Kulis, S., Hecht, M. L., & Sills, S. (2004). Ethnicity and ethnic identity as predictors of drug norms and drug use among preadolescents in the U.S. Southwest. *Substance Use and Misuse, 39*, 1061–1094.

26. Phinney, J. S., & Ong, A. D. (2007). Conceptualization and measurement of ethnic identity: Current status and future directions. *Journal of Counseling Psychology, 54*, 271–281; Umaña-Taylor, A. J., Updegraff, K. A., & Gonzales-Backen, M. A. (2011). Mexican-origin adolescent mothers' stressors and psychosocial functioning: Examining ethnic identity affirmation and familism as moderators. *Journal of Youth and Adolescence, 40*, 140–157.

27. Kroger, J., & Marcia, J. E. (2011). The identity statuses: Origins, meanings, and interpretations. In S. J. Schwartz, K. Luyckx, & V. L. Vignoles (Eds.), *Handbook of identity theory and research* (pp. 31–53). New York: Springer.

28. Spears Brown, C. (2011). American elementary school children's attitudes about immigrants, immigration, and being an American. *Journal of Applied Developmental Psychology, 32,* 109–117.

29. Schwartz, S. J., Syed, M., Yip, T., Knight, G. P., Umaña-Taylor, A. J., Rivas-Drake, D., and Lee, R. M. Ethnic and Racial Identity in the 21st Century Study Group. (2014). Methodological issues in ethnic and racial identity research with ethnic minority populations: Theoretical precision, measurement issues, and research designs. *Child Development, 85,* 58–76.

30. Bailey, E. J. (2013). *The new face of America: How the emerging multiracial, multiethnic majority is changing the United States.* New York: Praeger.

31. Syed, M., & Azmitia, M. (2010). A narrative approach to ethnic identity in emerging adulthood: Bringing life to the identity status model. *Developmental Psychology, 44,* 1012–1027.

32. Portes & Rumbaut. (2006).

33. French, S. E., Seidman, E., Allen, L., & Aber, J. L. (2006). The development of ethnic identity during adolescence. *Developmental Psychology, 42,* 1–10.

34. Pahl, K., & Way, N. (2006). Longitudinal trajectories of ethnic identity among urban Black and Latino adolescents. *Child Development, 77,* 1403–1415.

35. Syed, M., & Azmitia, M. (2009). Longitudinal trajectories of ethnic identity during the college years. *Journal of Research on Adolescence, 19,* 601–624.

36. Rivas-Drake, D., Seaton, E. K., Markstrom, C. A., Quintana, S. M., Syed, M., & Lee, R. M. & Ethnic and Racial Identity in the 21st Century Study Group. (2014). Racial identity in childhood and adolescence: Implications for psychosocial, academic, and health outcomes. *Child Development, 58,* 40–57.

37. Spears, R., Doosje, B., & Ellemers, N. (1997). Self-stereotyping in the face of threats to group status and distinctiveness: The role of group identification. *Personality and Social Psychology Bulletin, 23,* 538–553.

38. Zane, N., & Mak, W. (2003). Major approaches to the measurement of acculturation among ethnic minority populations: A content analysis and an alternative empirical strategy. In K. M. Chun, P. B. Organista, & G. Marín (Eds.), *Acculturation: Advances in theory, measurement, and applied research* (pp. 39–60). Washington, DC: American Psychological Association.

39. Kiang, L., Yip, T., & Fuligni, A. J. (2008). Multiple social identities and adjustment in young adults from ethnically diverse backgrounds. *Journal of Research on Adolescence, 18,* 643–670; Schwartz, S. J., Unger, J. B., Zamboanga, B. L., & Szapocznik, J. (2010). Rethinking the concept of acculturation: Implications for theory and research. *American Psychologist, 65,* 237–251.

40. Arnett Jensen, L. (2008). Immigrants' cultural identities as sources of civic engagement. *Applied Developmental Science, 12*(2), 74–83.

41. Jiménez, T. R. (2011). *Immigrants in the United States: How well are they integrating into society?* Washington, DC: Migration Policy Institute.

42. Portes & Rumbaut. (2001). For some exceptions, see Portes & Rumbaut. (2006); Suárez-Orozco, C., Suárez-Orozco, M. M., & Todorova, I. (2008). *Learning a*

new land: Immigrant students in American society. Cambridge: Harvard University Press.

43. Benet-Martínez, V., & Haritatos, J. (2005). Bicultural identity integration (BII): Components and psychosocial antecedents. *Journal of Personality, 73*, 1015–1050; Chen, S. X., Benet-Martínez, V., & Bond, M. H. (2008). Bicultural identity, bilingualism, and psychological adjustment in multicultural societies: Immigration-based and globalization-based acculturation. *Journal of Personality, 76*, 803–838.

44. Rudmin, F. W. (2003). Critical history of the acculturation psychology of assimilation, separation, integration, and marginalization. *Review of General Psychology, 7*, 3–37.

45. Portes & Rumbaut. (2006).

46. Nishina, A., Bellmore, A., Witkow, M. R., & Nylund-Gibson, K. (2010). Longitudinal consistency of adolescent ethnic identification across varying school ethnic contexts. *Developmental Psychology, 46*, 1389–1401.

47. Phinney, J. S. (2003). Ethic identity and acculturation. In K. M. Chun, P. B. Organista, G. Marín (Eds.), *Acculturation: Advances in theory, measurement, and applied research* (pp. 63–81). Washington, DC: American Psychological Association; Kim, B. S. K., & Abreu, J. M. (2001). Acculturation measurement: Theory, current instruments, and future directions. In J. G. Pontcrotto, J. M. Casas, L. A. Suzuki, & C. M. Alexander (Eds.), *Handbook of multicultural counseling* (2nd ed., pp. 394–424). Thousand Oaks, CA: Sage.

48. Knight, G. P., Vargas-Chanes, D., Losoya, S. H., Cota-Robles, S., Chassin, L., & Lee, J. (2009). Acculturation and enculturation trajectories among Mexican-American adolescent offenders. *Journal of Research on Adolescence, 19*, 625–653.

49. Pew Research Center. (2010). *Public supports Arizona immigration law*. Retrieved August 4, 2011, from http://pewresearch.org/pubs/1591/public-support-arizona-immigration-law-poll; Pew Research Center. (2010). *Hispanics and Arizona's new immigration law*. Retrieved August 4, 2011, from http://pewresearch.org/pubs/1579/arizona-immigration-law-fact-sheet-hispanic-population-opinion-discrimination.

50. Kolb, E. (2009). *The evolution of New York City's multiculturalism: Melting pot or salad bowl?* Self-published through Books on Demand.

51. Park, C. C. (2011). Young children making sense of racial and ethnic differences: A sociocultural approach. *American Educational Research Journal, 48*, 387–420.

52. Spears Brown. (2011).

53. Aboud, F. E. (1984). Social and cognitive bases of ethnic identity constancy. *Journal of Genetic Psychology, 145*, 217–229.

54. Williams, J. L., Tolan, P. H., Durkee, M. I., Francois, A. G., & Anderson, R. E. (2012). Integrating racial and ethnic identity research into developmental understanding of adolescents. *Child Development Perspectives, 6*(3), 304–311.

55. Schwartz, S. J., Zamboanga, B. L., & Weisskirch, R. S. (2008). Broadening the study of the self: Integrating the study of personal identity and cultural identity. *Social and Personality Psychology Compass, 2*, 635–651.

56. Sneed, J. R., Schwartz, S. J., & Cross, W. E., Jr. (2006). A multicultural critique of Eriksonian-based research and theory: A call for integration. *Identity: An International Journal of Theory and Research, 6*, 61–84.

57. Schwartz, S. J., Kim, S. Y., Whitbourne, S. K., Zamboanga, B. L., Weisskirch, R. S., Forthun, L. F., Vazsonyi, A. T., Beyers, W., & Luyckx, K. (2013). Converging identities: Dimensions of acculturation and personal identity status among immigrant college students. *Cultural Diversity and Ethnic Minority Psychology, 19*, 155–165.

58. Schwartz, S. J., Zamboanga, B. L., Weisskirch, R. S., & Rodriguez, L. (2009). The relationships of personal and ethnic identity exploration to indices of adaptive and maladaptive psychosocial functioning. *International Journal of Behavioral Development, 33*, 131–144; Schwartz, S. J., Mason, C. A., Pantin, H., Wang, W., Brown, C. H., Campo, A. E., & Szapocznik, J. (2009). Relationships of social context and identity to problem behavior among high-risk Hispanic adolescents. *Youth and Society, 40*, 541–570.

59. Syed, M., Walker, L. H. M., Lee, R. M., Umaña-Taylor, A. J., Zamboanga, B. L., Schwartz, S. J., Armenta, B. E., & Huynh, Q.-L. (2013). A two-factor model of ethnic identity exploration: Implications for identity coherence and well-being. *Cultural Diversity and Ethnic Minority Psychology, 19*, 143–154; Usborne, E., & Taylor, D. M. (2010). The role of cultural identity clarity for self-concept clarity, self-esteem, and subjective well-being. *Personality and Social Psychology Bulletin, 36*, 883–897.

60. Umaña-Taylor, A. J., Yazedjian, A., & Bámaca-Gómez, M. Y. (2004). Developing the Ethnic Identity Scale using Eriksonian and social identity perspectives. *Identity: An International Journal of Theory and Research, 4*, 9–38.

61. Schwartz, S. J. (2001). The evolution of Eriksonian and neo-Eriksonian identity theory and research: A review and integration. *Identity: An International Journal of Theory and Research, 1*, 7–58.

62. Hammack, P. L. (2008). Narrative and the cultural psychology of identity. *Personality and Social Psychology Review, 12*, 222–247.

63. Devos & Heng. (2009); Devos & Ma. (2006).

64. Roberts, R. E., Phinney, J. S., Masse, L. C., Chen, Y. R., Roberts, C. R., & Romero, A. J. (1999). The structure of ethnic identity of young adolescents from diverse ethnocultural groups. *Journal of Early Adolescence, 19*, 301–322; Syed & Azmitia. (2009).

65. Syed & Azmitia. (2010).

66. Vignoles, V. L., Regalia, C., Manzi, C., Golledge, J., & Scabini, E. (2006). Beyond self-esteem: Influence of multiple motives on identity construction. *Journal of Personality and Social Psychology, 90*, 308–333.

67. Sellers, R. M., Copeland-Linder, N., Martin, P. P., & Lewis, R. L. (2006). Racial identity matters: The relationship between racial discrimination and psychological functioning in African American adolescents. *Journal of Research on Adolescence, 16*, 187–216; Sellers, R. M., Smith, M. A., Shelton, J. N., Rowley, S. A. J., & Chavous, T. M. (1998). Multidimensional Model of Racial Identity: A reconceptualization of African American racial identity. *Personality and Social Psychology Review, 2*, 18–39.

68. Brittian, A. S., Umaña-Taylor, A. J., Lee, R. M., Zamboanga, B. L., Kim, S. Y., Weisskirch, R. S., Castillo, L. G., Whitbourne, S. K., Hurley, E. A., Huynh, Q.-L., Brown, E. J., & Caraway, S. J. (2013). The moderating role of centrality on associations between ethnic identity affirmation and ethnic minority college students' mental health. *Journal of American College Health, 61*, 133–140.

69. Stepick, A., Dutton Stepick, C., & Vanderkooy, P. (2011). Becoming American. In S. J. Schwartz, K. Luyckx, & V. L. Vignoles (Eds.), *Handbook of identity theory and research* (pp. 867–894). New York: Springer.

70. Rumbaut, R. G. (2008). Reaping what you sow: Immigration, youth, and reactive ethnicity. *Applied Developmental Science, 12*(2), 108–111.

71. Schildkraut, D. J. (2010). *Americanism in the twenty-first century: Public opinion in the age of immigration.* Cambridge: Cambridge University Press.

72. Umaña-Taylor, A. J., Bhanot, R., & Shin, N. (2006). Ethnic identity formation during adolescence: The critical role of families. *Journal of Family Issues, 27*, 390–414.

73. Schwartz et al. (2007).

74. Umaña-Taylor, A. J., Updegraff, K. A., & Gonzales-Backen, M. A. (2011). Mexican-origin adolescent mothers' stressors and psychosocial functioning: Examining ethnic identity affirmation and familism as moderators. *Journal of Youth and Adolescence, 40*, 140–157.

75. Wei, M., Wang, K. T., Heppner, P. P., & Du, Y. (2012). Ethnic and mainstream social connectedness, perceived racial discrimination, and posttraumatic stress symptoms. *Journal of Counseling Psychology, 59*, 486–493.

76. Schwartz et al. (2013); Zamboanga, B. L., Schwartz, S. J., Jarvis, L. H., & Van Tyne, K. (2009). Acculturation and substance use among Hispanic early adolescents: Investigating the mediating roles of acculturative stress and self-esteem. *Journal of Primary Prevention, 30*, 315–333; Zamboanga, B. L., Raffaelli, M., & Horton, N. J. (2006). Acculturation status and heavy alcohol use among Mexican American college students: An investigation of the moderating role of gender. *Addictive Behaviors, 31*, 2188–2198.

77. Syed et al. (2013).

78. Kidwell, J. S., Dunham, R. M., Bacho, R., Pastorino, E., & Portes, P. R. (1995). Adolescent identity exploration: A test of Erikson's theory of transitional crisis. *Adolescence, 30*, 785–793; Schwartz, S. J., Zamboanga, B. L., Weisskirch, R. S., & Rodriguez, L. (2009). The relationships of personal and ethnic identity exploration to indices of adaptive and maladaptive psychosocial functioning. *International Journal of Behavioral Development, 33*, 131–144.

79. Rumbaut, R. G. (2008). Reaping what you sow: Immigration, youth, and reactive ethnicity. *Applied Developmental Science, 12*(2), 108–111.

80. Tummala-Narra, P., Inman, A. G., & Ettigi, S. P. (2011). Asian Indians' responses to discrimination: A mixed-method examination of identity, coping, and self-esteem. *Asian American Journal of Psychology, 2*, 205–218.

81. Huntington, S. P. (2004). *Who are we? The challenge to America's national identity.* New York: Simon and Schuster; Schildkraut. (2010).

82. Sellers, R. M., Copeland-Linder, N., Martin, P. P., & Lewis, R. L. (2006). Racial identity matters: The relationship between racial discrimination and psychological functioning in African American adolescents. *Journal of Research on Adolescence, 16,* 187–216.

83. Yoo, H. C., & Lee, R. M. (2008). Does ethnic identity buffer or exacerbate the effects of frequent racial discrimination on situational well-being of Asian Americans? *Journal of Counseling Psychology, 55,* 63–74.

84. Brittian et al. (2013).

85. Cornelius, W. (2002). Ambivalent reception: Mass public responses to the "new" Latino immigration to the United States. In M. M. Suárez-Orozco & M. M. Páez (Eds.), *Latinos: Remaking America* (pp. 165–189). Berkeley: University of California Press; Hondagneu-Sotelo, P. (2007). *Domésticas: Cleaning and caring in the shadows of affluence.* Berkeley: University of California Press.

8

Bilingualism and Language Learning

MARIELA M. PÁEZ AND CRISTINA J. HUNTER

Clara is a Spanish-speaking, U.S.-born student attending first grade in a public early childhood education center (pre-K through first grade). She lives at home with her parents and four siblings. Her parents are immigrants from El Salvador and have been in this country for more than 12 years. They are both literate in Spanish but have limited knowledge of English. Currently, only her father is employed, and given reported income levels, the family can be described as low-income. At home, Clara speaks a mix of English and Spanish, while her parents speak to her only in Spanish. She attended preschool as a four-year-old at the same school and has been learning English in this context. In kindergarten, her Spanish skills as measured by standardized assessments were similar to her English skills. By the time she got to first grade, Clara showed stronger English skills (e.g., vocabulary, word reading, and comprehension) and diminishing Spanish skills.

Clara's mother, Vilma, is very involved in the school; she attends a monthly family literacy program connecting classroom and home activities through read-alouds. As part of her participation in this program, Vilma reads in Spanish to Clara every week and has been able to create links between Spanish language use at home and English learning at school. The parents feel that it is important for their children to maintain the Spanish language for both cultural and instrumental reasons. The school follows an English-only curriculum with instructional support for bilingual students. The principal, a Spanish native speaker, makes notable efforts to connect with the families with children attending her school and provide a supportive, culturally responsive environment. The family lives in a Latino neighborhood predominantly composed of immigrants from Central and South America. The high number of immigrant parents and children in this community can be seen in different contexts such as schools, churches, and other organizations.

As in many countries around the world, immigrant-origin children in the United States are placed in the position of having to learn multiple languages in order to navigate their different social and cultural environments. Children learn and develop their language skills within these sociocultural contexts, including their experiences at home, at school, and in their wider communities. Thus, bilingualism or multilingualism develops because children are exposed to more than one language and are placed in different contexts that demand the use of these languages.[1] While exposure to more than one language is common, the process of becoming bilingual and the factors that impact second-language acquisition are very complex. As revealed in the case of Clara, there are numerous factors and contexts to consider when trying to understand the learning and development of bilingual children.

Dual-Language Learners and Pathways to Language Learning

There are numerous terms for bilingual and multilingual children used in different disciplines, with little agreement about which term best describes these students.[2] A widely used term in education and policy fields is *English-language learners* (ELL), which refers to students who speak a language other than English at home. Federal legislators and the U.S. Department of Education also use the term *limited English proficient* (LEP) to identify students who are enrolled or are about to enroll in elementary or secondary education programs and have insufficient mastery of English to meet state standards and excel in an English-language classroom.[3] An alternate term, *heritage-language speakers*, is used "to refer to a language student who is raised in a home where a non-English language is spoken, who speaks or at least understands the language, and who is to some degree bilingual in that language and in English."[4] Notably, this term is mostly used by foreign-language educators and scholars who are involved with the study, maintenance, and revitalization of non-English languages in the United States. This focus on maintenance is important given the current vulnerable state of bilingualism for immigrants and children of immigrants, who have limited opportunities and motivation to continue developing their native, or heritage, languages.

In this chapter, we use the term *dual-language learners* (DLL), which has recently emerged in the research literature on second-language acquisition, to refer to children who are learning two or more languages. Importantly, it emphasizes that some children continue to develop and learn in their first language while also learning English, as in the case of young bilingual children whose first language is not yet fully developed by the time they enter school. While all of the terms just discussed display a bias toward learning two languages, we acknowledge that multilingualism is a global phenomenon and is growing in the United States.[5]

As the number of immigrants and children of immigrants in the United States has increased, so has the number of DLL students, who are currently the fastest growing segment of the public school population.[6] According to recent statistics, the number of DLL children (ages five to 17) rose from 4.7 to 11.2 million between 1980 and 2009, showing an increase from 10 to 21 percent of the school population.[7] The DLL population is concentrated in five states (California, Texas, New York, Florida, and Illinois) that account for 64 percent of this population.[8] These large states have been dealing with the challenge of educating diverse learners for some time. However, the education of DLL students has become a national priority due to the increase of this population in all regions of the country. In fact, the National Center for Education Statistics recently started classifying its reported statistics on ELL students as referring to those being served in programs of language assistance, such as English as a Second Language (ESL) and bilingual education. With this new definition, the number of students classified as ELLs is now much smaller than the number of those who speak a language other than English at home. Data from 2010–2011 show that 10 percent, or an estimated 4.7 million students, were classified as ELLs participating in language programs in public schools.[9]

The demographic profile of DLLs and their families is complex since they come from different ethnic groups and reflect a diversity of values, beliefs, and practices as well as resources. There are more than 350 languages represented within the DLL population, but Spanish predominates, with 72 percent of students (eight million) speaking Spanish at home.[10] Even though there unquestionably is variation within this group, certain general characteristics have been noted. The majority of

DLL students are U.S.-born citizens, and a large number of them come from Spanish-speaking homes, live with families who are at or below the poverty line, live in two-parent households, have parents with low levels of formal schooling, and live in urban areas with a high concentration of DLL students.[11] Some of these demographic characteristics, such as living in two-parent households and having a family that places a high value on education, support DLL children's healthy development and learning.[12] However, these immigrant families and their children face many challenges that are primarily driven by their poverty and limited economic resources.

Most children and youth in immigrant families are considered DLL learners at some point in their lives,[13] but there are different pathways to becoming a bilingual individual. Some children (*simultaneous bilinguals*) are exposed to and given the opportunity to learn two or more languages from birth, while others (*sequential bilinguals*) are exposed to a second language after having already acquired one language.[14] This process of second-language learning can be *additive* in that children maintain their skills in their first language (L1) while learning a second language (L2), or it can be *subtractive* in that children might fail to maintain or continue to develop their first language while learning their second language.[15] However, describing the pathways to learning languages is more complex than classifying learners within these bimodal categories. Bilingualism and second-language learning are complicated processes characterized by unique pathways and developmental patterns, so learners' variable successes cannot be explained by a single factor or theory.[16]

A family's use of language at home often establishes the foundation for the process of bilingualism in immigrant-origin children and youth. Beyond the home context, these children and youth encounter school, community, and societal influences that further shape their language-learning outcomes. A current review of the research literature on developing literacy in second-language learners shows that both individual and social factors work together to facilitate second-language development.[17] In addition, recent research with DLL students demonstrates that although differences in individual student characteristics partially explain the variation in English-language-learning outcomes, social context factors are also important.[18] *Social context factors* are elements of the complex worlds in which children live that directly influence their learning outcomes by providing some with more or better opportunities and providing others with less advantageous opportunities or offering them less frequently.[19] Given the complexity of factors that can influence language learning, scholars studying second-language acquisition acknowledge the importance of utilizing a sociocultural perspective when studying language development. For example, Brisk developed a model for understanding how linguistic, cultural, economic, political, and social factors impact students directly or indirectly through schools, peers, families, neighborhoods, and media.[20] This model has not been tested empirically, but it is supported by cumulative evidence from different research studies on bilingualism and second-language development. In this chapter, we bring together knowledge and evidence from various research perspectives that emphasize different contexts and factors that are important for second-language development and learning.

Research on Bilingual Children's Language Development Across Contexts

Research on second-language development has identified individual, familial, educational, and societal factors that influence language and literacy development.[21]

Individual Factors and Developmental Trajectories

Researchers of child development and linguists have been studying developmental trajectories for DLL students and have accumulated considerable evidence about factors that account for individual differences. In fact, most researchers of DLLs acknowledge that there is substantial individual variation not just in children's rates of language acquisition but also in the profiles of learners and in their ultimate levels of attainment.[22] Individual characteristics of children that explain differences in second-language acquisition include motivation, personality, aptitude, age or cognitive maturity, and knowledge of the structure of a first language.[23] In addition to these internal factors, there is evidence of variation due to external factors such as the use of and exposure to languages and the quality of language interactions at home and at school.[24]

Even with these documented variations and the unique profiles of DLL students, the task of researchers is to find some common developmental patterns that can help us understand and support these students' learning and achievement. Thus, we turn to some of the research in the area of language and literacy that illustrates these developmental trends.

For DLLs, the development of language and literacy involves the integration of component skills such as sound-symbol awareness, grammatical knowledge, and vocabulary knowledge as well as more elusive sociocultural variables critical to the development of reading and writing.[25] Bilingual learners can and do develop second-language literacy while they are acquiring second-language oral proficiency. Furthermore, the oral, reading, and writing skills of a bilingual learner interact, creating complex relationships of mutual support.[26] We also know from DLL children's developmental trajectories that these students do not approach native-speaker proficiency in all linguistic domains at the same pace.[27] For example, longitudinal developmental studies have found that DLL students develop word-decoding skills at the same rate that monolingual peers of the same age do, while they may lag behind in other areas of language acquisition such as vocabulary.[28]

Although most language and literacy studies have been conducted with Spanish-speaking populations, comparative research with diverse bilingual populations has found similar patterns of developmental differences across domains. For example, research comparing Hebrew-English, Spanish-English, and Chinese-English bilingual students with English monolingual students has shown that bilinguals have an advantage in skills such as phonological awareness but also have vocabulary deficits.[29] In addition, this line of comparative research has also demonstrated bilinguals' potential for transferring knowledge from one language to the other, especially when the languages share linguistic characteristics such as similar writing systems (e.g., the Spanish and English alphabets).

These studies of DLLs' language and literacy development make several important points. First, they offer considerable evidence that uneven development is common for DLLs, especially during early childhood. This evidence demonstrates that not all DLLs develop in the same way; certain domains of language and literacy progress at different rates given different learning conditions. However, most of these studies focused on bilingual children from low socioeconomic backgrounds, so it is not clear how much of the language gap experienced by DLL children is due to their socioeconomic backgrounds or their dual-language exposure.[30] The limited research on dual-language learners from high socioeconomic backgrounds indicates that these children catch up to monolingual norms during the elementary grades and that some even exceed their monolingual peers' achievement in English.[31] Finally, the majority of research has been conducted with Spanish-speaking DLL students, so our knowledge of diverse language groups is limited.

From a different research perspective, psycholinguists' studies of second-language acquisition have focused on the relationship between cognitive skills and bilingualism. Research conducted by Ellen Bialystok and colleagues has established a foundation for examining how particular aspects of cognitive functioning such as executive functioning develop more rapidly in children who have bilingual experiences. These studies tend to be cross-sectional and employ a comparative design— that is, they compare monolingual and balanced bilingual (i.e., those who are equally adept in both languages) students to examine differences in cognitive skill that can be attributed to one group's bilingualism.[32] This line of research is promising as more studies are exploring the link between bilingualism and important cognitive skills such as attention and inhibitory control.[33] However, methodological issues limit the conclusions that can be drawn from this body of research, including the lack of representation of different immigrant and language groups, the low number of longitudinal studies that examine developmental patterns, and the varied definitions and measures of bilingual status. More research is needed in order to better understand the applications of these findings to diverse populations of bilinguals and immigrant-origin children and youth.

Researchers have also investigated the social-emotional development of DLL students. A review of recent studies in this area focused on key social-emotional developmental constructs such as attachment, social competence, social cognition, emotion regulation, and behavior regulation in early childhood DLLs.[34] In sum, findings suggest that fluent bilingualism provides social-emotional benefits. Fluent bilingual Spanish speakers demonstrate stronger task-orientation and instruction-following skills than monolingual students.[35] Bilingual children also display greater sociolinguistic awareness[36] and self-control, though some also display more behavioral problems.[37] Similar to limitations found in studies of the cognitive development of DLL children, however, methodological concerns limit the conclusions of and potential for generalizing these study findings. Importantly, the authors of the review note that there is not enough research to disentangle the associations between bilingualism and these skills given the powerful effect of socioeconomic status and other less studied factors such as immigrant status and heritage culture. Moreover, the review stresses the need for additional research focused on social-emotional development to better understand the impact of language on this area. In particular, studies should investigate the long-term effects of early social and linguistic experiences on social-emotional outcomes such as attachment and regulation.

In sum, research with DLLs demonstrates the importance of individual and developmental factors in understanding bilingualism. In particular, research establishes the critical role of language and literacy development for DLLs while also identifying this area as particularly challenging for some DLLs, such as Spanish-speaking students from low-socioeconomic backgrounds. Research also shows the importance of considering bilingualism when studying cognitive and socioemotional development. However, research on how bilingualism or multilingualism influences different developmental domains has been limited. We know more about what influences language and literacy development than what influences other areas of growth in DLL children. In addition to individual developmental factors, we need to consider contextual factors related to the home and classroom environments.

The Role of Family and Home Language Experiences

Research stemming from child language and sociolinguist perspectives demonstrates the powerful contributions of family and home environments to children's language and early literacy development. Studies have shown that achieving school literacy is a much easier task for children from homes with certain characteristics, such as parents who model literacy activities, the availability of a wide range of reading materials, frequent joint book-reading and discussions of the books, and rich verbal exchanges.[38] The relationship of parental talk and the home language and literacy environment to child outcomes has been documented for diverse populations, even at the earliest stages of literacy acquisition. For example, children growing up in homes where they hear more parental talk have larger productive and receptive vocabularies.[39] In addition, differences in the quantity and quality of exposure to language have been found to correlate with certain demographic characteristics of the home such as the mother's level of education[40] and socioeconomic background.[41] However, the majority of this research base has been developed with studies of English-only students. What about DLL children? Children who are growing up in bilingual environments might encounter different degrees of exposure to and different qualities of language and literacy experiences in their homes.[42]

Studies of DLL students have confirmed the importance of the home language and literacy environment in predicting outcomes for these students, specifically Latino children. Findings demonstrate that Latino family home resources and parental involvement are significant predictors of kindergartners' early literacy skills.[43] Furthermore, a review of studies on the influence of family-based factors in Latino families found evidence indicating that early literacy experiences in the home supported subsequent literacy development in school for this population.[44] In addition, research has shown that low-income Spanish-speaking children tend to have relatively meager early literacy experiences at school and at home. Although Latino parents want to help their children succeed academically,[45] especially in the earliest stages of schooling, these children's home environment may not provide optimal conditions for literacy enhancement, such as parents who have time to read with children and can provide a wide range of text-based materials and activities.[46]

Findings from studies with second-language learners that investigated the influence of parents and families support three conclusions: (1) language-minority families are willing and often are able to support their children academically; (2) home literacy experiences are generally associated with superior literacy outcomes, but findings are not consistent; and (3) there are mixed correlation findings in the relationship between home language use and literacy outcomes—thus, some studies showed a positive association between bilingual home language use and literacy and other studies showed a negative association.[47] Research has identified a number of important social and cultural characteristics that foster variability of literacy experiences in home contexts.[48] A number of family factors that have been identified include socioeconomic status (SES), parental education and literacy levels, and home support for literacy development.[49] However, more research is needed to determine the influence of other factors on literacy. For example, we know very little about the effect of immigration status and experience, commitment to maintaining the first language, language loss, parental literacy in either the first or second language, or parental resources and cultural capital for selecting particular educational programs.

The Role of Schooling and Language Instruction

Most of the research and policy attention to DLLs has centered on the role of schools and on promoting academic achievement for these students (see Marks, Seaboyer, and García Coll, "Academic Achievement," chapter 13 in this volume). Successfully educating DLL students is a major challenge throughout the United States given their increasing number and risk for low academic achievement. National data have consistently shown that DLL students are performing at rates below those of non-DLL students, particularly in the areas of reading and math. Results from the 2009 National Assessment of Educational Progress (NAEP) indicate that DLL fourth graders scored 36 points below non-DLLs in reading and 24 points below them in math. The gaps between DLL and non-DLL eighth graders were even larger, with gaps of 47 points in reading and 42 points in math between the achievements of the two groups. Data for twelfth-grade students during the same year (2009) showed a persistent gap between the two groups, with DLLs scoring 50 points below non-DLLs in reading and 38 points below them in math. These are considerably large gaps and even larger than the differences reported for poverty, as evidenced in the scores of students eligible for free or reduced-price lunches.[50]

The academic vulnerability of the DLL population, including an achievement gap demonstrated in national assessments and other academic outcomes such as increased high school dropout rates and low college attendance, has been documented for several years.[51] Thus, educators, researchers, and policy makers have emphasized the urgency of addressing the needs of these learners, particularly those from Spanish-speaking backgrounds, who make up the largest DLL population in the United States. Research and policy efforts have focused on increasing DLLs' English-language skills and proficiency as a means of improving their academic achievement. Indeed, a focus on language is important since knowledge of English is necessary not only for performing well on national academic tests but also for successfully navigating the contexts of school, community, and the broader society.

In fact, school contexts can significantly impact outcomes for DLLs and second-language learning. Variation in instructional approaches and language programs can result in different language proficiency achievements of children and youth. Across the United States, there are different types of programs serving students who speak a language other than English at home. These broadly fall in two categories: programs that provide instruction only in English and those that involve instruction in two languages.[52] The availability of these programs and opportunities to enroll in them are determined by state and local policies. In California, Arizona, and Massachusetts, program options are limited due to an existing ban on the use of immigrant children's primary language for instruction. Other states' educational policies allow for more options, which have resulted in more variety in educational programs.

A key issue in the education of DLL students is the language used for instruction in different program models. The most prevalent include English-only programs, transitional bilingual programs, and two-way bilingual language programs. Four major reviews of scientific studies have concluded that students in bilingual programs typically score higher on tests of English than children in all-English immersion programs do.[53] Among language approaches in bilingual education, two-way bilingual programs are emerging as an effective and increasingly common method for addressing the needs of DLL students.[54] Although there is growing evidence that bilingual and first-language instruction is as effective as English immersion, these educational programs remain controversial.[55] Moreover, there is dissension between the findings on effective program models and practices and the current policies of educational systems across the nation.[56]

In addition to research on program models, there is a body of research that addresses instructional strategies and interventions with

DLL students. A recent review of instructional factors that improve DLL students' academic achievement synthesizes the findings in three major points.[57] First, evidence strongly supports the use of immigrant-origin students' first language for teaching reading since such use promotes high levels of reading achievement in English. Second, techniques that constitute good instruction and an effective curriculum for learners in general (such as employing a combination of direct, interactive, and collaborative teaching approaches or teaching foundational skills for promoting literacy) are important for DLL students. However, these strategies and curriculum approaches need to be modified in order to be effective for DLL students. This conclusion is the third major research finding—instruction for DLLs must take into account their language skills and limitations.

Further research is needed to assess the impact of new policies and programs on the education of DLLs. In addition, the majority of studies have been conducted with students in early elementary grades; only a handful have surveyed students at the secondary level. In fact, there has not been much research on language instruction of DLL students at opposite ends of the educational spectrum—early childhood grades and high school. Additional research is also needed on special populations within the DLL category, such as newcomers (immigrants who have recently arrived in this country) and students whose formal schooling has been interrupted.

The Role of Community, Language Status, and Prestige

In addition, the process of learning a second language can vary according to the context of the community, including the status of a language and the particular characteristics of a language. Differentiating between a majority-minority ethnolinguistic community is important because it determines the types of opportunities or forms of exposure that children have in particular settings.[58] For example, in the United States, individuals may be exposed to frequent and varied input in English since it is spoken by most members of the larger community. In addition, the prevalence of English use in the community can also affect individuals' motivation for and attitudes about learning that language. A less studied and yet equally important area of influence on second-language development is the role of societal factors, both cultural and institutional, that frame the influence of elements in more proximal contexts such as individual, family, and school. Students are socialized within these proximal contexts that are part of broader sociocultural conditions within which they learn how to communicate, behave, and relate according to cultural norms and expectations. Research demonstrates the influence of factors such as different status levels of languages, attitudes toward different ethnic groups, social integration, and social and educational adjustment on second-language development.[59] The most recent review identified a small number of studies investigating the influence of language status and prestige on first- and second-language literacy development; however, the research base in this area is limited, so the review was not able to draw firm conclusions.[60] Among the studies included, there was evidence of the impact of language status on achievement through its effect on self-concept, motivation, and/or learning opportunities.[61] Another area of this review considered the influence of policies at the district, state, and federal levels, suggesting that policies that value more than one language can minimize the negative effects of DLL status on student outcomes.

Most of the research in this area stems from a sociocultural perspective and includes case studies and ethnographies, which are difficult to summarize and are often excluded from research syntheses. Examples of this type of research include studies of the adaptation of Asian Indian immigrants in the United States,[62] descriptions of Puerto Rican community cultural and language socialization patterns,[63] and the school and language experiences of Mexican American students.[64] This line of research is very valuable as it provides a rich, descriptive, qualitative account of language learning for particular DLL groups. More attention should be paid to this research as it could inform the practices and policy that can support DLLs' school readiness and academic achievement.

Cultural and societal factors are critical influences on second-language learning and development. While some researchers argue for stronger evidence to ascertain the influence of specific factors with empirical links, what would be more beneficial to the field is to acknowledge the importance of these factors and to investigate how they shape and interact with factors across other contexts. More research is needed in this area to expand the knowledge base for particular groups of DLLs and also to provide more empirical evidence to understand sociocultural factors related to community, language status, and prestige. Special consideration should be given to factors relevant to immigrant children and youth, such as the dynamic nature of language preference, the importance of language maintenance, the impact of language policies on home practices and school environments, and information about new and emerging immigrant communities.

Future Research Directions

Cutting across disciplines are several themes for future research with immigrant-origin children and youth and their development across contexts. This chapter has focused on DLLs and research on second-language development, highlighting areas for further investigation. Additional research is needed to advance understanding of how individual, family, school, and community factors impact DLL students' language and literacy development. Studies need to take into account interactions among factors as well as mediating effects driven by socioeconomic backgrounds and other immigrant-related experiences. Longitudinal studies that track different developmental pathways according to the quantity and quality of an individual's exposure to different languages—while controlling for other important factors related to the home and school environment—would significantly contribute to the research literature. Similarly, we need a better understanding of how knowing or learning more than one language impacts a child's functioning and/or development across domains such as cognitive skills, socioemotional development, and computational skills.

Several exemplary research studies conceptualize language as one of multiple factors that impact immigrant-origin children's and youth's adaptation to and achievement in school. For example, research by Carhill, Suárez-Orozco, and Páez[65] has increased our understanding of factors that account for academic English-language proficiency in a group of adolescent first-generation-immigrant students from China, the Dominican Republic, Haiti, Central America, and Mexico. Findings from this study support conceptualizing social context factors as well as individual and home factors as variables that affect second-language learning. Similarly, the program of research by Suárez-Orozco and

Suárez-Orozco[66] represents a model for the type of investigation that is needed in the field. These scholars approach the study of immigrant youth from a longitudinal multidisciplinary perspective, taking into account individual, family, and school factors pertinent to this population. These research programs also contribute to the literature by investigating diverse groups of bilingual and multilingual students, including speakers of languages other than Spanish. More research is needed on immigrant children and youth from different language groups such as Chinese, Filipino, Hindi, and Vietnamese, which are the top languages of immigrant groups entering the United States after Spanish. Additional research in these areas would result in a more comprehensive understanding of second-language development and learning, which in turn could support the overarching goal of providing effective educational programs that promote school readiness, academic achievement, and success for all immigrant-origin students.

NOTES

1. Menyuk, P., & Brisk, M. (2005). *Language development and education: Children with varying language experiences*. Basingstoke, UK: Palgrave Macmillan; McCabe, A., Tamis-LeMonda, C. S., Bornstein, M. H., Cates, C. B., Golinkoff, R. M., Hirsh-Pasek, K., Hoff, E., Kuchirko, Y., Melzi, G., Mendelsohn, A., Páez, M., Song, L., Wishard Guerra, A. (2014). Multilingual children: Beyond myths towards best practices. *SRCD Policy Report, 27*(4), 1–21.

2. Garcia, O., Kleifgen, J. A., & Falchi, L. (2008). *From English language learners to emergent bilinguals*. New York: Campaign for Educational Equity. Retrieved June 3, 2012, from http://www.equitycampaign.org/i/a/document/6468_Ofelia_ELL__Final.pdf.

3. No Child Left Behind (NCLB) Act of 2001, Pub. L. No. 107-110, § 115, Stat. 1425 (2002).

4. Valdés, G. (2001). Heritage language students: Profiles and possibilities. In J. K. Peyton, D. A. Ranard, & S. McGinnis (Eds.), *Heritage languages in America: Preserving a national resource* (pp. 37–77). Washington, DC: Center for Applied Linguistics / Delta Systems.

5. McCabe et al. (2014).

6. Aud, S., Hussar, W., Kena, G., Bianco, K., Frohlich, L., Kemp, J., & Tahan, K. U.S. Department of Education, National Center for Education Statistics. (2011). *The Condition of Education 2011* (NCES 2011-033). Washington, DC: U.S. Government Printing Office.

7. Ibid.

8. Capps, R., Fix, M., Murray, J., Ost, J., Passel, J., & Herwantoro, S. (2005). *The new demography of America's schools: Immigration and the No Child Left Behind Act*.

Washington, DC: Urban Institute. Retrieved June 1, 2012, from http://www.urban.org/url.cfm?ID=311230.

9. Aud et al. (2011).

10. Ibid.

11. Capps et al. (2005); Garcia et al. (2008); National Center for Children in Poverty. (2007). *Low-income children in the United States: National and state trend data, 1996–2006*. New York. Retrieved June 1, 2012, from http://www.nccp.org/publications/pdf/text_761.pdf.

12. Castro, D. C., Espinosa, L., & Páez, M. M. (2011). Defining and measuring quality in early childhood practices that promote dual language learners' development and learning. In M. Zaslow, I. Martinez-Beck, K. Tout, & T. Halle (Eds.), *Quality measurement in early childhood settings* (pp. 257–280). Baltimore: Paul H. Brookes.

13. García, E. E., Jensen, B. T., & Scribner, K. P. (2009). The demographic imperative. *Educational Leadership, 66*(7), 8–13.

14. Paradis, J., Genesee, F., & Crago, M. B. (2011). *Dual language development and disorders: A handbook on bilingualism and second language learning* (Vol. 11). Baltimore: Paul H. Brookes.

15. Lambert, W. E. (1981). Bilingualism and language acquisition. In H. Winitz (Ed.), *Native language and foreign language acquisition* (pp. 9–22). New York: Academy of Science.

16. Snow, C. (1992). Perspectives on second-language development: Implications for bilingual education. *Educational Researcher, 21*(2), 16–19; Fillmore, L. W. (1991). When learning a second language means losing the first. *Early Childhood Research Quarterly, 6*(3), 323–346.

17. August, D., & Shanahan T. (Eds.) (2006). *Developing literacy in second-language learners: Report of the National Literacy Panel on Language-Minority Children and Youth*. Mahwah, NJ: Lawrence Erlbaum.

18. Brisk, M. (2006). *Bilingual education: From compensatory to quality schooling* (2nd ed.). Mahwah, NJ: Lawrence Erlbaum; Goldenberg, C., Rueda, R., & August, D. (2006). Sociocultural influences on the literacy attainment of language-minority children and youth. In D. August & T. Shanahan (Eds.), *Developing literacy in second-language learners: Report of the National Literacy Panel on Language-Minority Children and Youth* (pp. 269–318). Mahwah, NJ: Lawrence Erlbaum; Lightbown, P., & Spada, N. (2006). *How languages are learned*. Cambridge: Cambridge University Press.

19. Goldenberg et al. (2006).

20. Brisk. (2006).

21. August & Shanahan. (2006).

22. Ibid.

23. Paradis et al. (2011); Tabors, P. (2008). *One child, two languages: A guide for early childhood educators of children learning English as a second language* (2nd ed.). Baltimore: Paul H. Brookes.

24. Paradis et al. (2011).

25. Castro, D. C., Páez, M. M., Dickinson, D. K., & Frede, E. (2011). Promoting language and literacy in young dual language learners: Research, practice and policy. *Child Development Perspectives, 5*(1), 15–21.

26. Brisk, M. E., & Harrington, M. M. (2007). *Literacy and bilingualism: A handbook for all teachers* (2nd ed.). Mahwah, NJ: Lawrence Erlbaum.

27. Paradis et al. (2011).

28. Oller, D. K., Pearson, B. Z., & Cobo-Lewis, A. B. (2007). Profile effects in early bilingual language and literacy. *Applied Psycholinguistics, 28,* 191–230; Páez, M., Tabors, P. O., & López, L. M. (2007). Dual language and literacy development of Spanish-speaking preschool children. *Journal of Applied Developmental Psychology, 28*(2), 85–102; Mancilla-Martinez, J., & Lesaux, N. K. (2011). The gap between Spanish speakers' word reading and word knowledge: A longitudinal study. *Child Development, 82*(5), 1544–1560.

29. Bialystok, E., Luk, G., & Kwan, E. (2005). Bilingualism, biliteracy, and learning to read: Interactions among languages and writing systems. *Scientific Studies of Reading, 9,* 43–61.

30. For a detailed discussion of DLLs and SES, see Hoff, E. (2012). Interpreting the early language trajectories of children from low-SES and language minority homes: Implications for closing achievement gaps. *Developmental Psychology, 49*(1), 4–14.

31. Umbel, V. M., Pearson, B. Z., Fernández, M. C., & Oller, D. K. (1992). Measuring bilingual children's receptive vocabularies. *Child Development, 63,* 1012–1020; Castro, Paez, Dickinson, & Frede. (2011).

32. Bialystok, E. (1999). Cognitive complexity and attentional control in the bilingual mind. *Child Development, 70*(3), 636–644; Bialystok, E. (2001). *Bilingualism in development: Language, literacy and cognition.* Cambridge: Cambridge University Press; Bialystok, E., & Martin, M. M. (2004). Attention and inhibition in bilingual children: Evidence from the dimensional change card sort task. *Developmental Science, 7*(3), 325–229; Bialystok, E., Martin, M. M., & Viswanathan, M. (2005). Bilingual across the lifespan: The rise and fall of inhibitory control. *International Journal of Bilingualism, 9*(1), 103–119.

33. Carlson, S. M., & Meltzoff, A. N. (2008). Bilingual experience and executive functioning in young children. *Development Science, 11*(2), 282–298.

34. Center for Early Care and Education Research—Dual Language Learners (CECER-DLL). (2011). *Research brief #7: Social-emotional development in dual language learners: A critical review of the research.* Chapel Hill: University of North Carolina, FPG Child Development Institute.

35. Han, W. (2010). Bilingualism and socioemotional well-being. *Children and Youth Services Review, 32,* 720–731; Han, W., & Huang, C. C. (2010). The forgotten treasure: Bilingualism and Asian children's emotional and behavioral health. *American Journal of Public Health, 100*(5), 831–838.

36. Cheung, H., Mak, W. Y., Luo, X., & Xiao, W. (2010). Socio-linguistic awareness and false belief in young Cantonese learners of English. *Journal of Experimental Child Psychology, 107,* 188–194.

37. Dawson, B. A., & Williams, S. A. (2008). The impact of language status as an acculturative stressor on internalizing and externalizing behaviors among Latino/a children: A longitudinal analysis from school entry through third grade. *Journal of Youth and Adolescence, 37*, 399–411.

38. Snow, C., Burns, M. S., & Griffin, P. (Eds.). (1998). *Preventing reading difficulties in young children.* Washington, DC: National Academy Press.

39. Hart, B., & Risley, B. (1995). *Meaningful differences in the everyday experience of young American children.* Baltimore: Paul H. Brookes.

40. Hoff-Ginsberg, E. (1991). Mother-child conversation in different social classes and communicative settings. *Child Development, 62*(4), 782–796.

41. Hoff, E., Laursen, B., & Tardiff, T. (2002). Socioeconomic status and parenting. In M. H. Bornstein (Ed.), *Handbook of parenting* (2nd ed., pp. 231–252). Mahwah, NJ: Lawrence Erlbaum.

42. De Houwer, J. (2009). Implicit measures: A normative analysis and review. *Psychological Bulletin, 135*(3), 347–368; Parra, M., Hoff, E., & Core, C. (2011). Relations among language exposure, phonological memory, and language development in Spanish-English bilingually developing 2-year-olds. *Journal of Experimental Child Psychology, 108*(1), 113–125.

43. Lin, Q. (2003). *Parent involvement and early literacy.* Cambridge: Harvard Family Research Project. Retrieved June 1, 2012, from http://www.hfrp.org/publications-resources/publications-series/family-involvement-research-digests/parent-involvement-and-early-literacy?print=1.

44. Reese, L., Garnier, H., Gallimore, R., & Goldenberg, C. (2000). Longitudinal analysis of the antecedents of emergent Spanish literacy and middle-school English reading achievement of Spanish-speaking students. *American Educational Research Journal, 37*(3), 633–662.

45. Goldenberg, C. (1987). Low-income Hispanic parents' contributions to their first-grade children's word-recognition skills. *Anthropology & Education Quarterly, 18*(3), 149–179.

46. Delgado Gaitan, C. (1991). Involving parents in the schools: A process of empowerment. *American Journal of Education, 100*(1), 20–46.

47. August & Shanahan. (2006).

48. Delgado Gaitan (1991); Gallimore, R., & Goldenberg, C. (1993). Activity settings of early literacy: Home and school factors in children's emergent literacy. In E. Forman, N. Minick, & C. A. Stone (Eds.), *Contexts for learning: Sociocultural dynamics in children's development* (pp. 315–335). New York: Oxford University Press.

49. Snow, C. (2006). Cross-cutting themes and future research directions. In D. August & T. Shanahan (Eds.), *Developing literacy in second-language learners: Report of the National Literacy Panel on Language-Minority Children and Youth* (pp. 269–318). Mahwah, NJ: Lawrence Erlbaum.

50. Aud et al. (2011).

51. Education Week editors. (2012). Latinos' school success: A work in progress. *Education Week, 31*(34). Retrieved June 1, 2012, from http://www.edweek.org/ew/

articles/2012/06/07/34execsum.h31.html?intc=EW-DC12-TOC; National Center for Education Statistics. (2012). *The condition of education 2012* (NCES 2012-045, Table A-33-1). Washington, DC: U.S. Department of Education. Retrieved June 1, 2012, from http://nces.ed.gov/fastfacts/display.asp?id=16.

52. Francis, D., Lesaux, N. K., & August, D. (2006). Language of instruction. In D. L. August & T. Shanahan (Eds.), *Developing literacy in second-language learners: Report of the National Literacy Panel on Language-Minority Children and Youth* (pp. 365–410). Mahwah, NJ: Lawrence Erlbaum.

53. Francis et al. (2006); Genesse, F., Lindolm-Leary, K., Saunders, W., & Christian, D. (2005). English language learners in U.S. schools: An overview of research. *Journal of Education for Students Placed at Risk, 10*(4), 363–385; Slavin, R., & Cheung, A. (2005). A synthesis of research of reading instruction for English language learners. *Review of Educational Research, 75*(2), 247–284; Rolstad, K., Mahoney, K., & Glass, G. (2005). The big picture: A meta-analysis of program effectiveness research on English language learners. *Educational Policy, 19*(4), 572–594.

54. Barnett, W. S., Yarosz, D. J., Thomas, K. J., & Blanco, D. (2007). Two-way and monolingual English immersion in preschool education: An experimental comparison. *Early Childhood Research Quarterly, 22,* 277–293; Howard, E. R., Sugarman, J., & Christian, D. (2003). *Trends in two-way immersion education: A review of the research (Report 63)*. Baltimore: Center for Applied Linguistics, CRESPAR/Johns Hopkins University. Retrieved June 13, 2012, from http://www.csos.jhu.edu/crespar/techReports/Report63.pdf.

55. Barnett et al. (2007).

56. Garcia et al. (2008).

57. Goldenberg, C. (2008). Teaching English language learners: What research does and does not say. *American Educator, 8*(23), 42–44.

58. Paradis et al. (2011).

59. For a review, refer to Brisk. (2006).

60. Goldenberg et al. (2006).

61. Ibid.

62. Gibson, M. A. (1988). *Accommodation without assimilation: Sikh immigrants in American high school*. Ithaca: Cornell University Press.

63. Zentella, A. C. (1997). *Growing up bilingual*. Malden, MA: Blackwell; Espinosa, L., Laffey, J., & Whittaker, T. (2006). *Language minority children analysis: Focus on technology use*. Final report. Washington, DC: CREST/NCES.

64. Valdés. (2001).

65. Carhill, A., Suárez-Orozco, C. & Páez, M. (2008). Explaining English language proficiency among adolescent immigrant students. *American Educational Research Journal, 45,* 1155–1179.

66. Suárez-Orozco, C., & Suárez-Orozco, M. M. (2001). *Children of immigration*. Cambridge: Harvard University Press; Suárez-Orozco, C., Suárez-Orozco, M. M., & Todorova, I. (2008). *Learning a new land: Immigrant students in American society*. Cambridge: Harvard University Press.

9

Child Language Brokering

MARJORIE FAULSTICH ORELLANA AND SHU-SHA ANGIE GUAN

Estephanie is the youngest of three children. Her father had moved to the United States from Mexico before she was born; her mother and older siblings had remained in Mexico for several years until her father secured a green card and earned enough money to send for them. Eventually, the family reunited in San Diego, where Estephanie was born. As a result, Estephanie was the only child in the family who had U.S. citizenship status.

Because Estephanie was the youngest in her family, she had fewer household responsibilities than her older siblings, who were expected to cook, clean, and watch over her while their parents were at work. But she helped her family with myriad everyday tasks, including many things that required English-language skills: making and answering phone calls, scheduling appointments, reading the mail, researching information on the Internet, filling out forms, and speaking on behalf of her parents to teachers, doctors, store personnel, and people on the street. Most of her friends did the same for their immigrant families, though Estephanie never really talked with them about this work; it was just something you did to help your family.

When Estephanie was young, she would sometimes accompany her father on trips to visit family and friends in Mexico City. Her siblings were not able to cross the border, so Estephanie's citizenship status gave her privileges within the family. It also provided her with opportunities to maintain and strengthen her Spanish-language abilities and supplied a measure of protection when she served as the family translator in public spaces. After all, the fact that her family needed help translating marked them as immigrants, and they were uncomfortable speaking in public themselves, even after they had mastered some degree of English, because they spoke with heavy accents.

Immigrant families face many challenges as they settle in their new homelands. They must adjust to new social, cultural, and linguistic contexts. Some move from rural areas to urban centers; many leave behind their extended family support systems; for some, even their nuclear families are split across national borders, as Estephanie's was for a time. They send their children to schools that have different schedules, curricula, expectations, and values than schools in their home country did. They take jobs that make new demands on them and their family time. They may be subjected to evaluation and judgment by teachers, doctors, social workers, store personnel, and even strangers on the street—exposed by their accents, phenotype, need for translation, or cultural values, practices, and beliefs.

To meet the demands of life in a new locale, many immigrants rely on their children's help. They do so because children often have skills and knowledge that adults do not have—the ability to speak English without a marked accent and an understanding of how things are done in this country that they acquire through their experiences in school. Additionally, because many immigrants bring collectivist cultural orientations that emphasize interdependent social ties and participation in the maintenance of the household,[1] parents may *expect* children to help with family needs. Thus, in immigrant households, children are often called on to leverage their linguistic, cultural, social, and pragmatic knowledge in order to help their families as they navigate life in a new land.

In this chapter, we explore how immigrant families organize to accomplish the tasks of everyday life, with a particular eye to the work that children do as language and culture brokers for their families. We focus on this practice of *language brokering* because it is ubiquitous in immigrant communities, consequential for youth development, and integrated into many everyday household tasks as families adjust to life in a new cultural, social, and linguistic environment. It is a dimension of more general forms of family obligation such as caring for siblings, running errands, and taking care of household responsibilities since many of those tasks involve speaking, reading, and writing in English. It both shapes and is shaped by families' cultural values, beliefs, and norms, and it both shapes and is shaped by particular family dynamics.

At the outset, it is important to emphasize that immigrant families vary on many dimensions. These include family size and composition, length of U.S. residence, educational experiences, social class background, citizenship status, and access to social, cultural, financial, legal, material, and linguistic resources, among many other factors. All of these variations matter for everyday living and for how household tasks in general and language-brokering work in particular are distributed in families. We must keep these variations in mind as we consider how families organize as they "settle" in their new homelands and how language brokering shapes youth development. In general, it is important to note that immigrant families tend to be more multigenerational than nonimmigrant families are, including having more extended family members in residence. They share caregiving responsibilities among a greater number of people, and this distribution matters for household responsibilities and language-brokering work.

Language and Culture Brokering

Let us return to the portrait of Estephanie that we sketched in the opening vignette in order to examine more closely her experiences as a language broker and consider how this language-brokering work was set within the context of other household responsibilities as well as how it changed over time in relation to other aspects of Estephanie's development. We discuss this case in relation to what we know about a wide range of language-brokering experiences and household responsibilities on the basis of our interviews with many immigrants of different ages and detailed observations of immigrant families in several contexts over long periods of time.[2]

First, we can see from Estephanie's experiences how language brokering is integrated into other family settlement processes and how it both shapes and is shaped by family dynamics as these unfold in relation to particular tasks, situations, and contexts. The practice can change over time as families' needs and circumstances change and as family members develop, learn new things, have new experiences, and take on new challenges. Estephanie, who was 19 and a second-year college student when we interviewed her, told us that when she was a child, she initially viewed the translation/interpretation work she did for her parents "like a game." She found it fun when she was asked "simple things like 'How do you say this?'" She was happy to help her family, proud that she could speak two languages, and pleased with the attention she received. Much of her work involved "everyday" things that did not feel very hard to do.

But as Estephanie got older and "knew more," some language-brokering work became more frustrating, anxiety provoking, and burdensome. More often, she was asked to handle things on her own rather than to work with her older siblings. She was also asked to do more public and difficult translation work, not just everyday things at home. This work exposed her to the public eye and made her feel that her immigrant family was being judged for the ways they did things; anti-immigrant (and especially anti-Mexican) sentiment was growing in her community, so the larger sociopolitical context also colored her experiences.

Estephanie also had to deal with a few "crisis" situations. She described one difficult situation that she managed as a young teen:

> Five years ago, maybe seven years ago, [my father] fell at work and something from the ladder—they had to like remove it. It was a really important surgery. So whatever a letter said, we had to really understand. So there would be—they would ask my sister, and when she wouldn't do it, they would ask me. And when there were words I didn't understand, they would go back to my sister. Like a single word could be crucial to the case[;] that's why we made sure we understood everything. . . . I felt more pressure to get it right. . . . Or even when I translated, I felt like I wasn't doing well enough—like, what if they understood it differently than what I explained? So I would go to Google and translate the word to Spanish.

This is the kind of language-brokering situation that has drawn a good deal of attention in the news media; it is a high-pressure scenario with potential consequences for the health and well-being of Estephanie's father and for his understanding of his situation and his rights as a patient. As Estephanie noted, in encounters such as this one, even the mistranslation of a single word could matter—or, at the very least, participants may *feel* that it mattered and feel responsible for anything that went wrong. (It is important to note that most everyday translation involves texts with redundancy and paralinguistic and contextual cues that allow participants many ways of understanding the meaning even when individual words are unknown. But these factors do not eliminate the burdens that language brokers may experience.)

We see from Estephanie's description of this encounter, however, that she did not act alone; she collaborated with her sister. Often language brokering, like other household work, is shared in families, and parents as well as siblings pool their linguistic, social, and cultural knowledge to accomplish the tasks at hand.[3] Indeed, many parents both speak and understand some English; they call on their children to *assist* with brokering language but not necessarily to *do* it all by themselves. This action is consistent with larger cultural values of collectivity and interdependence. Thus, the ages of family members and the composition of the family can affect the degree of support that language brokers can muster for their work. Eldest children in immigrant families generally carry more of the burden—as well as reap the potential benefits—of language brokering. However, as we can see in Estephanie's case, who is selected as "designated family translator" may depend on many things, including perceptions of the child's abilities, their willingness to help, and their citizenship status. Gender may also be a factor in terms of who is expected to translate for whom in particular tasks and activities.

Generally, language brokering is just a part of larger tasks that the family accomplishes as a collective: filling out forms; researching information on the Internet; reading and making sense of financial, legal, medical, instructional, political, and educational documents; helping siblings with homework; and more. Estephanie noted that she drew support from online resources when dealing with her father's work accident. Access to the Internet and knowledge of how to navigate it can make a big difference for family translators as they search for information to help their families navigate a new land. Youth often broker technology even as they broker language and culture.[4]

How Language Brokering Shapes Youth Development

Given the many variations of language-brokering practices as well as other intertwined family characteristics such as citizenship status and language ability that are evident in Estephanie's vignette, it is perhaps no wonder that many different "effects" of language brokering have been noted by developmental psychologists and educational researchers. Language brokering demands many cognitive, linguistic, social, cultural, and pragmatic skills and strategies, and the experience of performing these tasks may in turn sharpen children's competencies. On the other hand, the practice can involve high-pressure situations that may seem burdensome to youth. Some researchers have argued that the practice can expose young people to information beyond their years and create "role reversal" in families by giving children too much power. In this section, we consider some of the potential developmental implications of language brokering for immigrant youth as well as research evidence for such outcomes.

Socioemotional Development. Many studies investigating language brokering have asked questions about the positive or negative effects on youth's socioemotional development, seeking "global" effects of the practice. Researchers have found a relationship between language brokering and depression,[5] adolescent stress,[6] and internalizing symptoms[7] or depression.[8] But brokering can provide opportunities for youth to build not only relationships with their parents[9] but also their ethnic identities, given the importance of social and linguistic interactions with and in relation to others in identity formation processes.[10] Higher levels of and more positive feelings about language brokering have been linked to higher levels of ethnic identity, or one's sense of belonging and commitment to one's ethnic group.[11] And language brokering is related to *biculturalism*, the involvement and comfort felt with both heritage and host cultures.[12] A possible explanation for this result is that language brokering encourages the maintenance of ties to heritage cultural practices as well as to the heritage language.

Language brokering also appears to enhance youths' understanding of other people and other cultures. On the basis of ethnographic research, Orellana built the case for how language brokering may shape the development of *transcultural dispositions*—psychosocial competencies such as keen reading of social cues, the ability to see the world through the perspective of others (perspective taking), and flexibility in understanding and using language for particular audiences and cultures. More recently, brokering for parents has been associated with transcultural perspective-taking capacities (being able to understand different cultural perspectives), and brokering for others (other family members, teachers, and friends) has been associated with empathic concern, a component of empathy.[13]

As the body of research on language brokering has grown, we have developed much more nuanced understandings of its socioemotional impact. As we saw in Estephanie's case, some translation situations can be stressful, but not all are; and the burdens that Estephanie experienced were shared with family members. There were also other stressors on her family—their mixed citizenship status, for example—that were intertwined with the need for language brokering, a situation that would make it difficult to tease out just what aspects of family life actually "caused" any negative outcomes. Other factors are the general acculturative stress that immigrants have been shown to experience and the particular ways in which this stress may affect children.[14]

Qualitative evidence makes clear that brokering situations in which families' health, well-being, and financial or legal security are threatened are stressful for children—as they would most likely be for anyone of any age. Estephanie has distinct memories of the time when she had to translate for her father's operation. Hall and Sham describe similar anxiety expressed by a child broker who had to interpret between his father, a restaurant owner, and an agent of the Health and Safety Environment Department. The teen reported "shaking with fright" as his dad told him not to answer the agent's questions for fear they would lose their restaurant.[15] Reynolds and Orellana discuss the pain that children experienced when they translated in places where their families were viewed in racist and xenophobic ways.[16] Similarly, Guske describes the pressure that immigrant youth in Germany experienced in medical, financial, and legal situations and how this feeling was aggravated when parents did not realize how difficult translation could be.[17]

Intergroup differences that have been found in some quantitative studies also bear consideration. Chao, for example, found that translating for mothers and fathers predicted higher levels of internalized symptoms (depression-anxiety, somatic complaints, and withdrawal symptoms) among Chinese and Korean American ninth graders from eight high schools in Los Angeles. But she found no association between translating for parents and psychological symptoms among Mexican American adolescents.[18] Chao speculates that these ethnic differences may be due either to culturally specific views about children's contributions to family functioning or to study limitations (i.e., small sample size). However, there may be other reasons for ethnic differences: how particular groups are viewed in particular contexts may color children's experiences of language brokering, as evidenced in studies of Arabic[19] and Korean American youth.[20]

Within-group differences have also been identified. Among Mexican American adolescents, for example, Love and Buriel found that brokering for greater numbers of people was associated with higher levels of depression.[21] However, Mexican American adolescent girls who had brokered in more places and had reported having been given more responsibilities within the family had lower levels of depression. The authors suggest that because girls from traditional immigrant families often have less status and independence within the family, language brokering may boost the girls' status and affect their lives in ways that it might not for boys. This supposition accords with research on the developmental effects of more general forms of family "helping" behaviors and the factors that lead to positive outcomes such as youths' ability to find meaning and value in their work.[22]

More recent research suggests that there are factors that can mitigate the negative effects that may be associated with some language-brokering experiences. This research also locates language brokering within the complex dynamics of immigrant family settlement processes and considers the nuanced and multifaceted effects of the practice on children and their families. Suárez-Orozco and Suárez-Orozco, for example, note that the financial, legal, and emotional stability of the post-migration family environment can vary greatly, a situation that in turn influences all family processes.[23]

Feelings about Brokering. Most, if not all, language brokers likely encounter some stressful and anxiety-provoking situations such as the one Estephanie detailed. But for some youth, these experiences are relatively few and do not color their overall view of the practice. Youth vary in how they feel about their language-brokering experiences, just as they vary in their views of household responsibilities, with some reporting overall positive feelings and others reporting decidedly negative ones.[24] For the most part, young children seem to feel that language brokering is "just normal" or "just something you do to help your family."[25]

Views about language brokering also seem to change as youth grow older. There may be several reasons for this development. First, adolescents and young adults may be asked to broker in more complicated circumstances than younger children are, as Estephanie noted. They may be expected to translate in more contentious situations and exposed to racism and xenophobia. Developmentally, they may be more aware of their own ethnic identifications and of how they and their families are being viewed in these public encounters. They may also begin to compare their own experiences with those of other youth. This comparison may change their understandings of their own family processes, and they may come to regard what they once considered "just normal" as somehow deviant, nonnormative, and *wrong*.[26]

Research indicates that young people who associate negative feelings such as anger, anxiety, shame, embarrassment, nervousness, pressure, fear, and discomfort with their language-brokering experiences are more likely to have lowered self-esteem and to engage in adolescent substance use than youth who report feeling good about their experiences are.[27] Perhaps youth who associate negative feelings with language brokering have indeed *had* more negative experiences performing it. Or perhaps they have had more brokering experiences overall.

However, as we saw in Estephanie's case, not all language brokering involves high-stress situations, and not all youth shoulder heavy burdens of language brokering. There is both qualitative and quantitative evidence that children garner pride from being able to help their families, build understanding, and acquire resources for their families and others. Children's engagement in prosocial behaviors may also produce payoffs in terms of the development of prosocial competencies and other competencies that may serve them in future educational, service, and employment domains.

Mitigating Negative Effects. As the body of research on language brokering has grown, it has begun to illuminate factors that may either exacerbate or mitigate the potential negative effects of language brokering on youth. Qualitative research has led to a more nuanced understanding of the practice and facilitated the exploration of more complex models of its impact on youth development. Quantitative research has moved toward assessing indirect as well as direct relationships. Consequently, we have a deeper understanding of how context matters in language brokering.

First, as we saw in Estephanie's case, language brokering is generally a *family* practice—one that is distributed among siblings and in which parents participate alongside their children.[28] It is part of a larger set of household responsibilities and is shaped by the dynamics of family relationships as well as by the general levels of stress that the household may experience. If there is tension in family relationships, that tension may both shape and be exacerbated by language-brokering activities. Research suggests that when there is trust and support from parents and others in youths' social networks, potentially stressful situations may not be experienced as being so burdensome.[29] Greater warmth within the parent-child relationship may also be protective, and there is evidence that higher levels of parent-child bonding are associated with more positive feelings about brokering.[30] Work by Hua and Costigan suggests that frequent language brokering may be more strongly associated with poor psychological outcomes for children who perceive their parents as being highly psychologically controlling (i.e., who use coercive methods to ensure obedience).[31] And problematic family relationships in which children report not enjoying time spent with their family, not being able to depend on family members, or feeling annoyed by them have been linked to more negative feelings about language brokering.[32] These negative relational outcomes may also be explained by parental behaviors associated with language brokering such as praise or criticism.[33]

Some researchers have suggested that families' levels of *acculturation*—or their familiarity with their new cultural context—need to be considered when examining the effects of language brokering on youth development. Families with little local cultural knowledge may both need and demand more language brokering from their children.[34] Lower levels of acculturation can lead to increased acculturative stress; work by Kam suggests that this increase may be linked to children's negative feelings about brokering and higher rates of risky behaviors.[35] It is important to remember, however, that family contexts in which greater language brokering is needed—that is, those in which both parents speak very limited English and have little knowledge of the local culture—are also associated with greater levels of immigration stress, occupational stress, parental depression, and lower parental involvement.[36] Having to function within these types of high-stress family contexts may be one explanation of why youth who broker more frequently report having poorer psychological well-being.

Immigrant-origin children's own cultural value orientations can also moderate the relationship between brokering and negative outcomes. In one of the few longitudinal studies on language brokering, Wu and Kim found that adolescents in the United States who had a strong sense of family obligation (a cultural value orientation that emphasizes prioritizing, respecting, and helping one's family) reported having an increased sense of mattering to their parents, which in turn was associated with a higher sense of competency and lower rates of perceiving language-brokering activities as burdensome.[37] Hua and Costigan's research on adolescents in Canada provides a different perspective; these researchers found that children who endorsed higher family obligation values were more likely to internalize symptoms at higher brokering frequencies.[38] What these seemingly contradictory findings about the indirect effects on different outcomes suggest is that a sense of family obligation can help youth experience a greater sense of mattering to their parents but that this strong sense of responsibility to others may also create self-imposed pressures that affect their psychological well-being.

Finally, qualitative evidence points to families' different ways of supporting children in their work as language brokers. When language brokering is a shared experience—with the family pooling its linguistic, cultural, and social knowledge to accomplish the work—not only are the burdens on children lessened, but learning and development may be enhanced as well.

Cognitive and Linguistic Development. There is growing evidence that language brokering can be beneficial in terms of linguistic and cognitive growth. Malakoff and Hakuta suggest that children's rule-governed code-switching during language brokering is evidence of their metalinguistic awareness of the nature and nuances of different languages.[39] To broker effectively, children must assess the mode and message in one language and decide on the most appropriate way to convey that information in the second language. This task demands—and thus develops—metalinguistic processing. Qualitative analyses of how children handle different kinds of language-brokering circumstances make evident the linguistic, social, cultural, and pragmatic demands of the tasks.[40] This situation was evident in Estephanie's case, in which such competencies were perhaps also facilitated as family members worked together to make sense of information and convey it to others.

Virtually no quantitative research has explored the direct links between language brokering and linguistic or cognitive development, but some research has pointed to academic payoffs. Buriel and colleagues, for example, found that higher levels of language brokering were associated with higher self-reported grades.[41] In an extension of this study, Acoach and Webb found that language brokering had a direct effect on academic self-efficacy (i.e., a sense of one's competency in school), and this result in turn had a direct effect on the grade point average of high school students.[42] Dorner and colleagues found that when compared with nonbrokers, fifth graders who were active language brokers scored higher on standardized reading and math tests, even after controlling for early test scores.[43]

Changing Family Dynamics

As we have argued throughout this chapter, language and culture brokering are part of a larger set of family obligations that immigrant youth are often called on to engage in as their families navigate life in a new land. Children may also have to assist with household tasks (cleaning, cooking, running errands) or to participate in sibling care. They may feel obliged to help their families out in many ways, including by leveraging their linguistic and cultural skills.

Most research on the impact of language brokering on child development has been with populations who may be said to come from "collectivist" cultures in which children are *expected* to contribute to the family good. Thus, families may regard their children's participation as family language brokers in the postmigration stage as an extension of home cultural practices now placed in a new context rather than as a changed family dynamic. Families may *expect* youth to contribute to the collective good, and children too may—at least initially—see this situation as "just normal."

At the same time, some of the specific demands of language brokering may be new ones for youth to shoulder as their families reorganize to meet the demands of living in a new land. And changes in family processes in and of themselves likely put stress on families, a development that in turn can heighten the stress children experience doing this work. Moreover, youth have to navigate both their families' expectations of them and the assumptions that teachers and other authority figures have about what children should be allowed or be expected to do.

Implications for Policy and Practice

In this chapter, we have examined the work that children do as language and culture brokers for their immigrant families as their families organize to accomplish the tasks of daily life in a new country. We have surveyed research on the varied and multidimensional effects that this practice has on youth development. The impact of the practice is also influenced by many factors both specific to language brokering (i.e., the supports available and ways in which children experience the activities) and more general to family dynamics.

Immigrant-origin children's work as language brokers is a specialized dimension of their more general contributions to household settlement processes. Children play an important role in most immigrant households because their skills and labor are *needed* for survival. Further, many immigrants endorse obligations to family as an important cultural value, so children are *expected* to contribute their language and cultural skills for the good of the collective.

Teachers, social workers, and other professionals often express concern about the possible negative effects of language brokering on child development. Our review of the literature helps to complicate the discussion as we consider what children learn from the practice as well as how it may impact them socially and emotionally. Understanding how the practice can be *both* beneficial *and* burdensome may help practitioners and policy makers support youth and mitigate against the worst effects. After all, whether or not we think children "should" be doing these things, they *will* be doing so because their skills are both needed and expected and because language brokering is part and parcel of the immigrant settlement process. But *how* they participate—and how others support them in that work—can matter greatly for their own learning and development. It behooves educators, social workers, psychologists, and others who are concerned about youth development to carefully consider how to support children and families in immigrant communities so that the most damaging effects of this practice are mitigated and its benefits enhanced.

NOTES

1. Fuligni, A. J., Tseng, V., & Lam, M. (1999). Attitudes toward family obligations among American adolescents with Asian, Latin American, and European backgrounds. *Child Development, 70*, 1030–1044; Greenfield, P. M. (2009). Linking social change and developmental change: Shifting pathways of human development. *Developmental Psychology, 45*, 401–418; Triandis, H. C., & Suh, E. M. (2002). Cultural influences on personality. *Annual Review of Psychology, 53*, 133–160.

2. Orellana, M. F. (2009). *Translating childhoods: Immigrant children, language, and culture.* New Brunswick: Rutgers University Press.

3. Eksner, J., & Orellana, M. F. (2012). Shifting in the zone: Latina/o child language brokers and the co-construction of knowledge. *Ethos, 40*(2), 196–220.

4. Bacigalupe, G., & Parker, K. Transnational connections through emerging technologies. (Chapter 3, this volume); Katz, V. S. (2014). *Kids in the middle: How children of immigrants negotiate community interactions for their families.* New Brunswick: Rutgers University Press; Katz, V. S. (2010). How children of immigrants use media to connect their families to the community: The case of Latinos in South Los Angeles. *Journal of Children and Media, 4*, 298–315.

5. Love, J. A., & Buriel, R. (2007). Language brokering, autonomy, parent-child bonding, biculturalism, and depression: A study of Mexican American adolescents from immigrant families. *Hispanic Journal of Behavioral Sciences, 29*, 472–491.

6. Jones, C. J., & Trickett, E. J. (2005). Immigrant adolescents behaving as culture brokers: A study of families from the former Soviet Union. *Journal of Social Psychology, 145*, 405–427; Kam, J. A. (2011). The effects of language brokering frequency and feelings on Mexican-heritage youth's mental health and risky behaviors. *Journal of Communication, 61*, 455–475.

7. Chao, R. K. (2006). The prevalence and consequences of adolescents' language brokering for their immigrant parents. In M. H. Bornstein & L. R. Cote (Eds.), *Acculturation and parent-child relationships: Measurement and development* (pp. 271–296). Mahwah, NJ: Lawrence Erlbaum.

8. Love & Buriel. (2007).

9. Chao. (2006).

10. Bucholtz, M., & Hall, K. (2005). Identity and interaction: A sociocultural linguistic approach. *Discourse Studies, 7*, 585–614; Phinney, J. S. (1989). Stages of ethnic identity development in minority group adolescents. *Journal of Early Adolescence, 9*, 34–49.

11. Weisskirch, R. S. (2005). The relationship of language brokering to ethnic identity for Latino early adolescents. *Hispanic Journal of Behavioral Sciences, 27*, 286–299; Weisskirch, R. S., & Alatorre, S. A. (2002). Language brokering and the acculturation of Latino children. *Hispanic Journal of Behavioral Sciences, 24*, 369–378.

12. Acoach, C. L., & Webb, L. M. (2004). The influence of language brokering on Hispanic teenagers' acculturation, academic performance, and nonverbal decoding skills: A preliminary study. *Howard Journal of Communications, 15*(1), 1–19; Buriel, R.,

Perez, W., De Ment, T. L., Chavez, D. V., & Moran, V. R. (1998). The relationship of language brokering to academic performance, biculturalism, and self-efficacy among Latino adolescents. *Hispanic Journal of Behavioral Sciences, 20*(3), 283–297; Love & Buriel. (2007); Tse, L. (1996). Language brokering in linguistic minority communities: The case of Chinese- and Vietnamese-American students. *Bilingual Research Journal, 20*, 485–498.

13. Guan, S. A., Greenfield, P. M., & Orellana, M. F. (2014). Translating into understanding: Language brokering and prosocial development in emerging adults from immigrant families. *Journal of Adolescent Research, 29*(3), 331–355.

14. García Coll, C. T., & Magnuson, K. (1997). The psychological experience of immigration: A developmental perspective. In A. Booth (Ed.), *Immigration and the family: Research and policy on US immigrants* (pp. 91–131). Hillsdale, NJ: Lawrence Erlbaum.

15. Hall, N., & Sham, S. (2007). Language brokering as young people's work: Evidence from Chinese adolescents in England. *Language and Education, 21*, 16–30.

16. Reynolds, J. F., & Orellana, M. F. (2009). New immigrant youth interpreting in white public space. *American Psychologist, 111*, 211–223.

17. Guske, I. (2010). Familial and institutional dependence on bilingual and bicultural go-between-effects on minority children. *MediAzioni, 10*. Retrieved from http://mediazioni.sitlec.unibo.it.

18. Chao. (2006).

19. Nash, A. (2012, May). "When I open the door to my parents' house, I enter the door to a whole new world": The context of language brokering among Arab American youth. Paper presented at the First International Conference on Non-Professional Interpreting and Translation NPITI. Forli, Italy.

20. Kwon, H. (2013). The hidden injury of class in Korean-American language brokers' lives. *Childhood, 0*, 1–16.

21. Love & Buriel. (2007).

22. Fuligni, A. J., Yip, T., & Tseng, V. (2002). The impact of family obligation on the daily activities and psychological well-being of Chinese American adolescents. *Child Development, 73*(1), 302–314; Juang, L. P., & Cookston, J. T. (2009). A longitudinal study of family obligation and depressive symptoms among Chinese American adolescents. *Journal of Family Psychology, 23*(3), 396–404; Telzer, E. H., & Fuligni, A. J. (2009). Daily family assistance and the psychological well-being of adolescents from Latin American, Asian, and European backgrounds. *Developmental Psychology, 45*, 1177–1189.

23. Suarez-Orozco, C., & Suarez-Orozco, M. (2001). *Children of immigration.* Cambridge: Harvard University Press.

24. Morales, A., & Aguayo, D. (2010). Parents and children talk about their language brokering experiences: The case of a Mexican immigrant family. *MediAzioni, 10*, 215–238.

25. Cline, T., De Abreu, G., O'Dell, L., & Crafter, S. (2010). Recent research on child language brokering in the United Kingdom. *MediAzioni, 10*, 105–124; Weisskirch, R. S., Kim, S. Y., Zamboanga, B. L., Schwartz, S. J., Bersamin, M., & Umaña-Taylor, A. J.

(2011). Cultural influences for college student language brokers. *Cultural Diversity and Ethnic Minority Psychology, 17*(1), 43–51.

26. For a discussion, see Orellana. (2009).

27. Kam. (2011); Weisskirch, R. S. (2006). Emotional aspects of language brokering among Mexican American adults. *Journal of Multilingual and Multicultural Development, 27*(4), 332–343; Weisskirch, R. S. (2007). Feelings about language brokering and family relations among Mexican American early adolescents. *Journal of Early Adolescence, 27*(4), 545–561.

28. Eksner & Orellana. (2012).

29. Hall & Sham. (2007); Love & Buriel. (2007).

30. Buriel, R., Love, J. A., & De Ment, T. D. (2006). The relation of language brokering to depression and parent-child bonding among Latino adolescents. In M. H. Bornstein & L. R. Cote (Eds.), *Acculturation and parent-child relationships: Measurement and development* (pp. 249–270). Mahwah, NJ: Lawrence Erlbaum.

31. Hua, J. M., & Costigan, C. L. (2012). The familial context of adolescent language brokering within immigrant Chinese families in Canada. *Journal of Youth and Adolescence, 41*, 894–906.

32. Weisskirch. (2007).

33. Guan, S. A., & Shen. J. (2014, March 15). Language brokering and parental praise and criticism among young adults from immigrant families. *Journal of Child and Family Studies.* 1–9.

34. Jones & Trickett. (2005); Jones, C. J., Trickett, E. J., & Birman, D. (2012). Determinants and consequences of child culture brokering in families from the former Soviet Union. *American Journal of Community Psychology, 50*, 182–196; Weisskirch & Alatorre. (2002).

35. Kam. (2011).

36. Martinez, C. R., McClure, H. R., & Eddy, J. M. (2009). Language brokering contexts and behavioral and emotional adjustment among Latino parents and adolescents. *Journal of Early Adolescence, 29*, 71–98.

37. Wu, N. H., & Kim, S. Y. (2009). Chinese American adolescents' perceptions of the language brokering experience as a sense of burden and sense of efficacy. *Journal of Youth and Adolescence, 38*(5), 703–718.

38. Hua & Costigan. (2012).

39. Malakoff, M., & Hakuta, K. (1991). Translation skill and metalinguistic awareness in bilinguals. In E. Bialystok (Ed.), *Language processing in bilingual children* (pp. 141–166). Cambridge: Cambridge University Press.

40. García-Sánchez, I. M. (2010). (Re)shaping practices in translation: How Moroccan immigrant children and families navigate continuity and change. *MediAzioni, 10*, 182–214; Hall & Sham. (2007); Harris, B., & Sherwood, B. (1978). Translating as an innate skill. In D. Gerver & H. Sinaiko (Eds.), *Language, interpretation, and communication.* New York: Plenum; Orellana, M. F. (2001). The work kids do: Mexican and Central American immigrant children's contributions to households and schools in California. In Immigration and education. Special issue of *Harvard*

Educational Review, 71(3), 366–389; Orellana, M. F., Dorner, L., & Pulido, L. (2003). Accessing assets: Immigrant youth's work as family translators or "para-phrasers." *Social Problems, 50*(4), 505–524; Reynolds & Orellana. (2009).

41. Buriel et al. (1998).

42. Acoach & Webb. (2004).

43. Dorner, L. M., Orellana, M. F., & Li-Grining, C. P. (2007). I helped my mom, and it helped me: Translating the skills of language brokers into improved standardized test scores. *American Journal of Education, 113*(3), 451–478.

PART III

Developmental Outcomes

MONA M. ABO-ZENA AND AMY K. MARKS

Returning to our central framing question of how immigrant-origin children and youth are similar to or different from other child and youth populations, this last section considers developmental outcomes. Just as the contexts and processes central to the developing immigrant child are varied in their nature and properties, so too are the outcomes of immigrant youth's development. Outcomes—typically measured as health and educational statuses—are potent and vital markers of the well-being of the immigrant youth population. Researchers have long tracked physical health, academic success (or failure), and the behavioral and mental health of immigrant families, sometimes with startling results. Since at least the 1930s, researchers have documented one such surprising group-level trend: a paradox in outcomes among immigrants.[1] The *immigrant paradox* posits that it is the newest immigrants who have the best outcomes. For decades, many newcomer immigrants have had the lowest rates of infant mortality, the healthiest body mass indexes (BMIs), and the lowest rates of delinquency and have attained the highest levels of education when compared with their more acculturated (or U.S.-born) same-ethnicity peers. This trend is paradoxical because at the same time that newcomer youth are faring well in these key developmental outcomes, they are also more likely to reside in the poorest neighborhoods and households and to attend schools with the fewest resources.

Most importantly, there are many nuances in and exceptions to the immigrant paradox patterns in immigrant-origin children's and youth's health, behavior, and education. Such variations exist across cultural and gender groups and by developmental age range. Each of the authors in this section of the book tackles the challenging task of depicting the nuanced variability within and among cultural groups on a variety of key outcomes. Some research lends support to an immigrant paradox pattern in areas of health and behavior, whereas others do not. It is in examining these differences that we can and should refer back to the contexts and processes that frame this book to seek new directions in order to understand why some immigrant-origin children thrive while others struggle or fail.

When considering child and adolescent development, it is important to ponder the question "Developmental toward what end or ends?"[2] The chapters in this section explicitly delineate what immigrant-origin children and adolescents are developing toward. The chapters also draw on the contexts and processes discussed in the previous sections in order to highlight *how* these children and youth are challenged by and supported in achieving these developmental ends. In this section, we offer insights into the developmental experiences of highly diverse immigrant-origin children, providing a contrasting perspective to the "normative" standard for development—White middle-class children.[3]

Considering the most fundamental of developmental outcomes, Robert Crosnoe, Aida Ramos-Wada, and Claude Bonazzo in chapter 10 explore the physical health of immigrant children and youth. In particular, they seek to understand the unique health considerations and paradoxes in the physical health of immigrant youth. School and community medical professionals serve an immigrant child and youth population that is increasingly diverse in its languages, cultures, and religions. This chapter provides an overview of the ways in which acculturation shapes the physical health and development of these immigrant children. The authors particularly investigate the ways in which contextual variability according to race, socioeconomic status, gender, and culture of origin intersect with receiving communities to promote or challenge the optimal growth of immigrant children and youth.

In a study closely related to immigrant-origin children's and youth's physical health, in chapter 11, Pratyusha Tummala-Narra expands the focus to include their mental health and clinical issues. The mental health field is currently at a crossroads when it comes to serving and supporting immigrant-origin families. There is a rapidly growing need for behavioral health services for immigrant families, while at the same time there is a call for practitioners to become culturally "competent" enough to meet the unique needs of these diverse families. Chapter 12 examines the barriers to optimal mental health treatment and outcomes, including problems with access to care, the cultural stigmatizing of mental health disorders, and practitioners' common misunderstandings of their clients' cultural contexts. For professionals, the chapter outlines the most current standards of care related to case conceptualization and treatment adaptation.

Both physical and mental health outcomes are often associated with other behavioral outcomes, particularly risk behaviors. In chapter 12, Hoan N. Bui outlines how research on the behavioral outcomes of immigrant children and youth has uncovered many important developmental considerations involving race, country of origin, and socioeconomic status. This chapter reviews the current data and findings available from large, nationally representative studies of immigrant-origin children's and adolescents' risk-taking behaviors. Data on family, school, and neighborhood contexts informs a discussion of the ways in which settings interact with immigrant-origin youth to either promote or protect immigrant children and adolescents from developing behavior problems.

One of the most common reasons parents give for migrating to the United States is to provide their children with a better life. For most parents, this means enrolling their children in the U.S. public education system. In chapter 13, Amy K. Marks, Lourah M. Seaboyer, and Cynthia García Coll discuss the tremendous variations in the academic achievement of immigrant children and youth. This chapter reviews the current state of research on academic achievement, considering immigrant children's and youth's performance on standardized test scores as well as their graduation outcomes, academic engagement and aspirations, school involvement or sense of belonging, and peer processes. The authors draw from research conducted with national data as well as from studies attending to variability in racial, ethnic, and socioeconomic status related to immigrant children's and youth's achievement.

Beyond family and school contexts, the ways in which immigrant youth are integrated into and civically engaged in U.S. society have implications not only for their own well-being but also for the kind of civil society we will become during the coming decades. In chapter 14, Lene Arnett Jensen and Justin Laplante explore questions and answers regarding the outcome of civic involvement of immigrant youth. Research on the civic engagement of immigrant-origin youth has been conspicuously sparse. While some contemporary media reports have claimed that immigrants represent a threat to U.S. civil society because of their alleged divided loyalties, a growing body of evidence suggests that such fears may be misplaced. For example, Latino and Asian immigrant youth demonstrate a pattern of being highly engaged in civic activities in ways that researchers using traditional measures have not considered—such as translating for others, serving as advocates, and working to register voters. Chapter 14 discusses the important roles that factors such as immigrant generation, authorization status, language fluency, socioeconomic status, religiosity, and country of origin as well as current sociopolitical debates play in influencing immigrant youth's civic engagement.

NOTES

1. Marks, A. K., Ejesi, K., & García Coll, C. (2014). The U.S. immigrant paradox in childhood and adolescence. *Child Development Perspectives, 8*(2), 59–64.

2. Rogoff, B. (2003). *The cultural nature of human development*. New York: Oxford University Press.

3. Spencer, M. B. (2006). Phenomenology and ecological systems theory: Development of diverse groups. In W. Damon & R. M. Lerner (Eds.), *Handbook of child psychology: An advanced textbook* (pp. 829–893). Hoboken, NJ: Wiley.

10

Paradoxes in Physical Health

ROBERT CROSNOE, AIDA RAMOS-WADA, AND
CLAUDE BONAZZO

> Rosa was a mother who participated in a study I conducted in Texas on
> the connection between early health and learning among the children of
> Mexican immigrants. She had a four-year-old son enrolled in a public pre-K
> program and was intensely focused on providing the best care for him and
> offering him all of the opportunities she could so that he could have a better
> life. Rosa was also poor, had little education, and was uncomfortable speak-
> ing English. She had no access to health insurance through her sporadic job
> as a housecleaner, and because of the immigration-related enrollment re-
> strictions the state had put in place in the wake of welfare reform, she was
> not eligible for federal health programs such as Medicaid. Consequently, her
> child had limited access to quality health care other than emergency rooms
> and received little, if any, preventative well-child care.[1]

In many ways, Rosa's family is typical of the Mexican immigrant population and the broader immigrant population in the United States. Poverty
rates are high among immigrant families, but they are underrepresented
in the caseloads of health and human services for low-income families.[2]
This combination is a recipe for children's poor health. However, Rosa's
son, while suffering from more health illnesses (such as colds and ear
infections) than many of the White, African American, and Latino/a
children at his pre-K did, was certainly not in poor health overall. More
broadly, the health outcomes of immigrant children are often much
better than expected given their circumstances, a situation that gives
credence to the notion of an immigrant paradox in health.[3] This paradox
idea was originally based on data showing that Latin American immigrants in the United States have a life expectancy that is much closer to
(and perhaps even higher than) that of U.S.-born Whites despite their

having socioeconomic profiles much closer to (and even lower than) those of U.S.-born African Americans.[4] More and more, the paradox is becoming a frame for studying immigrants' health much earlier in their life course.

This chapter reviews the evidence from social science and medical research that sheds light on this potential immigrant paradox in health—when, where, and for whom it holds or does not apply. In doing so, two important points need to be kept in mind. First, the existence of the paradox does not necessarily mean that immigrants are doing better than everyone else. Rather, it means that they are doing better than their social and economic positions suggest that they should be. Second, the paradox may apply in general but not hold in specific domains of health for certain subgroups or at certain life stages. The health literature is so voluminous that it cannot be reviewed in its entirety. Instead, this chapter is more selective in its coverage. In line with the developmental and ecological spirit of this book, a particular health topic has been chosen to highlight what is occurring in major periods of the early life course and to demonstrate how physical, social, and cultural forces and contexts intersect to strengthen or weaken the immigrant paradox around this topic. Specifically, the chapter focuses on infant mortality, childhood illness and disease, and adolescent health behavior, giving additional attention to a topic that cuts across life stages: obesity.

Infant Mortality

One powerful tool for gauging the general well-being of a population is its infant mortality rate. At the beginning of life, the immigrant paradox is quite striking, just as it is at the end of life. The *infant mortality rate* refers to the number of babies born in the United States (per 1,000 births) who die before their first birthday. Most deaths occur within the first hours or days after birth. The overall rate for the United States is about six deaths per 1,000 births. The rate for Whites, the most socioeconomically advantaged and powerful racial/ethnic group in the country, is about five deaths per 1,000 births. The rate for African Americans, historically the most disadvantaged and disenfranchised group, is much higher, at around 13 deaths per 1,000 births. Thus, racial/ethnic disparities in infant mortality are quite striking. Just as striking, however, are immigration-related disparities within and across racial/ethnic groups.[5]

Within all major racial/ethnic groups in the United States, the children of foreign-born parents have lower infant mortality rates than do the children of native-born parents. Within both the Latino/a and White populations, this difference equals about one death per 1,000 births, a very large disparity. Within the African American population, it is much larger, nearly four deaths. Among Asian Americans it is smallest, around half a death. Moreover, the surprisingly low rate of infant mortality among Latino/as in the United States—one of the most often cited examples of the immigrant paradox—is almost solely accounted for by the large proportion of immigrants within the Latino/a population. In other words, the overall low rate of Latino/a infant mortality can be attributed to the strong infant health among first-generation Latino/a immigrant families. Again, the paradox for immigrants in general and Latin American immigrants in particular reflects a disconnect between their socioeconomic statuses (a *macro context* in ecological terms) and infant mortality rates. Socioeconomic disadvantage is the best predictor of infant mortality, and immigrants tend to be more socioeconomically disadvantaged than their U.S.-born counterparts. Therefore, infant mortality should be higher among immigrants than among natives, and it should be higher in racial/ethnic groups with greater proportions of immigrants. However, neither of these expectations happens to be true.[6]

One major factor in this paradox is *immigrant selectivity*, a social phenomenon that reflects macro- and micro-level immigration contextual processes.[7] Within any given country, those who leave for the United States differ from those who do not; hence, the former are more selective. They may themselves be healthier or have other characteristics that promote health in their children. For example, some families may come from community settings with established connections to migratory routes and social capital that may facilitate their overall well-being during migration. Consequently, any health advantages of immigrants in the United States could merely reflect differences in what brought them to this country and what kept others in their home countries from emigrating. Immigrant selectivity does indeed account for a large portion of the immigrant paradox, but it does not completely explain it. Similarly, immigrants may return to their home countries in times of sickness and distress, so some deaths may not show up in U.S. records. Although an important component of the immigrant paradox is overall mortality, this explanation does little to illuminate the immigrant paradox in infant mortality. Instead, contextual factors are at work, many having to do with family life and the broader cultures of immigrant communities. When immigrant mothers are compared with their native-born counterparts (within and across racial/ethnic groups), they tend to have better health behavior while pregnant (e.g., avoiding smoking and drinking and maintaining better nutrition) and can draw on stronger networks of social support. Thus, a combination of migration trends at the population level and ecological resources at the individual level likely explains why the health of immigrant babies in the United States defies the odds.

Illness and Disease in Childhood

Does the immigrant paradox in infancy extend into childhood? Birth outcomes largely depend on the health behavior of mothers and on children's congenital issues, but childhood introduces new problems in the form of infectious illnesses—acute problems such as ear infections, gastrointestinal sickness, and colds; serious problems such as flu and pneumonia; and chronic issues such as asthma. Although such illnesses can strike anywhere across the life span, they are particularly significant in childhood because children are increasingly exposed to new pathogens in their everyday ecologies while their immune systems are developing. Moreover, childhood health outcomes are strongly related to health-care utilization, and the majority of immigrant families have limited access to such care.[8]

Unfortunately, less is known about immigration-related disparities in childhood illnesses than about health statuses in infancy (or later, health behaviors in adolescence). In part, the relative dearth of evidence reflects data limitations. Many large-scale health studies do not have young children in their samples, or if they do, the studies do not allow immigrants to be readily identified. At the same time, many large-scale studies that include young immigrant children in their samples provide only limited information on health. Some work, however, has been conducted in this area, and it provides mixed support for the existence of the immigrant health paradox during this developmental stage.

Evidence from the Early Childhood Longitudinal Study–Kindergarten Cohort (ECLS-K), an education-focused national study of elementary school students, indicates that children with immigrant parents suffer more physical health problems (including acute illnesses such as ear infections) during their transition into formal schooling than children from nonimmigrant families of the same race or ethnicity do. These disparities are primarily explained by the socioeconomic disadvantages of immigrant families, but they persist despite socioeconomic controls for children from Latin American immigrant families. They stand in stark contrast to disparities in *mental* health, which significantly favor the children of immigrants. However, these patterns should not be interpreted too simplistically. The physical health patterns could reflect the underrepresentation of Latino/a immigrant children in child-care centers and preschools, which would delay peer exposure to pathogens. The mental health patterns could reflect underreporting due to racial/ethnic and immigration-related differences in stigma and stress. Still, these results are telling relative to the clear trend toward immigrant health advantages in the infant-mortality literature discussed previously.[9]

Findings from community studies often echo this national pattern. In a sample from Southern California, the children of Mexican immigrants were found to be at higher risk for serious infectious disease than were the children of U.S.-born parents. They were more likely to experience ear infections and pneumonia, especially if their parents were newly arrived and spoke little English. Notably, the children in this sample all had had healthy birth outcomes. In addition to this study's results, other research has found that tuberculosis infection is substantially higher among the children of immigrants than it is in the general population, even though tuberculosis infection is declining overall in the United States. These trends are often attributed to poverty and its many environmental correlates and could reflect a legacy from immigrant families' origin countries.[10]

As an exception to this general pattern, several studies have reported that asthma prevalence is significantly lower among immigrant children than it is among their peers from nonimmigrant families. This advantage weakens across generations and as length of residence increases and is especially apparent in the Mexican immigrant population. It is unclear why asthma disparities operate differently, so these findings call for more exploration of changes in children's everyday ecologies over time and of potential increases in utilization of health care (and, therefore, increases in diagnoses of conditions such as asthma) the longer that immigrant parents reside in the United States.[11]

Such evidence offers some insight into the greater tendency for immigrant parents (as opposed to U.S. natives) to report that their young children are in poor health. In ECLS-K, immigrant parents from Asia and Latin America rated their children's physical health significantly lower than their U.S.-born counterparts and White parents did, even when key socioeconomic and environmental factors were taken into account.[12] For this chapter, we analyzed the same parent assessments in the Early Childhood Longitudinal Study–Birth Cohort (ECLS-B), a companion to the ECLS-K that focuses on younger children. The results were similar to those of the ECLS-K. Mexican immigrant parents gave the lowest ratings of their children's health, a disparity that increased over time as the children approached the start of elementary school. Such disparities in parental health ratings are significant given how strongly these global health ratings predict future health problems and hospital visits.[13]

Infectious health problems in childhood, therefore, may be an exception to the general rule of an immigrant paradox discussed previously for infancy and discussed next for adolescence. Significantly, contextual or ecological influences on health are often discussed in the literature on childhood health among immigrant families but are infrequently examined directly. Possibly, contextual forces related to immigrant selectivity or migratory social capital advantages do not extend into the childhood period with the same protective impacts observed in infant mortality. Future research should consider how concrete environmental attributes of the settings of children's daily lives—especially policy-amenable aspects of child care, schools, communities, and health care—change as children develop and as both they and their parents spend more time in the United States and potentially become more assimilated.

Risky Health Behavior in Adolescence

The increased tendency for teenagers to take risks with their health has been extensively documented. Teenagers are more likely than children or adults to engage in many forms of risky sex, problematic substance use, or other kinds of dangerous behavior such as reckless driving. This pattern is rooted in several factors, including the increased peer orientation that is a byproduct of the developmental task of individuating themselves from their parents as well as the divergent developmental timetables in areas of the brain that control sensation seeking and self-regulation.[14] Still, this increased risk-taking is widespread but not universal. Immigration is one factor producing significant variation.

In short, ample evidence suggests that the immigrant paradox applies to adolescent health-risk behavior. Much of this evidence comes from the National Longitudinal Study of Adolescent Health (Add Health), a nationally representative study of U.S. teenagers in the 1990s, but other national and community studies have also contributed findings.[15] Foreign-born youth tend to have lower levels of substance use (e.g., cigarettes, alcohol, marijuana, and other illegal drugs) than U.S.-born youth do and are less likely to have sex and to have unprotected sex.[16] These patterns extend fairly consistently across most racial/ethnic groups (e.g., Asian Americans and Latino/as) as well as subgroups within them (e.g., Mexicans and Cubans among Latino/as).[17]

The reduced risk-taking among youth from immigrant families, however, tends to weaken over time. This reduction is less apparent among U.S.-born youth with immigrant parents than it is among foreign-born youth in immigrant families. Even among youth who are foreign-born themselves, low rates of risky behaviors fade as their length of residency in the United States increases. The risky behavior of immigrant youth who have been in the United States longer than 10 years looks similar to that of U.S.-born youth.[18] In general, substance use, sexual activity, and other risky behaviors are associated with higher levels of acculturation to U.S. society, as facilitated by factors such as English-language use.[19] Similarly, risky behavior rates are lower among adolescents from immigrant families when they live in neighborhoods high in ethnic concentration—but only if those neighborhoods are not also socioeconomically disadvantaged.[20] Therefore, risky behavior may be a product of immigrant youth's becoming more integrated into the U.S.-based peer culture. At the same time, immigrant youth do show an uptick in risky behavior when they experience discrimination, a finding suggesting that in some cases youth's risk-taking may reflect problems with that process of social integration.[21]

Several microsystemic contextual mechanisms have been identified by research on these immigration-related disparities in health-risk behavior. Particularly important are the strong family orientations and responsibilities of youth from immigrant families and the greater value that they place on school. Such youth also tend to be less peer oriented than the general adolescent population is, especially in terms of their orientation to peers from nonimmigrant backgrounds, a factor that is important since peer influences are among the strongest factors contributing to risky behavior. These mechanisms support the conclusion that immigrant youth become more prone to risky behavior as they are absorbed into the social worlds of their American peers and, consequently, are drawn away from their families and other conventional institutions—in line with theoretical models of adolescent development that emphasize tensions between adult and peer worlds.[22]

Obesity across the Early Life Course

Rising obesity rates in the United States cut across stages of the life course. Therefore, obesity is a good topic to examine when considering the health of immigrant children *and* adolescents. Some evidence suggests that the immigrant paradox does apply to obesity but with important caveats.

Generally, foreign-born youth are less likely to be obese than U.S.-born youth are.[23] Indeed, estimates from the National Survey of Children's Health indicate that the former have 26 percent lower odds than the latter of having body mass indices in the obese range, controlling for socioeconomic circumstances and other demographic factors.[24] These disparities seem to reflect immigration-related differences in diet since immigrant families tend to eat lower-fat foods and be less likely than nonimmigrant families to eat fast food. These disparities do not, however, seem to reflect differences in another factor significantly relevant to obesity: physical activity. Children from immigrant families are actually less likely to engage in physical activity than are their peers from nonimmigrant families, a finding indicating that immigrant youth have less understanding about the benefits of such activity and more time constraints. Also, given these youth's lower average socioeconomic statuses, the findings reflect the general impact of poverty on physical activity.[25]

This immigrant advantage in obesity is primarily concentrated in the first generation (i.e., youth who are foreign-born). It is weaker or even nonexistent in later generations (e.g., in the U.S.-born children of immigrants). Even within the first generation, this advantage weakens as more time is spent in the United States and as markers of acculturation increase.[26] Immigration-related disparities in obesity also vary by race or ethnicity—being weaker among Latino/as and stronger among Whites and African Americans.[27] Another source of variation is age related, with the immigrant paradox being stronger in early childhood and adolescence than in childhood, especially for boys.[28] Cross-national comparisons are also revealing. Unlike the situation in the United States, immigration-related differences in obesity in many European countries favor natives (i.e., they tend to be thinner) rather than immigrants.[29] Economic development is also a major factor in national variation in the immigration-related disparities in obesity. In many developing countries that send migrants to the United States, socioeconomic status is positively associated with body mass index, while the association is inverse in the United States. Consequently, low-income immigrant youth from less developed countries have a lower BMI than higher-income youth in those countries do and, within the United States, than the children of immigrants from developed counties do.[30] On balance, then, assimilation into U.S. society seems to promote obesity, a finding that calls for paying more attention to the ways in which youth from immigrant families are exposed over time to ecological contexts (such as neighborhoods with limited options for healthy eating or safe recreation) and processes (such as eating outside the home) that put their physical health at risk.

Thus, immigration-related trends in obesity tend to defy the socioeconomic odds in the United States since not only obesity but also the socioeconomic factors that protect against obesity are less prevalent in immigrant groups than in the general population. These links among immigration, socioeconomic status, and obesity are more complicated, however, in transnational perspective. Furthermore, the immigrant advantage varies more substantially than simple conclusions about the immigrant paradox suggest and requires a more careful unpacking of the evolving ecologies of development among immigrant youth.

Conclusion

Overall, the health of immigrant children and adolescents in the United States appears to be good, especially relative to the health of youth who are not immigrants and do not have immigrant parents. This general picture also subsumes a good deal of variation that is likely to interest researchers studying children and youth within their everyday ecological contexts.

Variations in the immigrant paradox in health tend to reflect various dimensions of time: developmental time and timing of immigration. On the one hand, the duration of time since immigration (on the part of children in terms of length of residence, on the part of families in terms of immigrant generation) is consistently related to a decline in observed immigrant advantages in multiple markers of health in the early life course. This fadeout most likely reflects the absorption of immigrant children and youth—who tend to assimilate more quickly than their parents do—into pockets of U.S. culture that do not generally promote health and, due to this absorption, their movement away from strong family and community networks that promote health. On the other hand, evidence for the immigrant paradox is also most consistent for aspects of health behavior (as opposed to health status) among adolescents. This pattern suggests that immigration is a qualifier to a common developmental theme in the United States—adolescents engaging in risky behavior as they individuate from parents, take more control of their lives, and become more peer oriented. Immigration may slow down or reduce this normative process, contributing to a healthier behavioral profile among immigrant youth during this stage of their life span than that of their nonimmigrant peers.

The immigrant paradox and its variations discussed here lead to some conclusions about policies and interventions targeting population health among children and adolescents. Such efforts might be more successful if they promoted healthy practices (such as providing nutrition education) among young children and school-age children from immigrant families—especially those of Mexican and other Latin American origins—who have lived longer in the United States, focused on improving the ecological conditions in which these children live their lives (such as providing community environmental programs), expanded access to health care for young children from immigrant families in general and for undocumented and mixed-status families in particular (e.g., through local and state programs that supplement the more immigration-restrictive federal health-care services),[31] and, more generally, attempted to improve the basic socioeconomic circumstances of such immigrant families by supporting broader policies such as comprehensive immigration-reform legislation as a means of reducing the poverty-related factors that most undermine the health of immigrant children and youth.

NOTES

1. Crosnoe, R., Bonazzo, C., & Wu, N. (2015). *Healthy learners: Poverty, immigration, and opportunity in early childhood education.* New York: Teachers College Press.

2. Fortuny, K., & Chaudry, A. (2011). *Children of immigrants: Growing national and state diversity.* Washington, DC: Urban Institute; Hernandez, D. J., Macartney, S., Blanchard, V. L., & Denton, N. A. (2010). Mexican-origin children in the United States: Language, family circumstances, and public policy. In N. Landale, S. McHale, & A. Booth (Eds.), *Growing up Hispanic: Health and development of children of immigrants* (pp. 169–185). Washington, DC: Urban Institute.

3. Perreira, K., & Ornelas, I. J. (2011). The physical and psychological well-being of immigrant children. *Future of Children, 21,* 195–218.

4. Markides, K. S., & Eschbach, K. (2005). Aging, migration and mortality: Current status of research on the Hispanic paradox. *Journals of Gerontology, Series B: Social Sciences and Psychological Sciences, 60B,* 68–75.

5. Arias, E. (2010). United States life tables by Hispanic origin. *National Vital Health Statistics, 2*(152), 1–41.

6. Hummer, R. A., Powers, D., Gossman, G., Pullum, S., & Frisbie, W. P. (2007). Paradox found (again): Infant mortality among the Mexican origin population of the United States. *Demography, 44,* 441–457.

7. Ibid.

8. Fuller, B., Bridges, M., Bein, E., Jang, H., Jung, S., Rabe-Hesketh, S., Halfon, N., & Kuo, A. (2009). The health and cognitive growth of Latino toddlers: At risk or immigrant paradox? *Maternal and Child Health, 13,* 755–768; Guendelman, S., English, E., & Chavez, C. (1995). Infants of Mexican immigrants: Health status of an emerging population. *Medical Care, 33,* 41–52; Mendoza, F. S., & Dixon, L. B. (1999). The health and nutritional status of immigrant Hispanic children: Analyses of the Hispanic Health and Nutrition Examination Survey. In D. J. Hernandez (Ed.), *Children of immigrants: Health, adjustment, and public assistance* (pp. 187–243). Washington, DC: National Academy Press; Yu, S. M., Zhihuan, J. H., & Singh, G. K. (2004). Health status and

health services utilization among U.S. Chinese, Asian Indian, Filipino, and Other Asian/Pacific Islander children. *Pediatrics, 113,* 101–107.

9. Crosnoe, R. (2006). Health and the education of children from race/ethnic minority and immigrant families. *Journal of Health and Social Behavior, 47,* 77–93.

10. Guendelman et al. (1995); Nelson, L. J., Schneider, E., Wells, C. D., & Moore, M. (2004). Epidemiology of childhood tuberculosis in the United States, 1993–2001: The need for continued vigilance. *Pediatrics, 114,* 333–341.

11. Brim, S. N., Rudd, R. A., Funk, R. H., & Callahan, D. B. (2008). Asthma prevalence among U.S. children in underrepresented minority populations: American Indian / Alaska Native, Chinese, Filipino, and Asian Indian. *Pediatrics, 122,* 217–222; Eldeirawi, K., McConnel, R., Freels, S., & Persky, V. W. (2005). Associations of place of birth with asthma and wheezing in Mexican American children. *Journal of Allergy and Clinical Immunology, 116,* 42–48; Subramanian, S. V., Jun, H. J., Kawachi, I., & Wright, R. J. (2009). Contribution of race/ethnicity and country of origin to variations in lifetime reported asthma: Evidence for a nativity advantage. *American Journal of Public Health, 99,* 690–697.

12. Crosnoe. (2006).

13. Case, A., Lubotsky, D., & Paxson, C. (2002). Economic status and health in childhood: The origins of the gradient. *American Economic Review, 92,* 1308–1334.

14. Steinberg, L. D. (2008). A social neuroscience perspective on adolescent risk taking. *Developmental Review, 28,* 78–106.

15. Bui, H. N. (2013). Racial and ethnic differences in the immigrant paradox in substance use. *Journal of Immigrant Minority Health, 15*(5), 866–881; Peña, J. B., Wyman, P. A., Brown, C. H., Matthieu, M. M., Olivares, T. E., Hartel, D., & Zayas, L. H. (2008). Immigration generation status and its association with suicide attempts, substance use, and depressive symptoms among Latino adolescents in the USA. *Prevention Science, 9,* 299–231; Perreira & Ornelas. (2011).

16. Gfroerer, J. C., & Tan, L. L. (2003). Substance use among foreign-born youths in the United States: Does the length of residence matter? *American Journal of Public Health, 93,* 1892–1895; Guarini, T. E., Marks, A. K., Patton, F., & García Coll, C. (2011). The immigrant paradox in sexual risk behavior among Latino adolescents: Impact of immigrant generation and gender. *Applied Development Science, 15,* 201–209; Perreira & Ornelas. (2011).

17. Eitle, T. M., Gonzalez Wahl, A. M., & Aranda, E. (2009). Immigrant generation, selective acculturation, and alcohol use among Latina/o adolescents. *Social Science Research, 38,* 732–742; Harachi, T., Catalano, R. F., Kim, S., & Choi, Y. (2001). Etiology and prevention of substance use among Asian American youth. *Prevention Science, 2,* 57–65; Le, T., Goebert, D., & Wallen, J. (2009). Acculturation factors and substance use among Asian American youth. *Journal of Primary Prevention, 30,* 453–473.

18. Gfroerer & Tan. (2003); Perreira & Ornelas. (2011).

19. Bui. (2013); Cavanagh, S. E. (2007). Peers, drinking, and the assimilation of Mexican American youth. *Sociological Perspective, 50,* 393–416.

20. Eitle et al. (2009); Frank, R., Cerdá, M., & Rendón, M. (2007). Barrios and burbs: Residential context and health-risk behaviors among Angeleno adolescents. *Journal of Health and Social Behavior, 48,* 283–300.

21. Kulis, S., Marsiglia, F. F., & Nieri, T. (2009). Perceived ethnic discrimination versus acculturation stress: Influences on substance use among Latino youth in the Southwest. *Journal of Health and Social Behavior, 50*, 443–459.

22. Bui. (2013); Cavanagh. (2007); Prado, G., Huang, S., Schwartz, S. J., Maldonado-Molina, M. M., Bandiera, F. C., de la Rosa, M., & Pantin, H. (2009). What accounts for differences in substance use among U.S.-born and immigrant Hispanic adolescents? Results from a longitudinal prospective cohort study. *Journal of Adolescent Health, 45*, 118–125.

23. Perreira & Ornelas, 2011; Popkin, B. M., & Udry, J. R. (1998). Adolescent obesity increases significantly for second- and third-generation U.S. immigrants: The National Longitudinal Study of Adolescent Health. *Journal of Nutrition, 128*, 701–706.

24. Singh, G. K., Kogan, M. D., & Yu, S. M. (2009). Disparities in obesity and overweight: Prevalence among U.S. immigrant adolescents by generational status. *Journal of Community Health, 34*, 271–281.

25. Gordon-Larsen, P., Harris, K. M., Ward, D. S., & Popkin, B. M. (2003). Acculturation and overweight-related behaviors among Hispanic immigrants to the U.S.: The National Longitudinal Study of Adolescent Health. *Social Science and Medicine, 57*, 2023–2034; Perreira & Ornelas. (2011); Singh et al. (2009); Unger, G. B., Reynolds, K., Shakib, S., Spruijt-Metz, D., Sun, P., & Johnson, C. A. (2004). Acculturation, physical activity, and fast-food consumption among Asian-American and Hispanic adolescents. *Journal of Community Health, 29*, 467–481.

26. Singh et al. (2009); Van Hook, J., & Balistreri, K. (2007). Big boys and little girls: Gender, acculturation, and weight among young children of immigrants. *Journal of Health and Social Behavior, 51*, 200–214.

27. Harris, K. M., Perreira, K. M., & Lee, D. (2009). Obesity in the transition to adulthood: Predictions across race/ethnicity, immigrant generation, and sex. *Archives of Pediatric and Adolescent Medicine, 163*, 1022–1028.

28. Perreira & Ornelas. (2011); Van Hook & Balistreri. (2007).

29. Kirchengast, S., Schober, E., Waldhor, T., & Sefranek, R. (2004). Regional and social differences in body mass index, and the prevalence of overweight and obesity among 18-year-old men in Austria between the years 1985 and 2000. *Collegium Anthropologicum, 28*, 541–552.

30. Van Hook, J., & Balistreri, K. (2007). Immigration generation, socioeconomic status, and economic development of countries of origin: A longitudinal study of body mass index among children. *Social Science and Medicine, 65*, 976–989.

31. Crosnoe, R., Pedroza, J. M., Purtell, K., Fortuny, K., Perreira, K., Ulvestad, K., Weiland, C., Yoshikawa, H., & Chaudry, A. U.S. Department of Health and Human Services, Office of the Assistant Secretary for Planning and Evaluation. (2012). *Promising practices for increasing immigrants' access to health and human services* (ASPE Issue Brief). Retrieved from http://aspe.hhs.gov/hsp/11/immigrantaccess/practices/rb.shtml.

11

Mental Health and Clinical Issues

PRATYUSHA TUMMALA-NARRA

Marie is a 14-year-old Haitian immigrant student who recently met with her guidance counselor at school because she had become increasingly withdrawn in the classroom and had stopped communicating with her teachers and classmates. She attends an ethnically diverse school, where she has several friends, most of whom are also Haitian American. She moved to the United States after the 2010 earthquake in Haiti, which devastated her home, because her parents decided that she should live with relatives in the United States. Marie left Haiti shortly after witnessing the death of her cousin in the earthquake; she has not spoken about this tragedy with her relatives or anyone else in the United States other than her guidance counselor, who speaks Haitian Creole. To the counselor, she described feeling unsure about her future and about whether she will see her family in Haiti again.

Taran is a 10-year-old Indian American boy who was born and raised in the United States. His parents migrated to the United States from India in the 1990s and established a small business. Taran's father is Sikh, and his mother is Hindu. Taran has been increasingly withdrawn at school and has been refusing to eat regular meals at home. Taran's parents brought him to a psychotherapist after their primary-care physician suggested that he talk with a therapist. Taran is reluctant to talk with a therapist who is not from a South Asian background because he thinks that someone from outside his community will not understand his problems. He feels ashamed and angry about being teased for his brown skin and Indian background. He feels proud of his heritage but is saddened because whenever people see his father, they see only his turban and make negative judgments about the man, his family, and his community. Taran thinks that no one in his family or school can really understand how he feels.

First- and second-generation immigrant children and adolescents compose the fastest growing segment of the child population in the United States, with one-fourth of adolescents being of immigrant origin.[1] Latino and Asian immigrant youth in particular are the fastest growing populations today.[2] However, the internal stories of immigrant children and youth like Marie and Taran are often invisible to family, friends, adults, and peers at school and, more broadly, to the public. Many first- and second-generation immigrant children and youth demonstrate remarkable resilience in the face of numerous types of acculturation-related stress, as evidenced in their ability to navigate across multiple cultural contexts and cope with language and communication barriers, poverty, trauma, and discrimination. At the same time, the stress contributing to their mental health issues and immigrant children's and adolescents' low utilization of mental health services have largely been understudied, with a majority of the literature focusing on the needs of adult immigrants. This chapter explores the ecological contexts of immigrant children and youth and the specific stressors (e.g., acculturative stress, trauma, and discrimination) that contribute to their mental health problems.[3] Although immigrant youth and families from many cultures face considerable stress in their adjustment to life in the United States, this chapter focuses on the experiences of racial minority immigrant children and adolescents.

Mental Health of Immigrant-Origin Youth

The prevalence of mental health problems among immigrant youth and the conceptualization of treatment should be considered within the context of immigration and acculturation. Research suggests that mental health problems among immigrant youth are related to interactions among individual, social, and cultural contexts, with rates and types of symptomatology, or the combined symptoms of a disease, varying across subgroups. For example, newcomer youth may be at risk for internalizing problems such as depression.[4] Many studies to date have called attention to the relatively high rates of combined symptoms such as anxiety and depression that in turn contribute to problems with academic and social functioning and increased risk for self-destructive behavior such as suicide attempts. For example, Latino/a youth, particularly

Mexican American and Afro-Latinos, report higher rates of depression than non-Latino White youth do.[5] First-generation Latina girls in particular report more depressive symptoms and suicide attempts than do first-generation Latino boys.[6]

Although Asian American youth have long been construed as a "model minority," with the assumption that they experience fewer mental health problems than youth from other ethnic groups do, research indicates that mental health concerns among Asian American youth are prevalent and often go unrecognized. Specifically, assuming that Asian Americans are academically and/or financially successful contributes to the perception that there are minimal mental health needs among Asian American communities. However, a recent study indicates that second-generation Asian American children are at greater risk for developing physical health problems; internalizing feelings such as sadness, loneliness, and anxiety; and having problematic interpersonal relationships than U.S.-born White children are.[7] Additionally, there is variation in the academic performances of Asian American youth that is largely unrecognized. Asian American youth who underperform or do not meet the expectations inherent in the model minority stereotype may be especially vulnerable to isolation. Those who achieve academically may experience the model minority stereotype as one that carries both a positive image and a psychological burden.

In the area of mental health variations due to migratory experiences, there has not been much research addressing mental health needs among undocumented immigrant youth or children and adolescents with unauthorized parents despite the fact that unauthorized immigrants tend to experience relatively high levels of traumatic exposure, have fewer economic resources, and may be particularly vulnerable to exploitation.[8]

Despite numerous challenges faced by first-generation immigrants (those born outside the United States), there is evidence that second- and third-generation immigrants (those born in the United States) and those with higher levels of acculturation have worse mental and physical health than members of the first generation do.[9] This *immigrant paradox* is thought to be partly explained by stressors such as the family conflict and increased awareness of and exposure to discrimination faced by the second and third generations and by the first generation's protective factors such as speaking a non-English language at home and having a supportive family environment.[10] However, it is important to note that there have been some mixed findings concerning the immigrant paradox and behavioral problems among immigrant-origin children, with first-generation and second-generation children experiencing different advantages and disadvantages in their psychosocial adjustment.[11] Nonetheless, a majority of research with immigrant youth suggests that even after controlling for social class, second- and third-generation adolescents experience higher levels of behavioral problems such as risky sexual and violent behaviors and substance abuse than their first-generation peers do.[12] In addition, early adolescence is a particularly vulnerable time to develop internalizing problems such as depressive symptoms.[13]

The immigrant paradox should be further considered in light of variations in the presentation of psychological symptoms across immigrant generations, with the first generation being more likely to report somatic, or physical, symptoms than the second and third generations are and perhaps being more likely to seek help from professionals to cope with them.[14] The problem of recognition of immigrants' distress, however, exists across generations. For example, teachers may not interpret immigrant children's and adolescents' psychological issues as problematic or as indications of their distress. In fact, teachers' ratings of immigrant students' symptoms have been found to be lower than students' self-reported symptoms are.[15] The increase in combined mental health symptoms in second and later immigrant generations and the lack of attention given to their mental health needs are issues of concern, especially since most immigrants relocate to the United States in order to secure a better future for their children.

The vignettes of Marie and Taran presented earlier highlight some major stressors experienced by many immigrant children and adolescents and challenges faced by youth across immigrant generations in securing help for their mental health issues. Although there are several factors that protect against distress, such as family support, mental health concerns are often rooted in stress associated with one or more of the following areas: acculturation, discrimination, and interpersonal violence and trauma.[16] The following sections describe how acculturation, discrimination, and trauma across different contexts (e.g., home, school, the community, and the broader society) shape immigrant youth's experiences of distress and well-being.

Acculturation

The Context of the Family. First-generation youth face separation from extended family—and sometimes from parents and siblings—and the loss of a familiar cultural environment, contributing to their feelings of anxiety, sadness, and cultural confusion.[17] Some youth struggle with English-language learning and communicating effectively with peers, teachers, and school administrators. Others become culture and language brokers for parents and family members, providing a bridge between their culture of origin and the new culture and between home and school. Culture and language brokering can be a double-edged sword in that youth who fulfill this role for their families have been found to experience both positive outcomes (e.g., greater family adaptability and better decision-making abilities) and negative ones (e.g., greater family stress and lowered academic and social functioning).[18] Research concerning language brokering suggests that immigrant-origin adolescents' experiences of stress and resilience coexist as parents and children simultaneously struggle with adjusting to a new cultural environment. Other types of stress within the family may reflect variations in acculturation among family members. For example, children who acculturate in ways similar to those of their parents or adult caregivers may experience less conflict in the home, whereas children who adapt in ways that contrast significantly with those of their parents or adult caregivers may experience greater conflict and challenges with communication.

The effects of acculturative stress are evident in intergenerational conflicts, which are common in immigrant homes. These conflicts are unique when compared with more typical intergenerational conflicts that exist across cultures and migration histories. Specifically, parents and children may subscribe to some of the same cultural values and yet can also vary significantly in their other cultural values and beliefs, resulting in an acculturation gap.[19] For example, an adolescent girl of Pakistani Muslim origin who has a close, supportive relationship with her parents may feel that her parents cannot relate to her growing desire to date a boy whom she has met in school. Her parents' belief that she should only date when she is an adult stands in sharp contrast with the mainstream culture's acceptance of dating during adolescence. Her parents, consistent with their cultural and religious beliefs, may worry that dating prior to marriage would compromise their daughter's sexual purity, a situation that would then limit her chances of marrying a desirable husband when she is older. Although the daughter may identify with values inherent in both her Pakistani and American backgrounds, she may feel increasingly disconnected from either or both her parents and her peers. From the perspective of diagnosis and treatment, a clinician must consider the dual experiences of immigrant-origin youth, in which their relationships with parents, siblings, and extended family members involve a desire simultaneously to maintain close family ties and to create a bicultural or multicultural identity. Notably, in some cases, youth may experience conflict when attempting to maintain a connection with their families in a way that impedes their identifying with mainstream cultural values and norms.

Cultural expectations of gender roles may vary considerably between the culture of origin and the host culture, with women and girls at times experiencing increased opportunities for academic and professional growth and at other times coping with new demands such as adhering to body-image ideals of thinness and light skin color.[20] In families with a collectivistic orientation (e.g., Asian, Latino, Afro-Caribbean, and Arab cultures), girls tend to be monitored in their social interactions more than boys are, and both boys and girls are socialized to value interdependence among family members and within their ethnic and/or religious communities.[21] This valuing of interdependence contrasts with the Euro-American emphasis on individual autonomy and separation-individuation. The valuing of interdependence and what is viewed as an authoritarian parenting style can be misinterpreted by mental health professionals as factors leading to pathological dependence, especially during late adolescence and emerging adulthood, when youth in the United States are increasingly expected to make decisions about their lives independent of their families. However, in many immigrant families, an individual's decisions about issues such as education, career, and marriage are made with the guidance of older family members. It is worth noting that such advice from parents, grandparents, aunts, uncles, and others can be beneficial to adolescents as they navigate multiple cultural contexts. However, problems in communication and gaps in acculturation can also create stress in these family relationships, contributing to mental health concerns. In fact, an acculturation gap accompanying family conflict and poor communication among family members has been associated with poor mental health outcomes and parenting stress.[22]

The Context of the Ethnic Community. The context in which immigrant youth live can have important consequences for their identity development. For example, an immigrant child who lives in a geographical area where there are few or no other children of his ethnic background or who speak his heritage language is not likely to have much opportunity for *refueling,* which is the ability to access physical and psychological spaces where he can comfortably speak the heritage language and engage in heritage customs and traditions.[23] Furthermore, this child may receive messages from peers that his heritage language and culture have less value than the English-speaking mainstream culture. Negative messages about the heritage culture shape the child's *social mirror,*[24] therefore causing him to internalize attitudes about himself and his family, ethnic community, and heritage culture. In a different case, a child may be strongly identified with her heritage culture through regular interactions with her ethnic and/or religious community. Although a strong connection with one's ethnic community can be a protective factor in coping with stress, immigrant youth can also experience this connection as an identifier of cultural, racial, and/or religious difference that marginalizes them from the mainstream culture. In either case, youth across different immigrant generations experience important shifts in racial and cultural identity that shape and are shaped by their interactions with family, friends, and important adults such as teachers and religious authorities or figures.

Research indicates that a positive ethnic identity is associated with more favorable mental health outcomes among immigrant youth than a negative identity is.[25] However, there are variations in the relationship between ethnic identity and specific combined symptoms across ethnicity. For example, Rogers-Sirin and Gupta found that ethnic identity was associated with less depressive combined symptoms for Asian and Latino immigrant youth but that ethnic identity was associated with fewer physical symptoms for Asian immigrant youth but not for Latino/a immigrant youth.[26] Recent studies also suggest that immigrant-origin youth are actively involved in exploring multiple aspects of identity and specifically in exploring their sense of identification with and belonging to heritage culture(s) and mainstream U.S. culture.[27] Collectively, these findings suggest that immigrant youth's identity development has important implications for psychological well-being.

Discrimination

The majority of recent immigrants in the United States are members of racial minorities, and for many immigrants, U.S. race-based hierarchies are unfamiliar. Although immigrants may have previously experienced other forms of discrimination related to sex, social class, sexual orientation, disability, or religion, they may be facing racial discrimination specific to the U.S. context for the first time. It is important to note that first-generation immigrants who arrive in the United States as adults may have a different experience with race in this country than first-, second-, and third-generation immigrant youth do. Racial minority immigrant-origin youth typically are socialized in racial labels and hierarchies from a young age, so they may be more likely to identify as people of color than first-generation adult immigrants are. Immigrant-origin youth experience the feeling of social difference early in their lives. They may be frustrated because others do not make an effort to pronounce their names correctly, because their parents appear to be visibly different from members of the dominant culture, and because they experience different expectations at home and school than their U.S.-born peers do. It is more common in immigrant homes for first-generation parents to discuss cultural values, traditions, and customs than to discuss race and racism.[28] Furthermore, immigrant children from the same heritage culture who arrive in the United States during different historical periods may define themselves differently along racial lines. These differences highlight the ways in which the development of racial identity varies across immigrant generations and across waves of immigration.

Experiences of discrimination have important implications for identity formation and psychological well-being. Numerous studies have found a negative association between perceived discrimination and mental health.[29] Among refugee youth, perceived discrimination is associated with both depressive symptoms and posttraumatic stress symptoms.[30] Immigrants and refugees who have visible markers of difference such as skin color, hair texture, and eyelid shape are identified as racial minorities, a label that can reshape individual and collective identities. Whereas both first- and second-generation immigrants may be ambivalent about ascribed racial identifications, second-generation immigrants may be more likely to internalize a minority identity, an action that carries both positive and negative meanings.[31] Immigrant-origin youth experiencing minority stress (experiences of stereotyping and discrimination) are at higher risk for mental health problems, including depression, anxiety, and psychosomatic complaints.[32]

In some adult immigrant communities, racism-related stress has been found to be higher among the second generation than among the first.[33] Most second-generation individuals and children of first-generation immigrants likely do not have the option of choosing "marginated" experiences—that is, those in which they can interact almost exclusively within their ethnic communities.[34] Children of immigrants instead engage with the mainstream culture early in their socialization through interactions at school and in their neighborhoods. Experiencing racism can be detrimental for immigrant youth as they attempt to develop identifications with both the heritage and the mainstream cultures, leaving them disillusioned or disconnected from both cultural contexts. This outcome can be especially problematic when youth also face discrimination within their ethnic communities, perhaps being targeted for their sexual orientation or social class, as well as from outside their communities.

The sociopolitical context in the host culture further contributes to these youth's experiences of discrimination and minority identity. For example, anti-immigrant sentiment and deportation policies exacerbate a sense of danger and uncertainty among youth and their families.[35] In fact, legal status in the United States has been associated with anxiety among first- generation Latino/a youth, particularly due to their loss of control over their legal status and its potential impact on their future.[36] Since the terrorist attacks of September 11, 2001, several immigrant groups such as Arab Americans and South Asian Americans have continued to be disillusioned about their status as Americans and their lack of personal safety in the face of verbal and physical harassment and racial profiling.[37] Additionally, the real threat of deportation is a significant source of stress and anxiety for more than one million children in the United States who are unauthorized, for more than four million children who live with their undocumented parents, and for children who live in families with members of mixed citizen status. Children whose parents have been detained in immigration raids have been found to experience anxiety, sadness, changes in sleep and eating patterns, and withdrawal even after a nine-month follow-up.[38]

Family and Peer Support. Family and peer support are critical sources of resilience for immigrant children and adolescents coping with emotional distress.[39] In fact, it is common for youth to feel both burdened and proud as they attempt to fulfill the hopes and dreams of their parents and extended family for a better life; in this situation, the family unit in particular takes a central position in youth's identity development. Furthermore, immigrant-origin children and adolescents, many of whom live in collectivistically oriented homes, tend to seek advice from family members and friends when coping with emotional distress.[40] Informal sources of support, such as family, friends, and community members, are a primary avenue of help for immigrant-origin youth. Identity development relies heavily on the degree of family support and conflict experienced by immigrant-origin youth. Although adolescence is a critical time for developing peer relationships in general, in some cases coethnic peer groups become primary sources of ethnic identity and racial identity formation, especially when there is a high degree of family conflict or when parents and caregivers are unavailable to youth, perhaps due to long work hours, death, divorce or separation, deportation, or physical and mental health issues. Nevertheless, the family remains the primary bastion of support for many first- and second-generation immigrant youth's emotional well-being.[41] Further research is needed to explore the roles of peers and family for adolescents who identify with multiple minority positions such as racial and sexual identities.

Interpersonal Violence

Traumatic experience coexists with disproportionate rates of poverty among immigrant youth. Specifically, 31 percent of Latino/a children and 15 percent of Asian children live in poverty, as compared with 11 percent of White children who do.[42] Along with cumulative experiences of racism, rates of exposure to interpersonal and community violence among immigrant and refugee youth are relatively high.[43] For example, a study of Latino/a children of middle-school age from low-income backgrounds found that participants were exposed to an alarmingly high lifetime level of violence (89 percent).[44] Traumatic experiences can contribute to a wide range of combined psychological symptoms among youth, including distrust of authorities, fear of school, difficulty concentrating, eating disorders, depression, anxiety, loss of motivation, decline in academic performance, and intergenerational conflict.[45] Rates of posttraumatic stress disorder (PTSD) are especially high among refugees. For example, rates of PTSD have been estimated at between 11.5 percent and 65 percent among refugee children and adolescents from Cambodia, Bosnia, Afghanistan, Palestine, and Tibet.[46]

Studies of interpersonal violence among immigrant communities have focused primarily on domestic violence, and few studies have focused on immigrant-origin children who have witnessed domestic violence.[47] A traumatic experience can occur prior to migration, during transit to the United States, and/or after migration.[48] Exposure to trauma across different points in the migration process is especially pronounced among refugee youth, many of whom have to cope with war trauma in addition to other forms of interpersonal violence. In some cases, immigrant children are separated from parents and other important adult figures, as happens with many Caribbean youth whose parents send them to live with relatives or family friends in the United States to escape poverty and political instability.[49] Children who are especially vulnerable to exploitation after immigrating include those victimized by labor and sex trafficking. There are numerous systemic causes for trafficking of youth globally, such as poverty and sexism. Victims' experiences and needs are mostly invisible, and these children typically do not have any access to help.[50]

Violence within the Ethnic Community. Other types of interpersonal violence such as childhood physical and sexual abuse have received far less attention in the psychological literature, yet such incidents can be devastating, especially when youth experience oppression both within and outside the home. In particular, some immigrant youth cope with multiple types of traumatic experience such as enduring violence at home and discrimination in the form of racism, sexism, homophobia, classism, or prejudice against people with disabilities at school. While violence against children in immigrant homes has been documented, within many immigrant communities there tends to be significant denial of its occurrence that interferes with child and adolescent victims' ability to access adequate help. There may be culturally specific worldviews regarding the physical disciplining of children that clash with mainstream U.S. views, contributing to a reluctance to discuss family conflict and violence. Unfortunately, there often is stigma attached to violence within the home, and victimized immigrant-origin children and adolescents are frequently silenced by members of their families and communities. Sexual violence in particular is considered a taboo topic in many immigrant communities, so research on this issue and on implementation of culturally competent interventions is sorely needed.

Traumatic exposure can further influence children's identity development. For example, a child who is sexually victimized by a family member may struggle with deciding to seek help outside of the family if she believes that disclosing the abuse would bring shame to her family's reputation. In fact, she may be explicitly told by other family members not to disclose the victimization to outsiders, limiting her access to help and ability to form authentic connections within the family. This situation can be particularly challenging for immigrant-origin youth as they form cultural identifications within and outside their families and ethnic and religious communities in the face of traumatic stress (e.g., anxiety, depressed mood, or hyperarousal). Although few studies have addressed identity development among youth growing up with unauthorized legal status, fears of deportation are likely to diminish their feelings of belonging in the mainstream culture.[51] Experiences of racial and political violence can also undermine youth's identification with and sense of inclusion in the mainstream culture and sense of home. This result was evident, for example, in the racial profiling prevalent in the aftermath of the terrorist attacks of 9/11 as many second- and third-generation Arab Americans and South Asian Americans questioned their acceptance by other Americans.

A Contextual Approach to Mental Health Interventions

Barriers to Help. Most immigrant children and youth tend to seek help through informal sources of support, such as friends and family members, and tend to underutilize mental health services. Several barriers to immigrant community members' accessing of adequate mental health services have been documented in the literature, including social-cultural, contextual-structural, and clinical-procedural obstacles.[52] Sociocultural barriers are cultural differences in descriptions of symptoms (e.g., physical symptoms), conflicting cultural explanations for causes of and recovery from mental health problems (e.g., using traditional healing as opposed to seeking help from a therapist), and stigma attached to mental illness. Examples of contextual-structural barriers include federal and state policies that limit access to health care, lack of culturally competent services, lack of awareness of how to access services, and lack of access to interpreters. Clinical-procedural barriers include problems such as clinician bias, misdiagnosis, the universal application of Euro-American models of pathology in assessment, and failure to attend to cultural expressions of resilience.[53]

Racial minority youth have less access to services and receive lower-quality treatment for coping with mental health issues, especially internalizing behaviors (e.g., depression and anxiety), than their White peers do, even when social class and insured status have been considered.[54] A substantial proportion of immigrant youth drop out of psychological treatment after only one session, probably due to their lack of connection with a therapist or counselor whom they perceive as not understanding their sociocultural background.[55] Recent studies indicate that a majority of immigrant-origin youth are not aware of mental health resources available to them. For example, García and colleagues found that fewer than 25 percent of Latino/a youth reported knowing about specific mental health resources and that participants living in urban settings were more likely to instead identify a community resource that would be helpful to a Latino/a adolescent with mental health issues.[56] Additionally, many participants reported that they would be willing to seek help from a professional for a mental health problem if they could access culturally and linguistically appropriate services. Contrary to the notion that immigrants do not want to seek help from people outside the community, García and colleagues noted that youth were willing to seek help for coping with their mental health issues.[57]

Adolescence is a critical time period for identifying mental health issues, so adult gatekeepers play an important role in recognizing mental health concerns. Family members may attend more to externalizing behaviors than to internalizing ones due to differences in cultural norms regarding healthy or typical behavior and approaches to healing. For example, if parents and caregivers value interdependence and harmony in the family unit, they may interpret internalizing symptoms such as anxiety and depressed affect as quietness and deference to older family members.[58] Parents and caregivers may also prefer to treat such symptoms through traditional healing practices such as herbal medicine, Ayurveda, and acupuncture and by consulting with elders and religious leaders in their communities, whose counsel may be effective in helping youth. Additionally, parents may be less apt to seek professional help if they have heard of relatives' or friends' negative experiences with mental health professionals and if they are concerned about having to report their authorization or legal status to such professionals.

Cultural Competence in Assessment, Diagnosis, and Treatment. Challenges in the assessment and diagnosis of mental health issues among immigrant populations have been well documented.[59] Some of these challenges include the lack of culturally valid diagnostic instruments, clinician bias, a failure to consider culturally embedded expressions of resilience, and the Euro-American focus of the *Diagnostic and Statistical Manual of Mental Disorders (DSM)*.[60] Furthermore, training in culturally appropriate instruments and in cultural formulation with different immigrant populations is limited in graduate training programs and internship programs. Unfortunately, the lack of consistency in attention to sociocultural context in assessment and diagnostic practices often contributes to the overdiagnosis and underdiagnosis of racial minority members' mental health problems. The problem of overdiagnosis of certain mental health problems such as attention deficit hyperactivity disorder (ADHD) among Latino boys, for example, may mask experiences of traumatic stress that manifests in a complex of symptoms that resemble ADHD. The problem of underdiagnosis is evident when a clinician interprets the client's distress as based solely on cultural factors rather than on personality variables that may be shaped by cultural beliefs and values. In either case, the actual nature of the presenting psychological issue is misinterpreted.

Over the past decade, culturally adapted interventions delivered in the client's heritage language have been found to be effective, and ethnic matching in the treatment dyad has been found to improve treatment outcomes in many cases, although ethnic matching does not necessarily predict the effectiveness of a treatment for all subgroups of immigrant-origin individuals.[61] It is important to note that immigrant-origin youth and adults may differ in their preferences for therapists of similar or different ethnic, racial, and/or religious backgrounds. There has been increased interest in the use of evidence-based practice in psychology (EBPP), which aims to develop and implement empirically supported intervention. Although the development of EBPPs with immigrant communities is in its infancy, there have been a few studies suggesting that cognitive-behavioral therapy, particularly due to its problem-solving focus, is effective for members of some immigrant adolescent subgroups (e.g., Latino/as and Haitians) coping with depression and trauma.[62] School-based programs have also been found to be effective in helping immigrant-origin students and their families deal with traumatic stress and depressive symptoms.[63] In particular, these interventions focus on increasing awareness of mental health concerns and collaborating with school personnel, students and their families, and community stakeholders. Additionally, some programs focused on the delivery of mental health services to immigrant communities have created innovative, culturally appropriate interventions that consider variations in clients' styles of adapting to the host culture. Although these programs have not yet conducted systematic research on the effectiveness of these interventions, knowledge gained from these services regarding cultural competence in practice with specific immigrant communities forms the ground for practice-based evidence.[64]

Culturally competent therapeutic interventions with immigrant-origin adolescents should consider practice-based evidence and EBPPs that are based on studies including members of immigrant populations. Culturally competent practices attend to the therapist's cultural knowledge, conscious and unconscious attitudes and beliefs toward clients of diverse cultural backgrounds, and use of culturally appropriate interventions.[65] Practitioners providing clinical interventions with immigrant-origin youth should consider several recommendations. They should first assess the language fluency and usage of child and adolescent clients and their family members and identify linguistically and culturally appropriate diagnostic tests. The assessment of pathological functioning and combined symptoms should be accompanied by the assessment of resilience as defined by contextual factors such as cultural beliefs.[66] Diagnosis and case conceptualization should be based on the client's and their family's cultural explanations of psychological distress, views of normal development, and culturally congruent approaches to healing. *Family* is broadly defined in many immigrant families, with grandparents and other relatives often living in the same home as parents and children. The inclusion of family members and friends in interventions may be critical to providing adequate support for immigrant youth as they navigate their comfort with a mental health professional and to addressing acculturation gaps and communication difficulties. However, practitioners should be careful when determining whether to include family members in cases in which clients have been or are being victimized by one or more family members. It is also important to keep this concern in mind when collaborating with members of a client's ethnic or religious community.

Effective practice includes a careful assessment of a client's migration history, acculturation, traumatic exposure, and personal and family access to resources such as finances, health insurance, immigration status, transportation, and interpreters. Such a history encompasses language fluency and usage, cultural and religious identifications, experiences of discrimination, and family separations.[67] Culturally competent assessment also includes attention to changes in the family structure and roles of men and women, to changes in the school environment and peer relationships, and to the personal meanings that child and adolescent clients attach to these shifts.

Culturally competent practice requires ongoing self-examination, engagement with training opportunities, and consultation. In fact, clinicians' own orientation to diversity issues is associated with self-perceived cultural competence when working with ethnic minority clients.[68] Practitioners should examine their conscious and unconscious beliefs about the client's cultural background and ethnic and religious communities. Microaggressions related to race, sex, age, sexual orientation, immigration status (unauthorized), social class, and disability can be especially challenging when establishing trust since they contribute to impasses in the therapeutic relationship.[69] Psychological theories of psychopathology and psychotherapy (e.g., cognitive-behavioral, psychodynamic, humanistic, and family systems) should be considered through a social contextual lens so that interventions are culturally appropriate. It is important that practitioners take a collaborative approach with clients when conceptualizing problems and treatment planning and that they promote collaborative relationships with important adults in the client's life (e.g., parents, grandparents, teachers, guidance counselors, psychopharmacologists, family physicians, and religious leaders or healers). Such collaboration can also involve work with community liaisons and community members who play a critical role in reaching out to communities that may not have access to information about mental health care or may be reluctant to seek help. Finally, practitioners should consider the complexity of mental health issues faced by immigrant-origin youth and validate youth's experiences of uncertainty, ambivalence, confusion, and pride as they negotiate a host of social, cultural, and interpersonal challenges and various intersections of identity (e.g., race, sex, and social class) that may be distinct from those of their parents and grandparents.

NOTES

1. American Psychological Association (APA), Presidential Task Force on Immigration. (2012). *Crossroads: The psychology of immigration in the new century, report of the APA Presidential Task Force on Immigration.* Washington, DC: APA.

2. Rogers-Sirin, L., & Gupta, R. (2012). Cultural identity and mental health: Differing trajectories among Asian and Latino youth. *Journal of Counseling Psychology, 59*(4), 555–566.

3. APA. (2012).

4. Patel, S. G., & Kull, M. A. (2011). Assessing psychological symptoms in recent immigrant adolescents. *Journal of Immigrant Minority Health, 13*, 616–619.

5. García, C. M., Gilchrist, L., Vazquez, G., Leite, A., & Raymond, N. (2011). Urban and rural immigrant Latino youths' and adults' knowledge and beliefs about mental health resources. *Journal of Immigrant Minority Health, 13*, 500–509.

6. Ibid.; Dawson, B. A., Perez, R. M., & Suarez-Orozco, C. (2012). Exploring differences in early involvement and depressive symptoms across Latino adolescent groups. *Journal of Human Behavior in the Social Environment, 22*, 153–171.

7. Huang, K., Calzada, E., Cheng, S., & Brotman, L. M. (2012). Physical and mental health disparities among young children of Asian immigrants. *Journal of Pediatrics, 160*(2), 331–336.

8. Potochnick, S. R., & Perreira, K. M. (2010). Depression and anxiety among first-generation immigrant Latino youth: Key correlates and implications for future research. *Journal of Nervous and Mental Disease, 198*(7), 470–477.

9. Alegria, M., Mulvaney-Day, N., Torres, M., Polo, A., Zhun, C., & Canino, G. (2007). Prevalence of psychiatric disorders across Latino subgroups in the United States. *American Journal of Public Health, 97*(1), 68–75; García Coll, C., & Marks, A. K. (Eds.) (2012). *The immigrant paradox in children and adolescents: Is becoming American a developmental risk?* Washington, DC: American Psychological Association.

10. Bauer, A. M., Chen, C., & Alegria, M. (2012). Associations of physical symptoms with perceived need for and use of mental health services among Latino and Asian Americans. *Social Science & Medicine, 75*, 1128–1133; Turney, K., & Kao, G. (2012). Behavioral outcomes in early childhood: Immigrant paradox or disadvantage? In C. García Coll & A. K. Marks (Eds.), *The immigrant paradox in children and adolescents: Is becoming American a developmental risk?* (pp. 79–107). Washington, DC: American Psychological Association.

11. Hernandez, D. J., Denton, N. A., Macartney, S., & Blanchard, V. L. (2012). Children in immigrant families, demography, policy, and evidence for the immigrant paradox. In C. García Coll & A. K. Marks (Eds.), *The immigrant paradox in children and adolescents: Is becoming American a developmental risk?* (pp. 17–36). Washington, DC: American Psychological Association.

12. Ibid.

13. Dawson et al. (2012).

14. Hernandez et al. (2012).

15. Patel & Kull. (2011).

16. APA. (2012).

17. Akhtar, S. (2011). *Immigration and acculturation: Mourning, adaptation, and the next generation.* New York: Jason Aronson.

18. Martinez, C. R., McClure, H. H., & Eddy, J. M. (2009). Language brokering contexts and behavioral and emotional adjustment among Latino parents and adolescents. *Journal of Early Adolescence, 29*(1), 71–98; Trickett, E. J., & Jones, C. J. (2007). Adolescent culture brokering and family functioning: A study of families from Vietnam. *Cultural Diversity and Ethnic Minority Psychology, 13*(2), 143–150.

19. Birman, D. (2006). Acculturation gap and family adjustment: Findings with Soviet Jewish refugees in the U.S. and implications for measurement. *Journal of Cross-Cultural Psychology, 37*, 568–589.

20. Tummala-Narra, P. (2007). Skin color and the therapeutic relationship. *Psychoanalytic Psychology, 24*(2), 255–270.

21. Suárez-Orozco, C., & Qin, B. (2006). Gendered perspectives in psychology: Immigrant origin youth. *International Migration Review, 40*(1), 165–198.

22. Costigan, C. L., & Dokis, D. P. (2006). The relations between parent-child acculturation differences and adjustment within immigrant Chinese families. *Child Development, 77*, 1252–1267; Kim, M., & Park, I. J. K. (2011). Testing the moderating effect of parent-adolescent communication on the acculturation gap–distress relation in Korean American families. *Journal of Youth and Adolescence, 40*, 1661–1673.

23. Akhtar. (2011).

24. Suárez-Orozco, C., & Suárez -Orozco, M. M. (2001). *Children of immigration.* Cambridge: Harvard University Press.

25. Smith, T. B., & Silva, L. (2011). Ethnic identity and personal well-being of people of color: A meta-analysis. *Journal of Counseling Psychology, 58*(1), 42–60; Rogers-Sirin & Gupta. (2012).

26. Ibid.

27. Ibid.; Sirin, S. R., & Fine, M. (2008). *Muslim American youth: Understanding hyphenated identities through multiple methods.* New York: NYU Press; Marks, A. K., Patton, F., & García Coll, C. (2011). Being bicultural: A mixed-methods study of adolescents' implicitly and explicitly measured multiethnic identities. *Developmental Psychology, 47*(1), 270–288.

28. Tummala-Narra, P., Inman, A. G., & Ettigi, S. (2011). Asian Indians' responses to discrimination: A mixed-method examination of identity, coping, and self-esteem. *Asian American Journal of Psychology, 2*(3), 205–218.

29. Awad, G. H. (2010). The impact of acculturation and religious identification on perceived discrimination for Arab / Middle Eastern Americans. *Cultural Diversity and Ethnic Minority Psychology, 16*, 59–67; Sirin, S. R., Ryce, P., Gupta, T., & Rogers-Sirin, L. (2013). The role of acculturative stress on mental health symptoms for immigrant adolescents: A longitudinal investigation. *Developmental Psychology, 49*(4), 736–748; Tummala-Narra, P., Alegria, M., & Chen, C. (2012). Perceived discrimination, acculturative stress, and depression among South Asians: Mixed findings. In Secondary Analysis of the National Latino Asian American Study (NLAAS) Dataset—Part I. Special issue of *Asian American Journal of Psychology, 3*(1), 3–16.

30. Ellis, B. H., MacDonald, H. Z, Lincoln, A. K., & Cabral, H. J. (2008). Mental health of Somali adolescent refugees: The role of trauma, stress, and perceived discrimination. *Journal of Consulting and Clinical Psychology, 76*(2), 184–193.

31. Tummala-Narra et al. (2011).

32. Sirin et al. (2013).

33. Tummala-Narra et al. (2011).

34. Pumariega, A. J., Rothe, E., & Pumariega, J.B. (2005). Mental health of immigrants and refugees. *Community Mental Health Journal, 41*(5), 581–597.

35. Suárez-Orozco, C., Yoshikawa, H., Teranishi, R. T., & Suárez-Orozco, M. M. (2011). Growing up in the shadows: The developmental implications of unauthorized status. *Harvard Educational Review, 81*(3), 438–620; APA. (2012).

36. Potochnick & Perreira. (2010).

37. Sirin & Fine. (2008).

38. Chaudry, A., Capps, R., Pedroza, J., Castaneda, R. M., Santos, R., & Scott, M. M. (2010). *Facing our future: Children in the aftermath of immigration enforcement.* Washington, DC: Urban Institute.

39. Mulvaney-Day, N. E., Alegria, M., & Sribney, W. (2007). Social cohesion, social support, and health among Latinos in the United States. *Social Medicine & Medicine, 64,* 477–495.

40. Tummala-Narra et al. (2011).

41. Suárez-Orozco & Suárez-Orozco. (2001).

42. Kataoka, S. H., Novins, D. K., & DeCarlo Santiago, C. (2010). The practice of evidence-based treatments in ethnic minority youth. *Child and Adolescent Psychiatric Clinics of North America, 19*(4), 775–789.

43. Ellis, B. H., MacDonald, H. Z, Lincoln, A. K., & Cabral, H. J. (2008). Mental health of Somali adolescent refugees: The role of trauma, stress, and perceived discrimination. *Journal of Consulting and Clinical Psychology, 76*(2), 184–193; Kataoka, S. H., Stein, B. D., Jaycox, L. H., Wong, M., Escudero, P., Tu, W., Zaragoza, C., & Fink, A. (2003). A school-based mental health program for traumatized Latino immigrant children. *Journal of the American Academy of Child and Adolescent Psychiatry, 42* (3), 311–318.

44. Gudino, O. G., Nadeem, E., Kataoka, S. H., & Lau, A. S. (2011). Relative impact of violence exposure and immigrant stressors on Latino youth psychopathology. *Journal of Community Psychology, 39*(3), 316–335.

45. Suárez-Orozco et al. (2011); APA. (2012).

46. Ellis et al. (2008).

47. Raj, A., & Silverman, J. G. (2003). Immigrant South Asian women at greater risk for injury from intimate partner violence. *American Journal of Public Health, 93,* 435–437.

48. Foster, R. P. (2001). When immigration is trauma: Guidelines for the individual and family clinician. *American Journal of Orthopsychiatry, 71*(2), 153–170.

49. Nicolas, G., Arntz, D. L., Hirsch, B., & Schmiedigen, A. (2009). Cultural adaptation of a group treatment for Haitian American adolescents. *Professional Psychology: Research and Practice, 40*(4), 378–384.

50. Bernat, F. P., & Zhilina, T. (2010). Human trafficking: The local becomes global. *Women and Criminal Justice, 20,* 2–9.

51. Suárez -Orozco et al. (2011).

52. APA. (2012).

53. Ibid.

54. Cummings, J. R., & Druss, B. G. (2011). Racial/ethnic differences in mental health service use among adolescents with major depression. *Journal of the American Academy of Child and Adolescent Psychiatry, 50*(2), 160–170; Merikangas, K. R., He, J., Burstein, M., Swendsen, J., Avenevoli, S., Case, B., Georgiades, K., Heaton, L., Swanson, S., & Olfson, M. (2011). Service utilization for lifetime mental disorders in U.S. adolescents: Results of the National Comorbidity Survey-Adolescent Supplement (NCS-A). *Journal of the American Academy of Child & Adolescent Psychiatry, 50*(1), 32–45.

55. Carson, N. J., Stewart, M., Lin, J. Y., & Alegria, M. (2011). Use and quality of mental health services for Haitian youth. *Ethnicity & Health, 16*(6), 567–582.

56. García, C. M., Gilchrist, L., Vazquez, G., Leite, A., & Raymond, N. (2011). Urban and rural immigrant Latino youths' and adults' knowledge and beliefs about mental health resources. *Journal of Immigrant and Minority Health, 13*(13), 500–509.

57. Ibid.

58. Gudino, O. G., Lau, A. S., & Hough, R. L. (2008). Immigrant status, mental health need, and mental health service utilization among high-risk Hispanic and Asian Pacific Islander youth. *Child Youth Care Forum, 37*, 139–152.

59. Park-Taylor, J., Ventura, A. B., & Ng, V. (2010). Multicultural counseling and assessment with children. In J. G. Ponterotto, J. M. Casas, L. A. Suzuki, & C. M. Alexander (Eds.), *Handbook of multicultural counseling* (3rd ed., pp. 621–631). Los Angeles: Sage; APA. (2012).

60. Park-Taylor et al. (2010); APA. (2012).

61. Alegria, M., Vallas, M., & Pumariega, A. J. (2010). Racial and ethnic disparities in pediatric mental health. *Child and Adolescent Psychiatric Clinics of North America, 19*, 759–774; APA. (2012).

62. Nicolas, G., Arntz, D. L., Hirsch, B., & Schmiedigen, A. (2009). Cultural adaptation of a group treatment for Haitian American adolescents. *Professional Psychology: Research and Practice, 40*(4), 378–384; APA. (2012).

63. Kataoka et al. (2003).

64. APA. (2012).

65. Sue, D. W., Arredondo, P., & McDavis, R. J. (1992). Multicultural counseling competencies and standards: A call to the profession. *Journal of Counseling and Development, 70*, 477–486.

66. Tummala-Narra. (2007).

67. Comas-Diaz, L. (2006). Latino healing: The integration of ethnic psychology into psychotherapy. *Psychotherapy: Theory, Research, Practice, Training, 43*, 436–453; Pumariega et al. (2005).

68. Tummala-Narra, P., Singer, R., Li, Z., Esposito, J., & Ash, S. (2012). Individual and systemic factors in clinicians' self-perceived cultural competence. *Professional Psychology: Research and Practice, 43*(3), 165–174.

69. Sue, D. W., Bucceri, J., Lin, A. I., Nadal, K. L., & Torino, G. C. (2007). Racial microaggressions and the Asian American experience. *Cultural Diversity and Ethnic Minority Psychology, 13*(1), 72–81; Leary, K. (2000). Racial enactments in dynamic treatment. *Psychoanalytic Dialogues, 10*, 639–653.

12

Behavioral Outcomes

HOAN N. BUI

On April 4, 1991, the Nguyễn brothers—Lợi (age 21), Pham (age 19), and Long (age 17)—asked their parents' permission to go fishing with their friend Cường Trần (age 16). However, the boys did not go fishing. Instead, they went to an electronics store in a mall near their home in Sacramento, California, and held 38 people hostage at gunpoint in a horrifying eight-hour siege that ended with six people dead, including three of the boys, and 11 injured hostages. Law-enforcement authorities indicated that the hostage takers were members of an Asian gang called the Oriental Boys.

The Nguyễn brothers and their parents, who had escaped dictatorship in Vietnam by sea in a small boat and arrived in the United States as refugees 10 years earlier, had faced many barriers to cultural and economic integration. During the long siege, the boys complained about their lives in the United States: they experienced strict discipline at home, their parents were poor, and they could not find jobs. Prior to the hostage and shooting incident, Long and Cường had been expelled from school for stealing sports equipment and trying to set the school on fire. Cường also had shoplifting charges, and Long had vandalism charges for having broken into a Coke machine. The Vietnamese interpreter for the police said, "I don't think of these boys as a Vietnamese problem. They are an American problem. These kids have been here for 10 years now. They've adopted this culture already. They're like bananas—they look yellow on the outside, but inside they're White already."[1]

Parents' concern for their children is often perceived as a main incentive for their decision to immigrate; they frequently have high hopes for their offspring's future and success in the United States.[2] These hopes appear to be based on numerous success stories of immigrants, who have come to the United States since the early 17th century to seek freedom and a better life or to realize their dreams of prospering financially. Many have made great fortunes, contributed tremendously to U.S. society, and become renowned in various fields such as the sciences, education, the arts, business, industry, and politics.[3] However, not all immigrants and their children are able to "make it." Along with valedictorians and high achievers, there are immigrant youth whose American dreams are shattered as they experience the consequences of delinquency, dropping out of school, arrests, and incarcerations.[4]

Research has identified the relationships among immigration, crime, delinquency, and risk behaviors. Studies have shown that foreign-born (i.e., first-generation) immigrant youth as a group exhibit lower levels of risk behaviors than U.S.-born (i.e., second- and later-generation) immigrant-origin youth do, a finding often called the *immigrant paradox* because foreign-born youth frequently appear to succeed despite their disadvantaged economic situations.[5] Early studies of the experiences of immigrants who came from European countries at the turn of the 20th century indicate that crime problems were attributed to the children of immigrants, who were more likely than their U.S.-born White counterparts to be involved in delinquency.[6] Theories of delinquency that were developed in the first half of the 20th century suggest that problems in migration adaptation were major factors contributing to delinquency among children of immigrants.[7] More recent research has suggested similar connections between the rise of violent youth gangs and the involvement of children of immigrants in youth gangs. These findings are not surprising given that many of today's U.S.-born immigrant youth are concentrated in urban areas, where juvenile crime and gang involvement are most common.[8]

Understanding the behaviors of immigrant youth is important because risk behaviors affect the well-being and safety not only of immigrants and their children but also of their community and the entire country. Theories and empirical studies suggest that behavior in early childhood is linked to divergent trajectories throughout the life course and that risk behavior in adolescence tends to persist into adulthood because of the accumulation of disadvantage and the stability of delinquency and antisocial behavior over time.[9] A low level of delinquency, substance use, and sexual activity among foreign-born youth can be seen as a benefit of immigration, but higher levels of involvement in these behaviors among the second generation, which accounts for a substantial majority (85 percent) of the immigrant youth population, present a pressing need to understand the social context of delinquency and risk behaviors among immigrant youth in order to implement appropriate interventions.[10] This chapter discusses the social contexts of immigrant-origin youth's delinquency and risk behaviors with a focus on the environmental systems with which they have the most contact.

Ecological Perspective for Understanding Immigrant Youth's Behaviors

The ecological perspective proposed by Ury Bronfenbrenner emphasizes the interactions and influences of environmental systems on youth's developmental outcomes.[11] These environmental systems—which include the family, school, neighborhood, ethnic community, and larger U.S. society—exert lifetime influences on socialization, but these influences are particularly salient during adolescence. As individuals interact with others, the environmental systems also interact to shape youth's interaction experiences. This perspective is consistent with delinquency theories suggesting that families, schools, neighborhoods, and larger social contexts influence child and adolescent delinquency and risk behaviors. According to social control theories, close and warm family relationships as well as strong attachments to one's family can prevent youth's negative behaviors through effective parental supervision and discipline. Conversely, family conflicts diminish family attachments and undermine parental control, thus facilitating delinquency and risk behaviors.[12] Similarly, the quality of familial relationships can influence adolescent sexuality through parental monitoring and communication of sexual values and attitudes.[13] A youth's commitment to school and aspirations for attaining higher levels of education are major elements of the investment in conventional lines of action that can prevent delinquent or criminal behavior.[14] On the other hand, adverse neighborhood conditions such as the presence of negative role models, unconventional values, and ineffective social control can facilitate delinquency, substance abuse, and sexual activity by exposing youth to the condition of social disorganization.[15] Youth then engage in negative behaviors in response to the stress caused by the social contexts characterized by economic inequality.[16]

Environmental systems can influence the development and behaviors of immigrant-origin youth through their effects on acculturation and/or assimilation during immigrants' process of adaptation to the host country. *Acculturation*, the changes in attitude and/or behavior resulting from contacts with another culture, often occurs on a number of dimensions such as the language, cultural beliefs, values, and behaviors of the dominant society.[17] For example, the United States has higher levels of substance use and abuse than many other countries do. Drug use is part of its youth culture, with between 37 and 48 percent of 10th to 12th graders having tried illicit drugs. Long-term immigrants' exposure to mainstream U.S. society often leads to patterns of alcohol and drug use that approximate substance use among the U.S.-born population.[18] On the other hand, *assimilation* involves the incorporation and fusion of immigrants into groups and/or the larger society in a common life.[19] The classic assimilation perspective advanced by Milton Gordon assumes that assimilation has a positive effect on adaptation outcomes and maintains the importance of assimilation for upward mobility.[20] Cultural assimilation can involve immigrants' and their children's acquiring English proficiency and valuable new job skills, attaining higher levels of education, and completing other accomplishments that can ease their entry into U.S. society and improve their chances for success in the U.S. economy.[21]

However, acculturation and assimilation do not always occur smoothly or automatically lead to positive developmental outcomes. Recent (or revisionist) assimilation perspectives suggest that there may be negative effects of acculturation. With greater socialization and more time spent in U.S. institutions, neighborhoods, and youth culture, the children of immigrants are likely to adopt the behavioral norms of the host society, including its risk behaviors, and may lose connection with the values of their heritage culture; they may also be subject to negative economic and social forces that likely promote negative behaviors.[22] Studies show that acculturation measured by immigrants' language use (English), preference for U.S. culture (music, newspapers, TV, and radio), and length of U.S. residency has been associated with substance use and delinquency.[23] Adaptation to and assimilation into environments plagued by social problems can facilitate immigrant-origin youth's risk behaviors.[24] In addition, immigrant youth can experience tension in their adjustment to the new society as they strive to be accepted by the majority population and simultaneously cope with socializing agents in their family and neighborhood who may wish to deter the acculturation and assimilation processes.[25] Family tensions can alienate immigrant youth from other family members, increase their number of peer associations, and encourage delinquency and risk behaviors such as substance abuse and sexual activity. In short, because immigrants and their children often undergo complex social, interpersonal, psychological, and context-sensitive processes of adaptation to the host society, it is important to understand the role of environmental systems in shaping youth behaviors within the contexts of acculturation and assimilation.

Effects of Neighborhoods, Communities, and the Society at Large on Adaptation

The social environment within which acculturation occurs can play an important role in shaping youth's behavioral outcomes. Research has demonstrated that the link between immigration and crime is not universal but rather varies with race and ethnicity, location, and specific types of behaviors. For example, among early migrants, Irish immigrants born in Ireland and living in Detroit had higher arrest rates for public-order offenses such as drunkenness than other foreign-born immigrant groups and U.S.-born people did.[26] Among more recent immigrants, research has demonstrated that Puerto Rican newcomers living in New York City had high rates of violent crime, while those living in other urban areas had rates comparable to those of U.S.-born Whites.[27] In California, male immigrants from Southeast Asia were found to be more likely than U.S.-born Whites to engage in crimes that produced financial gain, including theft, auto theft, and petty theft. In particular, the Vietnamese were more likely to be arrested for all crimes than Whites and more established Asian groups such as the Chinese and Japanese were.[28] In addition, the immigrant paradox was observed to occur among Blacks and Hispanics but not among Asians and Whites, whose levels of engagement in violent and property crimes were similar across immigrant generations.[29]

Portes and Zhou have developed the concept of *segmented assimilation*, which emphasizes that the social context of immigrant resettlement is an important factor in immigrant youth's life experiences. Segmented assimilation maintains that adaptation outcomes vary, depending on the characteristics of the social sectors into which particular immigrant groups assimilate.[30] One path of assimilation involves parallel integration into the White middle class, another path leads to permanent poverty and assimilation into the underclass, and a third path of assimilation occurs for immigrant groups that experience rapid economic advancement while preserving their immigrant community's values and tight solidarity. These different adaptation outcomes, which in turn are associated with immigrant youth's behaviors, are determined by the resources available to immigrants and their children as well as by the barriers they face during the adaptation process. Strong coethnic immigrant communities are considered a key resource for many immigrant parents in their struggle to successfully raise their children in urban areas and protect them from social ills because these communities can supply immigrant families with social capital by maintaining positive cultural norms, preventing family disruption, and reinforcing parental authority over children.[31] This view has been supported by studies that reveal negative relationships between immigrant density in neighborhoods and levels of substance use and delinquency among second-generation youth.[32]

The positive aspects of coethnic communities are not unlimited, however. Due to class, racial, and ethnic segregation, immigrant Blacks and Latinos are often concentrated in impoverished and disorganized neighborhoods that expose immigrant youth to the harmful subculture that marginalized U.S.-born youth have developed to cope with their lack of economic resources and opportunities for a better existence.[33] These negative environments also stymie parents' expectations and plans for their children's upward mobility.[34] Alienation from the mainstream society, thwarted opportunities for change, a lack of positive role models, a deviant subculture, and economic pressures can leave immigrant youth vulnerable to the underground economy, making criminal and destructive behaviors tempting.[35] Research has shown that living in predominantly Mexican-heritage and impoverished Latino neighborhoods that are mostly populated by nonimmigrants is a risk factor for substance abuse among highly acculturated Mexican American and Latino immigrant youth.[36]

Immigrants' resettlement in places where racial and ethnic prejudice and discrimination exist can negatively affect their adaptation and behavioral outcomes. Racial and ethnic prejudice and discrimination can emerge in immigrant gateways if U.S.-born individuals living there have previously only had limited exposure to immigrants and cultural diversity.[37] Research on school segregation has presented evidence of U.S.-born students keeping their distance from new immigrant students in emerging immigrant communities.[38] When a member of a minority group is exposed to stressful situations such as discrimination or language difficulties, he or she is increasingly vulnerable to maladaptive behavior, especially when he or she has few personal resources such as financial or social supports to moderate the effects of these stressors.[39] Immigrant youth who are more acculturated to the dominant culture may be more vulnerable to the effects of discrimination because they are less aligned with their traditional culture and more sensitive to negative attitudes about and stereotypes of their group.[40] Youths' feelings of marginalization and mistrust combined with a lack of status and economic opportunities can produce problematic behavior such as criminal activity, delinquency, and substance use.[41] Studies have found that immigrants who had experienced many forms of racial discrimination were more likely to use tobacco, alcohol, and controlled substances than those who had not.[42] Research suggests that patterns of criminal activity among Southeast Asian immigrants in California were caused by stress resulting from dealing with poverty, unemployment, discrimination, and acculturation problems. Studies also found that Black immigrant youth in New York adopted violent behaviors to protect themselves from perceived or actual threats from others in their neighborhoods.[43]

The cultural context of the society at large and neighborhood characteristics can also influence adolescent sexual behavior. For immigrant youth, a critical aspect of adaptation is renegotiating or redefining gender roles in the new cultural context.[44] In many non-Western nations, including the Asian and Latin American countries from which most current U.S. immigrants originated, cultural values stress familism and traditional roles for women over individual sexual fulfillment. Women's roles are formed around concepts of femininity that emphasize women's sexual purity, chastity, and obedience to males.[45] In these traditional cultures, adolescent sexual activities are uncommon, especially among girls, while sex outside marriage has become the norm rather than the exception for teens in the United States.[46] Thus, immigrant youth, especially females, often live in two worlds in which they experience contradictions between their heritage culture and U.S. culture.[47] Less acculturated female youth may internalize their heritage country's traditional gender-specific norms characterized by passivity and submissiveness during interactions with males. Through media, which are a potent source of sex socialization, youth are acclimated to the new culture of sexuality, and those who are highly acculturated may adopt gender roles shaped by U.S. values that emphasize gender equality in social status, power, and sexual freedom.[48] Research has found that adaptation to U.S. culture has been associated with an increase in permissive attitudes toward premarital sex, liberal sexual views, sexual empowerment, and regarding birth outside of marriage as acceptable.[49] In addition to the influences of society at large, neighborhood contexts affect teens' sexual activities. Research indicates that low-income neighborhoods have been associated with higher levels of teenage sexual activity, perhaps because of negative role models living in these areas.[50] Sexual freedom can have negative consequences for adolescents since early sexual activity is associated with alcohol and drug use, multiple sex partners, sexually transmitted diseases, adolescent pregnancies, inconsistent use of sexual protection, and intimate-partner violence. Thus, a high level of acculturation within negative neighborhood contexts can increase the likelihood of immigrant youth's problem behaviors.

Schools, Peers, Acculturation, and Behavioral Outcomes

As a primary context for social interactions, schools have important implications for youth's behavior and for determining whether adolescents will follow a socially acceptable path or become involved in deviant behaviors such as delinquency and substance use.[51] For immigrant youth, schools, which are places where they learn the new language, become educated, cultivate interpersonal skills, and form peer groups, are also a key driver of acculturation.[52] Research demonstrates that most foreign-born children arrive at school with favorable attitudes about education; they also have more positive feelings about their schools and are more accepting of the educational values of their school than their U.S.-born peers are. These differences in attitude are not explained by these children's socioeconomic backgrounds.[53] Perhaps immigrant parents often have high expectations regarding their children's education, thus exerting pressure on the children to do well in school.[54] Because parents' aspirations can influence children's attitudes, children of immigrants may attribute extrinsic or instrumental values (e.g., good jobs, high income) to their schooling, which in turn can motivate them to work hard.[55] However, not all immigrant youth succeed at school. The school experience can be frustrating for many because of language difficulties.[56] Acculturation stress associated with learning a new language can negatively affect youth's educational experience, including school failure, and can contribute to youth's involvement in negative behaviors. Language barriers experienced by immigrant parents can pose an additional problem because they impact parents' ability to help their children with homework, keep track of their progress in school, and monitor their attendance.[57] Students with limited English proficiency often have lower academic achievement and far more modest educational goals than those who are fluent in English.[58] Poor academic performance and low aspirations can discourage youth from trying to learn and may drive them out of school to join gangs and consort with delinquent peers.[59]

Studies have also found diminished educational aspirations and low achievement among second- and third-generation immigrant children, which can result from their assimilation into a negative school environment.[60] The school climate, a part of the school environment, is often measured by formal and informal rules that govern individual and group interactions as well as by the values and belief systems of a school, including peers' norms, expectations for success, and attitudes toward discipline.[61] As such, the school climate is indicative of the quality of students' school experiences that shape their academic achievement, attitudes, and social and emotional adjustment as well as their negative behaviors. Research indicates that students attending schools that have an overall high level of student attachment to school are less likely to engage in substance abuse than students attending schools with less attachment are.[62] However, as a major social context for interactions, schools can also enable the spread of negative behaviors among students, and their adaptation to these behaviors can result in negative outcomes. Research has shown that the risk of cigarette smoking is significantly associated with peer networks and increasing rates of prevalent school smoking.[63]

Race and class segregation can also significantly impact students' experiences with school climate. Black and Hispanic immigrants tend to live near U.S.-born Blacks and Latinos in low-income communities, and their children often attend segregated schools with a disproportionate number of students with limited English proficiency.[64] Studies have revealed that schools attended by Latino children of immigrants, especially Mexican children, have a perceived negative climate and more behavior problems than schools attended by Asian American youth do. Findings also show that Southeast Asian children often attend the most unsafe schools, including those with a high occurrence of gang activity and violent fights.[65] These problem behaviors are likely to be transmitted to immigrant youth when they form friendships with peers at school and adapt to the negative school environment and culture. Indeed, youth often engage in substance abuse due to peer pressure or their desire for acceptance in peer-group networks. Those who attend schools in neighborhoods where youth gangs are prevalent can join gangs as an adaptive strategy for protection. Because gangs engage in criminal activities, gang membership eventually leads to delinquency and crime.

Peer groups, which are often formed at school, provide an important socialization context for youth in general and a means of acculturation for immigrant youth in particular. Peers' influence derives from youth's perceptions of their peers' attitudes and behaviors as well as from their peers' actual attitudes and behaviors, so peer relationships can be an important factor contributing to youth's negative behaviors.[66] Like many adolescents, immigrant youth may turn to peers rather than family members for information and emotional support.[67] Because recent immigrants have largely come from Latin America and Asia, immigrant youth tend to differ from their U.S.-born counterparts in racial and ethnic background, appearance, religion, and language. Since being different holds crucial social significance for an individual's acceptance into peer networks and school culture, peer approval and the ability to blend into mainstream society may become important for immigrant youth.[68]

Consequently, immigrant youth may identify even more with peers in their attempts to belong.[69] Through face-to-face peer interactions, peer relationships facilitate acculturation, which reinforces itself because high levels of acculturation make it unlikely that immigrant youth will have best friends from their panethnic group, nationality, or culture.[70] Studies indicate that peer norms for substance abuse have the greatest effect on the likelihood of youth's substance abuse, and research on immigrant youth has revealed peers' significant mediating effects on the relationship between acculturation and substance use.[71] Peer influence is also an important factor in adolescents' decisions about sex and sexual risk-taking behaviors. Research has indicated that affiliation with delinquent peers and having sexually active friends were two significant influences on adolescents' participation in early intercourse.[72]

Immigrant Families and Parent-Child Conflicts

The family can be a source of protection, constraint, and/or frustration for immigrant youth. Youth may benefit from the structure and work ethic of immigrant families; most children of immigrants (82 percent) live in two-parent families with working parents (95 percent of fathers and 60 percent of mothers), and the proportion of two-parent families among foreign-born youth is higher than that among their U.S.-born peers.[73] Due to differences in the educational levels of members of various racial and ethnic immigrant groups, parents' level of education is a resource for some immigrant youth but a constraint for others. Many immigrants from Asia and Europe have higher levels of education than do immigrants from other areas of the world, in part because a majority of them migrate to the United States in the professional emigration category, which requires immigrants to have at least a U.S. baccalaureate degree or a foreign equivalent.[74] Consequently, immigrant youth from Europe and Asia are more likely than their U.S.-born peers to have parents with a college education, but the opposite is true for immigrant youth from Mexico and Latin America.[75] Because educational achievement is associated with occupational status and generally higher income, high levels of parental education can contribute to the financial stability of immigrant families, while low levels cause financial problems. The structural stability of intact families as well as the financial stability associated with parents' high levels of education and employment can facilitate youth's educational achievements and goal attainment as well as positive behavioral outcomes. Research has found that children who live in intact families with working parents perform better academically and have lower dropout rates and lower levels of delinquency than those who live in other types of families.[76] Family income often determines residential locations and quality of school climate, which in turn can influence youth's behavior.

Relationships in immigrant families are also especially complicated as a result of acculturation. Immigrant youth can be protected within the boundaries of their ethnic culture and its traditional behavior expectations, or they can turn away from their ethnic culture and family traditions.[77] Often when parents migrate to a new country, they bring with them their heritage culture's child-rearing practices and notions of children's development that may not be consistent with practices in the new culture. Intrafamily conflicts are less common among new immigrants because they still hold traditional values that stress strong family relationships and amicable social interactions between children and adults.[78] Because of collectivism and close family relationships, such as those of Latinos and Asians, some cultures may place adolescents' behavior in the context of the family, causing youth to consider the impact of their behavior on their families.[79] In addition, parents can influence adolescents by monitoring and attempting to control their behavior or by communicating positive values and attitudes about negative behavior.[80] Among new immigrants, parents' high hopes for their children's education, which may have influenced their decision to migrate, and traditional notions of family stability and children's familial obligation to stay out of trouble can easily be internalized by children and have been linked to children's educational success and mental, physical, and behavioral development.[81]

Acculturation can also cause parent-child conflicts in immigrant families, which in turn can have significant negative consequences for family relationships and youth's behavior. Children typically acculturate more rapidly than adults do, thus adopting values and beliefs that differ from those of their parents.[82] More acculturated youth frequently face conflicting sets of expectations from their parents and from members of the larger society with whom they have contact.[83] Among Asian immigrants, for example, parents' harsh discipline and expectations of obedience often clash with children's desires for autonomy.[84] Immigrant parents' acculturation can promote changes in their parenting, resulting in less disciplining or inconsistent disciplining of their children as well as less effective monitoring and supervision of them.[85] Language gaps between parents and children caused by different rates of acculturation can also result in a lack of effective communication between them. Because children tend to learn to speak English more quickly than their parents do, gaps between parents' and children's English proficiency can impede communication, creating opportunities for family conflicts.[86] Such problems in family discourse can also make it difficult for parents to discuss sex with their children, who may feel more comfortable turning to peers for information and advice.

Intergenerational conflicts stemming from different rates of acculturation can have significant negative consequences for youth's behavior because they weaken family cohesion and attachments, disrupt the family's social control over children, and alienate youth from their family. These conditions are considered chief sources of delinquency.[87] In addition, immigrant youth's acculturation also weakens the influence of traditional family structures and social networks that can help youth cope with risk behaviors.[88] Studies have demonstrated that good family relationships serve as a protective factor against substance abuse but that gaps in acculturation between parents and children increase parent-child conflicts, and low family functioning affects adolescents' psychological well-being and produces negative behavioral outcomes, including anxiety, anger, depression, school misconduct, substance abuse, delinquency, and risky sexual behavior.[89]

Conclusion

Immigrant youth's adaptation to their new country involves acculturation and assimilation, which can either negatively or positively impact behavioral outcomes. Acculturation and assimilation can be beneficial for immigrant youth when they have opportunities to adapt to middle-class U.S culture and practice middle-class behavior, thus enabling their upward mobility and integration into the middle class. Conversely, acculturation and assimilation can be problematic when immigrant youth lose touch with their cultural heritage and experience family conflicts.[90] Assimilating into negative social environments can lead to maladaptive behaviors when immigrant youth adopt the norms and values of the underclass, including substance abuse, participating in crime, and dropping out of school. Higher reported levels of risk behaviors among second-generation youth compared with those of their foreign-born peers suggest negative effects of acculturation and assimilation, but generational differences in risk behavior are not universal across racial/ethnic groups.[91] Rather, acculturation and assimilation are shaped by many interrelated social, familial, and personal factors that interact to produce different adaptation outcomes. Capital resources, resettlement locations, and racial attitudes determine the type of people with whom immigrants and their children are likely to associate, the quality of the education that immigrant youth receive, the culture into which they assimilate, and consequently, the types of behaviors they adopt.[92] Socioeconomic advantages reflected in parents' high levels of education and substantial financial resources are associated with their children's greater access to educational opportunities that provide them with more chances for upward mobility.[93] On the contrary, life in impoverished and disorganized communities exposes immigrant youth to negative cultural norms that discourage youth's commitments to conventional value systems, weaken family bonds, and reduce parents' ability to supervise and influence their children's behavior.[94]

Families and schools have complex effects on immigrants' adaptation to the new culture. Foreign-born youth can benefit from the stability of their intact families, but there is less stability for second-generation youth, who have lower rates of intact families. In addition, some aspects of acculturation can lead to family conflicts that alienate immigrant youth from their families.[95] Peer relationships formed at schools also distance youth from their families, thus reducing the family's social control and diminishing the supportive role that family can play in youth's lives. Strong coethnic communities can provide support and cultural resources to immigrant families in their struggles to successfully raise children in the new society, but most new immigrants, especially those from Latin America, live in impoverished and isolated minority communities with few positive resources.[96] Biculturalism and bilingualism have been linked to favorable academic and behavioral outcomes because they can enable good communication between parents and children, which can help maintain close family relationships and provide support to protect immigrant youth from the negative influences of acculturation.[97] Parents' and children's discussions about culture can also facilitate ethnic pride and ethnic identity, which have been found to influence patterns of positive behavior.[98] However, marginalized immigrant youth with limited English proficiency who are isolated in segregated immigrant communities are unlikely to benefit from biculturalism and bilingualism, which require fluency in two languages (English and the language of the heritage country) and a strong involvement in both U.S. culture and the heritage culture.

Because immigrant youth differ greatly in their social, cultural, and economic backgrounds as well as in their family circumstances, they have complex adaptation experiences that result in wide variations in achievement and behavioral outcomes.[99] Since the 1960s, a majority of immigrants to the United States have come from Mexico, Latin America, and the Caribbean with few economic resources and little social capital; their children account for the majority of immigrant youth in the United States.[100] Without social policies that provide support and facilitate opportunities for the social integration of these children, they face a great risk of downward assimilation with negative behavioral outcomes, including substance abuse, delinquency, early sexual intercourse, and teenage parenthood.

NOTES

1. Nhu, T. T. (1991, April 19). Sacramento siege. *San Jose Mercury News.*

2. Rumbaut, R. (2005). Children of immigrants and their achievement: The roles of family, acculturation, social class, ethnicity, and school contexts. In R. D. Taylor (Ed.), *Addressing the achievement gap: Theory informing practice* (pp. 23–59). Greenwich, CT: Information Age.

3. Barkan, E. R. (Ed.). (2001). *Making it in America: A sourcebook on eminent ethnic Americans.* Santa Barbara, CA: ABC Clio.

4. Zhou, M., & Bankston, C. L. (2006). Delinquency and acculturation in the twenty-first century: A decade's change in a Vietnamese American community. In R. Martinez, Jr., and A. Valenzuela, Jr. (Eds.), *Immigration and crime: Race, ethnicity, and violence* (pp. 117–139). New York: NYU Press.

5. Bui, H. N. (2011). Segmented assimilation: Racial differences in the relationship between immigration status and delinquency. In C. García Coll & A. Marks (Eds.), *The immigrant paradox in children and adolescents: Is becoming an American a developmental risk?* (pp. 135–158). Washington, DC: American Psychological Association.

6. National Commission on Law Observance and Enforcement. (1931). *Report on crime and the foreign born*. Washington, DC: U.S. Government Printing Office.

7. Shaw, C. R., & McKay, H. D. (1942). *Juvenile delinquency in urban areas*. Chicago: University of Chicago Press.

8. Bankston, C. L. (1998). Youth gangs and the new second generation: A review essay. *Aggression and Violent Behavior, 3*(1), 35–45.

9. Loeber, R. (1982). The stability of antisocial and delinquent child behavior: A review. *Child Development, 53*, 1431–1446.

10. Bui. (2011); Passel, J. (2011). Demography of immigrant youth: Past, present and future. *The Future of Children, 21*(1), 19–41.

11. Bronfenbrenner, U. (1979). *The ecology of human development: Experiments by nature and design*. New York: Oxford University Press.

12. Hirschi, T. (1995). The family. In J. Q. Wilson & J. Petersilia (Eds.), *Crime* (pp. 121–140). San Francisco: Institute for Contemporary Studies Press.

13. Raffaelli, M., Kang, H. & Guarini, T. (2011). Exploring the immigrant paradox in adolescent sexuality: An ecological perspective. In C. García Coll and A. Marks (Eds.), *The immigrant paradox in children and adolescents: Is becoming an American a developmental risk?* (pp. 109–134). Washington, DC: American Psychological Association.

14. Hirschi, T. (1969). *Causes of delinquency*. Berkeley: University of California Press.

15. Sampson, R. J., Raudenbush, S. W., & Earls, F. (1997). Neighborhoods and violent crime: A multilevel study of collective efficacy. *Science, 277*, 918–924.

16. Merton, R. (1938). Social structure and anomie. *American Sociological Review, 3*, 672–682.

17. Berry, J. V. (1980). Acculturation as varieties of adaptation. In A. M. Padila (Ed.), *Acculturation: Theory, models, and some new findings* (pp. 207–236). Boulder, CO: Westview.

18. Degenhardt, L., Chiu, W., Sampson, N., Kessler, R. C., Anthony, J. C., Angermeyer, M., Bruffaerts, R., Girolamo, G., Gureje, O., Huang, Y., Karam, A., Kostyuchenko, S., Lepine, J. P., Mora, M. E. M., Neumark, Y., Ormel, J. H., Pinto-Meza, A. P., Posada-Villa, J. P., Stein, D. J., Takeshima, T., and Wells, J. E. (2008). Toward a global view of alcohol, tobacco, cannabis, and cocaine use: Findings from the WHO World Mental Health Surveys. *PLoS Medicine, 5*, 1053–1067.

19. Gordon, M. (1964). *Assimilation in American life: The role of race, religion, and national origin*. New York: Oxford University Press.

20. Ibid.

21. Harris, K. M. (1998). Health status and risk behavior of adolescents in immigrant families. In D. Hernandez (Ed.), *Children of immigrants: Health, adjustment, and public assistance* (pp. 286–374). Washington, DC: National Academic Press.

22. Ibid.

23. Bui. (2011).

24. Shaw & McKay. (1942).

25. Harris. (1998).

26. Waters, T. (1999). *Crime and immigrant youth*. Thousand Oaks, CA: Sage.

27. Martinez, R., & Lee, M. (2000). On immigration and crime. *Criminal Justice, 1*, 485–524.

28. Kposowa, A. J., & Tsunokai, G. T. (2003). Offending patterns among Southeast Asians in the state of California. *Journal of Ethnicity in Criminal Justice, 1*(1), 93–113.

29. Bui. (2011).

30. Portes, A., & Zhou, M. (1993). The new second generation: Segmented assimilation and its variants. *Annals of the American Academy of Political and Social Sciences, 530*, 74–96.

31. Portes, A., & Rumbaut, R. (2001). *Legacies: The story of the immigrant second generation*. Berkeley: University of California Press.

32. Kulis, S., Marsiglia, F. F., Sicotte, D., & Nieri, T. (2007). Neighborhood effects on youth substance use in a southwestern city. *Sociological Perspectives, 50*(2), 273–301.

33. Anderson, E. (1994). The code of the streets. *Atlantic Monthly, 273*, 81–94.

34. Portes & Zhou. (1993).

35. Tonry, M. (1997). Ethnicity, crime, and immigration. In M. Tonry (Ed.), *Ethnicity, crime, and immigration: Comparative and cross-research perspectives* (pp. 1–29). Chicago: University of Chicago Press.

36. Frank, R., Cerdá, M., & Rendón, M. (2007). Barrios and burbs: Residential context and health risk behaviors among Angeleno adolescents. *Journal of Health and Social Behavior, 48*(3), 283–300.

37. Conger, D., & Atwell, M. S. (2011). Immigrant gateway communities: Does immigrant student achievement vary by location? In C. García Coll and A. Marks (Eds.), *The immigrant paradox in children and adolescents: Is becoming an American a developmental risk?* (pp. 233–252). Washington, DC: American Psychological Association.

38. Ibid.

39. Guilamo-Ramos, V., Jaccard, J., Pena, J., & Goldberg, V. (2005). Acculturation-related variables, sexual initiation, and subsequent sexual behavior among Puerto Rican, Mexican, and Cuban youth. *Health Psychology, 24*(1), 88–95.

40. Berry. (1980).

41. Samaniego, R. Y., & Gonzales, M. A. (1999). Multiple mediators of the effects of acculturation status on delinquency for Mexican American adolescents. *American Journal of Contemporary Psychology, 27*(2), 189–210.

42. Du, P. L. (1997). Cultural and social factors and Vietnamese gangs. *Journal of Contemporary Criminal Justice, 13*, 331–339; Yoo, H., Gee, G., Lowthrop, C., & Robertson, J. (2010). Self-reported racial discrimination and substance use among Asian Americans in Arizona. *Journal of Immigrant & Minority Health, 12*(5), 683–690.

43. Kposowa & Tsunokai. (2003); Mateu-Gelabert, P. (2001). *Dreams, gangs, and guns: The interplay between adolescent violence and immigration in a New York City neighborhood*. New York: Vera Institute of Justice.

44. Hahm, H. C., Lahiff, M., & Barreto, R. M. (2006). Asian American adolescents' first sexual intercourse: Gender and acculturation differences. *Perspectives on Sexual and Reproductive Health, 38,* 28–36.

45. Averett, S. L., Rees, D. I., & Argys, L. M. (2002). The impact of government policies and neighborhood characteristics on teenage sexual activity and contraceptive use. *American Journal of Public Health, 92*(11), 1773–1778.

46. García Coll, C., & Marks, A. (2011). Introduction. In C. García Coll and A. Marks (Eds.), *The immigrant paradox in children and adolescents: Is becoming an American a developmental risk?* (pp. 3–13). Washington, DC: American Psychological Association.

47. Hahm et al. (2006).

48. Ibid.

49. Averett et al. (2002).

50. Ebin, V. J., Sneed, C. D., Morisky, D. E., Rotheram-Borus, M. J., Magnusson, A. M., & Malotte, C. K. (2001). Acculturation and interrelationships between problem and health-promoting behaviors among Latino adolescents. *Journal of Adolescent Health, 28*(1), 62–72.

51. Henry, K. L., and Slater, M. D. (2007). The contextual effect of school attachment on young adolescents' alcohol use. *Journal of School Health, 77*(2), 67–74.

52. García Coll & Marks. (2011).

53. Pong, S., & Zeiser, K. L. (2011). Student engagement, school climate and academic achievement of immigrants' children. In C. García Coll and A. Marks (Eds.), *The immigrant paradox in children and adolescents: Is becoming an American a developmental risk?* (pp. 209–232). Washington, DC: American Psychological Association.

54. Kao, G., & Tienda, M. (1995). Optimism and achievement: The educational performance of immigrant youth. *Social Science Quarterly, 76,* 1–19.

55. Ibid.

56. Ebin et al. (2001).

57. Bankston, C. L., & Cada, S. J. (1996). Adolescents and deviance in a Vietnamese American community: A theoretical synthesis. *Deviant Behavior, 17,* 159–181.

58. Rumbaut, R. (1998). Transformations: The post-immigrant generation in an age of diversity. In L. F. Tomasi (Ed.), *In defense of the alien* (pp. 229–259). New York: Center for Migration Studies.

59. Bankston. (1998).

60. Fuligni, A. J. (1997). The academic achievement of adolescents from immigrant families: The roles of family background, attitudes, and behavior. *Child Development, 68*(2), 351–364.

61. Pong & Zeiser. (2011).

62. Henry & Slater. (2007).

63. Alexander, C., Piazza, M., Mekos, D., & Valente, T. (2001). Peers, schools, and adolescent cigarette smoking. *Journal of Adolescent Health, 29*(1), 22–30.

64. Capps, R., Fix, M., Murray, J., Passel, J. S., & Herwantoro, S. (2005). *The new demography of American schools: Immigrants and the No Child Left Behind Act.* Washington, DC: Urban Institute.

65. Pong, S., & Hao, L. (2007). Neighborhood and school factors in the school performance of immigrants' children. *International Migration Review, 41*(1), 206–241.

66. Cavanagh, S. E. (2007). Peers, drinking, and the assimilation of Mexican American youth. *Sociological Perspectives, 50*(3), 393–416.

67. Ibid.

68. Harris. (1998).

69. Le, T. N., & Kato, T. (2006). The role of peer, parent, and culture in risky sexual behavior for Cambodian and Lao/Mien adolescents. *Journal of Adolescent Health, 38*(3), 288–296.

70. Kao, G., & Joyner, G. (2006). Do Hispanic and Asian adolescents practice panethnicity in friendship choice? *Social Science Quarterly, 87*(5), 972–992.

71. Alexander et al. (2001).

72. Le & Kato. (2006).

73. Bui. (2011).

74. Portes & Rumbaut. (2001).

75. Ibid.

76. Rumbaut. (1998).

77. Harris. (1998).

78. Szapocznik, J., & Kurtines, W. M. (1993). Family psychology and cultural diversity: Opportunity for theory, research and application. *American Psychologist, 48*(4), 400–407.

79. Ebin et al. (2001).

80. Raffaelli et al. (2011).

81. Fuligni, A. J. (2011). The intersection of aspiration and resources in the development of children from immigrant families. In C. García Coll and A. Marks (Eds.), *The immigrant paradox in children and adolescents: Is becoming an American a developmental risk?* (pp. 299–308). Washington, DC: American Psychological Association.

82. Szapocznik & Kurtines. (1993).

83. Zhou & Bankston. (2006).

84. Bankston. (1998).

85. Samaniego & Gonzales. (1999).

86. Qin, D. B., Chang, T. F., Han, E-J., & Chee, G. (2012). Conflicts and communication between high-achieving Chinese American adolescents and their parents. *New Directions for Child and Adolescent Development, 135,* 35–57.

87. Chin, K. (1990). *Chinese subculture and criminality: Nontraditional crime groups in America.* Westport, CT: Greenwood.

88. Terrell, M. (1993). Ethnocultural factors and substance abuse: Toward culturally sensitive treatment models. *Psychology of Addictive Behavior, 7*(3), 162–167.

89. Kim, I. J., Zone, N. W. S., & Hong, S. (2002). Protective factors against substance use among Asian American youth: A test of the peer cluster theory. *Journal of Community Psychology, 0,* 565–584.

90. Portes & Zhou. (1993).

91. Bui. (2011).

92. Rumbaut. (2005).

93. Fuligni. (2011).

94. Morenoff, J. D., & Astor, A. (2006). Immigrant assimilation and crime: Generational differences in youth violence in Chicago. In R. Martinez, Jr., & A. Valenzuela, Jr. (Eds.), *Immigration and crime: Race, ethnicity, and violence* (pp. 36–63). New York: NYU Press.

95. Qin et al. (2012).

96. Portes & Zhou. (1993).

97. Buriel, R. (2011). Historical origins of the immigrant paradox for Mexican American students: The cultural integration thesis. In C. García Coll & A. Marks (Eds.), *The immigrant paradox in children and adolescents: Is becoming an American a developmental risk?* (pp. 37–60). Washington, DC: American Psychological Association.

98. Hughes, D., Rodriguez, J., Smith, E. P., Johnson, D. J., Stevenson, H. C., & Spicer, P. (2006). Parents' ethnic-racial socialization practices: A review of research and direction for future study. *Developmental Psychology, 42*(5), 747–770.

99. Rumbaut. (2005).

100. Passel. (2011).

13

Academic Achievement

AMY K. MARKS, LOURAH M. SEABOYER, AND
CYNTHIA GARCÍA COLL

Izabel is in the fifth grade. She was born in the United States, though her older sister and parents were born in Portugal. She has average grades, likes R&B music, and describes herself foremost as "not mean." Izabel enjoys school for the most part and reports having high levels of school engagement and strong school values. She believes that getting good grades and doing your homework are very important since doing these things enables one to learn. Izabel consistently says that she likes her teachers and thinks that they like her as well. In fact, having good teachers is something that makes her proud of her school. However, despite these positive interactions, she is not always completely comfortable at school. She notes that students in her class do not get along well because "a lot of people bully a lot of other people" and that she feels a bit excluded while at school. She feels that "for no [particular] reason" some kids in her class do not like her. Nonetheless, she says she goes to school every day because she likes school. When Izabel arrives home from school, she usually starts her homework, which takes her anywhere from 60 to 90 minutes to complete. Although it is her least favorite part of school, she always does her homework because it helps her get good grades. Izabel also believes that graduating from high school is very important since doing so will allow her to "get a job." And although she only "kind of" thinks she might go to college someday, she knows her teachers and parents believe that she will.

Arun is also in the fifth grade but is a far-below-average student. He describes himself as "Cambodian, Khmer, and Asian." Like Izabel, he was born in the United States to immigrant parents. However, unlike Izabel, his parents were not voluntary migrants but instead fled the Khmer Rouge and arrived in the United States as refugees. In school, he likes "doing handwriting and having free time" and does not like "doing math or getting suspended." He espouses positive school values and says that he wants to graduate from high school. However, he indicates that he is often absent and only sometimes does his homework—for about 10 minutes a day, usually in the living room, where he is interrupted "all the time" by his brothers. Like Izabel, he is sometimes uncomfortable at school because "people [are] bothering" him. He believes that few teachers like him or would be willing to help him if he needed assistance, and he says that his classmates do not treat each other well—that "they always swear, and they hate each other."[1]

These vignettes compiled from interviews with second-generation immigrant-origin children depict many of the complexities surrounding academic achievement among immigrant youth. As we found in this longitudinal study, the academic pathways of immigrant children and adolescents are extremely varied. Some immigrant youth excel despite attending poor, underperforming schools, while others struggle and fail. The person–environment interactions evidenced in each student's successes, mixed outcomes, and/or failures paint a powerful picture of individuals' academic achievement at the intersections of public policy, family processes, school resources, and peer/teacher supports—or lack thereof. Very sadly, we learned that the young boy named Arun had dropped out of school at the start of sixth grade. Why do some immigrant children perform adequately—or even excel (like Izabel)—while others fail? This chapter takes a person–environment approach to understanding how individual, family, school, and community contexts intersect in the lives of immigrant youth to shape their academic achievement.

The Immigrant Paradox and Risk Perspectives

We begin our review by exploring two complementary patterns of academic achievement among immigrant children: the immigrant paradox (i.e., newcomer children's success despite their poor economic resources) and the risk model (i.e., newcomer youth with poor economic resources who struggle to achieve). Some researchers have noted that—as is the case with health outcomes (see Crosnoe, Ramos-Wada, and Bonazzo, "Paradoxes in Physical Health," chapter 10 in this volume)—first-generation immigrant youth often exhibit greater academic achievement in school than their more highly acculturated U.S.-born peers do. Even after taking into account the lower economic resources of newcomer families, children who are new to the United States tend to perform very well in school, particularly after achieving competency in English.[2] In other words, for older immigrant children and adolescents, there appears to be some evidence of the immigrant paradox in academic achievement. As is the case with other domains of development, the paradox pattern in academic achievement is strongest for some ethnic groups, particularly Asians. Favoring the paradox pattern, after taking into account families' socioeconomic statuses, Asian immigrant children are often documented as scoring higher on academic school readiness than U.S.-born children are. Using nationally representative data, researchers have found that first-generation immigrant children in kindergarten hold an advantage in reading achievement over third-generation immigrant children (U.S.-born children with U.S. born parents), a trend that remains significant over time, even after accounting for race and ethnicity.[3] Also, Asian immigrants are more likely than their Latino immigrant peers to attend schools with lower dropout rates[4] and to have higher rates of college attendance and bachelor's degree attainment than third-generation White immigrants are.[5] Such immigrant paradox patterns have also been documented in studies of adolescent academic success employing large nationally representative longitudinal data sets. Among the youth surveyed in the National Longitudinal Study of Adolescent Health (Add Health)[6] and the Adolescent Health and Academic Achievement Study (AHAA),[7] first-generation Hispanic and Asian immigrant adolescents were more likely to report greater positive academic trajectories over time— including continued high levels of school achievement and engagement, moderate levels with improvements, and low initial levels that improved drastically—than their second- and third-generation immigrant peers did. In figure 13.1, we also document the paradox pattern in an important academic behavior: preparedness for class. This figure shows that first-generation immigrant adolescents come to school unprepared less often than their second- and third-generation peers do.

In other studies, a "risk" model seems to apply better when one examines the academic trajectories of immigrant children. In other words, for some immigrant groups, including Mexican children and adolescents, there may be signs of struggle in newcomer immigrants' grades and test scores,[8] evidence typically linked with (and often explained by) poor school and low family economic resources. Such themes of paradox and risk in the research base are extremely nuanced, with mixed support by child ethnicity, receiving community contexts (i.e., the types of communities in which immigrants reside after coming to the U.S.) and child age. For example, even when controlling for families' socioeconomic statuses, evidence supporting the risk model shows that when entering kindergarten, immigrant children from Mexico score lower on standardized math scores than their U.S.-born Latino and White counterparts do.[9] Mexican-origin children are also more likely than children of other immigrant groups to attend schools with inadequate resources and problematic environments (see Marks and Pieloch, "School Con-

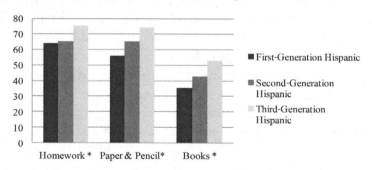

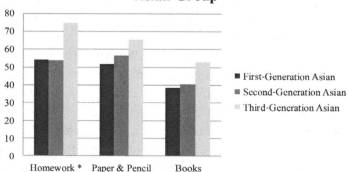

texts," chapter 2 in this volume). However, it is also worth noting that these early achievement-related disparities at school entry do appear to dissipate over the course of primary school attendance.[10] Such trends documented in the literature again point to the importance of context— that is, of having adequate resources at the school level starting in kindergarten and continuing through high school—in order to support the full potential of immigrant children's achievement. The fact that some ethnic and racial groups of immigrant children are less likely than others to receive adequate school resources or to achieve their educational potential represents a social problem that greatly needs to be addressed.

An area in which many young immigrant children across various ethnicities appear to excel is socioemotional school readiness (as measured by interpersonal competence). Academic achievement is not solely determined by cognitive scores and grades. It is also strongly influenced

---

Figure 13.1. Percentage of students never or sometimes unprepared for class, by ethnicity. Notes: * $p < .05$. Logistic regression models were used to predict academic preparedness (separately for homework, paper and pencil, books), with generation status as the independent variable while controlling for gender and socioeconomic status (SES). Models were conducted separately for Hispanics and Asians using data from the Add Health study. SES was a composite measure of the father's education level, mother's education level, father's occupation, mother's occupation, and family income. For Hispanics, generation status remained significant for all three types of academic preparedness (homework, paper and pencil, books), even when controlling for SES and gender. For Asians, in models predicting homework preparedness, generation status was a significant predictor in all models and remained significant after controlling for gender and SES. In models predicting Asian preparedness with paper and pencil, generation status was marginally significant ($p = .06$) and was reduced to not significant when controlling for gender and SES. In models predicting Asian preparedness with books, generation status was not significant ($p = .10$) and remained not significant when controlling for gender and SES. Hispanic country of origin included Mexican/Chicano (65.2%, $n = 662$), Puerto Rican (8.9%, $n = 90$), Cuban (3.4%, $n = 35$), and Other Hispanic (.5%, $n = 5$). Asian country of origin included Chinese (24.3%, $n = 132$), Filipino (19.0%, $n = 103$), Southeast Asian (16.2%, $n = 88$), Korean (9.4%, $n = 51$), Japanese (5.9%, $n = 32$), Pacific Islander (3.5%, $n = 19$), Middle Eastern (1.7%, $n = 9$), South Asian (1.1%, $n = 6$), West Asian (1.1%, $n = 6$), Other Asian (3.3%, $n = 18$). Percentages of country of origins may not add up to 100% because of missing responses.

by psychological attributes such as openness to learning, positive interpersonal skills, good self-esteem, and, for immigrant youth in particular,
pride in their ethnic and racial identities.[11] Izabel from the opening vignette, for example, was adept at interpersonal relations, building strong
alliances with her teachers, parents, and trusted friends, all of whom
helped her focus on her schoolwork, even when some of her peers engaged in negative social dynamics. In the data set of the Early Childhood
Longitudinal Program–Kindergarten Class of 1998–1999, Early Childhood Longitudinal Study–Kindergarten Cohort (ECLS-K), teachers
rated both Hispanic and Asian first-generation immigrant children as
better adjusted than children of U.S.-born White, Asian, Hispanic, and
Black parents.[12] Although research findings support both the paradox
and risk achievement adjustment patterns, taken together, these two
patterns clearly indicate that immigrant children and adolescents are
making exceptional use of their educations, often despite having few
economic resources. With first-generation immigrant children and adolescents having relatively low dropout rates compared with those of their
U.S.-born peers,[13] they primarily attend public schools that are underresourced (see Marks and Pieloch, "School Contexts," chapter 2 in this volume). It is therefore significant that, on average, immigrant youth from
various ethnic and racial backgrounds are doing so well academically.

Unpacking the Achievement of Immigrant Children: Interactions among Contexts

To better understand the ways in which immigrant children come to succeed or struggle in school, one needs to employ a person–environment
perspective. Since most research to date has focused on the proximal
contexts of development, such as family, schools, friends, and peers,
we also focus on these contexts.[14] When considering the early experience of an immigrant child's academic success, one important place
to start is with school readiness and the interplay between family and
school contexts. For example, English-language proficiency is vital for
academic success as soon as immigrant children enter kindergarten
and first grade. Immigrant parents often note that one of their primary
reasons for encouraging their young children to attend preschool and
kindergarten is to enable them to become proficient in English-language

use.[15] Immigrant children who are successfully bilingual are often more adept at comparing languages than monolingual children are. They also have stronger metalinguistic abilities, exhibit more optimal growth in academic-related cognitive skills, and have improved reading comprehension as they transition to school[16] (see also Páez and Hunter, "Bilingualism and Language Learning," chapter 8 in this volume). Practicing bilingualism and achieving dual-language proficiencies are important areas for immigrant children's academic achievement and are areas that require support from families, schools, and communities. For instance, in one study, both Hispanic English-language learners (ELL) and non-ELL Hispanic students had higher fourth-grade reading skill levels in states with stronger bilingual emphasis and more funding for these services than students in states with less emphasis and funding did. Furthermore, when teachers were better trained to work with multicultural families, non-ELL Hispanic students also performed better in reading.[17] Indeed, teachers who incorporated their students' cultural and linguistic perspectives into their teaching, promoted students' independence and critical thinking strategies, and used real-world applications to make material accessible to their students had the most positive impact on their ELL students' reading achievement.[18]

Perhaps equally important, supporting early bilingualism in both school and home contexts bolsters other aspects of immigrant children's achievement tool sets. As early as third grade (when students are age nine), a positive ethnic identity is directly associated with positive academic attitudes and bilingualism, which in turn support ethnic/racial minority children's academic achievement.[19] Having positive and secure ethnic and racial identities develops directly through positive family cultural socialization[20] and is very important for maintaining a positive academic attitude in the face of peer and/or teacher discrimination.[21] For example, Izabel reported being very proud of her Portuguese American heritage, a background that she regarded as synonymous with strong academic values. For Izabel, knowing that her parents were proud of her work at school and that they had immigrated to the United States to secure their children's education and prospects for a better life helped her work harder when it was time to focus on her homework. In turn, Izabel's teachers rated her as hardworking and pleasant and cast her as one of the students they expected to succeed. Such interactions among children, families, teachers, and schools continue into adolescence and the college years[22] and are vital to the future successes of immigrant youth.

Furthermore, children who are more secure in their ability to communicate in their family's native language tend to have closer relationships with their parents and more positive ethnic/racial identities—important family contextual characteristics that support the children's academic achievement.[23] On the other hand, immigrant-origin children and adolescents who do not practice their family's native language and/or have negative cultural identities may suffer in their relationships with family members, particularly with parents. High parent-child conflict due to different acculturation experiences (as when a child is highly acculturated to the United States and her peer/school culture while her parents are less acculturated) and different language practices can pose serious problems for the relationship. When Arun, the second child discussed in the chapter opening's vignette, was asked to identify himself, he did not know what to call himself—whether Asian, Cambodian, American, or some other label might fit. Confusion about his identity and peer processes was also apparent when he was asked about his in-group peer play preferences since he said that he did not want to play with other Cambodian children. As Arun reported, complex relationships at school—with other "kids" who were "mean"—made it difficult for him to listen in class. Without adequate time or structure at home to do his homework, Arun also had a very high absentee record at school, which he said he was not sure his parents knew about. Children with such family–school context conflicts may feel marginalized, and their academic achievement may suffer as a result.[24] In the adolescent years, youth with marginalized or isolated identities may reject both school and family—shunning the educational value systems of both their parents and their schools—and may become at risk for delinquency and other behavioral problems (see Bui, "Behavioral Outcomes," chapter 12 in this volume).

Researchers who are focused specifically on understanding the contexts that support strong overall academic success among first-generation Asian immigrant youth have pinpointed the important interplay among family, school, and community contexts.[25] As we consider how communities play dynamic roles in shaping academic achievement outcomes, it is important to remember that group-level patterns demonstrating success or failure can misconstrue the complexity of predicting whether a child from an immigrant family will eventually achieve their full academic potential. With these cautions in mind, researchers have noted that some groups of Asian immigrants (e.g., first-generation Chinese) may be particularly well equipped to complete secondary school and college through their cultural socialization with high education values and aspirations imparted by both their families and their communities. The benefit of living in ethnic enclaves such as Chinatown in Los Angeles that place a community-based emphasis on academic achievement, particularly for first-generation youth, is readily apparent. Advertisements on billboards and in newspapers offer tutoring, standardized-test scoring, and college-admissions supports in Chinese. One interesting line of theory posits that low-income Asian communities such as this one promote academic success for their children through "success frames"—that is, by using ethnicity and cultural values and customs specifically to overcome working-class disadvantages for social and educational mobility.[26] These frames combine community and family values that tightly link cultural practices and identity (e.g., being Chinese) as synonymous with high academic achievement. Such framing provides a scaffold for children to value their education and promotes strong academic behaviors that can ensure academic success.

On the other hand, these authors note, for children who cannot or choose not to adhere to the strict success frames advanced by their families, their disappointing educational experiences and failures may make them feel like outcasts. Other scholars have found similar tendencies in other ethnic and racial groups, indicating that making academic achievement part of the cultural identity of the child can have both benefits (high ethnic identity and high achievement = success) and risks (low ethnic identity and/or mixed/low achievement = failure). Indeed, in low-income or working-class immigrant communities that do not have organized community and school bilingual supports in place, children and adolescents may not internalize their full potential to succeed. Like Arun, children who at an early age do not have adequate interpersonal and instrumental resources to support their schooling quickly come to feel undersupported by teachers and can internalize such negativity, leaving them to struggle greatly. Notably, these relationships with teachers work in both directions. Strong relationships between children and their teachers may buffer immigrant youth from academic problems when other areas of their lives pose a threat to their success. Teachers are integral to the acculturation process, serving as guides in schools where youth are immersed in U.S. culture. Researchers have noted that in Asian and Hispanic samples, immigrant children on average tend to regard their teachers and school staff positively. In addition, when compared with their more highly acculturated peers, first-generation immigrants have demonstrated the strongest positive attitudes toward their teachers.[27] However, at the same time, teachers are more likely to have lower expectations for immigrant youth in general and for Hispanic children in particular.[28] Once again, ample evidence in such literature demonstrates that when the cycle of adequate interpersonal and instrumental support among home, school, and community is interrupted, the upward social and economic mobility of the child is threatened.[29]

Lastly, we need to consider how peer contexts also interact with families and schools to influence immigrant children's academic potential. The developmental literature well documents the fact that peers and friends can have a powerful influence on children's psychological well-being and academic success. When immigrant youth are surrounded by a peer or school culture that does not value academic achievement, it may be extremely difficult for them to achieve their potential.[30] For any child, being surrounded by a low-achieving peer group, including ones that engage in risky or delinquent behavior, is a potent risk factor for academic failure. Furthermore, when children perceive that they (or other members of their cultural or social group) may be victims of discrimination, such negative peer contexts can have very harmful effects on immigrant youth's potential for achievement. Research has shown that U.S.-born youth from immigrant families who perceive discrimination at school also tend to report high levels of depression.[31] The threat of discrimination is particularly high for immigrant children who may have minority status due to race, culture, language, or other attributed social difference from the perceived U.S. majority. For immigrant youth, then, the quality of the peer group, including the multicultural values and awareness purported by the school, is especially important for supporting academic achievement and potential.[32] And while some immigrant children are able to rise above the social threat of discrimination to achieve academic success, others may internalize negative stereotypes and believe that their possibilities for advancement are limited by their membership in a particular ethnic, racial, religious, or other socially constructed group.

On the other hand, positive interactions with peers and friends in the school context can provide immigrant students with a uniquely powerful support system and serve as important sources of socialization that inform children's identity development. Coethnic friendships can be particularly helpful for forming bonds and support systems to overcome immigration-related barriers. For example, undocumented Latino youth can experience extraordinary challenges and threats to their ability to advance their educations when compared with the circumstances of U.S.-born peers.[33] Such challenges include securing financial aid for college, obtaining a driver's license, and managing the severe stress of the threat of deportation (their own and that of loved ones)—all of which pose serious risks to undocumented youth's well-being and academic attainment (see Suárez-Orozco, "Family Separations and Reunifications," chapter 1 in this volume). Therefore, undocumented youth rely heavily on trusted friends and often on coethnic relations as well as on other peers, parents, and teachers for instrumental and psychological support in school.[34]

For many immigrant youth, their association with high-achieving peers also directly contributes to their academic success.[35] In studies of this issue, higher peer grade point average has been associated with higher immigrant-student grade point average and academic success. In the Add Health study, attending schools with high rates of coethnic friendships was directly associated with academic achievement and attainment, a relationship that was particularly true for Asian immigrant students. Additionally, social support across first-, second-, and third-generation peers for Latino boys and for third-generation peers for Latina girls has also been associated with higher academic achievement.[36] In this same sample, the academic experiences of Latino children with diverse groups of interethnic friends were enhanced when controlling for the significant impact of the educational level of friends' parents.[37] In other words, children with friends who have more educated parents may benefit from seeing examples of adults of their own ethnicity who have attained academic success and other achievements. Such increased social capital and cultural awareness can provide additional positive support to help youth achieve their educational goals. Taken together, the alignment of positive supports from family, peers, teachers, and schools to promote bilingualism, healthy ethnic-identity development, and strong academic aspirations provides the combined contextual support necessary for immigrant youth's optimal academic achievement.

Summary and Interventions to Support Academic Achievement

Current research provides clear evidence that immigrant children experience highly varied academic trajectories that are impacted by multiple intersecting contexts. It is necessary to take a person–environment approach to understand the complex interconnected relationships among individual, family, school, and community contexts that shape the academic achievement of immigrant children. Although this chapter has focused on the proximal contexts most frequently present in the research literature, it is also important to note that immigration itself is a macro-level context that interacts with the more proximal ones. Immigration laws, legal statuses within families and communities, the threat of deportation, systemic stereotypes about immigrants, and job insecurity are just a few of the immigration-related issues that can profoundly impact the academic achievement of immigrant youth. In particular, researchers are noting with increasing frequency how such macro-level risks play out in low-income and undocumented communities. This situation remains an understudied and crucial area for research as undocumented children are not only strong in number but also particularly vulnerable to being "lost" in the U.S. educational system once they reach the age of 18.

This chapter's exploration of immigrant academic achievement has also emphasized the variation in types of achievement patterns within and across ethnic groups and immigrant generations. Both risk and immigrant paradox patterns are common in the literature. Crosnoe has suggested that particularly for Mexican American immigrants, the "most consistent aspect of the paradox in this group is its inconsistency."[38] Children's relationships with parents, friends, and teachers may be risk factors or protective factors, depending on the setting and depending on ethnicity, country of origin, and migration status. Furthermore, despite the risk factors associated with immigrant status, some of these students continue to excel and make connections in their surrounding community, actions that foster upward social and economic mobility. At the same time, despite many immigrant children's strong positive school values and high levels of school engagement, they are still more likely to attend underperforming schools and to experience discrimination from teachers and peers. Future research and interventions should aim to reduce discrimination, to provide strong bilingual education, and to enhance students' academic success with community-based supports.

Some types of interventions appear to work best to support immigrant children's and adolescents' academic achievement. Academic interventions that focus on contextual determinants of academic achievement include those that address domains of school readiness, families, and peer influences (see Marks and Pieloch, "School Contexts," chapter 2 in this volume, on school-based interventions). One promising area of intervention seems to be peer support in the form of community-based peer mentorship.[39] In such programs, community members have organized coethnic peers to help newcomer Latino immigrant adolescents as they adjust to life and academics in the United States. While providing instrumental support for homework and practice with English-language learning, peer mentors also promote the healthy ethnic-identity exploration necessary for adolescents to achieve their full academic potential.

Many such interventions are needed since this is an underserviced area. It is important to note that most positive interventions with immigrant youth tend to be ones that work from a community perspective. Home-literacy initiatives, for example, have demonstrated strong support for improving immigrant youths' academic success. However, some qualitative literature suggests that parents regard these school-to-home literacy practices as contradictory to their cultural values, family routines, and expectations, with parents receiving instruction from the school rather than communicating with the school.[40] Indeed, some programs have indicated a need for more culturally competent parent trainings. Focus groups have suggested that home-literacy programs have been developed with the good intention of increasing literacy among struggling youth but have not taken into account the cultural values and practices of parents who are expected to be the primary providers of the intervention.[41]

On the other hand, at the neighborhood level, community centers with after-school care, homework help, language services, and subject-specific tutoring as well as role modeling by older youth provide opportunities for children that supplement their school educations. In addition, when compared with standard after-school homework help, small-group 10-hour, one week "camps" have been effective in improving first- through third-grade bilingual Hispanic immigrant children's comprehension of spelling and sight words, which persisted over the course of one year, and reading at the end of treatment only.[42] These types of community-based interventions can help alleviate the particular challenges that immigrant students face when parents do not know the language in which students' homework is given, work multiple jobs, or do not practice behaviors associated with increasing students' chances for success in U.S. schools (e.g., reading at home, helping with homework). It appears that community-based models that seek to enable immigrant families to strengthen their children's achievement by promoting bilingualism, positive peer-based ethnic-identity exploration, and home cultural-heritage practices offer the greatest promise for supporting U.S. immigrant children's achievement.

NOTES

1. García Coll, C., & Marks, A. K. (2009). *Immigrant stories: Ethnicity and academics in middle childhood.* New York: Oxford University Press. Excerpts adapted from pp. 103, 149–150.

2. García Coll, C., & Marks, A. K. (Eds.) (2012). *The immigrant paradox in children and adolescents: Is becoming American a developmental risk?* Washington, DC: American Psychological Association.

3. Palacios, N., Guttmanova, K., & Chase-Lansdale, P. (2008). Early reading achievement of children in immigrant families: Is there an immigrant paradox? *Developmental Psychology, 44*(5), 1381–1395.

4. Watkins, A. M., & Melde, C. (2010). Latino and Asian students' perceptions of the quality of their educators: The role of generational status and language proficiency. *Youth & Society, 42*(1), 3–32.

5. Hao, L., & Ma, Y. (2012). Immigrant youth in postsecondary education. In C. García Coll & A. Marks (Eds.), *The immigrant paradox in children and adolescents: Is becoming an American a developmental risk?* (pp. 275–296). Washington, DC: American Psychological Association.

6. Harris, K. M., Halpern, C. T., Whitsel, E., Hussey, J., Tabor, J., Entzel, P., and Udry, J. R. (2009). The National Longitudinal Study of Adolescent Health: Research design. Retrieved March 24, 2014, from http://www.cpc.unc.edu/projects/addhealth/design/.

7. Muller, C. (2005). The Adolescent Health and Academic Achievement Study. Retrieved March 24, 2014, from http://www.prc.utexas.edu/ahaa/.

8. Crosnoe, R. (2012). Studying the immigrant paradox in the Mexican-origin population. In C. García Coll & A. K. Marks (Eds.), *The immigrant paradox in children and adolescents: Is becoming American a developmental risk?* (pp. 61–76). Washington, DC: American Psychological Association.

9. Crosnoe, R., & López Turley, R. N. (2011). K–12 educational outcomes of immigrant youth. *Future of Children, 21*(1), 129–152.

10. Welsh, M., Parke, R. D., Widaman, K., & O'Neil, R. (2001). Linkages between children's social and academic competence: A longitudinal analysis. *Journal of School Psychology, 39*, 463–482.

11. Huffman, L. C., Mehlinger, S. L., & Kerivan, A. S. (2000). Risk factors for academic and behavioral problems at the beginning of school. In *Off to a good start: Research on the risk factors for early school problems and selected federal policies affecting children's social and emotional development and their readiness for school* (pp. 75–89). Chapel Hill: University of North Carolina; Marks, A. K., Godoy, C. M., & García Coll, C. (2013). An ecological approach to understanding immigrant child and adolescent developmental competencies. In L. Gershoff, R. Mistry, & D. Crosby (Eds.), *The contexts of child development* (pp. 75–89). New York: Oxford University Press.

12. Crosnoe & López Turley. (2011).

13. Greenman, E. (2013). Educational attitudes, school peer context, and the "immigrant paradox" in education. *Social Science Research, 42*(3), 698–714.

14. Chao, R. K., & Otsuki-Clutter, M. (2011). Racial and ethnic differences: Sociocultural and contextual explanations. *Journal of Research on Adolescence, 21*, 47–60.

15. Obeng, C. (2007). Immigrants' families and childcare preferences: Do immigrants' cultures influence their childcare decisions? *Early Childhood Education Journal, 34*, 259–264.

16. Palacios et al. (2008).

17. Francesca López., F., & McEneaney, E. (2012). State implementation of language acquisition policies and reading achievement among Hispanic students. *Educational Policy, 26*, 418–464.

18. López, F. A. (2012). Moderators of language acquisition models and reading achievement for English language learners: The role of emotional warmth and instructional support. *Teachers College Record, 114*(8), 1–30.

19. Brown, C., & Chu, H. (2012). Discrimination, ethnic identity, and academic outcomes of Mexican immigrant children: The importance of school context. *Child Development, 83*(5), 1477–1485; García Coll & Marks. (2009).

20. Hughes, D., Rodrigues, J., Smith, E., Johnson, D., & Stevenson, H. (2006). Parents' ethnic-racial socialization practices: A review of research and directions for future study. *Developmental Psychology, 42*(5), 747–770.

21. Greene, M., Way, N., & Pahl, K. (2006). Trajectories of perceived adult and peer discrimination among Black, Latino, and Asian American adolescents: Patterns and psychological correlates. *Developmental Psychology, 42*, 218–238.

22. Azmitia, M., Cooper, C. R., & Brown, J. R. (2009). Support and guidance from families, friends, and teachers in Latino early adolescents' math pathways. *Journal of Early Adolescence, 29*(1), 142–169: Azmitia, M., Syed, M., & Radmacher, K. (2013). Finding your niche: Identity and emotional support in emerging adults' adjustment to the transition to college. *Journal of Research on Adolescence, 23*(4), 744–761.

23. Marks et al. (2013).

24. Marks, A. K., Patton, F., & Coyne, L. C. (2011). Acculturation-related conflict across generations in immigrant families. In R. Moreno & S. S. Chuang (Eds.), *Immigrant children: Change, adaptation and cultural transformation* (pp. 255–270). Lanham, MD: Rowman and Littlefield; Marks, A. K., Patton, F., & García Coll, C. (2009). More than the A-B-C's and 1-2-3's: The importance of family cultural socialization and ethnic identity development for children of immigrants' early school success. In R. Takanishi & E. L. Grigorenko (Eds.), *Immigration, diversity, and education.* London: Routledge / Taylor and Francis Group.

25. Zhou, M., Lee, J., Vallejo, J. A., Tafoya-Estrada, R., & Xiong, Y. S. (2008). Success attained, deterred, and denied: Divergent pathways to social mobility in Los Angeles's new second generation. *Annals of the American Academy of Political and Social Science, 620*(1), 37–61.

26. Lee, J., & Zhou, M. (2014). The success frame and achievement paradox: The costs and consequences for Asian Americans. *Race and Social Problems, 1867*–1748.

27. Watkins, A. M., & Melde, C. (2010). Latino and Asian students' perceptions of the quality of their educators: The role of generational status and language proficiency. *Youth & Society, 42*(1), 3–32.

28. Gaytan, F. X. (2010). The role of social capital and social support from adults in the academic self-efficacy, identity, and engagement of Mexican immigrant youth in New York City. *Dissertation Abstracts International, 71.*

29. Crosnoe, R., & Lopez-Gonzalez, L. (2005). Immigration from Mexico, school composition, and adolescent functioning. *Sociological Perspectives, 48*(1), 1–24.

30. Crosnoe, R. (2005). Double disadvantage or signs of resilience? The elementary school contexts of children from Mexican immigrant families. *American Educational Research Journal, 42*(2), 269–303.

31. Tummala-Narra, P., & Claudius, M. (2013). Perceived discrimination and depressive symptoms among immigrant-origin adolescents. *Cultural Diversity and Ethnic Minority Psychology, 19*(3), 257–269.

32. Brown & Chu. (2012).

33. Gonzales, R. G. (2011). Learning to be illegal: Undocumented youth and the shifting legal contexts in the transition to adulthood. *American Sociological Review, 76*(4), 602–619.

34. Enriquez, L. E. (2011). "Because we feel the pressure and we also feel the support": Examining the educational success of undocumented immigrant Latina/o students. *Harvard Educational Review, 81*(3), 476–499.

35. Ryabov, I. (2009). The role of peer social capital in educational assimilation of immigrant youths. *Sociological Inquiry, 79*(4), 453–480.

36. Riegle-Crumb, C., & Callahan, R. M. (2009). Exploring the academic benefits of friendship ties for Latino boys and girls. *Social Science Quarterly, 90*(3), 611–631.

37. Ibid.

38. Crosnoe. (2012).

39. Yoshikawa, H., & Kalil, A. (2011). The effects of parental undocumented status on the developmental contexts of young children in immigrant families. *Child Development Perspectives, 5*(4), 291–297; Diversi, M., & Mecham, C. (2005). Latino(a) students and Caucasian mentors in a rural after-school program: Towards empowering adult–youth relationships. *Journal of Community Psychology, 33*(1), 31–40.

40. Dudley-Marling, C. (2009). Home–school literacy connections: The perceptions of African American and immigrant ESL parents in two urban communities. *Teachers College Record, 111*(7), 1713–1752.

41. Harpine, E., & Reid, T. (2009). Enhancing academic achievement in a Hispanic immigrant community: The role of reading in academic failure and mental health. *School Mental Health, 1*(4), 159–170.

42. Ibid.

14

Civic Involvement

LENE ARNETT JENSEN AND JUSTIN LAPLANTE

Immigrant youth constitute a vital, diverse, and distinct population whose understandings of and experiences in the civic realm are important in their own right. Their views and actions will also substantially impact the future of the United States—and potentially even our future world with its increasingly interconnected countries and cultures. We begin this chapter by listening to Anita, a 17-year-old second-generation immigrant whose parents came to the United States from India. She took part in one of our interview studies with immigrant families that included a focus on civic involvement. As we will see in the course of this chapter, Anita's account of how she is and is not civically involved, and why, captures in an authentic way the vitality, diversity, and distinctiveness that is characteristic of the civic lives of immigrant youth.

> INTERVIEWER: Are you involved in political activities . . . ?
> ANITA: No, not really. A lot of the protests, I have been asked to go. But I'm a little more conservative than most of my peers. . . . But I'm the president of the National Honor Society, and we organize a lot of community things. I volunteer in a hospital. I also tutor some kids through school.
> INTERVIEWER: Why is it important for you to be involved . . . ?
> ANITA: Because people have this perception that teenagers are, you know, ungrateful, lazy. And that's the first reason. You need to show that you're interested in what happens. Secondly, if you start out young, you'll probably keep doing it. . . . [Also, I tutor] because I think it's really sad to see a kid who wants to learn and do well, and [he] can't. A lot of people argue that, you know, if you come to public school, everyone has the same chance. But it's not true. If your par-

ents are always working because they have to support you, and you don't have a computer at home, things aren't equal. You're probably not going to do as well as other kids who have the fancy computers, and the textbooks, and parents [who] are college graduates. So I think that some kids need extra help, and I think they should get it. [Also,] you know, everyone has taken from this community. Like I feel, I feel so grateful just to be part, like [to] be able to work in America, [to] be able do all the stuff that I do and have everything I have. I really believe in giving back. And I think that the earlier you do it, the better. Because, as I said, it will probably stick with you, and you'll continue it as you grow up.

Anita went on to tell us about a number of her other civic activities. To us, her engagement and passion stand in contrast to the paucity of attention that researchers have devoted to the civic views and actions of immigrant youth.[1] Her engagement can also be a source of inspiration. To better understand the underpinnings of civic behaviors, we listen to what immigrant youth such as Anita have said about their motivation for civic involvement.[2] In this chapter, we also review and synthesize available research on the types and extent of civic involvement of immigrant youth in the United States and discuss how different micro- and macrolevel contexts encourage and discourage this involvement.

To What Extent Are Immigrant Youth Involved?

In order to capture the scope of immigrant youth's involvement in the civic realm, we need to include a wide array of relevant activities.[3] Sherrod, Flanagan, and Youniss have pointed out that political science research, both generally and on immigrant youth, has traditionally tended to focus on purely political behaviors and to utilize these as proxies for civic involvement.[4] As they have argued, and as illustrated by Anita's interview responses, such an approach misses the breadth and complexities of youth's involvement in civic activities. This situation is even more true for immigrant youth's civic engagement, which often takes nonpolitical avenues. For example, examination of political behaviors such as voting does not take into account youth under the age of 18 or immigrants who are not citizens, even if they are of voting age.[5] Therefore, it is important when thinking about civic involvement to broaden our conception beyond simple measures of political behavior; these may not be the most appropriate (or even possible) avenues of involvement for immigrant youth, who face specific structural barriers to their political engagement. Thus, we also need to include the civic volunteer activities that often occur through schools and various cultural, social, and religious organizations.[6]

Findings from currently available studies indicate that there are few differences between immigrant and nonimmigrant youth's political and civic involvement when factors such as levels of income and education are taken into account. Lower levels of income and education erect barriers that limit youth's availability to participate in civic activities, as when youth must spend time working to contribute to family income.[7]

Lopez and Marcelo conducted two national surveys that compared first-generation (i.e., foreign-born) immigrants, second-generation immigrants (i.e., those with at least one foreign-born parent), and native-born U.S. residents between the ages of 15 and 25. The surveys included more than 20 different civic, electoral, and political items. Results from one survey, which was conducted over the Internet, show almost no significant differences among the three groups. The results of the other survey, conducted via telephone, indicate that first-generation immigrants were less active than native-born residents in a number of political and civic areas when demographic differences such as socioeconomic status, gender, and region of the country were left unadjusted. However, when these differences were controlled for statistically, few group differences remained. The researchers point out that among the few remaining differences, some such as those relating to voting may reflect structural or legal barriers to young immigrants' involvement.[8]

Huddy and Khatib also surveyed first-generation, second-generation, and native-born youth. In two studies with students from Stony Brook University (the sample sizes were 300 and 341), they asked about both behaviors and attitudes. On seven different measures pertaining specifically to U.S. politics—including voting, patriotism, attention to politics, and knowledge of politics—there were essentially no differences among the groups. These studies did not control for demographic variation, but such differences might have been limited for samples consisting solely of students from the same college.[9]

A study by Stepick, Stepick, and Labissiere examined the activities of immigrant and nonimmigrant students at a college in Miami, Florida (1,334 first-year residents). Their study encompassed 23 different political, civic, and social activities such as discussing politics, volunteering, and watching younger siblings. Results reveal high levels of involvement for all students and few group differences. Averaged across all the activities, about 80 percent of all the college students reported having been engaged often or very often in these activities during their high school years. Among the group differences that did emerge, more native-born residents and second-generation immigrants had been registered to vote than first- and 1.5-generation immigrants (i.e., those born abroad who came to the United States prior to age 12) had. However, native-born residents scored lower than some or all of the immigrant groups did on helping non-English speakers, helping a recent immigrant, and helping an illiterate person.[10] These differences show how important context is for the specific types of engagement in which individuals participate. Immigrant youth have more contact with non-English speakers and with other immigrants, so they are more likely to be in a position to help them. In the United States, native-born and second-generation immigrants are natural citizens, so they are more likely to vote. For activities accessed equally by both immigrants and nonimmigrants, such as donating blood or volunteering, participation levels are similar for both groups.

In a review article on civic engagement among U.S. youth, Flanagan and Levine included a notable finding comparing immigrant and nonimmigrant youth.[11] On the basis of a Center for Information and Research on Civic Learning and Engagement (CIRCLE) report by Lopez, Levine, and colleagues, Flanagan and Levine observed that the proportion of youth who had taken part in a protest within the previous 12 months was 23 percent for first-generation immigrant youth, 18 percent for second-generation immigrant youth, and 10 percent for nonimmigrant youth. These numbers come from a nationally representative survey of 1,700 young people age 15 to 25.[12] It is important to note that this survey was conducted during the period of protests occurring in spring 2006 in reaction to proposed changes to U.S. immigration policy, including classifying undocumented immigrants as felons. These issues may explain why twice as many immigrant youth as nonimmigrant youth took part in the protests, again underscoring the importance of the broader context in influencing youth's choice of activities in which they become involved.

In an ethnographic study focused on immigrant adolescents and their families, Bloemraad and Trost also found high involvement in the 2006 protests. The study was not initially designed to address the protests but happened to include the period from March to August 2006 when they were occurring. In interviews with 40 low-income Mexican-origin immigrant families from California (a total of 79 adolescents and parents), 61 percent of adolescents and 62 percent of parents reported that they had taken part in activities centered around the protests, such as participating in a boycott or attending a march.[13] Here it is important to note differences between high-risk and low-risk involvement; some civic activities involve a higher risk, especially for undocumented immigrants. For example, there are potentially serious consequences for undocumented workers who participate in marches or protests. If the police were to show up, these workers might be identified as undocumented and then deported, a possibility that survey participants noted with caution when discussing their decisions to attend the 2006 protest marches. Conversely, boycotts have relatively few potential consequences in terms of immigrants being outed as undocumented. Of course, these problems and considerations uniquely arise for undocumented immigrants and their family members and often serve to keep such individuals "in the shadows."[14] However, in certain contexts, such as the spring 2006 protests, the issues are of such importance that protests can instigate outpourings of relatively high-risk involvement among immigrant youth and their parents in spite of the potential for serious consequences.

Taken together, the findings from these studies indicate that on overall rates of involvement in political and civic activities, immigrant youth's participation is fairly similar to that of their native-born peers with comparable demographic characteristics. However, immigrant youth often do not have demographic characteristics comparable to those of their native-born peers, so the unique interactions of contexts and immigrants' characteristics should be further researched. Clearly, more surveys of the civic and political behaviors of immigrant youth are needed. The available research also suggests that not all political and civic behaviors carry the same meanings, or risks, for immigrants and nonimmigrants or for immigrants of different generations and legal statuses. Immigrant youth may be more involved with issues relevant to immigrants, such as translation and protests pertaining to immigrant rights, but they may also be involved with issues that they have encountered among immigrants that also apply to others, such as literacy.

In What Specific Civic and Political Behaviors Are Immigrant Youth Involved?

There is not enough research available to provide reliable rates of immigrant youth's participation in specific types of civic and political behaviors. However, culling information from studies of immigrant youth helps to provide an understanding of the wide array of behaviors in which they take part. Some activities mainly occur at the individual level, such as keeping abreast of current events, registering to vote, or donating blood. Others revolve around the family system, such as discussing politics with family members and translating for non-English-speaking relatives. Some activities are broader in their focus, such as contacting a public official, raising money for charity, protesting, voting, joining a school club or sports program, boycotting, tutoring, helping senior citizens, or signing a petition. Of course, it is important to remember that these activities typically operate on multiple levels. For example, church is often attended with family and friends and frequently is a source for broader engagement with the community. Also, these types of engagement are not unique to immigrant youth.

Nevertheless, some forms of engagement are attractive to immigrant youth because of their particular experiences. For example, the bilingual or multilingual skills of many immigrant youth often enable them to act as translators for friends, family members, and others in their community who are less fluent in English.[15] For illustration, 84 percent of the 1.5-generation immigrant youth in the Florida sample described above had helped non-English speakers read and write, as compared with 58 percent of nonimmigrant youth performing such services.[16] In Bloemraad and Trost's previously described ethnographic study of immigrant families, the researchers found that fluency in English helped immigrant adolescents navigate mainstream U.S. media and translate information for their parents, who were less fluent in English. In turn, these services enabled greater family mobilization during the 2006 immigration pro-tests.[17] Researchers have also found that immigrant youth use their facil-ity with different languages when they tutor peers in school.[18]

Along with frequently being bilingual or multilingual, immigrant youth often have a bicultural or multicultural perspective. This multi-cultural mind-set can lend itself to civic engagement; by virtue of having been exposed to more than one culture and political system, individu-als can see both the problems and the benefits of the U.S. system from within and outside the system. Recall Anita in the chapter opening and how she spoke of being "so grateful just to be part, like [to] be able to work in America." Implicit here is a comparison with other places—a perspective more, if not exclusively, characteristic of immigrant youth. This bicultural or multicultural perspective, whether as upbeat as Anita's or not, can increase a person's motivation to work for change and to work to preserve what is valued.[19] Anita said, "I really believe in giving back."

Investigating the multicultural mind-set of immigrants, Myers and Zaman found differences in the ways in which immigrant and nonim-migrant youth conceptualized citizenship. On the basis of the question-naire and interview responses of 77 adolescents, they observed that immigrants tended to see themselves as "global citizens" rather than as citizens of one sovereign nation. Although nonimmigrant youth were aware of global issues or issues that cross national borders, they were nonetheless more likely to define citizenship in terms of their own na-tion.[20] As these immigrant youth become adults, this "global citizen" perspective could lead to their broader consideration of factors when making political or civic decisions. Rather than having a U.S.-centered framework, these immigrant adults will be able to take into account a multitude of perspectives and thus will be able to engage with an in-creasingly interconnected world.

In sum, the specific civic and political behaviors in which immigrant youth engage are myriad and highly varied. The multiplicity of these behaviors in part stems from the distinctive immigrant experiences of knowing more than one language and seeing the world from more than one cultural vantage point.

What Motivates Immigrant Youth to Become Involved?

Immigrant youth's motives for becoming involved in highly diverse civic activities are also multiple and different. Similar to the variety of ways in which immigrant youth become involved, their reasons for doing so range from the more personal, such as facilitating identity work or assisting with family matters, to the more distant, such as bettering their community or feeling related to their culture. Again, it is important to remember than these various levels interact and overlap.

As discussed earlier, immigrant youth's cultural identities can function as a conduit to their political and civic involvement. Chan found that cultural motives influenced Asian American immigrant college students' choices of civic participation. For example, they joined ethnic clubs and organizations as a way to explore their ethnic identity and meet other coethnic students. Their civic behaviors were also influenced by their relationships with family members such as older siblings who were engaged in particular volunteer opportunities (sometimes ethnically affiliated) and with friends who were involved in various service projects and often invited study participants to join. These avenues of initial involvement often snowballed into civic activities with other organizations.[21]

On the basis of ethnographic work with Bangladeshi, Indian, and Pakistani Muslim immigrant high school students, Maira used the terms *polycultural citizenship* and *flexible citizenship* to describe the intersection of cultural identities and civic involvement. She observed that immigrant youth drew on their multiple cultural identities (i.e., polycultural citizenship)—religious, nation of origin, panethnic—to explain their participation in U.S. civil society. Furthermore, they combined these diverse cultural identities in flexible or changing ways (i.e., flexible citizenship), depending on the specific nature of the civic participation at hand.[22]

In addition to mentioning identity motives, immigrant youth, just like nonimmigrant youth, invoke community motives when explaining their reasons for civic participation. Wanting to better society, feeling the need to give back to the community, and desiring to improve the conditions of various people are popular motives for civic participation. For example, Stepick, Stepick, and Labissiere quoted a first-generation

Haitian youth from their study in Florida who had volunteered in order to "help people."[23] An interview study in Canada found that African immigrant youth also focused on community considerations—for example, discussing the importance of voting, which they regarded as a duty of those who hold democratic citizenship.[24] These issues of citizenship might be more important to immigrant youth, who do not take their citizenship for granted, than they are to native-born youth.

In addition to these types of community motives, immigrants have spoken of "cultural motives" for their civic participation.[25] These are motives that reference either their cultural or national backgrounds or that pertain to their experiences as immigrants more generally. In a qualitative analysis of interviews with Indian and Salvadoran immigrants (80 adolescents and adults), Jensen identified seven different cultural motives for engagement. For example, "cultural remembrance" was a common motive involving immigrants' desire to remember and maintain the values and customs of their culture. This motive was often evidenced through their participation in cultural activities and classes, such as "taking an active role in Indian places, like the temple." Motives referred to as "traditions of service," immigrant adolescents and parents explained, involved activities in which their culture or religion prescribed engagement. Another common cultural motive was "bridging communities," which inspired immigrants to undertake a pursuit in order to gain an appreciation for U.S. culture while also sharing insights about their own backgrounds.[26] These cultural motives focus on engagement as a way for immigrants both to bond with others of similar cultural backgrounds and to traverse different cultural communities.

However, the multicultural backgrounds of immigrants are not always received positively. Immigrant youth also speak of discrimination, stereotypes, and barriers in regard to their cultural and immigrant backgrounds. These impediments can be systemic, legal, personal, or any combination thereof. Such negative experiences can inhibit youth's civic engagement and lead to isolation and withdrawal—although, paradoxically, they can also prompt immigrant youth's civic involvement and resilience in the face of discrimination.

As noted in the previous discussion of the 2006 protests over immigration reform, discriminatory and restrictive policies can galvanize immigrant youth and prompt their civic participation. Sief has highlighted the rallying effect that other restrictive policies, particularly those regarding immigrant youth's access to higher education, have had on promoting youth's civic engagement.[27] As Sief explains, the U.S. Supreme Court's *Plyler v. Doe* (1982) decision mandated that undocumented children cannot legally be excluded from K–12 education. In response to proposed changes to this law, such as Proposition 187, which would have required proof of citizenship for children to enroll in K–12 education in California, immigrant youth joined groups opposing the proposition.[28] However, after being eligible for public education from kindergarten through twelfth grade, undocumented students then encounter significant barriers to their higher education currently in place in the United States. Undocumented students do not have Social Security numbers, which are necessary to apply to colleges; often are not eligible for financial aid due to their undocumented status; and frequently are not fluent enough to navigate the complex and expensive application process for higher education. Consequently, groups that push for undocumented students to have more access to higher education, such as proponents of the DREAM Act or in-state tuition movements, are popular among immigrant youth, for whom these issues are especially salient. One such group, the Students Informing Now (SIN) collective, primarily provides immigrants with college information and assistance. The mission of this student group is "to give hope to those behind us, those who want to attend college but might not know they can."[29] These organizations provide ways for immigrant youth to become civically involved to combat perceived discrimination and legal barriers. The difficulties of immigrant life motivate these youth to help others facing situations similar to their own.

Immigrants have to deal not only with institutional barriers such as exclusionary laws but also with more personal instances of discrimination. Research has shown that such occurrences can also motivate immigrant youth's civic involvement. In discussing this phenomenon, Stepick, Stepick, and Labissiere present the example of Ronald, a second-generation Cuban adolescent who channeled a perception of discrimination into political engagement. In his interview, Roland referred to the negative media portrayals of Cubans during the Elián González case in 1999. This case involved a six-year-old Cuban boy who, unlike his mother, had survived their journey by raft when fleeing from Cuba to Miami. A controversy erupted over whether the boy should be returned to his father in Cuba, as the father and the Cuban government demanded, or should stay in the United States, as his U.S. relatives and the Miami Cuban community wanted. González was sent back to Cuba after U.S. government agents forcibly seized him from his Miami relatives. Commenting on the media portrayals of Cubans during this time, Ronald said, "That [the media coverage] was completely and totally out of proportion because all it would show in the news was people, you know, setting trash cans on fire, getting in fights with the cops. When you see stuff like that and it's about you, you realize that, you know, they wanted to make us look like the angry Cubans. Right? To make everybody hate us."[30] Motivated to take action to counter these media portrayals, Ronald and many other Cubans had attended peaceful daily vigils in front of the Miami house where Elián was living.

Describing a process of becoming motivated that is similar to—but also different from—the one that Stepick and colleagues observed, DeJaeghere and McCleary provide the example of a Mexican high school student in Michigan who experienced personal discrimination while attending a protest. The student recounted, "We walked to the capital protesting for the immigrants, telling our rights and singing. There were people [who] were telling us to go from their country, [saying] that we were invading their country, and telling us that we're a piece of shit and throwing . . . things [at us]."[31] DeJaeghere and McCleary theorize that experiences like this one in which immigrants are "being made as other" lead some immigrants to reject the image and its implications and instead work toward assuming more positive personal and public identities by taking part in civic and political activities. Sief concurs, stating that many immigrant youth become engaged in the civic realm to counter negative stereotypes.[32] However, most participants in the DeJaeghere and McCleary study reported that they had felt alienated and discriminated against, experiences that often produced negative emotional responses.[33] Even though some immigrant youth become civically or politically involved to counter negative stereotypes, their participation in these activities does not reduce or negate the pain caused by exclusion and discrimination. Their involvement can, however, demonstrate their resiliency. Immigrant youth, then, have many different motives for participating in civic and political activities. They share some motives with nonimmigrant youth, but others are relatively distinct to their experiences—for better and worse—of being immigrants and having ties to different cultures. However, even negative experiences such as encounters with stereotypes, barriers, and discrimination can serve as stimuli for civic and political participation.

What Roles Do Different Contexts Play in Immigrant Youth's Civic Involvement?

As is evident, immigrant youth are immersed in a variety of contexts that influence civic behavior, from macrosystems such as the political and legal spheres and media to microsystems such as educational institutions, family, and friends.[34] These contexts can either facilitate or hinder civic involvement.

At the political and legal level, there are many factors that influence immigrant youth and their civic engagement. Some immigrant youth point to positive aspects of the U.S. legal system as reasons for getting involved. Specifically, the protection of free speech is seen as a boon. As one immigrant explained, "What makes America different from a lot of [other] countries is that the freedom of speech grants people the right to say what they want on any issue, which is good. Definitely good—because it alerts people [to] things that they might not have been able to break down or able to notice."[35] Likewise, the United States provides opportunities for people to protest peacefully with minimal fear of legal repercussions. For example, Bloemraad and Trost tell of Señora Sanchez, a legal permanent resident who spoke of attending a rally with her daughter during the 2006 protests: "There were a lot of people and they invited me. . . . I am not like that [someone who participates] either. Not at all . . . I did not think that there would be so many people, and my older daughter could not believe what she was doing. I told her that there is nothing bad and we are just supporting people."[36] Sanchez's observations also highlight how, even for relatively high-risk participation activities such as protesting, the costs to individuals in the United States are less than they would be in some other parts of the world.

As noted earlier, experiences with legal barriers and discrimination can serve as rallying points for immigrant youth working for change. However, such experiences can also reduce immigrant youth's civic participation. In a study of more than 5,000 second-generation immigrant adolescents, Portes and Rumbaut found that negative responses to the statement "There is no better country to live in than the United States" were highest among youth who had reported experiencing discrimination.[37] Such responses were especially prevalent among youth from Haiti, Jamaica, and the West Indies, who Rumbaut noted may be the most likely to experience racial discrimination.[38] Negative perceptions of and negative experiences with the U.S. governmental system and discrimination, then, can hinder civic involvement among immigrant youth.

The media are an important platform for the representation, dissemination, and transmission of norms and images. Wray-Lake and colleagues noted that Arab immigrant youth who regarded media portrayals of their culture and religion as negative also were more distrustful of the U.S. government. In response to an open-ended question that states, "Movies and television programs sometimes show certain countries or groups of people as enemies of America. . . . These days what groups do you think are shown as enemies of America?" the researchers found that 61 percent of Arab immigrant youth in their study identified Arabs, Muslims, or Middle Easterners as groups depicted as "enemies" of the United States. Furthermore, these youths' responses were more negative regarding the belief that the U.S. government is responsive to everyone than were those of Arab immigrant youth who did not feel that their own cultural, religious, or national group was perceived in enemy terms.[39]

Negative media images of ethnic groups may thus lead to immigrant youth's less-than-positive views of the U.S. system of government and possibly to less civic involvement. However, media images—even negative ones—can also lead to immigrant youth's increased civic participation. As noted earlier, Stepick and colleagues found that the media attention given to the Elián González case mobilized Cuban immigrant youth to take political action, at least partly because they considered the portrayals of Cubans negative and inaccurate.[40] Similarly, Maira found that some South Asian Muslim immigrant youth paid close attention to media images of Muslims in the aftermath of 9/11 and then sought to counter stereotypic images in their everyday actions.[41] For example, one Asian Indian immigrant youth wrote the words "INDIA + MUSLIM" on her bag. To her, this display was a way of signaling that she was Muslim, that Muslims are diverse, and that Muslims are a visible and legitimate part of U.S. society. This youth said, "Just because one Muslim did it in New York, you can't involve everybody in there."[42]

Among microlevel contexts, school is an integral component of many immigrant youths' civic participation. We saw in the chapter opening that Anita tutored through her high school and also belonged to an honors society. Flanagan and Levine have argued that college is also a crucial context for civic behaviors because opportunities for youth's involvement are plentiful.[43] With respect to college, Bloemraad and Trost maintain that "youth participate [in civic activities in college] because little is stopping them, costs are modest, and they have time on their hands."[44] Flanagan and Levine have pointed out that although youth who do not attend college may participate in civic activities through church, work, the military, AmeriCorps, and community organizations, these institutions provide fewer occasions for civic engagement than college does. They also emphasize that the membership in many of the institutions that have historically catered to those who do not attend college, such as unions and fraternal social organizations, has decreased greatly and that these organizations do not provide as many opportunities for civic engagement as they once did.[45] While college is an excellent context for civic engagement for youth who attend, these opportunities are not as readily available to youth—immigrant and nonimmigrant—who do not.

Religious institutions, another microlevel context, have been and continue to be an important context in immigrants' social and civic lives.[46] One study of immigrant youth and adults found that half of the participants' civic activities occurred in the context of religious organizations.[47] (It is worth noting that this statistic is similar to one Putnam noted for the general U.S. population's rate of participation.)[48] Furthermore, the study indicates that religious organizations—unlike other institutions such as schools, social service groups, and cultural and political organizations—attract participants evenly across age groups as well as across national and religious backgrounds. While the religious context was important for immigrants' civic involvement, findings also show that few immigrants spoke of having religious or spiritual motivations when explaining their own civic involvement or why such involvement is important more generally. Only 12 percent of immigrant adults spoke of having religious or spiritual motivations; for immigrant youth, the comparable number was a mere 3 percent.[49] These findings suggest that although religions institutions provide important ways for immigrants to participate in civic activities, involvement with religion is not necessarily an important explanation for their doing so.

Given the high level of commitment to family that immigrant youth often evince,[50] it is important to understand the relationship between the religious context and the civic realm. In a study of high school students, Bogard and Sherrod found that immigrant youth who felt a strong allegiance to their family also strongly agreed with a measure of civic orientation that included items prescribing community service, staying informed, and helping the needy.[51] Bloemraad and Trost noted in their ethnographic research that political socialization was bidirectional, with parents and youth influencing one another. They observed that adolescents and parents accessed different social networks and different information sources. For example, parents tended to watch non-English, ethnic media, whereas youth were more tuned in to mainstream U.S. media and the Internet. In turn, parents and youth shared their different pieces of information. Doing this allowed them to exchange information about different ways to be involved and enabled them to participate in the 2006 protests together.[52] On the basis of research with Asian American immigrant college students, Chan also noted the importance of family for civic engagement. Parents, aunts, uncles, and older cousins not only modeled civic behavior for youth by belonging to and talking about particular groups and activities; they also invited youth to join the organizations and activities.[53]

Chan found that friends and peers similarly recruited immigrant youth in her study to join groups and activities.[54] Clearly, Anita's peers had tried to recruit her for political activities—albeit in her case not successfully. Nonetheless, friends are important during adolescence and emerging adulthood in general,[55] and immigrant youth are no exception. Chan noted that many of the Asian American immigrant college students in her research reported that they had first become involved in student organizations because their friends were involved and had invited them to join.[56]

Friends ask friends to participate in activities. Conversely, the lack of an invitation may also result in a lack of participation. For example,

Bloemraad and Trost mention an adolescent girl who, though sympathetic to the goals of the immigration protests of 2006, did not participate in them. When asked why she had not, she said that her friends had gone but that "they didn't even tell [her]" they were going. She said that if they had invited her, she would have gone.[57] Friends and peers, then, are an important context that lead some immigrant youth to become involved in civic behaviors—but without friends' or peers' invitations, the youth sometimes do not engage in them.

A wide variety of contexts at the macro- and microlevels influence immigrant youth's civic involvement or lack of it. Previous research has provided an initial understanding of some of the important contexts and the ways in which they facilitate or hinder involvement. However, more research on how the intersection of these contexts impacts the involvement of immigrant youth is needed since each individual is enmeshed in many contexts simultaneously. A greater understanding of the connections among contexts would provide a more complete picture of immigrant youth's civic engagement.

What Are Fruitful and Necessary Future Directions?

As we have seen, interesting and important research on the civic involvement of immigrant youth has been conducted, but many unanswered questions remain. Future studies should take into account the variation in immigrant youth's situations. Bloemraad and Trost's ethnographic work, for example, considers the importance of parents' documentation status to youth's civic engagement. The researchers found that two-thirds of the children whose parents were undocumented or legal permanent residents had participated in the 2006 protests, whereas about half of the children of naturalized parents had done so.[58] The sample size for this study was small, but it notes an important source of variation among immigrant youth. Wray-Lake, Syvertson, and Flanagan's study of Muslim immigrant youth suggests that considering how the dominant society views different immigrant groups can provide insights into immigrant youth's civic attitudes and behavior.[59] Flanagan and Levine have highlighted ways in which differences in immigrant youth's educational circumstances and levels of attainment may influence their opportunities for civic engagement.[60] When research is designed to consider these areas in which immigrant youth vary, we will gain a better understanding of the similarities and differences in their civic involvement.

In addition to focusing on the diversity of immigrant youth, it would be fruitful for future research to explore the implications of immigrant youth's multicultural skills and perspectives for civic involvement. Some work has already been conducted in this area,[61] even if many of the insights have come about through respondents' answers to questions designed for other purposes. Qualitative research designed to study immigrant youth's perceptions of the ways in which their navigation of different cultures relates to their civic attitudes and involvement should be undertaken next. Listening to immigrant youth like Anita is important. A qualitative approach could provide new emic insights, generate new theories, and place a primary focus on the everyday lived experiences of immigrant youths. Finally, from a developmental point of view, longitudinal research could help address unanswered questions about immigrant youth's civic engagement. Longitudinal work could clarify the extent to which immigrant youth's motives for civic involvement or for their lack of it change from early adolescence to adulthood. It could reveal the potentially positive benefits of their engagement in civic behaviors. Clearly, Anita thought that becoming involved in civic activities at an early age was important and beneficial for her: "I think that the earlier you do it, the better. Because, as I said, it will probably stick with you, and you'll continue it as you grow up."[62] As researchers, we should be inspired to test her thesis and draw from her experience. Longitudinal work could also provide opportunities to examine the waxing and waning importance of different contexts throughout immigrant youth's adolescence and into their adulthood. As noted previously, friends take on added significance in the lives of immigrant children as they move into adolescence. Likewise, their recruitment into civic activities and organizations may gain in importance. However, the influence of friends may wane as youth move into adulthood and as other contexts such as work increasingly become more relevant to them.

Conclusion

To return to the question asked at the outset: Why is it important to study immigrant youth's involvement in the civic arena? The world is changing. Globalization is occurring at a fast pace, and nations and peoples are no longer able to ignore the rapid increase in diversification. Immigrant youth are at the forefront of this diversification within and among nations. They will, in increasing numbers, become the citizens, leaders, and face of the United States in the years to come. With their multicultural perspectives, immigrant youth are well poised to navigate and bridge civic and political matters in U.S. culture by utilizing the myriad global interconnections that are changing the face of the civic and political realms.

NOTES

1. Stepick, A., & Stepick, C. D. (2002). Becoming American, constructing ethnicity: Immigrant youth and civic engagement. *Applied Developmental Science, 6*(4), 246–257.

2. Jensen, L. A., & Flanagan, C. A. (Eds.). (2008). Immigrant civic engagement: New translations. Special issue of *Applied Developmental Science, 12*(2), 55–56.

3. Putnam, R. D. (2000). *Bowling alone: The collapse and revival of American community.* New York: Simon and Schuster.

4. Sherrod, L. R., Flanagan, C., & Youniss, J. (2002). Editors' introduction. *Applied Developmental Science, 6,* 173–174; Sherrod, L. R., Flanagan, C., & Youniss, J. (2002). Dimensions of citizenship and opportunities for youth development: The *what, why, when, where,* and *who* of citizenship development. *Applied Developmental Science, 6,* 264–272.

5. Stepick, A., Stepick, C. D., & Labissiere, Y. (2008). South Florida's immigrant youth and civic engagement: Major engagement: Minor differences. *Applied Development Science, 12*(2), 57–65.

6. Youniss, J., Bales, S., Christmas-Best, V., Diversi, M., McLaughlin, M., & Silbereisen, R. (2002). Youth civic engagement in the twenty-first century. *Journal of Research on Adolescence, 12*(1), 121–148.

7. Perreira, K. M., Harris, K. M., & Lee, D. (2007). Immigrant youth in the labor market. *Work and Occupations, 34*(1), 5–34.

8. Lopez, M. H., & Marcelo, K. B. (2008). The civic engagement of immigrant youth: New evidence from the 2006 Civic and Political Health of the Nation Survey. *Applied Developmental Science, 12*(2), 66–73.

9. Huddy, L., & Khatib, N. (2007). American patriotism, national identity, and political involvement. *American Journal of Political Science, 51,* 63–77.

10. Stepick et al. (2008).

11. Flanagan, C., & Levine, P. (2010). Civic engagement and the transition to adulthood. *Future of Children, 20*(1), 159–179.

12. Lopez, M. H., Levine, P., Both, D., Kiesa, A., Kirby, E., & Marcelo, K. Center for Information and Research on Civic Learning and Engagement (CIRCLE). (2006). *The 2006 civic and political health of the nation: A detailed look at how youth participate in politics and communities.* College Park, MD: CIRCLE.

13. Bloemraad, I., & Trost, C. (2008). It's a family affair: Intergenerational mobilization in the spring 2006 protests. *American Behavioral Scientist, 52*(4), 507–532.

14. Suárez-Orozco, C., Yoshikawa, H., Teranishi, R. T., & Suárez-Orozco, M. M. (2011). Growing up in the shadows: The developmental implications of unauthorized status. *Harvard Educational Review, 81*(3), 438–472; Sief, H. (2011). "Unapologetic and unafraid": Immigrant youth come out from the shadows. In C. A. Flanagan & B. D. Christens (Eds.), Youth civic development: Work at the cutting edge. *New Directions for Child and Adolescent Development, 134,* 59–75.

15. Orellana, M. F., Dorner, L., & Pulido, L. (2003). Accessing assets: Immigrant youth's work as family translators or "para-phrasers." *Social Problems, 50*(4), 505–524; Younnis et al. (2002).

16. Stepick et al. (2008).

17. Bloemraad & Trost. (2008).

18. Jensen, L. A. (2008). Immigrants' cultural identities as sources of civic engagement. *Applied Developmental Science, 12*(2), 74–83.

19. Ibid.

20. Myers, J. P., & Zaman, H. A. (2009). Negotiating the global and national: Immigrant and dominant-culture adolescents' vocabularies of citizenship in a transnational world. *Teachers College Record, 111*(11), 2589–2625.

21. Chan, W. Y. (2011). An exploration of Asian American college students' civic engagement. *Asian American Journal of Psychology, 2*(3), 197–204.

22. Maira, S. (2004). Youth culture, citizenship and globalization: South Asian Muslim youth in the United States after September 11th. *Comparative Studies of South Asia, Africa, and the Middle East, 24*(1), 219–231.

23. Stepick et al. (2008).

24. Chareka, O., & Sears, A. (2006). Civic duty: Young people's conceptions of voting as a means of political participation. *Canadian Journal of Education, 29,* 521–540.

25. Jensen. (2008).

26. Ibid.

27. Seif. (2011).

28. Ibid.

29. Students Informing Now Collective. (2007). Students Informing Now (S.I.N.) challenge the racial state in California without shame . . . SIN Vergüenza! *Educational Foundations, 21,* 71–90.

30. Stepick et al. (2008), p. 61.

31. DeJaeghere, J. G., & McCleary, K. S. (2010). The making of Mexican migrant youth civic identities: Transnational spaces and imaginaries. *Anthropology & Education Quarterly, 41*(3), 228–244. (Quotation from p. 234.)

32. Seif, H. (2010). The civic life of Latina/o immigrant youth: Challenging boundaries and creating safe spaces. In L. R. Sherrod, J. Torney-Purta, & C. A. Flanagan (Eds.), *Handbook of research on civic engagement in youth* (pp. 445–470). New York: Wiley.

33. DeJaeghere & McCleary. (2010).

34. Bronfenbrenner, U. (1980). *The ecology of human development.* Cambridge: Harvard University Press; Bronfenbrenner, U., & Morris, P. A. (1998). The ecology of developmental process. In W. Damon (Series Ed.) and R. Lerner (Vol. Ed.), *Handbook of child psychology, Vol. 1: Theoretical models of human development* (pp. 993–1028). New York: Wiley.

35. Jensen. (2008), p. 81.

36. Bloemraad & Trost. (2008), p. 517.

37. Portes, A., & Rumbaut, R. G. (2001). *Legacies: The story of the immigrant second generation.* Berkeley: University of California Press.

38. Rumbaut, R. G. (2008). Reaping what you sow: Immigration, youth, and reactive ethnicity. In L. A. Jensen & C. A. Flanagan (Eds.), Immigrant civic engagement: New translation. Special issue of *Applied Developmental Science, 12*(2), 108–111.

39. Wray-Lake, L., Syvertson, A. K., & Flanagan, C. A. (2008). Contested citizenship and social exclusion: Adolescent Arab American immigrants' views of the social contract. In L. A. Jensen & C. A. Flanagan (Eds.), Immigrant civic engagement: New translation. Special issue of *Applied Developmental Science, 12*(2), 84–92.

40. Stepick et al. (2008).

41. Maira. (2004).

42. Ibid., p. 226.

43. Flanagan & Levine. (2010).

44. Bloemraad & Trost. (2008), p. 510.

45. Flanagan & Levine. (2010).

46. Foley, M. W., & Hoge, D. R. (2007). *Religion and the new immigrants: How faith communities form our newest immigrants.* New York: Oxford University Press.

47. Jensen, L. A. (2008). Immigrant civic engagement and religion: The paradoxical roles of religious motives and organizations. In R. Lerner, R. Roeser, & E. Phelps (Eds.), *Positive youth development and spirituality: From theory to research* (pp. 247–261). West Conshohocken, PA: Templeton Foundation Press.

48. Putnam. (2000).

49. Jensen. (2008). Immigrant civic engagement and religion.

50. Bloemraad & Trost. (2008).

51. Bogard, K. L., & Sherrod, L. R. (2008). Citizenship attitudes and allegiances in diverse youth. *Cultural Diversity and Ethnic Minority Psychology, 14*(4), 286–296.

52. Bloemraad & Trost. (2008).

53. Chan. (2011).

54. Ibid.

55. Youniss, J., & Smollar, J. (1985). *Adolescent relations with mothers, fathers, and friends.* Chicago: University of Chicago Press; Way, N., & Greene, M. L. (2006).

Trajectories of perceived friendship quality during adolescence: The patterns and contextual predictors. *Journal of Research on Adolescence, 16*(2), 293–320.

56. Chan. (2011).

57. Bloemraad & Trost. (2008), p. 523.

58. Ibid.

59. Wray-Lake et al. (2008).

60. Flanagan & Levine. (2010).

61. Ibid.

62. Jensen, L. A. (2008). Through two lenses: A cultural-developmental approach to moral psychology. *Developmental Review, 28*(3), 289–315; Youniss. (2002); Jensen. (2008). Immigrants' cultural identities.

15

Future Directions

Implications for Research, Practice, and Policy

CAROLA SUÁREZ-OROZCO, HIROKAZU YOSHIKAWA, AND
MARGARY MARTIN

As we have seen, the children of immigrants are an ever-increasing presence in schools and communities across the United States. For nearly five decades, there has been a continuous growth of this population, which sociologists and demographers have noted and with which educators in classrooms have (largely) floundered. Until a decade and a half ago, research that focused on children was largely limited to issues of language acquisition and identity.[1] However, along with increasing awareness of the burgeoning immigrant-origin child population has come the expansion of developmental scientists' research on aspects and implications of this phenomenon.

In creating this book, we turned to colleagues to consider the state of the field. What are the settings that contribute to various outcomes for immigrant-origin children? What processes are of particular significance for these children's development? How are they doing on a series of outcomes? How are they both similar to and different from nonimmigrant children? "How do various groups have both similar and discrepant experiences?"[2] How does immigrant generation matter?

The authors of this book's chapters have answered some of these questions, but no doubt more questions have been raised than answered. These are the questions that, moving forward, researchers will need to continue to ask themselves and to ask about the research they evaluate, the practices they engage with, in a variety of settings, and the policies they work toward implementing.

Methodological Considerations Moving Forward

What should researchers studying immigrant children consider?

As developmental scientists pursue research with child populations in general, given the high percentages of immigrant children involved (especially in urban centers but increasingly in suburban and rural areas as well), ignoring immigration status or generation should simply not be an option. We now know enough about the unique contexts and processes influencing immigrant children's development that such information should, at a minimum, be part of the demographic characterization of samples in child and family research. Further, neither immigrant status nor generation should be confounded with race or ethnicity or used as a control variable. To do so would be misleading since immigration, culture, race, and ethnicity are separate categories and are embedded within the context of several potential mediators, moderators, and outcomes.[3] Socioeconomic status, assessed in a number of ways (e.g., according to level of education attained in the country of origin, levels of professional attainment before and after migration, household income, and remittances made to family in the heritage country), should be considered since each has different implications for a variety of child outcomes.[4] In addition, research with immigrants should take into account the heterogeneity both between and within different immigrant communities.[5]

Cultural Validity and the Reliability of Constructs

Although constructs may be shared across groups, their expression may be culturally and socially defined. Thus, it is insufficient to conduct research on ethnically diverse populations without documenting (or at least considering) the diversity of patterns across groups. Valid and relevant assessment of a variety of constructs within and across different cultural groups and settings is essential in order to meaningfully document various outcomes of immigrant-origin children and adolescents and their families. To construct culturally valid research, developmental psychologists must further the understanding of how different cultural groups vary in their beliefs and cultural practices around whatever construct researchers are trying to document.[6]

In addition to identifying culture-specific expressions of well-being as well as those of distress, researchers must critically examine constructs that have been developed in a Western middle-class context before applying them to non-Western non-middle-class participants.[7] Combining "outsider" (*etic*) and "insider" (*emic*) approaches to diverse populations is important in both data collection and analysis.[8] Bicultural and bilingual researchers are better able than monolingual researchers are to establish rapport and trust within immigrant communities and to gain entry into populations that might otherwise be difficult to access. Furthermore, insiders are essential for appropriate linguistic and cultural translations of protocols. Their perspective is also necessary for accurate and culturally relevant interpretations of emerging findings.

Triangulation of Data and the Use of Multiple Informants

Using triangulated data collected from a variety of perspectives and including an assortment of strategies are crucial when one is conducting research with groups of diverse backgrounds. The utilization of such an approach provides more confidence that data are accurately capturing the phenomenon under consideration. By gathering a variety of perspectives—self-reports, parents' reports, teachers' reports (in the case of youth), and various stakeholder members' reports (in the case of adults)—and considering these alongside researchers' observations, concurrence and disconnections can be established among what informants say they do, what others say they do, and what the researchers observe them doing. Researchers should consider various levels of analysis in their research, including the individual, the individual's interpersonal relations (e.g., peers and family), the individual's context-specific social groups (e.g., work, school, neighborhood, and place of worship), and cultural dimensions.[9]

Developmental and Longitudinal Perspectives

Much of the research with immigrant communities is cross-sectional in nature. Although these data are valuable in their own right, by nature they limit researchers' ability to detect changes over time. This limitation has particular implications for researchers' ability to detect the immigrant population's adaptation over time as well as for developmental research. Though time-consuming and expensive to conduct, longitudinal research has much to offer and should be pursued whenever possible.[10] Future studies should also examine mediating factors (variables that explain the relationship between two other variables) and moderating factors (variables that explain the strength between two other variables) related to mental health and psychosocial adaptation and development.[11]

Use of Mixed Methods

A wide range of methodological strategies is required to identify cultural variations in individuals' expressions of well-being and distress.[12] Research with culturally and linguistically diverse populations requires a fundamental alteration of the most common investigative frameworks (e.g., rather than approaching culture through a preestablished middle-class U.S. framework, researchers should employ methodologies that will enable them to understand the worldview of the immigrant population).[13] Using multiple methods will help researchers address these complex methodological challenges.[14]

When working with immigrant-origin populations, research methodologies should consider the value of the following:

Qualitative data—collecting data to describe meaning (e.g., ethnographic observation, interviews, and focus groups)
Quantitative data—collecting data with an emphasis on statistical inference (e.g., questionnaires, surveys, and experiments)
Mixed methods—combining qualitative and quantitative strategies in varying sequences, depending on the research questions and intent of the study[15]

Well-designed, large-scale quantitative surveys can make it possible for researchers to generalize findings to particular immigrant populations; however, without also conducting qualitative research, it can be difficult for them to interpret that data. Qualitative methods provide an opportunity for researchers to better understand local terms and cultural norms across a variety of predictors and outcomes of interest.[16]

Ethical Considerations

Researchers should also be aware of particular ethical considerations when working with immigrant-origin populations. Power dynamics between researcher and participant are always a concern but are accentuated between the researcher and an immigrant participant, particularly when the participant is less educated or is from a nondominant group.[17] Researchers must explain how a study may contribute to improving the lives of its participants and/or the larger community and delineate any potential risks to participants. Researchers must also take steps to protect participants.

Since some portion of first-generation participants may be undocumented, researchers must consider that issue when formulating the study, recruiting participants, and conducting the study. In the current U.S. climate of concerns around deportation, extra precautions must be taken to shield the identities of participants. We recommend employing the usual research protections, including using assigned numbers to mask participants' identities in records, locking paper and digital records, and having participants sign consent forms with pseudonyms. In cases in which psychologists feel they might be in violation of federal or state laws, they should consult the *Ethical Principles of Psychologists and Code of Conduct* to resolve conflicts.[18] Researchers must uphold the strictest ethical standards in order to maintain the trust of the community and not place immigrant-origin child research participants and their families at risk.[19]

Practice Implications

What should professionals working with children of immigrant origin consider in their practices?

Promising Schooling Practices

What kinds of schooling practices ease the transition and integration of immigrant-origin youth into school and foster and enhance their academic performance? Some practices are simply sound for students in general, regardless of whether they are of immigrant origin—academic settings that are rigorous, relevant, and rich in relationships, for example.[20] Others practices are tailored to the needs of newcomers, English-language learners, or the children of immigrants, serving to ease their negotiation of the cultural transition and learning a new language.

Promising schools that serve these students well tend to provide rigorous curricula that are relevant to the lives of the diverse students they serve.[21] In addition to rethinking content and delivery, these schools seek multiple strategies to assess their students as well as ways to prepare them for high-stakes testing, in which immigrant-origin youth are at a notorious disadvantage.[22] Successful schools implement multiple forms of academic supports to help their students achieve. Further, promising schools place an expectation of postsecondary school attendance along with explicit supports to gain access.[23]

In addition, schools serving newcomer immigrant-origin youth and second-language learners must address their unique additional academic and socioemotional needs.[24] At the forefront is the need to develop both the social and academic language of their new country while mastering the content knowledge necessary to be successful in the new society. Most graduation pathways are quite unforgiving of the five to seven years it takes for most students to develop the academic language to the point of competitiveness with native peers.[25] Thus, immigrant students often are tracked into non-college-bound courses, falter in confidence, and fall behind their nonimmigrant peers.[26]

Further, immigration is a stressful process, removing youth from predictable contexts and stripping them of significant preexisting social ties.[27] Many children have been separated from their parents for protracted periods of time and may face emotionally complex reunifications.[28] Immigrant children must contend with the particular psychological acculturative challenges of navigating two worlds.[29] They are often asked to take on responsibilities beyond their years, including sibling care, translation duties, and advocacy for their families,[30] which at times may undermine parental authority. These often highly gendered roles may have both positive and negative consequences for development.[31] Children of immigrants also face the challenge of forging an identity and developing a sense of belonging to their new homeland while honoring their parental origins.[32] This acculturative stress has been linked both to psychological distress[33] and to academic problems.[34]

Thus, schools must be willing to address both the academic needs of newcomer youth and the acclimation to their new environment by providing (1) support in helping students navigate the cultural transition to the new country, (2) support for students who had gaps in literacy due to interrupted schooling, (3) instruction across content areas, (4) language-intensive instruction across the curriculum, and (5) language-learning accommodations.

Negotiating Cultural Transitions

Schools should be highly strategic in their approaches to help newcomer youth adjust to their new environs.[35] As new students come in, teacher teams should meet to discuss each one, and a series of assessments should be conducted in order to develop the best plan for the student. Teachers should try to meet with parents or caretakers in order to establish a relationship with the family and to learn about students' unique home and family situations. Information gleaned from these conferences should be shared when teachers meet across the teams working with each student. Students should be assigned to an adviser and advisory group in order to help students to adjust to their new school. If possible, the newcomer or beginning learner of a new language should be paired in the same group as another student who shares the same native language and is also proficient in the new language so that the more advanced new language speaker can translate. In advisory groups, students can discuss a range of topics, from difficulties with a class or missing families and friends back home to boyfriend/girlfriend issues.[36] As depicted earlier in this book, multidimensional supports and peer tutoring/mentorship are paramount to newcomer students' adjustment to school and ultimate academic achievement.[37]

Supports for Gaps in Interrupted Schooling and Literacy

Some students enter secondary school with limited prior education or significant interruptions in their schooling. These may occur for a variety of reasons including socioeconomic or gender inequities in original educational access, political strife that could have interrupted schooling, or hiccups in the migratory process that may have led to a sustained period out of school before reentry in the new land. Whatever the cause of an interruption in schooling, the consequence is often students who are overaged and underskilled and have considerable catching up to do in the classroom. This takes significant creativity, flexibility, and sustained effort on the part of school administrators and teachers.

Students with interrupted formal education (referred to in educational circles as SIFE students) should receive the same supports provided to other newcomer students and more. Recognition must be given to their overage status and particular emphasis should be placed on literacy. Typically, these students take longer than the standard four years to graduate from high school, often stretching to seven years. Support should be provided that balances as much independence as possible with knowledgeable encouragement, along with concurrent peer support. With the right amount of scaffolding, the daunting tasks of learning a new language, acquiring literacy, mastering content knowledge of a new culture, accruing course credits toward graduation, and passing high-stakes tests are achievable for many students who would have given up in another setting.[38]

Second-Language Learning

While not all immigrant students are second-language learners, many are. In some cases, immigration requires learning three or more languages. Competently learning a second language takes considerable time,[39] and the literacy and academic preparation of incoming students vary widely. While some students arrive from high-quality educational systems with high levels of native-language literacy, others arrive from war-torn zones where schools are shut down and have minimal literacy in native language. Thus, immigrant students entering schools in a new land with minimal native-language literacy or exposure to the new language of instruction will require very different kinds of systematic long-term curriculum plans, including English-language education, to be effective.

Successful schools for immigrant-origin youth have systematic second-language acquisition policies and practices atypical of most schools in the United States. Second-language instruction is most successful when learners are placed into a progressive and strategic program of instruction that first identifies a student's incoming literacy and academic skills and then builds appropriately thereafter.[40] Research shows that consistency of instruction is essential for students, as frequent transitions place them at considerable disadvantage.[41] Second-language learning is most successful when high-quality second-language instruction is provided with continued transitional academic supports—such as tutoring, homework help, and writing assistance—as the language learners integrate into mainstream programs.[42] In order to ensure a smooth transition between grades as well as the continual development of skills, teachers need to both understand and conform to the instructional model ascribed to by the school or district.[43] Further, assessment of skill growth should be done annually using portfolio assessment as well as testing in order to measure progress and to adjust interventions.[44]

Teaching across Content Areas

In addition to developing communicative proficiency in the language of the new country, second-language learners (SLLs) need to simultaneously build content literacies; many of them also have low cognitive academic language proficiency skills (CALP). Second-language acquisition programs (e.g., bilingual education, self-contained SLL programs) primarily focus on literacy development in terms of language proficiency, with only limited attention to academic second-language acquisition in content areas.[45] It is a challenge for students to learn content across the academic disciplines while at the same time acquiring new language and literacy skills, and it poses an instructional challenge to many teachers as well.[46] Teachers in exemplary schools have received extensive training in language-intensive curriculum; language learning is embedded across the entire curriculum. Writing is not simply an activity for language-arts classes. Students must be pushed daily to write and use their developing language skills in every class.

Language-Learning Accommodations

Students should be encouraged to use their first language to help them learn the second language, even if others do not know their mother tongue. Informally, other students should be encouraged to translate for the newest immigrants, to read and write in their first language during silent reading times, and to carry bilingual dictionaries, but they should consistently be gently prodded toward their new language over time.[47] The mother tongue is thus used strategically to aid the development of the new one.

Assignments should be modified to make them accessible to students, as such accommodations provide the much-needed scaffolding to newcomer students as they make the transition to their new educational setting. Instructions can be read aloud; written instructions can be thoughtfully simplified by making strategic word choices; students with complementary skills can be paired (clearly delineating roles and responsibilities; and one grade can be given for content and another for grammar/spelling). Students then begin to gain confidence in themselves and to take the necessary strides in their new language to gain the academic skills they will need to be successful in their new land.

Community-Based Practices

Many current interventions have not taken into consideration the growing demographic of immigrant-origin children and youth. Some programs, designed broadly, find themselves underserving this demographic. In a longitudinal study of 400 newcomer immigrant students, it was found that none took advantage of formal mentoring programs.[48] Thus, broad-reaching programs, such as mentoring school climate interventions to reduce bullying, and the like, may not be reaching as widely as they should the fastest growing child demographic in the nation. Other programs specifically designed for a particular population may inadvertently play a role in segregating these children. Serious assessments need to be done of how such programs are meeting or failing to meet immigrant student populations, and then work has to be done to modify or develop altogether new, targeted interventions to address the specific needs of the local immigrant-origin populations.

Some immigrant parents—particularly undocumented parents or nonnationalized parents—are reluctant to enroll their children in programs for which these children are eligible.[49] Access to means-tested programs could be facilitated through outreach and applications that facilitate enrollment by requesting a reduced set of information about household income as well as through simplified instructions.[50] Community-based organizations (CBOs) should play an important role in easing enrollment barriers for children in mixed-status families. CBOs, for example, should take pains not to be identified with the federal government or local law enforcement authorities. Organizations that develop trusting relationships and specific expertise with low-income immigrant groups, particularly those with high proportions of undocumented status, can access these often-otherwise-inaccessible networks. Working with groups of informal organizations—such as churches and other faith-based organizations—to provide information about programs that can benefit children's development, such as public prekindergarten, child-care subsidies, food stamps, or the Special Supplemental Nutrition Program for Women, Infants, and Children (WIC), is a helpful strategy. Further, CBOs and advocacy organizations should partner with government agencies to facilitate the gathering and sharing of information about low-income immigrant populations with immigrant families.[51]

Early Education and Prekindergarten

Public prekindergarten is an important and expanding part of many public school systems, with 40 states implementing them as of 2010 and roughly 27 percent of the nation's four-year-olds enrolled.[52] These programs have a robust effect on children's language and preliteracy skills, the very dimension that appears to be most at risk in studies of the young children of immigrant origin (particularly of poor and undocumented parents).[53]

Many public prekindergarten programs require the kind of paperwork that undocumented parents may feel reluctant to complete.[54] Prekindergarten programs that are not means tested have shown strong positive effects on children's cognitive skills.[55] Further, research suggests benefits to children's learning and development for more socioeconomically diverse preschool populations.[56] Thus, expansion of preschool programs makes good sense for this population.[57]

Prior to the typical age for public prekindergarten, efforts to facilitate enrollment in center-based care would aid cognitive development among children of immigrant-origin parents. Efforts targeting the paperwork process mentioned earlier could help. In addition, parenting and child-development programs provided in trusted settings such as primary-care clinics (during well-child visits, for example) have improved the cognitive development of infants and toddlers of low-income immigrant parents.[58] Home-visiting programs with standardized curricula and qualified, skilled visitors also show promise in improving children's developmental outcomes in low-income families.[59] Primary-care-based enrollment, particularly when information is obtained around the child's birth, has been more successful for means-tested program enrollment of U.S.-born infants of undocumented parents.[60]

Programming More Broadly

In nearly every major city in the United States, as well as increasingly across the nation in many rural and suburban areas, immigrant-origin children will be part of the constituencies of many after-school, mentoring, tutoring, and other service-provision programs serving children and adolescents. When immigrant-origin families find their way to these programs, those who are providing services should continually be assessing whether the services they are providing are meeting the needs of these children as well as they are those of non-immigrant-origin children in their program. And if not, how can services be better tailored? If immigrant-origin children are failing to appear at the doors of these programs, then service providers should ask themselves in what ways they can better reach out to families in culturally and linguistically synchronistic ways by working with partners from the community.

Policy Implications

What should policy makers tasked with promoting and protecting the well-being of immigrant-origin youth consider?

Educational Reform

In recent decades, standards-based reform, premised on the idea that the combination of setting high standards and establishing measurable goals would improve individual outcomes in education and reduce the achievement gap of underserved populations, swept the nation.

NCLB. The No Child Left Behind Act (NCLB), the federally mandated, standards-based education reform, was first enacted in 2002. NCLB required states to develop assessments of basic skills to be given to all students in certain grades, if those states were to receive federal funding.[61] NCLB was instrumental in revealing subpopulations of students from various economic, racial/ethnic, and language backgrounds who were not well served in schools. At the same time, it narrowed the focus of educational interventions considerably with a bias toward measurable outcomes based on the mastery of limited tasks. These, it should be noted, turned out to be low-hanging fruit—not necessarily nurturing the skills needed to be successful in college or in the knowledge-intensive economy in the world beyond it.[62]

Further, No Child Left Behind changed federal regulations for the education of English-language learners (ELLs) requiring annual English language proficiency assessments for these students.[63] Under NCLB, after only one year of entering the U.S. educational system, ELL students were now required to take a language arts as well as a math exam, though these assessments could be taken with accommodations (such as extended time or with the availability of a dictionary). More contentious were the new federal regulations that specified that after only two years, ELLs would be required to take the exams in English. Many states used standardized ELA exams to assess adequate yearly progress. This assessment flies in the face of research that has consistently shown that no matter the age, developing academic-English-language learning takes more time than that.[64] Thus, an impossible benchmark was set that would penalize schools with high numbers of ELLs, placing them at risk of losing standing and funding under NCLB.

We now are entering a new school-reform movement—the Common Core Standards. These too have been designed with the intention of raising teaching standards, with a new emphasis on higher-order thinking, creativity, and problem solving and putting into place a more coherent national curriculum. Like NCLB, it requires prescribed standardized assessments and is highly English-language dependent. Math assessments, for example, require not simply solving problems but explaining them, as well as word problems, placing a high demand for English-language skills with an added burden on ELLs. Again, this intensive, national school reform was not designed with the fastest growing child population taken into consideration. The implications for this population remain to be seen.

The Role of Erratic Policies for Language Acquisition. Nationally, as we have seen, we have erratic language-acquisition policies that make the process of new language attainment a challenge.[65] Currently, ELL students are placed in a variety of second-language instructional programs (pull-out programs, sheltered instruction, English as a Second Language [ESL], and dual-language instruction) as they enter their new school.[66] In many districts and across various states, students are then transitioned out of these settings often with little rhyme or reason for transition.[67] Yet this is an important equity policy issue.

Immigrant-origin children face the dual challenge of mastering content while concurrently attaining academic language proficiency in English. Well designed and implemented programs offer good educational results and buffer at-risk students from dropping out by easing transitions, providing academic scaffolding, and providing a sense of community.[68] There is, however, a huge disparity in quality of instruction between settings. There are nearly as many models of bilingual and second-language programs (with a wide array of practices and philosophical approaches) as there are school districts.[69] Many bilingual programs face real challenges in their implementation—characterized by inadequate resources, lack of certified bilingual teachers, and poor administrative support.[70] Because many bilingual programs are ambivalently supported throughout the nation, they do not offer the breadth and depth of courses that immigrant students need in order to get onto a meaningful college track. Hence, there is an ever-present danger that once a student enters the ESL, bilingual, or English-language-acquisition track, he or she will have difficulty switching to the college-bound track. Schools are seldom focused on meeting the needs of dual-language students—at best these students tend to be ignored, and at worst they are viewed as a problem contributing to low performance on state-mandated high-stakes tests.[71] We need to face this challenge systematically.

The Role of Educational Assessments. Nowhere is the issue of language acquisition more clearly contributing to the perpetuation of inequities than in the area of educational assessment and high-stakes testing.

Standardized tests, used both for screening learning differences and for high-stakes academic testing, tend to have been designed and normed for middle-class populations.[72] Such tests assume exposure to certain mainstream cultural knowledge and fail to recognize culture-of-origin content knowledge, leading to underestimating abilities and competencies.[73] Timed tests penalize second-language learners, who process two languages before they settle on a single answer.[74] Further, when culturally or linguistically sensitive approaches are not utilized, individuals' needs often go unrecognized, or conversely, they can be overpathologized.[75] In the current climate of high-stakes educational assessment, school districts are pressured to prematurely reclassify students from English-language learners to fluent English proficient;[76] there is huge variability between districts and states in these classifications. Seldom are these reclassification rituals tied to the research-based evidence on what it takes to reach levels of academic language proficiency required to be competitive on standardized assessments.[77] As high-stakes tests are pervasive in our educational culture—in grade school, through high school, to SATs and GREs, this issue has clear implications for English-language learners. How to appropriately and fairly assess learning differences—neither to overidentify children who are in the process of learning a new language nor to ignore real learning challenges—is a serious equity issue moving forward.

Addressing the Issue of Undocumented Immigrants

The sheer number of individuals affected by undocumented status—currently more than 4.5 million citizen-children of undocumented immigrant parents *plus* more than 1.5 million undocumented children and youth—indicates a large-scale national concern reaching well into the future. There is increasing evidence suggesting that parental undocumented status harms children's development, across early childhood, middle childhood, and adolescence.[78] Yet policies addressing immigration-related issues rarely consider the perspective of the children.[79] Moreover, as depicted earlier in this book, we now have a growing base of research demonstrating the many negative effects of family separations on the well-being of immigrant-origin youth. Sadly, we struggle as a society to find political solutions to documentation and immigration policies, which could protect many children from developing serious emotional, cognitive, and mental health problems due to family-member separations and deportations.

A Comprehensive Approach. The most sensible policy to benefit children would be a comprehensive approach providing for a pathway to citizenship for undocumented parents and their children.[80] This would reduce the stresses about removal experienced by both parents and children, bring the parents out of the shadows without fear of accessing sources of community support, and reduce the reluctance of parents to enroll their U.S.-citizen children in programs for which they are eligible, allowing these families to live and work in dignity.

Comprehensive reform has long been a subject of contentious debate in Congress under several presidencies. A variety of criteria for eligibility have been considered, including a minimum number of years of residence, years of continuous employment, and absence of a criminal background. Some proposals have included the payment of a fine and typically require that the undocumented be placed at the "back of the line" (not displacing those who have previously applied for legal permanent residency or citizenship under other circumstances).[81]

The length of the pathway to full citizenship has important implications for the development of the over five million children whom immigration reform may affect.[82] Recent proposals do not allow green-card access until at least 10 years after passage of federal legislation— representing over half of the full span of childhood. Those with provisional status (even legal permanent residents) often express fears of the consequences of using resources that may benefit their children, such as preschool education.[83] The longer a path to citizenship for parents, the greater the proportion of a child's life that would be affected by this status. As proposals move forward, it will be crucial to consider what different lengths of the pathway to citizenship mean for children of different ages, including citizen children as well as undocumented adolescents, adults, and parents.

Piecemeal Approaches. As comprehensive reforms have stalemated, piecemeal efforts have been implemented. For undocumented youth, a pathway to citizenship—through the Development, Relief, and Education for Alien Minors Act (the DREAM Act)—was proposed multiple times in Congress.[84] The 2009 version proposed granting qualifying people—those under 35 years old who arrived in the U.S. before age 16, have lived in the U.S. for at least five years, and have received a high school or equivalency diploma—a "conditional" status during a six-year period. The bill required this group to graduate from a two-year community college or complete at least two years toward a four-year degree or serve two years in the U.S. military. After this six-year period, those who meet at least one of these three conditions would be eligible to apply for permanent resident status.[85] The proposed act is restrictive toward potential DREAMer applicants who have not been able to go on to higher education. While the benefits of the DREAM Act (as currently proposed) hold promise for many, as it is currently proposed, it bars many in the undocumented population.[86]

A ray of hope for many undocumented youth came in the form of the Deferred Action for Childhood Arrivals (DACA) memorandum issued by the Obama administration in 2012, providing two-year, temporary protection from removal for some under the age of 31 who came to the U.S. as minors.[87] Those eligible for DACA are required to have continuously resided in the United States for the past five years; be physically present in the U.S. at the time of making their request for consideration of deferred action; have entered the U.S. without inspection or have had their lawful immigration status expire as of June 2012; either be currently in school, have graduated from high school, have obtained a GED certificate, or be a discharged veteran of the U.S. Coast Guard or armed forces; and have no criminal record. DACA provides for work authorization and a Social Security number, which in turn facilitates obtaining critical identification such as a driver's license. Early results indicated positive effects on those who have enrolled, although some groups, such as young undocumented parents, are underenrolled.[88]

In December 2014, President Obama announced the "Immigration Accountability Executive Action"[89] program, announcing new sweeping reforms that potentially could affect an estimated 3.9 million[90] to 5 million[91] individuals. These announced reforms expanded DACA by increasing the previous age cap from 31 to 35. Further, with the new Deferred Action for Parental Accountability (DAPA) provision, deportation protections were provided for parents of citizen children, though not for DACA recipients. This temporary, three-year measure specifies that applicants continuously reside in the United States for five years or more, pass a background check, and pay taxes.[92] This is a stopgap solution that immediately went up for debate in Congress.

Policies Modifying Enforcement Practices. Over 72,000 parents of U.S.-born citizen children were removed in 2013.[93] Removing a parent imposes a double penalty on children: the traumatic loss of a parent as well as lost earnings of that parent to support the child's development.[94] Both penalties impede the long-term prospects and productivity of the child.

The Secure Communities federal provisions encouraged federal, state, and local law enforcement to collaborate to apprehend and deport undocumented immigrants who had committed crimes. Begun under the George W. Bush administration, these provisions were greatly expanded to cover thousands of jurisdictions in the U.S. under the Obama administration. Revisions to the regulation focused enforcement on the most serious crimes. However, a causal impact study in 2014 found that implementation of the law led to no reductions in the FBI index crime rate or in any serious crime category (homicide, rape, robbery, or aggravated assault).[95]

In part on the basis of particularly harsh state actions against the undocumented (e.g., in Arizona and Alabama) and in the absence of congressional legislation, advocacy organizations and federal policy makers began to act on this issue. An Obama administration memo issued in the fall of 2011 outlined guidance for prosecutorial discretion to consider community and family ties (including having a U.S.-citizen child) during immigration-enforcement activities.[96] Lamentably, by mid-2012, however, it was made public that in practice, virtually no parents had been released from removal proceedings due to this provision.[97]

The crisis of unaccompanied Central American children in 2014 highlighted further issues with U.S. immigration policy.[98] The Trafficking Victims Protection Reauthorization (TVPR) Act,[99] coupled with a surge of drug and gang violence in Central America, led to a swell in child migration from that region. The TVRP Act specifically excluded Mexicans from protection, reflecting preferential rules for different countries.[100] Children began being sent back to violent situations without any attempt to systematically assess asylum requests or reunify children with parents. To address this crisis, investments in trauma assessment for asylum petitioners as well as basic judicial due process under U.S. and international law could be provided; legal supports are lacking for this large influx of unaccompanied children.[101] This crisis highlighted our massive investment in border controls ($18 billion in 2012, outweighing all other federal law enforcement combined) without comparable investments in the orderly processing of petitions and visas.[102] While border-enforcement spending has soared, nearly 400,000 people have been deported annually, and our private prison system has expanded exponentially; the green-card backlogs are now longer then ever.[103] For example, Mexican-origin adult children of U.S. citizens waiting for legal permanent resident status under family-reunification provisions were waiting an average of 20 years as of 2013 (substantially longer than those from most other countries).

Provision for Identification. For many mixed-status families, parents who lack access to widely recognized identification such as a driver's license face a barrier to access to everything from jobs to driving, to even entering their children's school events.[104] Some cities such as San Francisco, New Haven, Trenton, New York City, and Los Angeles allow municipal identification associated with that locality to help increase access to resources.[105] Providing driver's licenses to DACA recipients, as some states do, is another sensible approach.[106] In Boston, in response to advocacy pressures, consular identification and foreign passports now serve as acceptable forms of photo ID,[107] no longer banishing undocumented parents from school grounds. At a minimum, this allows parents to participate in their children's schools—which research has shown, and most everyone will agree, is an important requisite for children to thrive.

Moving forward, whenever policies are about to be enacted, time must be taken to examine whether the policies may exacerbate or reduce inequality for particular immigrant groups. Not to do so will simply continue to reinforce preexisting inequality in deeply concerning ways.[108] The (not so) new immigrant-origin child population is a vibrant and integral part of the tapestry of our nation today and will continue to be so in the decades moving forward. How we understand and serve them—whether as researchers, practitioners, or policy makers—will predict not only their future as individuals but also what kind of nation we will become.

NOTES

1. Suárez-Orozco, C., & Carhill, A. (2008). Afterword: New directions in research with immigrant families and their children. *New Directions for Child and Adolescent Development, 121,* 87–104.

2. García Coll, C. & Magnuson, K. (1997). The psychological experience of immigration: A developmental perspective. In A. Booth, A. C. Crouter, & N. Landale (Eds.), *Immigration and the family* (pp. 91–132). Mahwah, NJ: Lawrence Erlbaum. Quotation from p. 95.

3. American Psychological Association. (2010). *Resilience and recovery after war: Refugee children and families in the United States.* Washington, DC: Author. Retrieved from http://www.apa.org/pi/families/refugees.aspx; American Psychological Association, Presidential Task Force on Immigration. (2012). *Crossroads: The psychology of immigration in the new century: Report of the APA Presidential Task Force on Immigration.* Washington, DC: Author. Retrieved from http://www.apa.org/topics/immigration/report.aspx.

4. Diemer, M. A., Mistry, R. S., Wadsworth, M. E., Lopez, I., & Reimers, F. (2013). Best practices in measuring social class in psychological research. *Analysis of Social Issues and Public Policy, 13*(1), 77–113.

5. García Coll & Magnuson. (1997); García Coll, C., & Marks, A. (Eds.). (2011). *The immigrant paradox in children and adolescents: Is becoming American a developmental risk?* Washington, DC: American Psychological Association Press; Suárez-Orozco & Carhill. (2008).

6. García Coll & Magnuson. (1997). For a discussion of multicultural issues in the context of assessment, see American Psychological Association. (2002). *APA guidelines on multicultural education, training, research, practice, and organizational change for psychologists.* Washington, DC: Author. Retrieved from http://www.apa.org/pi/oema/resources/policy/multicultural-guidelines.aspx.

7. APA. (2010); APA. (2012).

8. APA. (2010); APA. (2012); Cooper, C. R., Jackson, J. F., Azmitia, M., Lopez, E. M., & Dunbar, N. (1995). Bridging students' multiple worlds: African American and Latino youth in academic outreach programs. In R. F. Macías & R. G. Ramos (Eds.), *Changing schools for changing students: An anthology of research on language minorities* (pp. 211–234). Santa Barbara: University of California; Suárez-Orozco & Carhill. (2008).

9. APA. (2010); APA. (2012); Suárez-Orozco & Carhill. (2008).

10. Fuligni, A. J. (2001). A comparative longitudinal approach to acculturation among children from immigrant families. *Harvard Educational Review, 71*(3), 566–578; APA. (2010); APA. (2012); Suárez-Orozco, C., & Suárez-Orozco, M. (2001). *Children of immigration.* Cambridge: Harvard University Press; Suárez-Orozco & Carhill. 2008.

11. APA. (2010).

12. Betancourt, T. S., & Williams, T. (2008). Building an evidence base on mental health interventions for children affected by armed conflict. *Intervention, 6,* 39–56.

13. APA. (2010); APA. (2012).

14. APA. (2010); APA. (2012); Betancourt, T. S., & Khan, K. T. (2008). The mental health of children affected by armed conflict: Protective processes and pathways to resilience. *International Review of Psychiatry, 20,* 317–328; Suárez-Orozco & Carhill. (2008).

15. APA. (2010); APA. (2012); Creswell, J. W., & Plano Clark, V. L. (2011). *Designing and conducting mixed methods research.* Thousand Oaks, CA: Sage.

16. APA. (2010); APA. (2012); Betancourt, T. S., Speelman, L., Onyango, G., & Bolton, P. (2009). A qualitative study of psychosocial problems of war-affected youth in northern Uganda. *Transcultural Psychiatry, 46,* 238–256.

17. APA. (2010); APA. (2012).

18. APA. (2010); APA. (2012).

19. APA. (2012); Hernández, M. G., Nguyen, J., Casanova, S., Suárez-Orozco, C., & Saetermoe, C. L. (2013). Doing no harm and getting it right: Guidelines for ethical research with immigrant communities. In M. G. Hernández, J. Nguyen, C. L. Saetermoe, C. Suárez-Orozco (Eds.), *Frameworks and ethics for research with immigrants: New directions for child and adolescent development, 141* (pp. 43–61). San Francisco: Jossey-Bass.

20. Suárez-Orozco, C., Martin, M., Alexandersson, M., Dance, L. J., & Lunneblad, J. (2013). Promising practices: Preparing children of immigrants in New York and Sweden. In R. Alba and J. Holdaway (Eds.), *The children of immigrant in school: A comparative look at integration in the United States and Western Europe* (pp. 204–251). New York: NYU Press.

21. Banks, J., and Banks, C. (2007). *Multicultural education: Issues and perspectives* (6th ed.). New York: Wiley; Suárez-Orozco et al. (2013).

22. Suárez-Orozco et al. (2013).

23. Ibid.

24. Marks, A., & Pieloch, K. School contexts. (Chapter 2, this volume).

25. Cummins, J. (2000). *Language, power, and pedagogy.* Clevedon, UK: Multilingual Matters; Hakuta, K., Butler, Y. G., & Witt D. (2000). *How long does it take English learners to attain proficiency?* University of California Linguistic Minority Research Institute Policy Report.

26. Marks & Pieloch. (this volume); Menken, K. (2008). *English language learners left behind: Standardized testing as language policy.* Clevedon, UK: Multilingual Matters; Suárez-Orozco, C., Suárez-Orozco, M. M., & Todorova, I. (2008). *Learning a new land: Immigrant students in American society.* Cambridge: Harvard University Press.

27. Suárez-Orozco & Carhill. (2008).

28. Suárez-Orozco, C., Bang H. J., & Kim, H. Y. (2011). "I felt like my heart was staying behind": Psychological implications of immigrant family separations and reunifications. *Journal of Adolescent Research, 21*(2), 222–257.

29. Berry, J. W., Phinney, J. S., Sam, D. L., & Vedder, P. (Eds.) (2006). *Immigrant youth in cultural transition: Acculturation, identity, and adaptation across national contexts.* Mahwah, NJ: Lawrence Erlbaum.

30. Orellana, M. F., & Guan, S.-S. A. Child language brokering. (Chapter 9, this volume).

31. Suárez-Orozco, C., & Qin, D. B. (2006). Psychological and gendered perspectives on immigrant origin youth. In Social sciences and migration and gender. Special issue of *International Migration Review, 40*(1), 165–199.

32. Suárez-Orozco & Suárez-Orozco. (2001); Schwartz, S. J., Cano, M. A. & Zamboanga, B. L. Identity development (Chapter 7, this volume).

33. APA. (2012); Birman, D., & Addae, D. Acculturation (Chapter 6, this volume); García Coll & Magnuson. (1997).

34. Suárez-Orozco et al. (2008); Birman & Addae. (this volume).

35. Suárez-Orozco et al. (2013).

36. Ibid.

37. Marks & Pieloch. (this volume); Suárez-Orozco et al. (2013).

38. Marks & Pieloch. (this volume); Suárez-Orozco et al. (2013).

39. Christensen, G., & Stanat, P. (2007). *Language policies and practices for helping immigrants and second-generation students succeed.* Washington, DC: Migration Policy Institute and Bertelsmann Stiftung; Hakuta et al. (2000); Páez, M. M., & Hunter, C. J. Bilingualism and language learning. (Chapter 8, this volume).

40. Christensen & Stanat. (2007).

41. Gándara, P., and Contreras, F. (2008). *Understanding the Latino education gap—Why Latinos don't go to college.* Cambridge: Harvard University Press.

42. Christensen & Stanat. (2007).

43. Sugarman, J., & Howard. E. R. (2001). *Development and maintenance of two-way immersion programs: Advice from practitioners.* Center for Applied Linguistics, Center for Research on Education, Diversity & Excellence. Retrieved from http://crede. berkeley.edu/products/print/pract_briefs/pb2.shtml.

44. Christensen & Stanat. (2007).

45. August, D., & Hakuta, K. (Eds.). (1997). *Improving schooling for language-minority children: A research agenda.* Washington, DC: National Academy Press.

46. Ibid.

47. Suárez-Orozco et al. (2013).

48. Suárez-Orozco et al. (2008).

49. Yoshikawa, H., Kholopstseva, J., & Suárez-Orozco, C. (2013). Developmental consequences of parent undocumented status: Implications for public policies and community-based organizations. *Social Policy Report, 27*(3).

50. Crosnoe, R., Purtell, K., Fortuny, K., Perreira, K. M., Ulvestad, K., & Weiland, C. (2012). Promising practices for increasing immigrants' access to health and human services. Report for the US Department of Health and Human Services, Assistant Secretary for Planning and Evaluation. Washington, DC; Yoshikawa, H., Weiland, C., Ulvestad, K., Fortuny, K., Perreira, K., & Crosnoe, R. (2013). *Ensuring access of low-income immigrant families to health and human services: The role of community-based organizations* (Policy Brief No. 4, Immigrant Access to Health and Human Services Project). Washington, DC: Urban Institute and U.S. Department of Health

and Human Services, Assistant Secretary for Planning and Evaluation; Yoshikawa, Kholopstseva, & Suárez-Orozco. (2013).

51. Yoshikawa, Kholopstseva, & Suárez-Orozco. (2013).

52. Barnett, W. S., Epstein, D. J., Carolan, M. E., Fitzgerald, J., Ackerman, D. J., & Friedman, A. H. (2010). *The state of preschool 2010*. New Brunswick, NJ: NIEER.

53. Gormley, Jr., W. T., Gayer, T., Phillips, D., & Dawson, B. (2005). The effects of universal pre-K on cognitive development. *Developmental Psychology, 41*(6), 872–884; Weiland, C., & Yoshikawa, H. (2013). Impacts of a prekindergarten program on children's mathematics, language, literacy, executive function, and emotional skills. *Child Development, 84*(6), 2112–2130; Yoshikawa, Kholopstseva, & Suárez-Orozco. (2013).

54. Yoshikawa, Kholopstseva, & Suárez-Orozco. (2013).

55. As found in Tulsa and Boston: Yoshikawa, H., Weiland, C., Brooks-Gunn, J., Burchinal, M., Espinosa, L., Gormley, W., Ludwig, J. O., Magnuson, K. A., Phillips, D. A., & Zaslow, M. J. (2013). *Investing in our future: The evidence base for preschool education* (Policy brief, Society for Research in Child Development and the Foundation for Child Development). Retrieved from http://fcd-us.org/sites/default/files/Evidence%20Base%20on%20Preschool%20Education%20FINAL.pdf.

56. Mashburn, A. J., Justice, L. M., Downer, J. T., & Pianta, R. C. (2009). Peer effects on children's language achievement during pre-kindergarten. *Child Development, 80*(3), 686–702; Yoshikawa, Kholopstseva, & Suárez-Orozco. (2013).

57. Yoshikawa, Kholopstseva, & Suárez-Orozco. (2013).

58. Mendelsohn, A. L., Valdez, P. T., Flynn, V., Foley, G. M., Berkule, S. B., Tomopoulos, S., Fierman, A. H., Tineo, W., & Dreyer, B. P. (2007). Use of videotaped interactions during pediatric well-child care: Impact at 33 months on parenting and on child development. *Journal of Developmental & Behavioral Pediatrics, 28*, 206–212.

59. National Forum on Early Childhood Policies and Programs (2007). *A science-based framework for early childhood policy*. Cambridge: Harvard Center on the Developing Child. Retrieved from http://developingchild.harvard.edu/index.php/resources/reports_and_working_papers/policy_framework/.

60. Yoshikawa, H. (2011). Immigrants raising citizens. *Undocumented parents and their young children*. New York: Russell Sage Foundation.

61. Durán, R. P. (2006). *State implementation of NCLB policies and interpretation of the NAEP performance of English language learners*. American Institutes for Research.

62. Goldrick-Rab, S., & Mazzeo, C. (2005). What no child left behind means for college access. *Review of Research in Education, 29*(1), 107–129.

63. Capps, R., Fix, M. E., Murray, J., Ost, J., Passel, J. S., & Hernandez, S. H. (2005). *The new demography of America's schools: Immigration and the No Child Left Behind Act*. Washington, DC: Urban Institute.

64. Cummins. (2000).

65. García. O. (2014). U.S. Spanish & education: Global and local intersection. *Review of Research in Education, 38*, 58–80; Gándara & Contreras. (2008); Thomas, W. P., & Collier, V. P. (2002). *A national study of school effectiveness for language minority*

students' long-term academic achievement. Center for Research on Education, Diversity & Excellence.

66. Gándara & Contreras. (2008).

67. Suárez-Orozco et al. (2008); Thomas & Collier. (2002).

68. Padilla, A., Lindholm, K. Chen, A., Durán, R. Hahuta, K. Lambert, W., & Richard Tucker. (1991). The English-only movement: Myth, reality, and implications for psychology. *American Psychologist, 46*(2), 120–130.

69. Ibid.

70. U.S. Department of Education. (2002). *1999–2000 schools and staffing survey: Overview of the data for public, private, public charter and Bureau of Indian Affairs elementary and secondary schools.* Washington, DC: Office of Educational Research and Improvement, National Center for Education Statistics. Retrieved from http://nces.ed.gov/pubsearch/pubsinfo.asp?pubid=2002313.

71. Menken. (2008); Suárez-Orozco, Suárez-Orozco, & Todorova. (2008).

72. APA. (2012); Birman, D., & Chan, W. (2008, May). *Screening and assessing immigrant and refugee youth in school-based mental health programs* (Issue Brief No. 1). Washington, DC: George Washington University, Center for Health and Health Care. Retrieved from http://www.rwjf.org/files/research/3320.32211.0508issuebriefno.1.pdf.

73. Rhodes, R., Ochoa, S. H., & Ortiz, S. O. (2005). *Assessment of culturally and linguistically diverse students: A practical guide.* New York: Guilford; Solano-Flores, G. (2008). Who is given tests in what language by whom, when and where? The need for probabilistic views of language in the testing of English language learners. *Educational Researcher, 37*(4), 189–199.

74. Solano-Flores. (2008).

75. APA. (2012); Lesaux, N. K., & Kieffer, M. J. (2010). Exploring sources of reading comprehension difficulties among language minority learners and their classmates in early adolescence. *American Educational Research Journal, 47*(3), 596–632; Suzuki, L. A., Ponterotto, J. G., & Meller, P. J. (2008). *Handbook of multicultural assessment: Clinical, psychological, and educational applications* (3rd ed.). San Francisco: Jossey-Bass.

76. Lesaux & Kieffer. (2010).

77. For a more detailed description of these issues, see APA. (2012); Cummins. (2000); Lesaux & Kieffer. (2010).

78. Yoshikawa, Kholopstseva, & Suárez-Orozco. (2013).

79. Suárez-Orozco, C., Yoshikawa, H., Tseng, V. (2015). *Intersecting inequalities: Research to reduce inequality for immigrant-origin children & youth.* New York: W. T. Grant Foundation.

80. Yoshikawa, Kholopstseva, & Suárez-Orozco. (2013).

81. Ibid.

82. Ibid.

83. Yoshikawa. (2011).

84. It was first proposed in the Senate in 2001; Yoshikawa, Kholopstseva, & Suárez-Orozco. (2013).

85. Miranda, L. (2010, December 1). The Dream Act: Good for our economy, good for our security, good for our nation. *White House Blog*. Retrieved from http://www.whitehouse.gov/blog/2010/12/01/get-facts-dream-act.

86. Batalova, J., & McHugh, M. (2010). *DREAM vs. reality: An analysis of potential DREAM beneficiaries*. Washington, DC: Migration Policy Institute. Retrieved from http://www.migrationpolicy.org/pubs/DREAM-Insight-July2010.pdf.. Parental responsibilities are likely to hinder individuals' ability to peruse higher education. Lopez, M. H. (2009). *Latinos and education: Explaining the attainment gap*. Washington, DC: Pew Hispanic Center. Retrieved from http://pewhispanic.org/files/reports/115.pdf. Additionally, there are over 279,000 undocumented parents who meet the DREAM Act's age requirements but do not have a high school diploma or a general education development (GED). Batalova & McHugh. (2010). Though they might be motivated by the prospect of obtaining a legal status to receive secondary education, family demands might make it a challenge to do so. Further, the DREAM Act excludes people who are older than 35 years of age, a group of undocumented individuals who have aged out and would not even have a chance to apply. Yoshikawa, Kholopstseva, & Suárez-Orozco. (2013).

87. U.S. Department of Homeland Security (2012). *Deferred action for childhood arrivals*. Washington, DC: Author. Retrieved from http://www.dhs.gov/deferred-action-childhood-arrivals.

88. Yoshikawa, Kholopstseva, & Suárez-Orozco. (2013); Gonzales, R., & Terriquez, V. (2013). *How DACA is impacting the lives of those who are now DACAmented*. Washington, DC: Immigration Policy Center.

89. American Immigration Council. (2014). *A guide to the Immigration Accountability Executive Action*. Washington, DC: American Immigration Council. Retrieved from http://www.immigrationpolicy.org/special-reports/guide-immigration-accountability-executive-action.

90. Krogstad, J. M., & Passel, J. (2014). *Those from Mexico will benefit most from Obama's executive action*. Washington, DC: Pew Research Center. Retrieved from http://www.pewresearch.org/fact-tank/2014/11/20/those-from-mexico-will-benefit-most-from-obamas-executive-action/.

91. White House. (2014, November 20). *Fact sheet: Immigrant Accountability Executive Action*. Washington, DC: White House. Retrieved from http://www.whitehouse.gov/the-press-office/2014/11/20/fact-sheet-immigration-accountability-executive-action.

92. American Immigration Council. (2014); White House. (2014).

93. U.S. Department of Homeland Security (2014). *Deportation of aliens claiming U.S.-born children: Second half, calendar year 2013*. Washington, DC: Author.

94. Chaudry, A., Capps, R., Pedroza, J. M., Castaneda, R. M., Santos, R., & Scott, M. M. (2010). *Facing our future: Children in the aftermath of immigration enforcement*. Washington, DC: Urban Institute.

95. Cox, A. B., & Miles, T. J. (2013). Policing immigration. *University of Chicago Law Review, 80*, 87–136.

96. Ibid.

97. Yoshikawa, H., & Suárez-Orozco, C. (2012, April 21). Deporting parents hurts kids. *New York Times*. Retrieved from http://www.nytimes.com/2012/04/21/opinion/deporting-parents-ruins-kids.html?_r=0.

98. Krogstad, J. M., Gonzalez-Barrera, A., & Lopez, M. H. (2014). *Children under 12 are the fastest growing group of unaccompanied minors at the U.S. border*. Washington, DC: Pew Hispanic Foundation. Retrieved from http://www.pewresearch.org/fact-tank/2014/07/22/children-12-and-under-are-fastest-growing-group-of-unaccompanied-minors-at-u-s-border/.

99. Martínez, O. (2014, August 18). Why the children from Central America will not stop fleeing. *Nation*. Retrieved from http://www.thenation.com/article/180837/why-children-fleeing-central-america-will-not-stop-coming#; Krogstad et al. (2014).

100. While it takes less than a week to get a visa to the U.S. as an Australian citizen, petitioners from Mexico or the Philippines can wait 20 years. From many countries, a third or more applicants are turned down at the consulate after paying application fees, at the whim of the interviewer.

101. Bergeron, C. (2013). Going to the back of the line: A primer on lines, visas, and wait times. Washington, DC: Migration Policy Institute; Zaragovia, V. (2014, June 30). Shortage of immigration judges complicates border crisis. *Texas Tribune*. Retrieved from http://www.texastribune.org/2014/06/30/shortage-of-immigration-judges-/.

102. Meissner, D., Kerwin, D. W., Chishti, M., & Bergeron, C. (2013). *Immigration enforcement in the United States: The rise of a formidable machinery*. Washington, DC: Migration Policy Institute.

103. Bergeron. (2013); ACLU. (2014). *Warehoused and forgotten: Immigrants trapped and forgotten in our shadow private prison system*. Houston: Author. Retrieved from https://www.aclu.org/sites/default/files/assets/060614-aclu-car-reportonline.pdf.

104. Yoshikawa, Kholopstseva, & Suárez-Orozco. (2013).

105. Semple, K. (2010, May 16). In Trenton, issuing IDs for illegal immigrants. *New York Times*. Retrieved from http://www.nytimes.com/2010/05/17/nyregion/17idcard.html?pagewanted=all&_r=0.

106. California, Connecticut, Florida, and Nevada do so (as of this writing). Yoshikawa, Kholopstseva, & Suárez-Orozco. (2013).

107. Montero-Sieburth, M. (2007). The roles of leaders, community and religious organizations, consular relationships, and student groups in the emerging leadership of Mexican immigrants in New England. *Journal of Latinos and Education, 6*(1), 5–33; Yoshikawa et al. (2013a).

108. Suárez-Orozco et al. (2015).

GLOSSARY

ACCULTURATION: A bidirectional process of an individual's psychological adaptation occurring with respect to both the new and the heritage cultures.

ACCULTURATIVE STRESS: Stressful life events associated with the acculturation process.

ASSIMILATION: A type of acculturation that involves adopting the new culture while simultaneously letting go of attachment to and practices of the heritage culture.

ASYLUM SEEKERS: Individuals who travel to the United States on their own and apply for asylum, which they may or may not be granted. These individuals arrive in the United States via student, tourist, and business visas or may be unauthorized. Asylum seekers apply to the U.S. Department of Homeland Security in the hope that they will be approved for refugee status on the basis of their previous, often traumatic, experiences prior to migration.

BEHAVIORAL ACCULTURATION: The extent of immigrants' or foreign-born individuals' participation in their culture of origin and/or new culture.

BILINGUAL EDUCATION: Any form of education in which academic content is taught in two languages with varying amounts of each language used in accordance with the program model.

CHILDREN OF IMMIGRANTS: Children whose parents are immigrants, including both first- and second-generation immigrant children and adolescents (used interchangeably with *immigrant origin*; for rationale, see Suárez-Orozco, C., & Suárez-Orozco, M. [2001]. *Children of immigration*. Cambridge: Harvard University Press).

COLLECTIVISM: Any philosophic, political, economic, or social outlook that emphasizes the interdependence of every human in some collective group and the priority of group goals over individual goals.

CULTURAL IDENTITY (ALSO KNOWN AS ETHNIC IDENTITY): Immigrants' or foreign-born individuals' sense of belonging to, positive regard for, and pride in their native culture.

CULTURE: See American Psychological Association. (2002). *APA guidelines on multicultural education, training, research, practice, and organizational change for psychologists*. Washington, DC: Author.

CULTURE-BOUND SYNDROME: Any combination of psychological or somatic symptoms that are considered a recognizable disease only by a particular culture or society.

CULTURE BROKERING: When children of foreign-born parents act as an aid for their parents to help them with culture and language of a new society (e.g., doctor appointments, parent-teacher conferences, financial and legal situations).

DAY LABORER: Any worker who is hired but only paid one day at a time, with no agreement between employer and employee that future work/pay will be available.

DISCRIMINATION: Unfair or harmful treatment of a person or group of persons on the basis of their membership in a minority-status social group (including racial, ethnic, religious, gender, sexuality, or linguistic groups).

DOWNWARD ASSIMILATION: Process of assimilating or integrating into underprivileged communities.

ECOLOGY: The study of the relationships among individuals and their settings.

EMERGING ADULT: The period of development roughly between the ages of 18 and 25, also referred to as *young adulthood*.

EMPLOYMENT-BASED IMMIGRATION: Situations in which individuals migrate from their country of origin to seek employment. This can apply to those who cannot find work in their country of origin, as well as highly skilled individuals who are sought after by companies outside their country of origin.

ESSENTIALISM: Belief system in which "races" are considered distinct entities with immutable biological differences.

ETHNICITY: A socially constructed way of categorizing people on the basis of cultural factors such as ancestry, religion, geographic origin, language, and cultural beliefs.

FAMILY PREFERENCE SYSTEM: Refers to a replacement system for simple "quotas" of visas distributed to immigrants from various regions. This system places immigrants into different groups called "preferences," which are based on their relationship with U.S. citizens, and each of these groups is allotted a certain number of visas that can then be distributed to those who qualify.

FICTIVE KIN: Kinship that is not based in genetics or marriage.

FIRST GENERATION: Born abroad, immigrating sometime during the life cycle (synonymous with foreign-born). Some common subcategories subsumed under the first generation can include

1.75 GENERATION (born abroad, arriving prior to school age)

1.5 GENERATION (born abroad, arriving after school age but prior to adolescence)

1.25 GENERATION (arriving after adolescence but before adulthood)

FOREIGN-BORN: Born abroad (synonymous with first generation).

FULL-IMMERSION OR NATIVE-LANGUAGE EDUCATION: Any form of education in which academic content is taught only in one language.

GENDER-BASED ASYLUM CLAIMS: Refers to requests for asylum (see *Asylum seekers*) on the basis of violence related to one's gender. For example, women may request asylum in an effort to escape female genital mutilation, rape, forced marriage, domestic violence, sexual slavery, and many other acts of violence committed against them because of their gender.

GREEN CARD: A U.S. Permanent Resident Card (USCIS Form I-551), formerly an Alien Registration Card or Alien Registration Receipt Card (INS Form I-151). This is an identification card attesting to the permanent resident status of an alien in the United States. It is known informally as a green card because it had been green in color from 1946 to 1964, and it reverted to that color again in May 2010.

HUMAN CAPITAL: Competences, knowledge, and personality attributes embodied in the ability to perform labor that produces economic value; attributes gained through education and experience.

HUMANITARIAN RELIEF: Material or logistical aid presented in response to an event that represents a critical threat to the health, safety, security, and well-being of a particular community or region.

IMMIGRANT: Born abroad; not born in the U.S.

IMMIGRANT HEALTH PARADOX: Also referred to as *epidemiological paradox* or *Latino paradox*; a pattern of research findings in which first-generation immigrants demonstrate more optimal physical, behavioral, and educational outcomes than their same-ethnicity second- or third-generation peers.

IMMIGRANT ORIGIN: Includes both first- and second-generation immigrant children and adolescents with immigrant parent(s).

LEGAL PERMANENT RESIDENCE: A noncitizen of the United States authorized to live, work, and study in the United States permanently. These individuals are holders of what is commonly referred to as the *green card*.

MICROAGGRESSION: Verbal or nonverbal snubs, which may be intended or unintended, directed at individuals of marginalized backgrounds.

MIGRANT WORKER: Refers to individuals who work outside their country of origin or individuals who migrate within a country to pursue work, such as seasonal employment.

MINORITY STRESS: Social stress that results from negative social experiences (such as microaggressions or stigmatization) that can occur from being part of a minority group.

MIXED STATUS: When some members of the same family have legal documentation status and others do not.

MULTICULTURAL IDEOLOGY: A philosophical orientation that embraces all cultures. Multicultural societies practice and celebrate many cultures within one larger society, emphasizing the positive aspects of its members' cultural differences.

NATIONAL IDENTITY: Immigrants' or foreign-born individuals' sense of belonging to a new society.

NATURALIZED CITIZEN: A foreign-born individual who has become a U.S. citizen by fulfilling requirements set forth in the Immigration and Nationality Act, including, in most cases, having resided in the United States for at least five years.

NEWCOMER: First-generation immigrants arriving within the past four years.

PARENTIFICATION: Children or adolescents prematurely taking on mature adult or parental roles, often before they are emotionally or developmentally ready.

POSTTRAUMATIC STRESS DISORDER (PTSD): A severe anxiety disorder experienced after traumatic events, particularly those involving psychological trauma. Typical symptoms include flashbacks or nightmares, avoidance of stimuli associated with the trauma, and increased arousal (through difficulty staying or falling asleep, anger, or hypervigilance). Formal diagnosis through *DSM-IV-TR* requires that symptoms last more than one month and cause significant impairment in social, occupational, or other important areas of functioning.

PREJUDICE: Preconceived negative feelings, opinions, or attitudes about a social group, including racial, religious, or national groups.

PROTECTIVE FACTORS: Conditions in contexts such as families and communities that, when present, increase the health and well-being of children. These attributes serve as buffers, helping parents find resources, supports, or coping strategies that allow them to parent effectively, even under stress.

RACE: A socially constructed way of categorizing people on the basis of phenotype such as facial features, skin color, hair, and the like. While race has been historically tied to alleged biological and inherited differences, its valence today is linked to sociocultural, political, and economic processes and dynamics.

RACIAL PROFILING: Authority figures using race or ethnicity as a basis for deciding whether to enforce laws or regulations or how to interact with community members.

RACISM: The belief that some races are inherently superior (physically, intellectually, or culturally) to others and therefore have a right to dominate them.

REACTIVE IDENTIFICATION: Immigrants or foreign-born individuals who embrace their cultural identity (from country of origin) while rejecting the new culture, after having been rejected by it.

REFUGEE: A person outside of their habitual residence who has a well-founded fear of persecution because of race, religion, nationality, or membership in a particular social group or political opinion and who is unable or unwilling to avail themselves of the protection of that country or return there for fear of protection.

SECOND GENERATION: Born in the U.S. (or in other immigration contexts in the new land) of foreign-born parent(s). Note that in the U.S., all second- generation immigrant adults and children are citizens as mandated by the 14th Amendment (1868).

SELECTIVE ASSIMILATION: Assimilation to a new country in which foreign-born individuals maintain their native culture in strong ethnic enclaves but successfully participate in the new culture as well, particularly economically.

SOCIAL JUSTICE PERSPECTIVE: A psychological orientation that is rooted in the belief that all people have a right to equitable treatment and a fair allocation of societal resources including decision making. To this end, social justice addresses issues of oppression, privilege, and social inequities. Psychologists committed to such a perspective direct efforts toward making society a better place for all by challenging systemic inequalities.

THIRD GENERATION: Born in the U.S. of parents who were born in the new land and thus the child of immigrant grandparent(s); no longer considered "immigrant origin," though there may be residual ethnic practices and identity.

UNDOCUMENTED: Individuals without legal authorization who reside in the country. These individuals are not U.S. citizens, do not hold current visas, and have not been permitted admission under a specific set of rules for longer-term residence and work permits.

U.S. CITIZENSHIP AND IMMIGRATION SERVICES (USCIS) H1-B PROGRAM: Used by U.S. businesses to employ foreign workers in specialty occupations that require theoretical or technical expertise in specialized fields, such as scientists, engineers, or computer programmers; capped annually at low numbers by country of origin.

VISA: A document (or in many cases a stamp in a passport) showing that a person is authorized to enter a territory. Typically a visa is attached to several conditions, such as the territory it applies to and the dates for which it is valid. A visa does not generally give a noncitizen any rights, including a right to enter a country or remain there. The possession of a visa is not in itself a guarantee of entry into the country that issued it, and a visa can be revoked at any time. The visa process merely enables the host country to verify the identity of the visa applicant before, rather than coincident with, applicant entry. Visas are associated with the request for permission to enter (or exit) a country and are thus, for some countries, distinct from actual formal permission for an alien to enter and remain in the country.

XENOPHOBIA: Expressed hatred or fear of foreigners or strangers.

ABOUT THE CONTRIBUTORS

MONA M. ABO-ZENA is Visiting Assistant Professor of Education and Human Development at Brown University. She coedited *Emerging Adults' Religiousness and Spirituality: Meaning-Making in an Age of Transition* (with Carolyn Barry).

DOROTHY ADDAE is a doctoral student in counseling psychology at the University of Miami.

GONZALO BACIGALUPE is Professor in the Family Therapy Program at the Department of Counseling and School Psychology in the College of Education and Human Development at the University of Massachusetts–Boston. He is also Ikerbasque Research Professor at the Stress and Resilience Research Team at the University of Deusto in Bilbao, Spain, and President of the American Family Therapy Academy.

DINA BIRMAN is Associate Professor of Educational and Psychological Studies at the University of Miami, School of Education and Human Development, and directs the new Community Well-Being Ph.D. program.

CLAUDE BONAZZO is a graduate student in the Department of Sociology at the University of Texas at Austin.

HOAN N. BUI is Associate Professor at the University of Tennessee–Knoxville. She is the author of *In the Adopted Land: Abused Immigrant Women and the Criminal Justice System* and numerous articles and book chapters on the experiences of immigrant women with domestic-violence victimization.

MIGUEL ÁNGEL CANO is Assistant Professor in the Department of Epidemiology at Florida International University.

ROBERT CROSNOE is the Elsie and Stanley E. (Skinny) Adams, Sr. Centennial Professor in Liberal Arts at the University of Texas at Austin, where he is also a faculty member in the Department of Sociology, Department of Psychology, and Population Research Center. His books include *Mexican Roots, American Schools: Helping Mexican Immigrant Children Succeed*; *Fitting In, Standing Out: Navigating the Social Challenges of High School to Get an Education*; and *The Accumulation of Social and Human Capital from Adolescence into Adulthood*. He is a member of the NICHD Early Child Care Network and the Governing Council of Society for Research in Child Development and is Deputy Editor of the *Journal of Marriage and Family*.

CYNTHIA GARCÍA COLL was the Charles Pitts Robinson and John Palmer Barstow Professor of Education, Psychology, and Pediatrics at Brown University until 2011. She then returned to Puerto Rico and is now Provost of the Carlos Albizu University. She has coedited and cowritten several books, including *Nature and Nurture: The Complex Interplay of Genetic and Environmental Influences on Human Behavior and Development*; *Immigrant Stories: Ethnicity and Academics in Middle Childhood*; and *The Immigrant Paradox in Children and Adolescents: Is Becoming American a Developmental Risk?* She was the 2009 recipient of the Society for Research on Child Development's "Cultural and Contextual Contributions to Child Development" lifetime award and the 2011 Lectureship Award of the Society for Developmental and Behavioral Pediatrics.

SHU-SHA ANGIE GUAN is a doctoral candidate in the Department of Psychology at the University of California–Los Angeles and a trainee in the FPR-UCLA Center for Culture, Brain, and Development.

CRISTINA J. HUNTER is Post-Doctoral Research Associate at Boston College. She has a Ph.D. in applied developmental/educational psychology from Boston College.

LENE ARNETT JENSEN is Associate Professor of Psychology at Clark University. Her publications include *New Horizons in Developmental Theory and Research* (with Reed Larson); *Immigrant Civic Engagement: New Translations* (2008, with Constance Flanagan); *Bridging Cultural and Developmental Psychology: New Syntheses for Theory, Research and Policy*; *Oxford Handbook of Human Development and Culture*; and *Moral Development in a Global World: Research from a Cultural-Developmental Perspective*.

JUSTIN LAPLANTE is a doctoral student in the psychology department at Clark University.

AMY K. MARKS is Associate Professor of Psychology and Director of Graduate and Undergraduate Studies in the Department of Psychology at Suffolk University. Her publication history includes coauthoring two recent books with Cynthia García Coll: *Immigrant Stories: Ethnicity and Academics in Middle Childhood* (2009) and *Is Becoming an American a Developmental Risk?*

MARGARY MARTIN is Visiting Assistant Professor in the Department of Education at Brown University. She is coauthor of *Schooling for Resilience: Improving the School Trajectory of Black and Latino Boys*.

MARJORIE FAULSTICH ORELLANA is Professor in the Graduate School of Education and Information Studies at UCLA, where she is codirector of the International Program on Migration. The author of *Translating Childhoods: Immigrant Youth and Cultures*, she is the current president of the Council of Anthropology and Education.

MARIELA M. PÁEZ is Associate Professor at the Lynch School of Education, Boston College. She has a doctorate in human development and psychology from the Graduate School of Education at Harvard University. She is the author of numerous articles and the coeditor of *Latinos Remaking America* (with Marcelo Suárez-Orozco).

KIMBERLY PARKER is an outpatient clinician in the metropolitan Boston area, where she works with children, couples, and families.

KERRIE PIELOCH is a doctoral student in child clinical psychology at Suffolk University.

AIDA RAMOS-WADA is Assistant Professor in the Department of Sociology at the University of Texas at San Antonio.

MEENAL RANA is Assistant Professor in the Child Development Department at Humboldt State University.

SETH J. SCHWARTZ is Professor of Public Health Sciences at the University of Miami Leonard M. Miller School of Medicine. He is senior editor of the *Handbook of Identity Theory and Research* and of the forthcoming *Oxford Handbook of Acculturation and Health*. He is president-elect for the Society for the Study of Emerging Adulthood and has been principal investigator on three NIH-funded studies.

LOURAH M. SEABOYER is a doctoral student in clinical psychology at Suffolk University.

CAROLA SUÁREZ-OROZCO is Professor of Human Development and Psychology at the University of California–Los Angeles. She has authored *Learning a New Land: Immigrant Students in American Society*, *Children of Immigration*, and *Transformations: Migration, Family Life, and Achievement Motivation among Latino Adolescents*, as well as *The New Immigration: An Interdisciplinary Reader*. In 2006, she was awarded an American Psychological Association Presidential Citation for her work on the cultural psychology of immigration and served as the chair of the APA Presidential Task Force on Immigration. She is the editor of the *Journal of Adolescent Research* and is a Senior Program Associate for the W. T. Grant Foundation.

PRATYUSHA TUMMALA-NARRA is Associate Professor in the Department of Counseling, Developmental, and Educational Psychology at Boston College. She has served as a member of the Committee on Ethnic Minority Affairs (CEMA) in the American Psychological Association and as a member of the APA Presidential Task Force on Immigration.

HIROKAZU YOSHIKAWA is the Courtney Sale Ross University Professor of Globalization and Education at the Steinhardt School of New York University. He currently serves on the Leadership Council and as the cochair of the early childhood development and education workgroup of the U.N. Sustainable Development Solutions Network. In 2012, he was nominated by President Obama and confirmed by the Senate as a member of the U.S. National Board on Education Sciences. In 2014, he was elected to the U.S. National Academy of Education. He is the author of *Immigrants Raising Citizens: Undocumented Parents and Their Young Children.*

BYRON L. ZAMBOANGA is Professor in the Department of Psychology at Smith College.

INDEX

Academic achievement, 9, 18, 86, 203, 259–72, 262, 302; case study, 259–60; community centers for, 271–72; English-language proficiency, 5, 178, 264, 302; immigrant paradox and risk model, 260–64, 270–71; interventions to support, 270–72; for newcomer youth, 7–8, 48, 261, 262; peer relationship contexts, 268–69; person-environment perspective on, 264–70; in primary schools, 51; school readiness, 49–50, 263–65; third generation declining, 8, 247, 261, 269

Academic language proficiency. *See* Cognitive academic language proficiency

Acculturation, 84, 120, 122–36, 323; of adult immigrants, 129; to antiacademic peer norms, 9; behavioral outcomes and, 246–49, 251–52; biculturalism and, 125; case study, 122; of children of immigrants, 129–30; contextual issues in, 126–28; cultural identity and, 150–52; culture and development, 123–24; culture brokering, 134–35; discrimination and, 127, 245; ethnic enclaves and, 127; ethnic identity as dimension of, 150–52; future directions, 135–36; gaps, 133–34; heritage culture and, 136, 137n17, 151; language brokering and, 193; measurement of, 128–29; mental health and, 222–25; parent-child conflicts and, 250–51, 266; physical health and, 202; press, 126, 127, 136; segmented assimilation, 144–45; selective, 65, 145; theory, 124–26. *See also* Behavioral acculturation; Identity acculturation

Acculturative stress, 121, 323; academic achievement and, 302; immigrant origin children response to, 6–7; of immigrant parents, 9–10, 134, 190, 193; intergenerational conflicts and, 222–23; language barriers, 247; mental health and, 219, 224, 302; religious values and beliefs and, 83

Adaptation, 34–36, 245; generational status and, 8; of immigrant origin children, 7; segmented assimilation and, 244

Add Health. *See* National Longitudinal Study of Adolescent Health

Additive acculturation, 125

Additive dual-language learners, 168

Adolescent Health and Academic Achievement Study (AHAA), 261

Adult immigrants, acculturation of, 129

Africa: center care use by immigrants from, 50; child fostering in, 43; ICT access and adoption, 63; migratory flow from, 2

African Americans. *See* Blacks

AHAA. *See* Adolescent Health and Academic Achievement Study

Amnesty, 15, 100

Arab immigrants: language brokering, 191; language school learning, 88; media portrayals of, 288; racial profiling of, 226–27, 229

Asian immigrants: academic achievement, 220, 261, 262, 262–64, 265, 267; acculturation gaps, 133–34; assimilation, 133; behavioral outcomes, 243; childhood illness and disease, 210; civic engagement, 204, 283, 288, 290; close family relations of, 250; criminal activity, 243, 245; discipline, 249–50; ethnic identity and, 133, 147, 149, 156–57, 224–25; infant mortality rate, 207;

Second generation (*cont.*)
    perpetual foreigner syndrome, 143; pop-
    ulation growth, 2, 20n7, 219; poverty,
    14; problematic schools, 51–52; racism
    stress, 226; religion and, 89; school drop
    outs, 48; voting registration, 279
Second-language learners (SLLs), 4, 178,
    304–5
Second-language oral proficiency, 170
Secure Communities federal provisions, 314
Segmented assimilation, 144–45, 244
Segregation, 101, 144–45, 248
Selective acculturation, 65, 145
Selective assimilation, 328
Self-categorization, 105, 144, 145, 147–48,
    150, 155
Separation phase, in family reunification,
    10, 28, 29, 35, 36–38, 42, 43
Sequential bilinguals, 168
Sex trafficking, 228
Sexual identity, 120
Sexuality, 229; adolescents sexual behav-
    ior, 211, 245–46; culture and religion
    influence on, 89–91; immigrant status
    and virginity loss, 90; socialization, 246;
    women's sexual roles, 245–46
SIFE. *See* Students with interrupted formal
    education
Simultaneous bilinguals, 168
SIN. *See* Students Informing Now
Sin País (Without Country) documentary,
    of Rigby, 61, 68, 74–75
SLLs. *See* Second-language learners
Social context factors, for bilingualism,
    168–69
Social control theories, 241
Social exclusion, 146–47
Social identity theory, 146, 155
Socialization, 86–87, 103, 130; in culture,
    123; identity centrality and, 155; peer
    groups influence on, 51, 248–49; from
    religion, 30, 81; sex, 246
Social justice perspective, 82, 108, 328
Social mirror, of immigrant families, 224;
    hate crimes, 17, 97; identity and sense of

belonging formation, 17; negative media
    coverage, 17, 97, 285, 288; xenophobia,
    13, 16–17, 29, 190, 192, 329
Socioeconomic status, 24n70, 263; child-
    hood illness and disease, 209; DLL
    and, 171, 172; infant mortality and, 207;
    obesity and, 213; physical activity and,
    212
Socioemotional development: of DLLs,
    171–72; externalizing and internalizing
    behaviors, 107–8; language brokering
    and, 189–91; school readiness, 263–64;
    of undocumented immigrant youth,
    106–8
South Asian immigrants: criminal activity,
    243, 245; problematic school settings,
    248; racial profiling of, 226–27, 229
Spiritual capital, 84–85
Spirituality: African-Americans and Carib-
    bean Black research, 92; depression
    and, 81; of emerging adults, 81, 83, 87,
    90–91; of first generation, 84; human
    development relevance, 82, 83. *See also*
    Religion
State-funded programs, for early educa-
    tion, 49
Stress: immigrant origin children response
    to, 6–7; minority, 226, 326; related to
    language brokering, 187, 189, 190, 193;
    traumatic, 229, 232. *See also* Accultura-
    tive stress; Posttraumatic stress disorder
Students Informing Now (SIN) collective,
    285
Students with interrupted formal education
    (SIFE), 304
Substance use, 210, 211, 242, 247–48
Subtractive acculturation, 125, 137n17
Subtractive dual-language learners, 168

Technologies, emerging: ambivalence
    toward, 71–74; deficits of, 74–75;
    developmental considerations, 68–71;
    emotional and cognitive development
    and, 69–70; emotional connections
    through, 62; family relations and,